THEOLOGIES OF RETRIEVAL

H C Biggs

THEOLOGIES OF RETRIEVAL

An Exploration and Appraisal

Editor
Darren Sarisky

t&tclark
LONDON · NEW YORK · OXFORD · NEW DELHI · SYDNEY

T&T CLARK
Bloomsbury Publishing Plc
50 Bedford Square, London, WC1B 3DP, UK
1385 Broadway, New York, NY 10018, USA

BLOOMSBURY, T&T CLARK and the T&T Clark logo are trademarks of Bloomsbury
Publishing Plc

First published 2017
Paperback edition first published in 2019

A catalogue record for this book is available from the British Library.

Library of Congress Cataloging-in-Publication Data
Names: Sarisky, Darren, editor.
Title: Theologies of retrieval : an exploration and appraisal / edited by
Darren Sarisky.
Description: 1 [edition]. | New York : Bloomsbury T&T Clark, 2017. | Includes
Bibliographical references and index.
Identifiers: LCCN 2017036092 (print) | LCCN 2017042427 (ebook) | ISBN
9780567666802 (ePDF) | ISBN 9780567666819 (ePUB) | ISBN 9780567666796
(hardback)
Subjects: LCSH: Theology. | Theology–Methodology. |Hermeneutics.
Classification: LCC BR118 (ebook) | LCC BR118 .T481552017 (print) | DDC
230.01–dc23
LC record available at https://lccn.loc.gov/2017036092

ISBN: HB: 978-0-5676-6679-6
PB: 978-0-5676-8879-8
ePDF: 978-0-5676-6680-2
ePub: 978-0-5676-6681-9

Typeset by Newgen KnowledgeWorks Pvt. Ltd., Chennai, India

To find out more about our authors and books visit
www.bloomsbury.com and sign up for our newsletters.

CONTENTS

Part III
TWENTIETH-CENTURY FIGURES

Part IV
THEOLOGICAL SOURCES

Part V
MAJOR DOCTRINES

CONTRIBUTORS

Michael Allen is J. D. Trimble Professor of Systematic Theology and academic dean at Reformed Theological Seminary, Orlando, Florida.

Brian Bantum is associate professor of theology at Seattle Pacific University, Seattle, Washington.

Gavin D'Costa is professor of Catholic theology at the University of Bristol.

Gabriel Flynn is associate professor in theology at Dublin City University.

Paul Gavrilyuk is Aquinas Chair in Theology and Philosophy at University of St. Thomas, St Paul and Minneapolis, Minnesota.

David Grumett is lecturer in Christian ethics and practical theology at the University of Edinburgh.

Stanley Hauerwas is Gilbert T. Rowe Professor Emeritus of Divinity and Law at Duke University, Durham, North Carolina.

Nicholas M. Healy is professor of theology and religious studies at St. John's University, New York, New York.

Ruth Jackson is research fellow at the Centre for Research in Arts, Social Sciences and Humanities at the University of Cambridge.

Michael C. Legaspi is associate professor of classics and ancient Mediterranean studies and Jewish studies at Pennsylvania State University, State College, Pennsylvania.

Andrew Louth is professor emeritus of patristic and byzantine studies at Durham University.

Jennifer Newsome Martin is assistant professor in the Program of Liberal Studies at the University of Notre Dame, South Bend, Indiana.

John Milbank is professor emeritus of religion, politics, and ethics at the University of Nottingham.

William E. Myatt is adjunct lecturer in theology at Loyola University Chicago and director of Development at Catholic Extension.

Kenneth Oakes is assistant professor of systematic theology at the University of Notre Dame, South Bend, Indiana.

Martyn Percy is dean of Christ Church and a member of the Faculty of Theology and Religion at the University of Oxford.

Fred Sanders is professor of theology at the Torrey Honors Institute of Biola University, La Mirada, California.

Darren Sarisky is tutor in doctrine and ministry at Wycliffe Hall and a member of the Faculty of Theology and Religion at the University of Oxford.

John Webster was professor of divinity at the University of St. Andrews.

INTRODUCTION

Darren Sarisky

Theologies of retrieval have had considerable impact within theological discussions during the twentieth and twenty-first centuries. This point can be substantiated with the mention, in very broad strokes, of a few examples. A first instance is postliberal theology, which seeks to root theological thinking in a determinate textual framework that a community can inhabit and on the basis of which they can navigate the world. Those for whom "the text absorbs the world"[1] operate with greater confidence in this textual framework than in generic categories of thought that are supposedly universally accessible. Another example is radical orthodoxy, which aims to break out of what its proponents view as a divorce in modernity between pure nature and supernatural grace by appealing to earlier stretches of the Christian theological tradition in order to reestablish a participatory outlook, according to which the entire created realm reaches out toward its supernatural end. In different ways, postliberal and radically orthodox theologians draw inspiration from some of the giants of twentieth-century theology, such as Karl Barth and the French *ressourcement* theologians, who were themselves mining older tracts of the Christian tradition as they formulated their own constructive proposals. Additional approaches to theology that emphasize retrieval are not hard to find. An indicator of the importance of this style of thinking is that a few significant syntheses have emerged recently that examine and reflect upon this trend.[2]

But what constitutes a theology as a theology of retrieval? Making some progress toward answering this question is one of the main goals of this volume as a whole, but consider the following as a first approximation. It is possible to characterize theologies of retrieval as one of two main ways in which a Christian theologian might respond to the conditions of the present. The first option is to commit to correlate elements of the Christian tradition with aspects of modern culture or to foster an open conversation between the theological tradition and a range of

---

1 George A. Lindbeck, *The Nature of Doctrine: Religion and Theology in a Postliberal Age*, 25th anniversary ed. (Louisville: Westminster John Knox, 2009), 140.

2 Rowan Williams, *Why Study the Past? The Quest for the Historical Church* (London: Darton, Longman and Todd, 2005); John Webster, "Theologies of Retrieval," in *The Oxford Handbook of Systematic Theology*, ed. John Webster, Kathryn Tanner, and Iain R. Torrance (Oxford: Oxford University Press, 2007), 583–99.

other fields, thus connecting the tradition to the present and providing a bridge to ensure that Christian proclamation is intelligible to contemporary minds. All theologies are marked in some way by the intellectual, social, and cultural contexts in which they originate and develop: theologies of retrieval are no exception to this. Yet theologies of retrieval, the second option, are less concerned to secure the plausibility of Christian theology by means of establishing similarities to presently influential ideas, and more focused simply on attending to, indwelling, and commending what they take to be the most compelling articulations of the Christian gospel. Theologies of retrieval are less taken up with the conditions of the possibility of Christian theology in the present than they are absorbed by the material content of theology, which is taken to have the requisite internal resources to respond to the challenges that face it. Theologies of retrieval are works in what Rowan Williams calls "creative archaeology,"[3] attempts to dig into a past era in order to open up new vistas for today. Theologies of retrieval unsettle present discussions by offering resources from beyond the current horizon with a view toward enriching ongoing debates.

Capitalizing on the recent gains that have been made in this mode of theological discourse, this edited volume has three broad goals: to advance the discussion by further pursuing some of the most important formal and material questions about retrieval; to recognize how the discussion has recently broadened out beyond previous boundaries and to further this process of widening the discussion; and, finally, to register some important objections to stressing retrieval in the ways that most of the contributions to this work do. The nineteen essays in this book attempt to work toward fulfilling these goals. What follows in the remainder of this introduction is not a detailed summary of the argument of each essay but an effort to spell out the main task for each of the book's parts, and thus to highlight the coherence of the whole. The book is divided into seven parts.

Theologies of retrieval depend, in some way or other, on judgments that theologians have made about the flow of the history of ideas. Thus intellectual history, which is the concern of Part 1, is a discourse that at least hangs in the background for retrieval works; at times, it even comes directly into the foreground of a discussion. Theologies in this mode sometimes depend on what seems to some to be a sweeping judgment about times during which particular problems arose, or on related presuppositions about stretches of history that were not afflicted by such difficulties, and that are thus especially promising for the task of retrieval. In other instances, theologies of retrieval operate with much less of a marked preference for any one particular period, thinking rather that theologians should connect with the history of the church in some way, and that they are justified in ranging widely for good sources, so long as they read them with discernment. In the first essay within Part 1, John Milbank explores the problems with and promise of the present moment for theology by reflecting on the work of Charles Péguy, a figure who has influenced Milbank himself as well as some of the French Roman Catholic

---

3 Williams, *Why Study the Past?* 100.

figures who are discussed elsewhere in this volume. The other essay in this section, from Stanley Hauerwas, delineates some complexities in any simple narrative that depicts "theological liberalism" as having no place for a notion of tradition; he also challenges the idea that all postliberal theologies represent a clean break from a more obviously "liberal" outlook that they seek to displace. The two essays consider major changes that have taken place in our intellectual culture (the stress of the first essay) and seek to nuance typical stories that are often rehearsed about the results of these changes (the emphasis of the second essay).

Part 2 examines the different ways in which theologians' confessional allegiances can influence how they approach the task of retrieval. There is one essay from an Orthodox perspective, a second from within the Protestant tradition, and a third on Roman Catholicism. It is arguable that the great divide in theology today is not between these three major confessional traditions just mentioned but rather between various types of correlationism or conversational theology, on the one hand, and theologies of retrieval, on the other. Accordingly, many similarities emerge when major theologians from the three traditions specify what they seek to retrieve, how they go about their task, and why it is an important job for them to perform, given their theological commitments. Of course, differences become clear as well when the three theologians articulate their approaches and those common in their tradition. The essays provide a combination of analytical historical work, interpreting major developments that have already taken place, and constructive proposals for how the work of retrieval ought to proceed.

Part 3 concentrates on a sampling of major figures from the recent history of Christian theology. The essays that constitute Part 3 deal with the same three confessional traditions that are represented in Part 2. The essays focus on the contribution made by a single theologian from each tradition, concentrating on how their theological outlooks were shaped by the most important sources they appropriated. The Orthodox theologian featured in this part is Georges Florovsky, the Protestant Karl Barth, and the Roman Catholic Henri de Lubac. Once again, both similarities and differences surface in the discussion.

Part 4 focuses on the primary sources of retrieval: Scripture and tradition. For Orthodoxy, Protestantism, and Roman Catholicism, Scripture is of the utmost importance as a text that forms theological discourse and exercises a normative function within it. The first essay in this section focuses on the current discussion of theological reading of Scripture as an effort to retrieve reading practices that are established in the Christian tradition as well as on the enterprise of biblical theology and the approach of Joseph Ratzinger. It inquires into the sort of retrieval involved in each case and offers critical assessment of the different hermeneutical frameworks. The next essay, which shifts to the topic of tradition, gives attention to the view of tradition that arose among several *ressourcement* theologians, who developed what is arguably the twentieth century's most sophisticated version of the concept. The final essay of Part 4 delves into precisely what it means to read classic theological texts, not as works that had a great deal of influence in the past but as texts that continue to have living voices today, ones which theologians may not only think *about* but may think *with*. This essay is constructive in orientation and focuses on the nature of retrieval as such.

Certain doctrinal loci are less important for theologies of retrieval than they are for correlationist approaches and related forms of theological discourse. In contrast, certain other doctrines take on a high profile within theologies of retrieval. Part 5 takes up a few doctrinal loci that are especially significant for retrieval projects because of the work that these notions do within these outlooks. These doctrines—the Trinity, creation, and ecclesiology as it connects with anthropology—are highly developed in the sorts of theology that are in focus in this book. The doctrine of the Trinity, for instance, is often proffered as the distinctively Christian way to identify God. It is a conceptual summary of what Christians, in contradistinction to Jews and Muslims, mean when they use the term "God." After surveying recent efforts to retrieve a doctrine of the Trinity, the essay on that topic proposes that there are several ways in which articulating a doctrine of the Trinity ought to involve a more thoroughgoing retrieval than one often finds in the supposed renaissance within contemporary Trinitarianism. All the essays that constitute Part 5 elaborate the doctrinal loci at issue in such a way as to make clear how they are employing the legacies of the Christian tradition as resources for their constructive proposals.

While theologies of retrieval concentrate especially on certain topics, other subjects that might have seemed to be difficult to handle from this point of view have begun to be featured more and more within theologies of retrieval. Race, gender, and the world religions are the topics dealt with by the essays in Part 6. There are now theologies with a focus on all of these crucially important contemporary issues that can fairly be said to evince an orientation to retrieval, though in the cases of race and gender, these theologies have a special sensitivity to the possibility that the Christian theological tradition has systematically excluded and marginalized the voices of nonwhites and women. The critical issues surrounding the definition of retrieval in these cases are sufficiently complex to defy easy summary; however, these essays represent test cases in the meaning of retrieval as well as important theological treatments in their own right of race and gender. The essay on world religions, which gives special focus to how the Roman Catholic tradition has dealt with the status of systems other than Christianity, is a good example of how theologies of retrieval need not come across as narrow simply because they are deeply rooted in a particular set of texts, institutional resources, and practices.

The final section of the book, Part 7, deals with two different types of objections. The essays in the previous six parts explore in detail and from many different angles what it means to do theologies of retrieval. The first essay in Part 7 deals with an especially significant objection to this whole way of operating. The essay turns to David Tracy and seeks to open up critical points of view on theologies of retrieval from within Tracy's evolving theological project. Tracy certainly has some room for retrieval, but for him, emphasizing retrieval as much as would any approach that can legitimately qualify as a theology of retrieval is just too simple. It overlooks difficulties and complexities that cannot be easily dismissed. Since his is one of contemporary theology's most well-developed critiques of the forms of thinking in focus in this volume, Tracy's perspective must be considered carefully. The other essay in the concluding part is not an objection against theologies of retrieval per se but a critique of one concrete case of retrieval, a particular sort of charismatic healing ministry operating in the West that claims to retrieve biblical resources. The author contends that this ministry is in important respects different than the biblical precedent upon which it supposedly draws, not simply by virtue of taking place many centuries after the events narrated in the New Testament, but especially because it reinforces the same patterns of marginalization that are challenged by the practices recorded in the biblical texts.

The overall goal of this collection is to gather contributions that further develop and refine theologies of retrieval. In other words, the aim is to nudge the whole debate forward. The essays answer important questions that already existing work raises, expand on suggestions that have not already been developed fully, summarize ideas in order to highlight themes that are relevant to the topic of this volume, and air critiques that should spur further debate. Many of these essays make significant contributions to Christian theology, and they could easily stand on their own as potent arguments on a relatively narrow individual topic. But, in bringing them together in this thematically unified collection, this book seeks to be more than the sum of its parts, for the text systematically explores and critically evaluates a whole approach to theology in a way that independent essays could not. Theologies of retrieval is by no means the name of a monolithic system, neither should it be seen as a well-defined school of thinking; instead, it is a set of overlapping concerns and substantive commitments shared by some of today's most important Christian theologies.

Part I

GENEALOGIES OF MODERNITY: REFLECTIONS ON THE
ROLE OF INTELLECTUAL—HISTORICAL JUDGMENTS

Chapter 1

"THERE'S ALWAYS ONE DAY WHICH ISN'T THE SAME AS THE DAY BEFORE": CHRISTIANITY AND HISTORY IN THE WRITINGS OF CHARLES PÉGUY

John Milbank

History and the event

(i)

History is arguably the central focus of Charles Péguy's life and work. He was an historical actor, a political agitator and polemicist; his poetry seeks not so much to invoke the past of the Gospels and of French history as to reperform, revivify and resurrect it in the present; and his philosophy is largely concerned with the nature of history and of time, but in a way that denounces any theoretically detached version of such concern as lying at the very heart of modern, post-Christian error. In this fashion his theoretical reflections form a bridge between his political agitation, which they sustain, and his poetic act of rememorization of Christian mystery. The latter was liturgically at one with his more hidden, more tragic, more familial and private mode of action, which he also regarded as a more historical and more genuinely social idiom of engagement.[1]

Sometimes these three facets of Péguy's engagement with history—and his historical engagement—are seen as comprising three different phases: of secular socialism, of critique of secular scientism and historicism, and of full if anomalous embrace of the Catholic faith. But although there is some truth to this perspective, to adopt it exclusively is surely to fall prey to the very illusion that Péguy most of all denounced: namely of substituting an "empirical" historical record for the reality of lived time that concerns the flux and fusion of memory. Thus, there were no circumscribed discrete sequential stages in Péguy or any other author's work. Rather, there were complex anticipations,

---

1 See Charles Péguy, "Memories of Youth," in *Temporal and Eternal*, trans. Alexander Dru (Indianapolis: Liberty Fund, 2001), 3–82. This is a somewhat abridged version of *Notre jeunesse* (Paris: Folio, 1993). Notably, the English version omits his paean to the atheist Jewish Dreyfusard whom Péguy regarded as his supreme mentor, Bernard Lazare.

overlappings, returns and retrievals. This fact can to some extent justify the treatment of an author's entire oeuvre as monolithic, with relatively little concern for periodization, adjustments, developments, and changes of mind. In Péguy's case, this kind of procedure seems abundantly warranted, so much so that he, supremely, matched his practice to his beliefs, in such a way that his writing always both looks to a later illumination and cycles endlessly back upon itself and to earlier authorial phases, from the micro- to the macrolevel—from the single phrase (replete with verbal assonance) through the sentence, the paragraph, and the book to his entire sequential series of writings, which involved much rewriting and reediting.

For this reason, Péguy's work lacks normal structuration, or narrative and argumentative development. And, as a result, it resists not only consecutive restructuring but also any verifiable exegesis, or even interpretation. It is apparently *illisible*, as suggested by Bruno Latour, forty-one years ago, on the anniversary of his birth (the year in which I am writing, 2014, being the anniversary of his death at the outset of the Battle of the Marne).[2] By only ever repeating himself with variation, Péguy leaves his assumptions, procedures, indications, and conclusions unsaid. In consequence, the reader must try to fill in these gaps, yet were she to do so in any spirit of systematic interpretative closure, she would surely betray the original open-ended seamlessness of Péguy's idiom, wherein, as Latour says, it is impossible to disinter idiom from content—for example, to see his long discussion of Victor Hugo's *Les Châtiments* as merely illustrative, rather than constitutive of the subject matter of *Clio II*. Because it is impossible to say what is fundamental in Péguy's works, as opposed to what is accidental and conditioned, the reader cannot genuinely interpret but only *gloss*, or repeat differently in a kind of continuation of the text in terms of combined method and content. Yet, as we shall see, to attempt this relation to Péguy is to enter into a literary and historical stance that he thinks should hold for every historical artifact considered as text and textual unfolding.

If one respects this character of his opus, as constantly bending back upon itself and endlessly regathering procedure from content and content from procedure, then it becomes clear that one cannot separate the earlier work from the transitional and the mature, nor the literary from the historical, political, philosophical, and theological. Péguy's socialism remains crucial to his theology, while inversely his Catholic poetic performances consummate his political commitments. And the theoretical–substantive hinge here is his middle-phase reflection on the relationship of time to eternity and of eternity to time. Once again, in considering it we find that Péguy's thoughts about historical method are inseparable from his philosophy of the actual course of human history.

This reflection focuses nevertheless upon a critique of secular progressivism. In the course of *Clio II* Péguy, the Republican, calls into question the usual leftist

---

2 Bruno Latour, "Les raisons profondes du style répétitive de Péguy," in *Péguy écrivain: colloque du centenaire* (Paris: Klincksieck 1973), 78–102.

attitude toward the French Revolution, which regarded it as the overcoming of abuses at the hands of the forward march of enlightened ideas concerning the rights of man.[3] Instead, Péguy suggests that the ancien régime more or less collapsed of its own accord. A once glorious Christian monarchy and aristocracy, not completely deaf to the call of charitable service, nor completely given over to the cult of money, eventually lapsed on account of its top-heavy decadence. Conversely, the revolution was not born primarily in a spirit of negative critique or the embrace of abstract ideals, but rather as a new *mystique,* an ineffably new sense of human companionship in a specific time and place, among a unique group of characters, which expressed itself most notably in the storming of the Bastille. This event took from the outset the idiom of a ritual, thereby becoming its own commemoration and only occurring as a *novum,* as a radical inauguration, because it had this paradoxical, originally repeated character.

But in his own day, in the early twentieth century, thinks Péguy, the revolutionary impetus has suffered a premature *viellissement,* such that the unique particular spirit pertaining amongst the Dreyfusards, which newly linked Jewish, Christian, and Republican *mystiques,* has proved the last authentic chapter in the history of French republicanism.[4] Already, by embracing the delusion of progress it has betrayed its ineffably ritual foundations to sink into the condition of a mere *politique.* Instead of being exclusively concerned with the absolute right and dignity of every human being in every time and place, and with the ever-renewed call to associate, it has surrendered to an essentially utilitarian constant sacrifice of all and every one for future generations, a sacrifice that must, therefore, be endlessly and nonsensically repeated. The vehicle of this monstrous process is the state, which has thereby finally lost touch with the antique city and civility in favor of a bureaucratic recording, docketing, and instrumental organization of human resources. *Laicité* has come to mean, not a possibly beneficial separation of religion from power that might accrue to the growth of spiritual freedom, but a dogmatic public denial of the eternal, with its immediate relation to every present moment (which is thereby precisely not *sublated* but sustained in its irreducible significance) in favor of the civil religion of futurity as our only source of shared purpose and of hoped-for redemption by endlessly improved descendants.

Because this new cult is a matter of quantification and calculation, the new sacred mediator is money, and one can infer that it is by virtue of this mediation that Péguy thinks we have now entered into a post-Christian age that simply gets by without any reference to notions of creation, sin, incarnation, redemption, grace, and damnation.[5] The ontologically given, plus temporal loss, gain, despair,

---

3 Charles Péguy, *Clio* (Paris: Gallimard, 1932).

4 Péguy, *Notre Jeunesse.*

5 Charles Péguy, *L'Argent* (Paris: De Equateurs, 2008). On Péguy's adoption of the originally Maistrian thematic of the proximity of the saint to the sinner, see Richard Griffith's very insightful paper, "'Le sacré et le dé-sacré': Péguy and the Maistrian Tradition of French Catholicism," given at the Oxford *Maison Française* colloquium for the centenary of Péguy's death.

and hope are now instead all pecuniary in character, such that most people are in danger of entering a lukewarm condition worse than that of sinners, who negatively grasp the drama of salvation and damnation. But there remain ministrators of the new sacrament of coinage and they are the new clerics, the "intellectuals" who claim to possess a social and historical equivalent of the experimental and technological understanding of nature. They may be situated in universities, but ultimately they work for the state and may well be recruited to the state administrative apparatus. And essentially they come in two forms: either they are a priori theorists of the social, the "sociologists" who have fantasized given ahistorical laws of a supposed social constant, in lieu of the constancy of eternity, or else they are empiricists, professional historians who have to give "total" and totally accurate accounts of historical events and epochs, in order to trace the advances or relapses of society through time. Péguy is thinking here of the legacy of Jules Michelet (whom he otherwise admired for disinterring the history of the people)—and since the advocacy of *histoire totale* was built upon this legacy, he can be read as offering a critique of the *Annaliste* approach, which came to dominate twentieth-century French historiography, in advance.

Against this new lay positivist historicism, Péguy marshals in *Clio II* a famously devastating critique.

It consists in four main arguments. First, the ancients and not the moderns were right: history is not an artificial technical process tending to aggregative advance, but remains the time of an organism and an animal, albeit a prodigiously intelligent and freely inventive one. Since civilizations are also cultures they naturally spring up, enjoy a short maturity, but then grow jaded in their habits and eventually wither away. As we shall later see, it is crucial to Péguy's quite drastic theology that even the Christian event and the Christian city have eventually not escaped this process and were perhaps always unlikely to do so. By insisting on inescapable *vieillissement*, Péguy points us, like many others shortly after him, such as Oswald Spengler, Arnold Toynbee and Christopher Dawson, toward an intercivilizational perspective on metahistory and away from narrowly ethnocentric fantasies of perpetual advance that nineteenth-century idealist metahistories had tended to promote. Within civilizations, for him, relative progress does not depend upon incremental improvements but rather on constant *renaissance*, constant return *ad fontes*, and constant startings-out all over again. As Latour points out, this motif of "return" in Péguy never implies reaction or conservation; instead, it means a revisiting of the neglected roots that remain forever new and surprising, forever ahead of a culture at its very origins.

Decadence, or *vieillissement* is, however, eventually almost inescapable, because cultures are founded neither upon material skills, which are unlikely to be lost and can readily be recovered, nor upon ideas, which can be written down and formalized and so always reapplied, even if they get temporarily neglected. Instead, cultures are founded upon a *mystique,* by which Péguy means an interpersonally shared set of ritual practices that link together the material and the symbolic and whose logic remains to a considerable degree ineffable and so, just for that reason, vital and inspiring. One can remark here that it is characteristic of

Catholic philosophers of history, from Vico through Pierre-Simon Ballanche and Friedrich Schlegel to Dawson and Eric Voegelin, to make the ritual and the religious ultimately determinative rather than the ideal *or* the material, which tend to be the oscillating preferences of Protestant metahistorians or their atheist successors. In this way, as Dawson especially emphasized, their approach is much more consonant with the conclusions of ethnography concerning the "prehistorical"— with which, nonetheless, our "history" can most plausibly be seen as being, after all, in continuity.[6]

The second argument has to do precisely with this question of origins. Historiography scours memorials in order to record facts with accuracy. But just this supposed realism must miss the reality of the event. All events, and especially significant ones, build up in secret, are more oral than written, and only acquire their character as events retrospectively, in terms of their later influence. Like a written work of literature, it is suggested in *Clio II,* any "record" of this process is no more than a "version," an interpretation of a more fundamental process. Because this process is always a dynamic inspiration, in order for it to be able to acquire the sort of significance that must always mark an event, it remains to a degree obscure and ineffable, locked into its original latency, which (similarly to Aristotelian "potential") is nevertheless an ontological reality, and indeed of the densest kind.

Thus one is left with the paradox that an event, in order to be such, must already have recorded itself, such that history must always already be its own historiography, and human lived reality is originally shadowed by literature and the real by the fictional. The "poetic" is double, such that without something having been "made up" in the realm of the imagination, nothing is materially "made" as event or factum. The authentic reality of the event requires this seeming supplement.

And yet, to compound the paradox, even if the supplement is not necessarily an "alienation" of an Hegelian kind, it also from the outset contains some element of decline or insufficiency (more like a Neoplatonic "emanation"), since the novel inspiration of the new irruption always fails to express itself with entire satisfaction, even though this expression does not come "after" the origin but is coincident with it. This means that the expression is only inadequate to the inspiration because it fails to be sufficiently inspired, fails to arrive at an adequate inspiration that would emerge already as a fuller expression. One sees the same tension in Péguy's attitude to thinking and to composition—on the one hand there is inexhaustible intuition, while on the other hand authentic intuition has always already begun to be the patient repeated work of discursive elaboration.

It is because of this compounded paradox that, throughout Péguy's oeuvre there is a tension between the theme of "the pure original" that is already pregnant with all that is to come and the necessity to "step out," to go forward and risk growth and life and death if one is to be complete and freshly authentic. This makes him, like no other since William Blake, a poet of innocence and experience

---

6　Christopher Dawson, *The Age of the Gods* (London: Sheed and Ward, 1933).

and of the interplay between them. Experience, as original repetition, has forever been already embarked upon, yet equally it adds nothing to an innocence that it always betrays and whose potentiality of original, playful, liturgical inspiration precontains the whole of what might be learned in advance and lies always ahead of anything that might be expressed or discovered. Thus the old man has lost the freshness of the child and is only once more equalized with him insofar as, at the end of his life, he has as much as the child still lying before him, in the shape of all eternity.

In consequence all the later Bastille days are pale echoes of the first, betraying its unrepeatable innocence, and yet equally, there was only a first day because there have been later ones and it was from the outset repeated in self-commemoration.[7] By a similar inversion, the later water lilies in Claude Monet's famous series appear as fresher and more "original" and "basic" than the earlier painted blooms. One might therefore say that for Péguy the event is already the second as well as the first item in a series because it is its own memorial and must have occurred at least twice in order to have occurred once. Yet at the same time the event is a fontal One that is not in a series at all, because it is the entire principle of the whole series. This amounts, in the wake of Henri Bergson, to a kind of application of Neoplatonic considerations to horizontal, temporal processes.

And in terms of either side of the paradox one is here remaining within real, lived, experienced and remembered time in keeping with Bergson's notion of *durée*. I only experience a past event because I remember it in significant connection with other, preceding or later events in an intimate fusion that is a stranger to any mere clock-time "spatialized" punctuality. Its significance is only sustained, and its strong event character only continues to loom, if it gets endlessly nonidentically repeated into the future. A failed revolution quite literally does not "happen" to the same degree as a successful one.

At the same time, Péguy's transferral of duration from a psychic to a historical plane involves on his part a certain disparagement of Bergson's duality between fused psychic inward time and the mere outer appearances of discrete events. On the contrary, for Péguy, if human time is always first of all public as both physically mediated through motion, and conventionally symbolic according to calendric markings, then duration consists, even for inward memory, in nothing but a catena of events, which, albeit they only arise as linked, remain also mysteriously discrete. The chain only consists in the links, even though no link is ever instanced on its own. And the mark of this discretion is that no real, actual, event is fully absorbable into a sequence. If it was ever "over" once and for all, or fully specifiable, it would be impossible for it either to be epistemologically notable or for it to have ontologically occurred in the first place. The most decisive events, without which there would be no human history whatsoever, arise just because they are saturated with significance—with other events, many words, and both verbal and physical

---

7 For much more on the paradoxes of repetition and discussions of Péguy, see Catherine Pickstock, *Repetition and Identity* (Oxford: Oxford University Press, 2013).

consequences that surround them in profusion, but for reasons we cannot quite fathom.

However, for Péguy the academicians unrealistically and uncritically ignore both sides of the paradox. They fail to see that historical causality is retrospective, that what once occurred depends upon what occurs next, and they equally fail to see that important events are such precisely because they are indefinable and endlessly debatable. In consequence a lived folk relationship to events, in private memory, rumor, and embellishment, as more accessible to the provincial lycée teacher than to the Parisian professor, lies always closer to historical reality than the ponderous researches of historians—a reflection that for Péguy renders much of the Renan-like business of Biblical criticism, in the face of the most saturated event of all, pitiably absurd. For the editor of the *Cahiers de la quinzaine* it is thereby the case that the sophisticatedly metaphysical keeps pace with innate folkloric wisdom, whereas the triumph of the "scientific" in the realm of the humanities is in reality the triumph of the middlebrowed and the time-serving. This, for him, has become the fate of his erstwhile fellow Dreyfusards, once upholding, pluralistically, the rights of the Jewish *mystique* that no true Catholic could ever disrespect, but now supporting a secular dogmatism in forgetfulness that the revolution itself was born in an atmosphere of liturgical disclosure.

The third argument has to do with a further implication of the event's saturated character. This is that there cannot be, in principle, any exhaustive history, even though the professors speak and act as if this were possible. An event may take a minute or a day, yet research into its reality necessarily takes longer and can never come to an end. That is because an occurrence is in excess of all its causal occasions that can be endlessly debated since they are without number, whether one divides up the local and immediate process of an event infinitesimally or alludes to its entire endlessly ramifying setting throughout all time and space. The whole stake of historiography resides in circumscribing the finite, yet it turns out that the event as an instance of peculiar finite uniqueness appears in this manner to coincide with the infinite. Thus there is never enough evidence for anything (especially for antiquity) or always far too much (especially for modernity). Nor, since an event only exists as repeated, can one really detach oneself from the past to produce only objective history, while even subjective history is problematic, since the same historical indeterminacy attends the questions of who one really is and what one's notions really amount to in the present. The only possible history would then consist in a mediation between the objective and the subjective, which would demand a submissive fidelity to some past horizon of significance and at the same time a commitment further to explore that horizon in the future.

Yet if it is the future conceived as aggregative that is alone projected by the historical past, as for prevailing positivism, then such an historiographical endeavor would be ruled out of court. Péguy seems therefore to imply not just that only committed history is possible but also that only a sacral history can outmaneuver the skeptical aporias that he has delineated. The "explanation" of an event has to yield place—like method to narrated substance—to the revelatory character of an event as *itself* disclosive and framing, as always a substantive horizon stretching further than any merely formal perspective. It follows that if we are to explain history in general, then this will require faith in the exploration of certain events and perhaps one supreme event as permitting us to construct narratives of universal human significance.

This implication is paralleled and more specifically developed in terms of the fourth criticism of the historical attitude of the new "age of the intellectuals." Here we switch from the level of empirical record to that of empirical example and sociological recommendation for action. On this level we can locate once more the theme of the civil religion of futurity. Péguy claims that this lay creed renders all notions of justice and therefore of ethics incoherent. For instead of eternity and the God of eternity we have substituted history and so her personified pagan guardian Clio, who had never, she tells us, expected to rule alone. There is no longer any eternal One to judge us here below; instead, each one of us is endlessly subject to the revisionary judgment of the indefinitely many people in the future who will be also be indefinitely displaced and in turn succeeded. Yet their verdicts upon us and our effects upon them are unknown; anticipation of them is useless and therefore should not be, as is currently the case, erected into a principle whereby to guide our social and individual practice. Furthermore, the uncertainty of this guidance can only encourage an erring on the side of a self-sacrificial or even self-obliterating action far in excess of any pathological religious self-abasement—here the following 100 years since 1914 have abundantly confirmed Péguy's diagnosis. Thus it would appear that after all the rights of Man and the sanctity of the passing interval can only be seen by the light of eternity. Paradoxically, it is eternity that saves the significance of the present moment and a sheerly temporal perspective that betrays and violates it. Equally it is an eternal sense of right that can correctly judge each passing epoch: such a judgment on the regime of Napoleon III Péguy sees as mediated by Hugo's *Châtiments,* wherein the sometimes bathetic final rhymes of stanzas negatively "crown" it with the verdict of self-failure and self-determined collapse.

In his *Clio I,* Péguy accordingly denounced "the lay curés who deny the eternal aspect of the temporal," implying that this destroys any sense of meaning in human history, since it is always grounded in mystical initiation (echoing perhaps Pierre-Simon Ballanche) and a genuine historiography must reflect upon this elusive reality.[8] Here, one should bear in mind that Péguy frequently alludes to the fact that the ancient pagan city was still based upon eternity and the soul, and that antique heroism, which he thinks transcends antique polytheism, would not have been possible without these beliefs, which sustained it through and past disaster.[9] So for him, the post-Christian is peculiarly terrible and perhaps arises because a later

---

8 For a slightly incomplete English translation, see *Temporal and Eternal,* 85–165.

9 In *Véronique,* Péguy says that the two greatest human civilizations, the ancient Mediterranean pagan and the medieval Christian, were both uniquely founded upon disaster. See Charles Péguy, *Véronique: Dialogue de l'histoire et de l'âme charnelle* (Paris: Gallimard, 1972), 269–71.

and corrupted Christianity (especially after René Descartes) had already in part enthroned the psychic and spiritual as entirely detachable from the body, and yet not immediately or necessarily involved with transcendence.[10] And quite certainly it is implied that modernity has prised away the Christian discovery of the tragic dignity of life in time from its contrasting reference to the eternal, in order to produce its barren cult of futurity.

In this way the post-Christian has bleakly and austerely compounded a modernity that was, in any case, according to *Clio I*, about to begin in the late antique world, but which the Incarnation interrupted—a pagan "presentist" modernity of hedonistic decadence, the lapsing of philosophy into occultism and of law into brutally organized Roman force. To the decadent sucking of the eternal and the psychic into the squandered present it has added the post-Christian cult of time as now the celebration of a secular, indefinite eschaton.

(ii)

Here one can pause to note that Péguy's account of Christian historicity is profoundly *non-Joachite*. The twelfth-century Abbot of Calabria had steered much Christian thought about history away from its patristic and specifically Augustinian moorings, which had regarded the Incarnation as the culmination of the post-Fall era involving a gradual disclosure of the divine Logos, or the second person of the Trinity.[11] With the incarnation of the Logos, the eschaton has already arrived and history is already fulfilled. Insofar as it nevertheless continues for a relatively short interval (of unknown duration) then, for Augustine, this is a history of sustained incarnation of the *totus Christi*,[12] which is the body of Christ as the church, the *Civitas Dei*. As for the fathers in general, so for Augustine, the entirety of the Old Testament spiritual senses are allegorically realized in this figure of the One Christ, which nonetheless included his extended, ecclesial body. Herein lies the full "spiritual" revelation to which the New Testament pointed, and which can only be adequately brought out and even essentially completed (as early medieval authors like Rupert of Deutz argued) by the patristic allegorical reading of the Bible itself.[13] Yet this "spiritual" disclosure is still that of the unexpected embodiment of God, which alone allows human beings, inversely, to recover their spiritual destiny of eventual beatification.

Péguy's approach effectively revives, in a novel and in some respects modern manner, just this Augustinian and Christocentric view of history. But it had been disturbed by Joachim, in an intervention that was to have a very long theological

---

10 Charles Péguy, "Note conjointe sur M. Descartes et la philosophie Cartésienne," in *Oeuvres en Prose, 1909–1914* (Paris: Gallimard, 1961), 1357–1552.

11 See Joseph Ratzinger, *The Theology of History in St Bonaventure* (Chicago: Franciscan Herald Press, 1989).

12 For this topos, see especially the *Enarrationes in Psalmos*.

13 Ratzinger, *Theology of History*, 1–55.

and then secular echo.[14] First, for the Calabrian, following the existing innovation of writers like Rupert of Deutz, Honorius of Autun, and Anselm of Haverberg, Augustine's specific statement that one cannot see in events occurring since Christ (like the coronation of Charlemagne) specific parallels to Old Testament events is effectively contradicted. For Augustine this refusal is inevitable if one considers that Christ, as God incarnate, has irrevocably and unsurpassably fulfilled all Old Testament intimations whatsoever. But Joachim takes over and extends certain existing denials of this view by other monastic writers, which effectively regard the era since Christ as a new worldly and not just a final, eschatological epoch. Hence for this outlook, political leaders like Charlemagne can be regarded as being prophesied by Old Testament counterparts. Such a perspective effectively starts to see Christ as much as a hinge or medium as he is an end or the beginning of the end.[15]

But in the second place Joachim went much further by suggesting that the era post-Christ was giving way to a new era of the Spirit, a postinstitutional epoch of pure and universal fulfillment of apostleship. This novel intellectual move invents the paradoxical notion of a future epoch purely within material time that is yet characterized by a spiritualization, or indeed a disincarnation. Joseph Ratzinger rightly here says that "spiritualization" or "pneumatization" does not as yet amount to "idealization," yet one could argue that the somewhat contradictory notion of an "etherealized" future on this same material earth must almost inevitably drift in an idealizing direction.[16] For it is just this paradox that, as Henri de Lubac argued, crucially encourages in the course of time a secularizing displacement of a spiritual eternity with a spiritualized future to come on earth. De Lubac saw this as eventually comprising the complementary reverse face of *pura natura*. Just as the idea of a fully integral nature without supernatural reference gives a space for the "sheerly secular" in advance, so the Joachite hope curiously accords this pure nature, when supernaturally purified, the accolade of the sheerly spiritual at a remove from human material, sexual, familial, and political necessities.[17] This hope is surely just the reverse of faith in the God incarnate, of the following of a God who has renewed us by becoming utterly immersed in normal, finite human processes.

Moreover, as Ratzinger showed in his doctoral thesis, while the spiritual Franciscans came to associate the advent of St. Francis and radical mendicancy with the breaking-in of the pneumatic eon, even the mainline members of the order, following the lead of St. Bonaventure, the Franciscan General, accepted the first part of Joachim's innovative approach (which he shared with some predecessors), though by no means the second. Thus for Bonaventure, beyond the level

---

14 See Henri de Lubac, *La postérité spirituelle de Joachim de Flore* (Paris: Cerf, 2014).

15 Ratzinger, *Theology of History*, 56–109.

16 Ratzinger, *Theology of History*, 187n82.

17 See John Milbank, *The Suspended Middle* (Grand Rapids, MI: Eerdmas, 2015), esp. 64.

of the allegorical sense that points entirely to Christ, there are certain prophetic *theoriae* that indicate events to come within the Christian epoch, including the appearance of St. Francis and St. Dominic.[18]

In consequence, this epoch has a gradually "spiritualizing" destiny—an eventual bent toward pure contemplation. This can appear paradoxical in view of the much greater engagement with the "world out there" of the mendicant orders, as compared with that of the monastics. Yet unlike the Dominicans, who were founded to preach and to oppose (Catharist) heresy, the Franciscans remained in a sense bifurcated between the drive to achieve a purer state of contemplation, beyond ritual and regular material support on the one hand, and a preaching mission on the other.[19] One can see in this dichotomy a tendency in effect to prise apart the supernatural and the natural into respective purities, whereas the Dominican quest further to know God remained inseparable from the desire to communicate him. Hence, in the latter case, the new adoption of a more "apostolic" destiny, demanding at once more spiritual rigor and more external exposure, remains thoroughly in keeping with the patristic and Augustinian understanding whereby spiritual growth or "deification" does not contradict but rather comprises a deepened incarnation or an entering into solidarity with this-worldly processes. Both aspects were of course involved also for the Franciscans, but they tended to be more in antithesis, or where they were reconciled to involve an identification with the precultural natural world, in refusal of the peculiar artifaction generic to human nature.[20] For the Dominicans, history after Christ remains the mediation of the God–Man through his extended complex sociopolitical (and thereby for now imperfect) body; for the Franciscans, especially Bonaventure, it becomes more a disincarnating drive toward the maximum achievement of perfect spiritual contemplation among essentially dispersed individuals.[21] Since this goal involves for them an eventual surrendering of the intellect

---

18 Ratzinger, *Theology of History,* 1–55 and 109–14.

19 See Simon Tugwell OP, "Introduction" to *Early Dominicans: Selected Writings* (New York: Paulist Press, 1982), 1–47.

20 See Giorgio Agamben, *The Highest Poverty: Monastic Rules and Forms of Life*, trans. Adam Kotsko (Stanford: Stanford University Press, 2013).

21 See Eric Voegelin, "Saint Francis," in *History of Political Ideas*, vol. 2, *The Middle Ages to Aquinas,* 135–43. Voegelin went perhaps further than anyone else in seeing the perception (at least) of St. Francis as *alter Christus* as ambivalent. Of course de Lubac is right to say (*La Postérité*, 139) that the newly "spiritual" man, St. Francis, was only such as *stigmatized,* but Voegelin (a Catholicizing Lutheran who was extremely close to de Lubac and is often building on his theological theses) probes the theological dangers that immediately opened from a tendency to read this as equalization with Christ *by a mere human being.* Read this way the stigmata ceases to be an incarnating balance to pneumatic perfection, but rather the very mark of corporeal denial. Thus this reading renders Francis's uniquely novel fate in terms of the same dubious paradox that with Joachim opens up the idea of a "spiritual future on earth"—namely a sheerly spiritual and beatified destiny in this life and in this current material body. Intimately connected with this is the tendency—as being newly explored by

to the emotions and to the will, one discovers here as de Lubac divulged (at least for the case of the Franciscan spirituals), a certain idolizing of "freedom" and understanding of the future as the release or "emancipation" of liberty that will eventually inform nearly all secular ideologies.

The subtle rift opened up in the Christian understanding of history by Joachim and the Franciscans in general (not merely the Franciscan spirituals) resonates even in our own day. Thus, for example, de Lubac, Jean Daniélou, and Ratzinger are at one in upholding the rejection of Joachim's second major thesis, the age of the Spirit, and in acknowledging the mainly shared ground here between Bonaventure and Thomas Aquinas. However, Ratzinger, at the youthful stage of his doctrinal thesis on Bonaventure's theology of history, appeared to grant equal validity to Thomas's more Augustinian account of history and to Bonaventure's more Joachite one, which accords with the latter's first major thesis, concerning the eventful parallels between the Old Testament and New Testament epochs. This allowance would appear to be in tension with Ratzinger's Augustinianism (which he always knew Bonaventure deviated from)[22] with his later, overwhelmingly Lubacian approach to theology, with his trenchant and admirable denial, especially as Pope, that there

Aaron Riches—of Franciscan Christologies (including in the case of Bonaventure) to be somewhat semi-Nestorian: the perfection of Christ as a human individual gets somewhat prised apart from his divine personification, which, to the contrary, Aquinas emphasizes to a quite hyperbolic degree.

22 He notes in *The Theology of History* that Aquinas's Trinitarian theology is far more Augustinian than that of Bonaventure. Today, in the wake of de Lubac, who pronounced Aquinas's Augustinianism to be "plus consequent" than that of the Franciscan General (*La postérité*, 159), we also realize that it is Aquinas who cleaves more truly to Augustine's theory of knowledge as illumination, with Aristotelian modifications (arguably quite consistent with Augustine, who never denies the crucial role of sensory mediation) far less drastic than Bonaventure's Avicennian ones that pull the doctrine at once in a somewhat ontologist and yet an a priorist direction. (Though as Ratzinger rightly notes, Bonaventure himself saw Aquinas's account of human knowledge as a *variant* of illuminationist theory.) This is in keeping with Bonaventure's equally Avicennian tendency to see the divine ideas as univocally exemplified albeit in differing degrees in both God and the created order, and so as reciprocally "alike" across the infinite/finite divide, in an effective bypassing of a true emanationist or participatory scheme. Just for this reason, Fernand van Steenberghen may have been right to see more seeds of a truly theologically independent philosophy in Bonaventure than in Aquinas—however much this appears to go almost clean against the surface of their texts. For in Aquinas a specifically independent metaphysics ultimately has to be referred in toto to theology, whereas in Bonaventure a few rather random philosophical theses taken largely from Avicenna, especially regarding the plurality of forms, are not all that well integrated into his exemplarist, Logos-centered theology, and tend rather to distort it. And while his metaphysics appears to be wholly a theology, the beginnings of a univocal reversibility of "likeness" as between forms in the Creator and in the Creation suggests that, after all God is "transcendentally" (as Scotus will later specifically say) included within a more general field of being. Ratzinger concedes much to Fernand van Steenberghen's

can ever be any total surpassing of the "Hellenizing" of Christian theology, and his highly nonvoluntarist and nonaffective upholding of the theological centrality of an integral reason (which fully includes an affective dimension).

Nevertheless, in his main mature period of theological writing one finds statements to the effect that Christology must not be conceived in terms of God's "taking further root in the world" but rather of Him encouraging the spiritual transcendence of the world, as if these two things were, indeed, in antithesis.[23] Yet one can note here that this "taking further root" is problematically identified with the church's more institutional aspect, rather than with incorporation and socialization as such, which surely have a far wider and indeed basically interpersonal remit. Likewise, Incarnation as "God's taking root" is associated by Ratzinger with an isolation of Christ's humanity from his divinity.

Yet it is hard to see that any such thing could have been involved in a supposed relatively early patristic sundering of ecclesiology from pneumatology, which is what Ratzinger is here claiming: "the Church was no longer understood charismatically from the angle of pneumatology, but was seen exclusively from the standpoint of the Incarnation as something all too earthbound and finally explained entirely on the basis of the power categories of worldly thinking" (even if Ratzinger thinks this final degeneration arose much later). But patristic Christological approaches to the church rather assumed something like a "communication of idioms," and while any "taking of God into the humanity" is refused by Athanasius, on account of the incommensurable ontological primacy of the divine, the "assumption of humanity into the Godhead" involves such a permeation of all of human nature by divinity that surely this can indeed be reversely seen from our perspective as a divine "taking root."

Moreover, in the best of patristic theology (in Augustine, for example), is not the physically organic sense of the church as the body of Christ balanced and qualified by the interpersonal sense of the church as Christ's bestowing on his followers the power to receive him—a bestowing that is exactly one with the eternal procession of the Spirit from the Son? But if, as for Ratzinger in this text, "it is a question here, not of the Spirit as a person within God, but as the power of God that opens with the Resurrection of Jesus," then could not there be a danger of thinking of the Spirit's action too impersonally and merely "dynamically" as the power of the united Godhead? And as reaching us problematically *apart* from our participation in the Trinitarian relations—this being problematic if the persons of the Trinity are *constituted* by their relations. In general Ratzinger admirably wishes to view Being and History together, and therefore to sustain a profound link between the eternal Trinity and the history of Salvation. Thus, he rightly deplores any tendency to so

rebuttal of Étienne Gilson's reading of Bonaventure as Augustinian, but today one might agree even more with the Belgian medievalist. See *The Theology of History*, 119–63.

23 Joseph Ratzinger, *Introduction to Christianity*, trans. J. R. Foster (San Francisco: Ignatius, 1990), 332–4.

"historicize" the credal invocation of the Trinity as to see the section on creation as only concerning God the Father. Yet any such theological reading of the creed surely occurred only much later, and it would seem odd to blame the same "historicization" for an excessive linking of the Spirit to its emergence from the incarnate Christ, thereby rendering the third section of the creed "a prolongation of the story of Christ in the gift of the Spirit and, therefore, as a reference to 'the last days' between the coming of Christ and his return."[24] This is odd, because "historicization" is here producing the opposite result of that complained of by Ratzinger in the case of the first part of the creed—namely the sundering of the action of the Father in creation from that of the other two persons. For in this instance, he is complaining of two tight a proximity between Son and Spirit! But in that case, then surely the historical focus on the event of temporal mediation of the Spirit through the Son is precisely *attaining* that unity of Trinitarian ontology with salvific history that Ratzinger so rightly seeks. The seeming desire here to grant more independence to a vertical descent of the Spirit is avowedly at one with a certain sundering of a tight link between the economic action of the Spirit with eschatology, and with the incarnate Christ regarded as already "the end." Instead, there seems to be present a highly Bonaventuran desire to associate the Spirit with a significance of a somewhat extra-Christic—because ever more spiritualizing and so disincarnating—history following after Christ, who has turned out to be not the final end after all.

A certain danger of wrenching pneumatology away from both Trinitarian and Christological doctrine is perhaps also shown in Ratzinger's demand for ecclesiology to "take its departure from teaching about the Holy Spirit and His gifts"— rather, it would seem, than from an equal co-beginning with the thematic of the body of Christ.[25] In apparent consequence, the "goal" of such a doctrine is said to be "the history of God with men" or, alternatively, of "the function of the story of Christ for mankind as a whole." These phrases *could* be read as subordinating, in a Bonaventuran manner, the Incarnation to the overall history of God's dealing with the world, before and after Christ, with the Christ event somehow subtly reduced to the "function" of an exemplary historical pivot. For such a perspective, it could be thought that the *entire* point of the Incarnation is to bring about a spiritualizing deification of all men rather than the entirely novel and paradoxical "inclusion" of God and Man together within a certain finite but infinite "form." This being now the only mode that, in a fallen world, deification can take—yet miraculously in excess of even deification: "And that a higher gift than grace/ Should flesh and blood refine/God's presence and his very self/And essence all divine?"[26]

---

24 Ratzinger, *Introduction to Christianity*, 332.

25 Ratzinger, *Introduction to Christianity*, 333.

26 John Henry Newman, "Praise to the Holiest in the Height," *Heart Speaks to Heart: Selected Spiritual Writings*, ed. Lawrence S. Cunningham (Hyde Park, NY: New City Press, 2004), 36.

Certainly one can agree with Ratzinger that the Incarnation and the giving of the Spirit belong together. Yet if the weight is placed too much on the latter instance, then this co-belonging is no longer united with the "substantive relations" of the Trinity, which Bonaventure indeed started to de-emphasize. One must surely rather insist that we can never vertically receive the Spirit at all, since it is the Spirit of the Father and the Son, unless we receive it also horizontally from the divine–human Christ and his ecclesial transmission through many human others. In this sense there can be no genuinely vertical "charismatic" aspect to history divorced from the horizontal, organic, traditioned, and also institutional dimension.

It may seem more than surprising to see Ratzinger as in any way acceding to such a divorce—yet this can be a logical consequence of a lingering admiration for some aspects of Bonaventure's approach to history. However, at many other times his later emphasis is more purely Augustinian and Thomistic, as when he explicitly stresses that the church's glory is mixed up with the mess, including the political mess of human existence,[27] and also when he rebuts the Lutheran sense of the church as a mere spatial "community" of coinciding individuals, as opposed to being a transmitted *successio* through time.[28]

All the same it might seem as if Ratzinger's youthful championing of Bonaventure is not without some later echo in his theology. But the Bonaventuran theology of history is problematic just to the degree that it sustains, in the wake of Joachim, the near contradiction of at once seeming to take more seriously the events of history since the Incarnation, and yet discounting these events except insofar as they are as it were "evacuated" events, bearing solely upon the spiritual. The most crucial sign of this paradox is the Franciscan insistence on absolute "highest" poverty, (though this is not even monastic possession in common) as the very *acme* of apostolic perfection. For thereby an ultimately interior willed attitude, in its formality—"non possessiveness"—can, they believe, only be guaranteed by the *external* practice and legal status of *simplex usus fati*. The exact opposite was true for Aquinas and most Dominicans: nonpossessiveness is an internal attitude because it is substantive and flexibly defined by ultimate intention; therefore, it is compatible with any eternal mode of actual property and does not require an external negative sign of authentication. In the Franciscan case, a rigid interiority is marked by ever the same univocal absence; in the Dominican case, a fluid interiority is blended with an analogically varying relation to practice.

By contrast with Ratzinger, Jean Daniélou, like de Lubac, remained more consistently Augustinian in his conception of history, *Anno Domini*, as an extension of the Incarnation.[29] On the one hand, this outlook, as we have seen, appears to give

27 Ratzinger, *Introduction to Christianity,* 343.

28 *Principles of Catholic Theology: Building Stones for a Fundamental Theology,* trans. Mary Frances McCarthy SMD (San Francisco: Ignatius, 1987), 290–4.

29 Jean Daniélou, "Christology and History," in *The Lord of History: Reflections on the Inner Meaning of History,* trans. Nigel Abercrombie (London: Longmans, 1958), 183–202, esp. 201.

less providential importance to specific events in the church's history and to that
degree can even be seen as "secularizing" these events. On the other hand, this
is just because it more consistently observes the logic of the Incarnation: all the
merely human is now of equal sacred significance, and the entirety of the church's
history is saturated with a divine–human meaning, which is ultimately but one.
Yet unity does not imply stasis: both Augustine and Aquinas insisted that the
Incarnation has improved the human condition and brought about progress in
time.[30]

This "secularizing" aspect of the Augustinian–Thomist approach to history can
be linked, as the youthful Ratzinger so profoundly noted, to Aquinas's attitude
toward infinite regress in the matter of causality. The angelic doctor only disal-
lowed this (and thereby one can see that his "cosmological argument" requires one
to accept—as one should—the Aristotelian–Neoplatonic, and not the Newtonian
account of ultimate causality) in the case of a vertical series of causes where the
causal power stands in a relevant sense asymmetrically higher than the caused
effect, as in the series beginning individual man and then rising to "elementary
body" and then to "the sun" and so forth.[31] Such a "substantive" series must,
Thomas argues, come to a definite end in a first cause. However this does not
rationally (as opposed to the requirements of faith, which appear to acquire an
origin of Creation in time)[32] preclude an *accidental* series of efficient causes, such
that man might have been generated by man ad infinitum.

From this daring concession to Aristotle, one can see just why Dante placed
Aquinas as proximate to Siger of Brabant in paradise, albeit as correcting him (just
as he places Bonaventure in a precisely parallel pairing with Joachim). However,
the Franciscan General rebuts such a view, and instead sees time itself as involved
in the metaphysical (and essentially Neoplatonic) *egressio* and *regressio* of being
that Aquinas also recognized. Thus time for Bonaventure literally begins and ends
in God.

In his doctoral thesis Ratzinger appears strongly to sympathize with this view as
newly allowing, in a manner inherently demanded by Christian faith, the knowledge of history to be fully scientific. He reasons that if events in time and in history
are just accidental and outside the range of true cognition, which is of universals,
then it is difficult to see how Christian claims to the unique and universal significance of specific happenings can gain any purchase—save, one could add, in rather
grossly fideistic terms.

---

30   For this reason it would not seem to be true that recognition of a "dynamic" aspect
to human history is solely down to Joachim.<AQ: Please clarify: is solely down to> So I am
slightly puzzled as to de Lubac's assigning a Joachite element to the nineteenth-century
French Christian socialist Pierre Buchez on the mere grounds of rightly locating a dynamic
and not just conservative aspect to his thought. See *La postérité spirituelle*, 520.

31   Aquinas, *ST* I. q. 46 a.2 ad 7.

32   But of course Origen had not thought so, while yet totally sustaining the radical
dependence of Creation. Today this must surely be an open question.

However, one can wonder whether the Bonaventuran response to this admitted problem is coherent or acceptable. Does it not tend to confuse horizontal with vertical or ontic with ontological dimensions? Indeed, it may be Bonaventure's already univocalist tendency to see the same discrete *formae* as assuming either infinite or finite actuality that encourages him to confuse and merge ontological with ontic commencement and inauguration. One can express this point inversely by saying that, while, in one sense, Aquinas' rational allowance of an eternal creation (the infinite series of accidental causes) appears to be a concession to Aristotle and to Siger's bifurcated truth, it can also, in another sense, be read as a far more radical grasp of the nature of Created dependency as not involving any change and therefore necessarily any "beginning" in the ordinary sense. So it is *not* that Aquinas is saying that, rationally speaking, the world may be uncreated and eternally immanent in a pagan fashion, but rather that *even* this "pagan eternity" if it be supposed, must be vertically accounted for as radically emergent, without reserve, ex nihilo from God.[33]

Does this Thomistic view, however, leave the temporal event as without scientific interest? A longer answer here would need to explore the ways in which Aquinas, somewhat in excess of Aristotle, in certain ways can make "accidental" properties (and especially the power of the human soul to know) nevertheless crucial to defining a thing's essence. But most crucially one could argue that the most extreme instance of this paradox in Aquinas concerns the way in which for him, as for the Fathers, Christ is fully human, existing in a state that normally requires personhood and yet is only a person—and even, at least in the *Summa Theologiae*, only in being—insofar as he is divine.[34] Thus for Aquinas, one might gloss, *the entire possibility* of a scientifically significant historical event depends upon the Incarnation, where the first and universal cause has assumed into itself a particular human being and specific human history. By doing so it has for Aquinas (as for the Fathers) also assumed into itself human nature as such, and so, one could venture, in addition human history as such. This history is exhaustively, after the Fall, the time of gradual Christological redemption and then, with and after Christ, the time of the end and the fulfillment of the end.

It is therefore in strictly Christological terms that Thomas brings together his metaphysics of God as esse with his account of history as throughout the history of salvation, since, for him, Christ's being (at least in the *Summa*) is entirely the divine "to be" itself, with no ontic addition or remainder. In this way all of history and indeed of cosmic time would be saved from the fate of pagan "accidental irrelevance" but in a manner different from that of Bonaventure's contrivance. From a Thomistic perspective, the problem with the latter would be that it substitutes for a Christological raising of history to scientific significance a kind of sanctification or ontologization of time as such—which could even be seen to foreshadow the intellectual move finally made by Martin Heidegger in the twentieth century.

33 Rowan Williams made this point to me long ago.
34 Aquinas, *ST* III, q.17 a.2.

In consequence, while Christ is radically the *medium* for Bonaventure, there remains a danger that he becomes the center of time such that this category exceeds him—just as the Godhead would exceed the eternal Son, were the latter not constituted by substantive relations (which thesis Bonaventure backs away from). With Aquinas, to the contrary, the Incarnation in a sense coincides with time tout court. For he says that, within all time, perfection precedes imperfection insofar as perfect states are the efficient causes of imperfect ones, while equally imperfection precedes perfection insofar as things but gradually attain their proper finality.[35] Thus time in general is constituted by the oscillation of these two priorities. Yet with Christ alone the two priorities occur simultaneously: Christ is at once the cause and the realization of his own perfection. Just because Christ in this way includes all temporal dynamics it was "fitting" (*conveniens*) for Christ to arrive after the beginning, but before the end of time. As Ratzinger observes, this suggests that, for Aquinas as for Bonaventure, Christ is a center and a middle; however, Thomas's noting of the unique coincidence of priorities radically ensures that for the angelic doctor Christ is only this as both absolute beginning and absolute end.[36] And given this coincidence, the further historical work of our deified perfection that arises from Christ as efficient cause is also the outworking of his perfection as final end, of a "fullness" that is already upon us, since the new law of the gospel already represents the breaking-in of the celestial City upon the realm of the ancient law.[37]

For this reason, the time of the church and the very nature of the earthly church should be primarily construed as belonging both to the time of Christ and to the time of the end. Of course, this remorselessly Christological focus does not deny that aspect of the church that is its continued constitution by the Holy Spirit: the point is rather that, from the Marian outset, the descent of the Incarnation has, as its other aspect, a spiritual ascent that is at one with human receptivity and response.

(iii)

In the terms of Péguy this means that Christian life "repeats" always the one Christ event, but nonidentically, in terms of an integral freedom that is enabled and not impaired by this "following." Péguy's outlook on history, while novel, has to be viewed as primarily Augustinian and non-Joachite just for this reason, despite his overwhelming and heuristically guiding rejection of the cult of futurity as tending

---

35 Aquinas, *ST* III, q. 1 a.6 resp.

36 Ratzinger rather oddly suggested, in the footnotes to his thesis, that in this passage Aquinas removed himself still further than did Bonaventure from the patristic association of the Incarnation with finality. But this does not well concur with his general account of Aquinas here, as I have tried to argue in the main text above. See also de Lubac, *La postérité*, 159.

37 Aquinas, *In 4 Sent.* d.1 q.1 a.2.

precisely to disincarnate humanity, by forcing us always to sacrifice the corporeal present in favor of an ideal and spiritual future. Instead of dangerous "metaphysical" schemes for creating a new sort of human being in the future, at once sheerly material and irreligious (*pura natura*) and yet also immanently spiritual and ascetic (secularized Joachimism), Péguy insisted that his mode of mutualist socialism (extremely close to Catholic social teaching) represented the modest, nonutopian, and achievable demand for a more just distribution of the world's economic resources.[38]

Nevertheless, despite his assault on the new lay priesthood who uphold the post-Christian cult of future freedom, in the same text, *Clio I,* Péguy also vocally denounced the church leaders who fail to see the temporal in the eternal, and even held this group to be the more culpable in terms of secularization. By ignoring the key Christian discovery of the significance of the temporal, they had helped ensure its colonization by sheerly lay forces. Once discovered, the temporal cannot be simply forgotten, yet if Christianity abandons it, then its significance will be read in merely material terms. But originally the new value of the temporal meant its significance for eternity itself as implied by the Incarnation and our sacramental inauguration into beatitude—initiations begun in time, yet forever upheld in both their commencement and irreversibility.

The new valuation of time concerned the process by which God went over into the temporal in order not to command but to redeem it, yet in the course of the ages *Anno Domini*, this "machine," as Péguy terms it, has been reversed such that all temporal concerns are sacrificed in terms of a crudely positivistic redemptive calculus (which perhaps anticipates the modern, monetary one) to supposedly eternal ones. Thus, lay interests have also been sacrificed to clerical interests and vocations to aid the world, and to an institutional concern to regulate and administer it. Understandably, (and one can think of Dante's much earlier lay protest here), the laity might want to emancipate themselves from such a distorted procedure that has come to confuse the priority of the spiritual with the hypocritical temporal interests of this priority's representatives. In the case of recent French history, this had even led the church to become newly complicit with outright anti-Semitism, such that Péguy's inability to enter into sacramental communion with the church was partly due to his repulsion to the thought of any association with erstwhile anti-Dreyfusards. Of course, one can wonder whether this alienation from the officially liturgical was part of what impelled him to such an acute sense of the permeation of *all* human reality by liturgical processes.[39]

From this double excoriation of the lay and the ecclesiastical clerisies, one can infer that for Péguy it is only a Christianity that takes into full account the unity of the temporal with the eternal that will be able to give a proper account of history as

---

38 See the discussion of his debate with Jean Jaurès over these issues in de Lubac, *La postérité spirituelle,* 751.

39 See Catherine Pickstock, *After Writing: On the Liturgical Consummation of Philosophy* (Oxford: Blackwell, 1997).

such. By this, he means a fully incarnational Christianity, and he would appear to suggest that the Christian *mystique* has failed because its incarnational aspect has never been realized sufficiently (even if, in the French Middle Ages, it was far more so than today). It has never quite been seen that the Incarnation implies an equal standing for lay existence and lay concerns and a service rather than a denial of the world and its loves and anxieties.

The Christian event

In terms of Péguy's four critical points about history and historiography, one can argue that the problems he identified are addressed through a Christian conception of a providential government of the historical process—but only if this is revised in Péguy's own peculiar theoretical direction, which involves a radicalization and thus a purification of orthodoxy, insofar as his aim is to render it more incarnational.

First, then, in terms of the organic character of history as unpredictable flourishing irruption and inevitable decay. Through his verbal practice in prose and especially through his poetry, Péguy links this to the pastoral character of the Gospels and to the endless agricultural analogies of Christ's parables. This suggests that Christianity, stemming from the birth of God in time, is a peculiarly rooted historical process, intertwining physical and spiritual growth, as manifest in the unique medieval instance of an advanced culture centered on town, village, monastery, and field rather than on big cities exploiting rural hinterlands. Péguy speaks of high medieval France as if it were in direct continuity with the Palestine of Christ's time. This view is surely not grounded in a fanciful nationalism (even if it is not quite free of that) but rather in his sense that Christendom, for all its terrible faults, most of all sought to embody the gospel injunctions, and that in many ways, Gothic France did indeed represent the acme and fulcrum of this endeavor.[40] As Latour has written, it is as if, in his long free-verse poems, with their imitations and extension of Biblical didacticism, incantation, repetition, and parallelism, Péguy was trying to write a fifth Gospel,

---

40 As Professor David Gervais pointed out at the Oxford colloquium, Péguy's praise in *Le porche du mystère de la deuzième virtu* of the supremacy of French gardens and the unmatched beauty of the French countryside might be expected to grate on English ears to the point of a nonreception of the poetry, yet it is pre-echoed by the invading English king in William Shakespeare's *Henry V.* One can note also how G. K. Chesterton and Hilaire Belloc's parallel Anglomania was also in part a Francophilia and suggest that the relative ignoring of Péguy in Britain by a cultured audience (though not by most of the best poets) is less to do with his incorrigible Frenchness than with the way in which there has been a general English metropolitan ignoring of writers sprung from the people and pursuing religious or socially conservative thematics—so also of native writers like Ivor Gurney, David Jones, and even D. H. Lawrence, early and late.

not in any Gnostic spirit, but precisely in order to state again with freshness and difference the original Gospel message. This alone, he must have thought, in such desperate times, might counter the decadence into which Christianity had entered.

Yet his attitude to this decline is complex. Above all, and not without Augustinian echoes, Péguy thought that God, by risking incarnation in time, had risked not just his Son's death but also the historical decline of belief in himself. To show himself in fully human form had been necessary because of sin, and in order to confront human beings honestly with his truth and to leave it to human freedom whether to accept or to reject it. It may well be, as Péguy argues in *Clio I*, that the post-Christian age renders surviving faith more than ever a matter of pure faith because it is now the product of a resisting liberty.

Yet at the same time, the divine in time is a peculiarly undying organism. Whenever there is distress, which will now increase, then, says Péguy in the same text, it will always be the case that the Christian offer of compassionate relief will come uniquely to the fore. Moreover, in the light of eternity, there is a hidden and now genuine progress, as Péguy elaborates in his long poem *Le porche du mystère de la deuxième virtu*.[41] All of human finite life goes in circles, and therefore we should repeatedly inscribe these circles not out of any purpose, not in order to arrive at any finite end, but playfully, like children and out of a hope that is not hope for *anything* definable, but obscurely for the remote hope of eternal bliss, in which pointlessness beyond point will be infinitely consummated. In the case of fallen, grown-up man, this endless finite cycling can readily give us a sense of futility and decay as habits grow stale and weary and "he that follows erases the steps of the one who precedes,"[42] yet, from the divine perspective it is rather that every time we go round the circle slightly differently, perform acts of daily love and service with a stylistic variation, that these variations constitute their own incremental rhythm and gradually "amount" to a developing line of accumulated merit. Just because God has become a child, lived in a family, inhabited for thirty years the normal human round, and then entered the public sphere only for a final three years and then to fail, the purely ludic, joyful aspect of life for its own sake as lived by the lilies of the field has been unprecedentedly affirmed by the event of the Incarnation. In consequence, despite its submission to ageing, the church is guaranteed never to pass nor finally to fail, because it escapes the fate of ruination attended upon sheer cultural artifice, being from the outset more bound to biological processes. The word has become flesh, and so spiritual resurrection is as assured as the following spring.

The second critique of the historians concerns the double paradox of origin and repetition. In the theological register, both facets are emphasized. Origins are singular, crucial, and frail yet vital. Every living thing and every cultural reality

---

41 For an English translation by David Schindler Jr., see *Portal of the Mystery of Hope* (London: Continuum, 1986).

42 Schindler Jr., *Portal of the Mystery of Hope*, 115.

grows from fragile buds that can be snatched away by the wind. All destruction is sure and easy and may be the work of a moment. Growth and achievement are conversely long, precarious, and hard and stem from a minute, minutely unique, and contingent instance. God entrusts himself to this process and decrees that processes begun with seeming randomness in time, like incarnation, the Eucharist, the cross, and sacramental initiation, will hold for all eternity. Indeed Péguy does not hesitate to say that if they are tied to eternity and if eternity is simple and unalterable, then incomprehensibly eternity must also take its origin from time.

Nor does this origin escape the pathos of every origin. Most human beings have never seen Christ physically on earth—and there can have been nothing like this. An overwhelming, unimaginable vividness was long delayed and now is forever vanished. Yet it is equally true that Christ has only come at all because he comes always; that the original vividness is there because of its Eucharistic repetition. And so too that Christ was uniquely incarnate God, the One before the series, also because he was simply an ordinary "one," the first in the series—the founder of a city, of the church, and the first of many saints, as Péguy so frequently declares. Thus, the ignoble suspicion that much of the story of Joan of Arc is mythical is of one piece with the same suspicion regarding the story of Christ: in both cases, popular memory can be taken as more reliable than the academic search for "evidence," since just this memory is constitutive—"retrospectively" and yet "originally" – of every genuine event as such, which must first be preserved in order for it be able to happen at all, and then be "investigated." What is more, those who first saw Christ often failed to recognize or abandoned him, not quite realizing who he was.[43] However, with the benefit of ecclesial hindsight, it could indeed be the case, as the peasant girl Jeanne d'Arc so obstinately insists in *Le Mystère de la charité de Jeanne d'Arc*, that the nobility and peasantry of Christian France would never have abandoned him in the garden of Gethsemane.[44]

But in the theological register also, the tension between the two sides of the paradox of origins becomes most acute. God himself before the creation of the world was perfect and replete—why did he step out beyond himself, adding to that to which nothing can be added, the finite to the infinite and the temporal to the eternal? By doing so, the dramatic glory of the tragic is gained, along with the fragile beauty of the finitely scarce, the melancholy of passing, and supremely the heroic triumph of freedom, which wagers, endures, and stays

---

43 Charles Péguy, "Un nouveau théologien: M. Fernand Laudet," in *Oeuvres en Prose, 1909-1914*, 899ff.

44 For a complete English translation, see *The Mystery of the Charity of Joan of Arc*, trans. Julian Green (London: Hollis and Carter, 1950). The more recent acting edition translated by Jeffrey Wainwright (Manchester: Carcanet, 1986) is taken from a Paris performance in 1986 that made some cuts in the text and also added material from Péguy's other St. Joan dramas.

firm in adversity. But nothing in all this can really balance out the apparent sullying thereby of God's innocent sufficiency by the paternal anxiety of care and the agony of loss.[45]

Péguy's "mythologization" of metaphysical perplexities here is by no means as naive as its exploited idiom, as we shall shortly see. Yet for the moment it is important to realize that it is the finite beginning, which in effect holds the synthetic balance between the eternal commencement and the eventual finite development, in a thoroughly incarnational manner. Thus "night," in *La porche du mystère de la deuzième virtue*, is the Bergsonian duration of being itself—unlike "day" seamlessly one, and only pierced by the days as if by holes, as the sea by islands, or "a great black wall" by windows.[46] As such a personification of overshadowing sophianic presence (because surely akin to created wisdom in the Bible) it is like God, simple and all-originating, besides being all-fertilizing, all comforting, and all healing through sleep. But, unlike God, it involves a merely finite potential and a mysterious merely finite advance embrace of every day to which it gives rise and which in the end it will foreclose in the final night of redemption: "the last day which is different from every other."[47] Similarly, in *Le mystère des saints-innocents*, the holy innocents murdered by Herod, despite their lack of lived finite life, are identified by Péguy (in accordance with tradition) as the 144,000 saints who stand immediately around the throne of God in the *Apocalypse*. No one stands hierarchically higher, because absolutely nothing is added by experience to pure innocence and its perfected play.[48]

This is not theological sentimentality but its absolute opposite: a rigorous refusal of every sentimental overvaluation of drama and the overcoming of temptation, which is still always an experience of contamination that necessarily corrodes. Yet at the same time, Péguy's elevation of innocence is balanced by his elevation also of the repentant sinner and of the ambivalent adult warrior. This is because, as he ceaselessly argues, it is exactly this quality of childlike innocence and hope that enables the saint and hero to bracket the terrible and the corrosive, and to endure or march past it. Hence, perfected innocence such as we must impute to those sacrificially substituted in the gospel birth narratives even for the divine substitute (another sense in which for Péguy Christ is but one citizen among many) is already in nuce, anticipation, and ultimate embrace—like that of night for every day—of the entire gamut of human experience insofar as it *is* human, which means fresh, original, and inspiring. The original is the already repeated, just as the nonidentically repeated remains the original, because the good in reality is one, and the deficiencies of experience are in the end nothing.

---

45 See *Clio I, Portal of the Mystery of Hope* and "The Mystery of the Holy Innocents" [*Le Mystère des saint-innocents*], in *The Holy Innocents and Other Poems*, trans. Pansy Pakenham (London: Harvill, 1956), 69–165.

46 Péguy, *Portal of the Mystery of Hope*, 123.

47 Péguy, *Portal of the Mystery of Hope*, 113.

48 See "The Mystery of the Holy Innocents."

Ultimately, this thematic is for Péguy Mariological as well as sophiological. Mary is humanly manifest night and childhood, since she is the one remaining-innocent adult human creation. But she is this absolute origin, only from the ever-repeated beginning in her of the incarnate word and the church. Nevertheless, at the heart of Péguy's Christianity (and in contrast to Protestant evasion) stands the extreme paradox that somehow divine grace and its eternal operation depend upon the Marian fiat. In a sense, for Péguy, an obscure peasant girl is the author of our redemption and even of our creation, whose eternal action is, from its own perspective, univocal, unilateral, and indivisible. The temporal thereby leads forth the eternal, just as a peasant girl once went ahead of the king at the head of the French army.[49]

In the third instance of critique, we saw that the narrated human event turns out paradoxically to imply in itself an infinite process and circumstance. Péguy's implicit resolution of this conundrum is surely that, just for this reason, the Incarnation is the only really defined and secured event—precisely defined and circumscribed by virtue of full coincidence with the infinite and eternal. This suggestion indicates that the finite, in order to be finite, requires at one finite point entire identification with the infinite and the participation of other finite things in that reality in order to ensure their own reality in declining degree. Just for this reason, the crucial mark of the Christian era is that it has proceeded entirely from one irreversible and entirely transfiguring event upon which the Christian city has been ceaselessly built.[50]

But it does not resolve the reverse conundrum of why the infinite should require the finite. Here, Péguy's mythological tropes seem to express a basic agreement with Eriugena, Bérulle, and Malebranche: in order for God to be God, He cannot lack even lack; the perfect cannot lack even the imperfect. Thus, the plenitudinous generosity of God must create and, finally, in order to resolve the conundrum of the outgoing glory of God (in creation and redemption) that is not-God in one sense and yet still God in another, must become himself incarnately finite while yet remaining reservedly and unreservedly infinite.

Given these extreme truths, it follows for Péguy that God has somehow done the impossible: put unriskable eternity at risk of rejection. As his crucial reading of the three parables of the lost coin, the lost sheep, and the lost son (the prodigal son) makes clear, this does not just mean rejection by another as pain, but the very loss of one's own being as incurred by a human father who has lost his son to death or error. The parables surely have to mean that the lost one counts more than the secured many, because every single one is vital to God, so much so that the missing and essential one will in effect be sought and loved yet more than

---

49 The parallel is pointed out by Latour. See, besides the article already cited, his later essay written forty-one years after the first for the centenary of Péguy's death, "Nous sommes les vaincus," in *Cahiers de l'histoire de la philosophie, volume du centenaire pour la Mort de Charles Péguy*, ed. Camille Riquier (Paris: Le Cerf, 2014), 15–18.

50 Péguy, *Véronique*, passim.

the others. God himself therefore is at stake here. Yet Péguy is not advocating any tragic and atheistic Hegelianism: he fully believes in divine immutability. It therefore has to follow that this belief can only be sustained if God wills in the end that all be saved, and also that in some mysterious, unknown way this, as much as God's eternal immutability, is both the case for always, and will also finally be the case.

For this reason, Péguy's apparently unorthodox universalism—which he shares nevertheless with other orthodox theologians like Origen, Gregory of Nyssa, Eriugena, and Julian of Norwich—follows for him from his logical rendering of orthodoxy. But it is also supported by other considerations that have more to do with history. In *La Mystère de la Charité de Jeanne d'Arc,* Jeanne suffers a "crack" in her devotion because she cannot accept that her prayers and sufferings will avail the damned not a whit.[51] But she also suggests with great cogency that if the damned cannot be saved, then no serious sinner can be either. For every grave state of sin involves despair, and Jeanne refuses Madame Gervase's pious Franciscan affirmation that we can never be sure of the divine will. Come off it, Jeanne says, we know very well when someone has damned themselves if nothing further intervenes. And what is more, Jeanne argues that the current condition of France under the ravages of war amounts to a state of literal hell on earth because, though murderous killers are thereby damned so are (with a slightly Nietzschean touch) their victims, who may have failed either to do their duty in resisting or were manipulated by their suffering into losing faith in God. Of course, one can object with Madame Gervase (Péguy's *usual* spokesperson) that that may in many heroic instances not occur, but it is here that Jeanne, the peasant girl, preserves Péguy's socialist perspective within her and his Catholicism. Most often, surely, those without their daily bread will lose their taste for the bread of the sacrament, even though they stand even more in need of Christ's body.[52] Thus, for Péguy, the incarnational and socialist exigency to save body as well

51 She also declares, though more mutedly than in the earlier Joan plays, that she would be prepared to be damned herself in order to save others—a theme that runs from Leon Bloy through to Georges Bernanos (who diagnoses it as the most diabolic of all temptations in his novel *Sous le soleil de Satan*). But it does not finally play a great role it would seem in Péguy—being more a mark of Jeanne's ardor; no doubt too hyperbolic at this point, but not when she argues against the idea of the futility of prayers for the damned.

52 As the play dates from 1910 this illustrates the survival into Péguy's Catholic period of his socialism. If in this period he exhibited a new sense of the dignity of the poor and even the necessity of poverty to sanctity, as Griffiths rightly points out, this perhaps exhibits at once a new realism about the impossibility of ever banishing all poverty (whose causes can be accidental); a sense that all misfortune can be purgative; and finally a sense that "dispossession" is in some sense necessary for all, such that the problem of the cult of money is as much or more that it encourages the misfortune of wealth as that it also brings about unjustifiable distress. But, as in the case of *Notre jeunesse*, Péguy surely never abandoned the imperative to relieve poverty nor to make war on its structural causes, as is evident in

as soul is at one with the theological thesis that it is only the apparently damned who require to be redeemed.

In order to save souls at all, we must indeed save them from hell, here and hereafter. Not to see that is to be deceived into supposing that sin itself is less than hell. Therefore, we have a moral obligation to oppose the whole hellish machinery—we have to feed bodies in order to feed souls; we have to oppose the mediation of lucre if we are to instill the mediation of grace, and we have to oppose war or violence as the very essence of evil. Yet, in contrast to Jean Jaurès and all pacifist tendencies on the left, there is no "right to peace" as there is to life and liberty—the interests of peace as a false universal cannot override the rights of a single innocent to justice. So because war as violence that is unfair coercion is the source of *all* injustice, we must make war most of all on war. But that counterviolence, if it is not to mean collusion in the effects of violence, must sometimes involve the ambiguity of actual violence and literal fighting, as it did for Jeanne, or for St. Louis King of France fighting in a crusade. Otherwise, there is not only no justice but also no charity, because souls will not yield if bodies are neglected. Thus, Péguy eventually marched to the line of the trenches in the faith that he was about to fight in a war to end all war. Yet, in his case, this faith was not a naive political miscalculation but rather the expression of the only attitude one could ever have that would justify any physical resistance whatsoever.

It is important also to see how this theme loops back into the question of the absolute contingency of historical origins. Would Jesus have fought the English and the Burgundians? Would the apostles? That the historical particularity of the Incarnation renders this question imponderable is surely part of Péguy's point about the radical historicity of the Incarnation despite its universality—a point that includes also the radical historicity of the church and of France in their peculiarly universal destinies. Christ as person and especially divine person cannot just be bound by his time, yet he is also so bound, such that we can never with surety be certain that he would have enacted charity in other circumstances in the same "pacifist" way. For even his relative peacableness cannot be prised apart from a divine strategy in one particular time and place, given that the adoption of that time and place was a tactical part of a universal and eternal strategy.

In that time and place Jesus came to found a different sort of postpolitical city that would yet providentially merge with the Roman city and the Roman empire. That was his task, and not to take over and defend any merely political governance. But who can say what he would have done in Gethsemane if supported by feudal loyalty and what relation of the transpolitical to the political city would then have immediately resulted? Very likely such support is only possible after the long, secure, and successful history of the church, but just because this machine has been established, and goes from eternity toward time, from spirit toward body, and even from the mystical body toward the political state (secondary to the social for Péguy, yet still vital to the social, since he was not a complete anarchist), it is now, as maybe not before, charitable and saintly for Jeanne and Louis to fight with physical weapons.

In contrast to Jeanne, the Franciscan Madame Gervase recommends world abandonment as the essence of the Gospels—not having a care as to work, nourishment, fighting, or procreation. But for Jeanne (and, it would seem, for Péguy) this is premature—for now, in the temporal middle there must be ever new births and new makings, if the great voyage and procession of souls toward God, on which he in some sense depends, is to be maintained.

Only when the time comes, at the end, in the final night, will Madame Gervase's perspective (which is not exactly wrong and is usually right) prove true: then the world will be decreated and all will return to God. Yet all the innocently repeated beginnings will forever remain and be eternally constitutive.

It is in this eschatological perspective that the fourth critique of secular historicism is finally engaged. The diversion of final judgment to an always postponed human future turns out to be a parody of Christian hope, as *Clio II* already indicates. Hope, argues Péguy, is the most anomalously remarkable and yet an equally crucial theological virtue as compared with faith and charity. Faith should readily arise, given the manifest glories of God; charity is surely elicited by suffering, but that we should go on hoping in the face of nonfulfillment seems far more surprising.[53]

But here Péguy presents hope as a little girl, who does not hope for anything in particular but continuously plays for the sheer fun of it running back upon her own steps and in hope of ever more diverting playfulness. This, he indicates, is how we should hope—realizing that in our circular nonquests something new is forever added, and that just because every day is seemingly like the last, it does not mean, even in our experience, that there will not be different, surprising days, saturated by new events and new disclosures. "There's always one day which isn't the same as the day before," says Jeanne's friend Hauvette.[54] Always a special day in our lives, always a seaside day, a Bastille day, Christmas and Easter day, and finally the day when days come to an end. From these finite days of opened hope derives not necessarily any world betterment for Péguy, and likely the inverse, as truth usually incites anger, but nevertheless certain patterns that provide the preconditions of transformation in terms of the offer of expiation, forgiveness, and mutual nurture. Out of these days we go on hoping, and this is what drives us to build cities and houses, found families, and risk the bringing of children into the world. For the

L'Argent. Equally he never abandoned the exigency of economic justice and of social and creative fulfillment for all, even if he later (and perceptively) implies that the removal of all social and educative hierarchy can only *ever* mean the encouragement of a debased monetary and bureaucratic hierarchy.

53 See *The Portal of the Mystery of Hope*.

54 See in the Carcanet acting edition, 84.

will to future destinies that we will not live to see in time is not a sacrificial sub-mission to their future verdicts on our pasts, but a continuation of the divine cre-ative risk not just on our children's behalf, and their children, and their children's children, but also for the whole human race in its eternal unity. A risk, says Péguy, which we take in hopeful confidence of a final and universal free decision, by free creatures, for eternal freedom.[55]

55 It is possible to read Péguy's insistence on the temporal, the embodied, the hopeful, the eschatological, the national, the military, and the political just as concerned with the reincorporation of Jewish thematics into Christianity. Thus his French patriotism has the very opposite implication as regards the Jews to that of Charles Maurras and his successors. One can equally see an echo (though likely unconscious) of kabbalistic and Hasidistic con-ceptions of salvation as a rescuing of the divine glory itself by gathering up its lost "scattered sparks" in Péguy's reiterated rendering of the three parables of loss.

Chapter 2

THE PAST MATTERS THEOLOGICALLY:
THINKING TRADITION

Stanley Hauerwas

The story that is Christianity

"Christianity is not one of the great things of history; history is one of the great things of Christianity."[1] Rowan Williams uses this pregnant observation from Henri de Lubac in support of his contention that Christians must study the past.[2] To "study the past" does not properly suggest what the significance of Williams's argument is for why the past matters theologically. Christians do not simply study the past, but rather the past continues to be crucial for the present. The past is not "back there" because it is not even the past.

Williams develops de Lubac's claim by suggesting that it is the Bible that makes history necessary. It does so because the people we now call Jews experienced a series of disruptions—for example, the exodus, the establishment of monarchy, the role of the prophets, the exile—that they could only make sense of by telling a story. Their struggle to tell a coherent story about their history of failures and displacements turns out to be just what makes history what it is, that is, a "set of stories we tell in order to understand better who we are and the world we're now in."[3]

According to Williams, what is true of the Hebrew Bible is perhaps even more the case in the New Testament. He observes by the time the first texts of the New Testament were being written, Christians were aware of tensions created by the question of whether they shared the same history with the Jews. Accordingly, the New Testament is not an account of "what really happened" but an attempt to make an intelligible story out of memories of very disruptive events for Jews and Gentiles alike. The New Testament writers had to develop a coherent story that

---

1 Henri de Lubac, *Paradoxes of Faith* (San Francisco: Ignatius Press, 1987), 145.

2 Rowan Williams, *Why Study the Past? The Quest for the Historical Church* (Grand Rapids, MI: Eerdmans, 2005), 6.

3 Williams, *Why Study the Past?* 1.

does justice to the novel presumption that in the life, death, and resurrection of Jesus, a decisive retelling was required about God's covenant with the Jews.[4]

This process, of course, did not end with the establishment of the New Testament canon. Christians were determined to read and write history in the light of what Michel de Certeau characterized as the revolution begun in Christ. That revolution the early Christians associated with the crucifixion and resurrection of Jesus that they believed had broken apart the familiar world. That revolution meant Christians must try to put the pieces back together in the light of what had happened in Christ. It soon became apparent to Christians that this is an unending process. That ongoing process is why Christians have had a strong investment in history as a discipline, because as for the Jews the past is always a problem that must be "talked through, mended and unified, in language. The strange and interruptive has to be made into a unity, has to be made intelligible, yet not reduced and made so smooth that you don't notice there is a problem."[5]

I have begun calling attention to Williams's understanding of the historical character of Christianity because I think it very important for any consideration of why Christianity is a faith that demands to be articulated through an ongoing tradition. To be sure, some Christians—call them liberal if you like—did and continue to reject some aspects of Christian tradition, which may give the impression that they do not believe tradition to be constitutive of Christianity. Yet this critical attitude toward tradition cannot help but reject some aspects of the tradition in the name of tradition. Thus Williams's argument for the acknowledgment that Christians must produce some "history" means there can be no avoiding some account of tradition as constitutive of the task to tell the story of our existence.

Put more polemically the presumption that one must choose between tradition and what is now identified as liberal theology is a mistake. Liberalism, at least liberalism understood as a stance within Protestant theology, is itself part of the tradition. It is so because the only way liberal theologians could make a case for why certain aspects of the Christian faith should be left behind or reconfigured in response to developments in modernity was by telling a story. No matter how hard Protestant liberal theologians may have tried to distance themselves from past understandings of what was assumed to be forms of orthodox theology, they could not help but reproduce the very mode of reasoning they were seeking to escape.

Yet it is certainly true that in recent times a recovery of the significance of tradition has taken place. It is not accidental, moreover, that de Lubac was one of the key figures in what is now identified as the *ressourcement* movement in Catholic theology in the last century. Other figures associated with the attempt to renew Catholic theology by recovering theological alternatives to neoscholastic theology would include Hans Urs von Balthasar, Marie-Dominique Chenu, Jean Daniélou, and Yves Congar. This significant movement, however, while certainly important

---

4 Williams, *Why Study the Past?* 6.
5 Williams, *Why Study the Past?* 9.

for the enrichment of the Catholic theological tradition, was not an attempt as it was in Protestantism to recover the role of tradition in order to enrich the theological resources for a theology that was thought to have grown too thin.

Neoscholastic theologians like Reginald Garrigou-Lagrange, for example, understood their work to be in a tradition. The *ressourcement* theologians thought, however, that the neoscholastics' understanding of tradition was too sterile.[6] They sought to enrich the tradition by recovering the theological insights often associated with the patristic fathers that challenged the neoscholastic categories. Much of their work found a home in Vatican II.

These developments in Catholic theology are extremely important, but the *ressourcement* movement in Catholicism was a quite different moment than the Protestant recovery of tradition. In this chapter, I attend primarily to developments in Protestantism because there we have a clearer view of the relation of tradition to liberalism. In particular I direct attention to developments in Protestant theology associated with the little-known but extremely important theologian Robert L. Calhoun, who in the second half of the last century taught at Yale Divinity School. Without Calhoun the recovery of tradition, which has become, perhaps misleadingly, known as the Yale School, would not have been possible. Calhoun quite simply created the knowledge of the doctrinal tradition that enabled George Lindbeck and Hans Frei to do their constructive work in theology.

To be sure there are other figures, for example Robert Jenson and Robert Wilken, who are not associated the Yale School but are theologians whose work has shown the significance of the theological tradition for the challenges of the present. By concentrating on developments at Yale, however, I hope to tell an important but little-known story of how a theological perspective was developed that did not entail the rejection of the concerns that had shaped the development of theological liberalism.

The recovery of tradition at Yale: the work of Robert Calhoun

In *After Virtue*, Alasdair MacIntyre characterizes "a living tradition" as "an historically extended socially embodied argument, and an argument precisely in part about the goods which constitute that tradition."[7] His understanding of tradition as argument is very important for the story I want to tell about the recovery of tradition by Calhoun and the subsequent development of what has become known as postliberal theology represented by Frei and Lindbeck. For as Lindbeck makes clear in a lovely reflection on his education under Calhoun, Calhoun

---

6 For an excellent set of essays on the *ressourcement* movement, see Gabriel Flynn and Paul Murray, eds., *Ressourcement: A Movement of Renewal in Twentieth-Century Catholic Theology* (Oxford: Oxford University Press, 2014).

7 Alasdair MacIntyre, *After Virtue*, 3rd ed. (Notre Dame, IN: University of Notre Dame Press, 2007), 222.

"called himself a liberal until the time he died, but he was a liberal who actually ended up being more orthodox doctrinally than someone like H. Richard Niebuhr."[8]

I call attention to Lindbeck's judgment about Calhoun because Lindbeck (and Frei) are well known, but Calhoun was not widely known when he taught at Yale (1923–65), nor is he well known today. Yet Frei and Lindbeck attribute how they learned to approach theology to Calhoun. His courses in the history of doctrine and the history of philosophy were renowned among colleagues and students at Yale.

Calhoun was an active participant in some of the activities of what was then called the Federal Council of Churches, but that was not sufficient to establish his reputation as a scholar of the Christian theological tradition. For that to have happened would have required him to publish his lectures. He seems to have simply seen no reason to do that. He was quite content to be a teacher.

He had, however, written his lectures, but in the classroom he delivered his lectures without notes. Students frustrated by not having his lectures to read would at various times record and transcribe his lectures. We are in Lindbeck's debt for finally making Calhoun's lectures on the early development of doctrine available in published form.[9]

Lindbeck's "introduction" to these lectures is crucial for understanding Calhoun's significance for the developments in theology now associated with Yale. Though "generous orthodoxy" is a description attributed to Frei, it rightly describes what Calhoun represented. Lindbeck remembers him as the greatest lecturer he has ever heard. He lectured in a manner that manifested his extraordinary learning—a learning, I might add, that he carried lightly. He lectured, according to Lindbeck, as if he thought through every sentence and paragraph to say what needed to be said about the theologian he was presenting. He was intent to provide as sympathetic account as he could of theologians with whom he might well disagree. In particular he wanted his students to understand those theologians who would later be called heretics because without them Christians would not know what they should not say.

Lindbeck draws on Virginia Corwin, one of Calhoun's PhD students, for her descriptions of Calhoun's effect. Corwin says,

> No student who has become a teacher can remember (Calhoun's lectures) without a stab of envy . . . . The thought of someone gone centuries ago—St. Augustine, for example, or Origin—takes shape before the mind, every essential

8 George Lindbeck, "Israel, Judgment, and the Future of the Church Catholic: A Dialogue among Friends," in *Postliberal Theology and the Church Catholic: Conversations with George Lindbeck, David Burrell, and Stanley Hauerwas*, ed. John Wright (Grand Rapids, MI: Baker, 2012), 125.

9 Robert Calhoun, *Scripture, Creed, Theology: Lectures on the History of Christian Doctrine in the First Centuries*, ed. George Lindbeck (Eugene, OR: Cascade, 2011).

detail in place . . . the line and structure of the whole dominate, and the part is held in true proportion . . . . This extraordinary effect of clarity is not achieved by sacrificing a (thinker) or his conception to a scheme of one's own . . . . Students know that they are watching a master teacher who is also an austerely honest historian, testing the theses of other scholars by reading the sources in their original language, by controlling the less well-known writings and personal letters, and making his independent report. He protests that he knows but little of the domain he traverses, but the listener is not deceived . . . . The response can only be one of keen pleasure.[10]

As one lucky enough to have had one of Calhoun's last courses in the history of doctrine, I can testify that Dr. Corwin's description is accurate. His commitment to help his students understand the development of Christian theology, developments the result of controversy and argument, meant, in the words of Robert Cushman, who was to become the dean of Duke Divinity School, that an appreciation of "premodern deposits of philosophical and Christian wisdom" was made possible. This was an achievement because Cushman observes it was at a time when theological studies in the mainline denominations and universities were "heavily weighted on the side of sciences of religion and post-Kantian thought."[11]

Cushman, who wrote a dissertation on Plato under Calhoun, judges that no other person did more to open a way "for a sympathetic rediscovery of classical Christian positions both Catholic and Protestant" than Calhoun. Accordingly Cushman suggests that Calhoun "mightily helped doctrinally illiterate children of liberal American Christianity in the thirties and forties recover a critical comprehension of the well-nigh unsearchable riches of inherited Christian wisdom." This had an unexpected result as not only did Calhoun's perspective make possible the reception of "neoorthodox theology" (i.e., Barth) but it also produced people able to be in conversation in Catholic and Protestant ecumenical movements.[12]

Cushman's judgments are no doubt true, but as Lindbeck noted above, Calhoun always thought of himself as standing in the Protestant liberal tradition. To be sure he was among those who abandoned in the face of war what was understood to be a far too optimistic account of the human condition, but according to Lindbeck that did not mean Calhoun became associated with what was called neoorthodoxy. Lindbeck suggests in effect Calhoun adopted "a view closer to traditional orthodoxy without abandoning his liberal convictions."[13]

"His liberal convictions," however, were primarily his conviction that theology had to be open to challenges of modernity. He was not a "liberal" if liberalism

10 Lindbeck, "Introduction," in *Scripture, Creed, Theology: Lectures on the History of Christian Doctrine in the First Centuries* (Eugene, OR: Cascade, 2011), ix–lxx, here xi.

11 Lindbeck, "Introduction," xv.

12 Lindbeck, "Introduction," xvi.

13 Lindbeck, "Introduction," xxii.

names that form of theology that tries to establish theological inquiry on some basis other than the authority of revelation and reflection on that revelation in the Christian tradition.[14] The very way Calhoun taught doctrine was an argument against the attempt by some forms of liberalism to ground Christian theology in reason qua reason. Calhoun knew the Enlightenment was over, which meant he saw clearly that Immanuel Kant was not the future for Christian theology.

Calhoun was a "traditionalist" if by that description one means someone who appreciated the mode of argument represented by patristic and medieval theologians. The care with which he explicated all the different sides in the development of the creeds, for example, testified to his conviction that the mode of argument used by the Fathers was appropriate to the subject matter. Frei in an *in memorium* for Calhoun describes the effect Calhoun had on his students this way:

> Calhoun taught us to use the time honored orthodox term "doctrine" once again with ease, and not to be afraid of the word "dogma." In his lectures . . . "orthodoxy" was a matter of broad consensus within a growing and living tradition with wide and inclusive perimeters. His theological teaching was above all generous, confident that divine grace and human reflection belonged together and that the revelation of God in Christ was no stranger to this world, for the universe was providentially led, and human history was never, even in the instances of the greatest follies, completely devoid of the reflection of the divine light.[15]

Calhoun's commitment to unpacking the arguments in order to understand developments in the tradition meant he was able to combine his liberalism with Christian traditionalism in a manner that did true justice to the integrity of both. Frei observes, for example, that Calhoun thought of philosophy, and in particular Plato, as an essential discourse for the development of Christian theology. He, therefore, according to Frei, agreed with Friedrich Schleiermacher that, freed of its unwarranted fear of the "secular," Christianity had been from its beginnings a faith that drew on its surrounding culture to be a "language-shaping force." Thus Frei contends that Calhoun "went about the business of showing how the one great, continuing tradition was built with the aid of . . . countless cultural contributions then and now."[16]

It would be a mistake, however, to suggest that Calhoun's theological convictions are or were crucial for how he taught the history of doctrine. Methodologically he insisted that the historian should be an agnostic. He neither sought nor did he make disciples. Yet he insisted that exactly because the historian has the obligation to represent the character of their subjects, they must attend to the religious devotion of the theologian, for it is finally the case that the primary locus of a theologian's work will depend on the practices that make the theologian a theologian.

---

14 Lindbeck, "Introduction," xxiv.
15 Lindbeck, "Introduction," xix.
16 Lindbeck, "Introduction," xx.

Accordingly, Calhoun refused to evaluate the theologians he presented by external standards. Instead he worked very hard to help students understand why, for example, theological work must be done if Christians are to be articulate about what they believe and why what they believe is necessary if they are to make sense of their lives.

Lindbeck rightly identifies Calhoun as a traditionalist, a category that Calhoun himself did not use, because Calhoun helped us see that the story of the development of doctrine is the condition necessary for any consideration of the validity and/or truth of the Gospel. He, for example, presented the creeds as "crucial for coherent construals of Scripture when it is treated as a unified whole . . . the historic and Trinitarian and Christological formulations, should continue to be regarded as criteriologically though not conceptually normative for mainstream Christianity."[17]

Calhoun helped students understand the inside of the people and movements that made Christianity Christianity. The result, according to Lindbeck, is that Calhoun worked very hard to provide a sympathetic picture of the theologians he thought crucial for understanding the ongoing exploration of what had happened in Christ. He would explain why Irenaeus thought the way he did, Tertullian the way he did, and Origen the way he did. As a result, when you came to the condemnations of Origen a few hundred years later, you understood why Origen was so misunderstood, and yet you were not out of sympathy with those who had condemned him.[18]

It is not possible to provide a detailed account of the narrative Calhoun developed in the course on doctrine, but I can give a general overview. He began the course with methodological considerations about the relation of revelation and theology; he then dealt with the New Testament and in particular questions surrounding the Jesus of history; and then he presented an account of Johannine theology. The latter was important because of how the Johannine books would shape later Christological controversies. The course was designed to climax in the disputes that resulted in the Nicene and Chalcedonian debates surrounding the Trinity and Christology. In order to get there, however, Calhoun dealt with the second-century apologists, heresies, the Apostles' Creed, Irenaeus, Tertullian, Alexandria, Clement, and Origen. The course was designed to help one appreciate that the development of doctrine was the result of the ongoing commitment of Christians to work out the implications of the reality that the God Christians worship is Trinity.

Lindbeck suggests that Calhoun's approach to doctrine allowed him to be at once a "traditionalist" who continued to understand himself to be in the tradition of liberal Protestant theology. That is particularly true if Schleiermacher is taken to be *the* representative of liberal theology. He treated Schleiermacher as a great theologian in the Reformed tradition who could not be blamed for the use of his theology to support positions that Schleiermacher avoided. Accordingly, we see in

---

17 Lindbeck, "Introduction," lvii.
18 Lindbeck, "Israel, Judgment, and the Future of the Church Catholic," 127.

Calhoun an account of the development of doctrine that is at once "traditional" and "liberal."

The implications of Calhoun's position can perhaps be best seen in Lindbeck's account of doctrine in *The Nature of Doctrine: Religion and Theology in a Postliberal Age*. The early methodological chapters in Lindbeck's book in which he contrasts the experiential-expressive account of theological claims with the cultural-linguistic alternative have tended to dominate discussions of his book in a manner that makes readers miss Lindbeck's primary purpose in writing the book, that is, to provide a comparative account of doctrine. Thus Lindbeck proposes a "rule-theory" account of doctrines that he thinks helps provide a way to understand how doctrines are at once constant yet subject to change.

The fruitfulness of Lindbeck's rule theory display of doctrine finds its most illuminating exemplification in his discussion of the development of the Nicene and Chalcedonian Creeds. Thus his regulatory principles: (1) there is only one God; (2) the stories of Jesus refer to a genuine human being who lived and died in a specific time and place; and (3) every possible importance is to be ascribed to Jesus that is not inconsistent with the first rule.[19] Lindbeck argues that these principles were clearly at work in the New Testament, which makes intelligible the diverse ways, some better than others, that Jesus was affirmed as God.

The various positions that we now call heretical must be part of the story because their mistakes are crucial for helping the church provide an appropriate account of the relation of the three principles. Lindbeck argues that it is probably the case that the "Nicene and Chalcedonian formulas were among the few, and perhaps the only, possible outcomes of the process of adjusting Christian discourse to the world of late classical antiquity in a manner conformable to regulative principles that were already at work in the earliest strata of the tradition."[20] It is hard to avoid the conclusion that Lindbeck's formulation of these Christological principals is the working out of how he learned to think as a student of Mr. Calhoun.

It is unclear to me how helpful it has been for the theological developments at Yale after Calhoun to be labeled "postliberal." But that label does at least indicate that, contrary to many critics of the theological developments represented by Lindbeck and Frei, they have not left behind much that has been learned from Protestant liberal theologians.[21] Frei's discussion of Schleiermacher and Karl Barth

19 George Lindbeck, *The Nature of Doctrine: Religion and Theology in a Postliberal Age*, 25th Anniversary ed. (Louisville: Westminster John Knox, 2009), 80.

20 Lindbeck, *Nature of Doctrine*, 81.

21 John Allen Knight provides a useful and informative account of the liberal/postliberal alternative in his *Liberalism versus Postliberalism: The Great Divide in Twentieth-Century Theology* (Oxford: Oxford University Press, 2013). Knight is a fair reporter of these alternatives, but I think he is quite wrong in his criticisms of Frei, whom he criticizes for having no referential account of language. Knight seems not to have learned from Ludwig Wittgenstein that the realism/idealism alternatives reproduce the modernist presumption that epistemology is everything.

in *Types of Christian Theology* makes clear that these theologians share much in common.[22] I call attention to Frei and Lindbeck because I think the kind of theology they have exemplified was made possible by the story of the development of doctrine represented by Mr. Calhoun.

There is the question, however, whether the politics exist to sustain this theological project. In the last chapter of *The Nature of Doctrine* Lindbeck observes that the disarray in church and society makes the transmission of the necessary skills to sustain the postliberal way of doing theology increasingly difficult.[23] The skills Lindbeck has in mind are as basic as learning the language of the faith as exemplified in Scripture.

In a "foreword" to the German edition of *The Nature of Doctrine*, a "foreword" now happily included in the twenty-fifth anniversary edition of the book, Lindbeck observes that there is much lacking in *The Nature of Doctrine*. In particular he suggests that "MacIntyre's treatment of what he calls 'traditions of inquiry' would have been helpful in specifying the relations of doctrine, theology, practice and religious communities."[24] I think Lindbeck is right about the importance MacIntyre's work can have for the position Calhoun (and Lindbeck and Frei) represented.[25] Let me try to explain why I take that to be the case.

MacIntyre on tradition

MacIntyre is, of course, first and foremost a philosopher, but I believe his work to have profound theological implications. I began the discussion of Calhoun's work with MacIntyre's claim that tradition is an extended, socially embodied argument. MacIntyre's emphasis on the importance of a tradition being socially embodied is extremely important because liberalism is not only a philosophical and theological position but also, more importantly, a determinative social theory and politics. Liberalism so understood means that Calhoun-like positions are necessarily in tension with the politics of modernity.

Of course liberalism is a hydra-headed beast. There is no strict relation between the many forms of political liberalism and the equally diverse reality of theological

---

22 Hans Frei, *Types of Christian Theology* (New Haven, CT: Yale University Press, 1992), 34–46.

23 Lindbeck, *Nature of Doctrine*, 110.

24 Lindbeck, *Nature of Doctrine*, xxxi.

25 David Trenery has written a terrific book comparing MacIntyre and Lindbeck. What follows owes much to his analysis. See his *Alasdair MacIntyre, George Lindbeck, and the Nature of Tradition* (Eugene, OR: Pickwick Publishers, 2014). For example, Trenery maintains that the text of *The Nature of Doctrine* "is a demonstration of the relevance of MacIntyre's account of tradition to understanding the way in which religions may respond to internal and external challenges to their coherence, and continue to develop their own tradition-constituted forms of rationality" (232).

liberalism. There are, moreover, many different kinds of liberal theories that in various ways seek to sustain an understanding of society, politics, and a liberal way of life. However, as I suggest below, MacIntyre's account of liberalism suggests why the church is a necessary social and political institution if Christian theology is to be properly disciplined by tradition.

MacIntyre develops his understanding of tradition and rationality in contrast to the liberal project's presumption—a presumption MacIntyre calls into question— that an account of rationality is possible that is free of any tradition.[26] The latter he thinks decisively represented by Kant's attempt to give an account of reason free of all contingencies. Kant's ambition was to show that by assuming a universal and impersonal stance it is possible for an agent to reason from the perspective of anyone and thus be free of any particularistic tradition (334). The difficulty with Kant's (and countless proposals after Kant) ambition to construct a morality for individuals free of all traditions was the inability to come to any agreements about what constitutes such universalizability. MacIntyre observes that the book review pages of philosophical journals are the graveyard that marks the failure to sustain the consensus that liberal theory assumes is not only possible but also necessary.

Liberalism, however, is not just a philosophical position. MacIntyre argues it is an ideal that many desire to be a social reality. Liberals seek to create social orders in which individuals can emancipate themselves from contingency and the particularity of tradition by each person being "anyone." The work of people such as John Rawls exemplifies MacIntyre's contention that liberalism entails a particular social theory and politics. Liberals sought as well as continue to seek to construct a social order on individualistic presumptions in the hope of establishing a tradition-independent mode of political life. The history of that project has exposed that ambition to be an illusion, but that same history has had the ironic result of transforming liberalism "into a tradition whose continuities are partly defined by the interminability of debate about principles" (335).

There is, moreover, a "morality" and corresponding social psychology associated with liberal social orders. Because liberals presume there is no overriding good that can make possible a narrative coherence for our lives, the compartmentalization of our lives cannot be avoided. Each individual is free to live by whatever conception of a good life appeals to them, but they are hounded by the knowledge that their understanding of what constitutes a good life is finally a matter of arbitrary preferences. Every individual is free to live by whatever conception that pleases them. The only thing they cannot do is believe that they have the right to impose their conception of the good on anyone else (336-7).

In contrast to the liberal tradition, MacIntyre develops an account of tradition-constitutive forms of rational inquiry. Such inquiry begins in and from some condition of pure historical contingency associated with a particular community. For MacIntyre the beginnings of a tradition are simply a given, but that does not mean the poetry that constitutes the beginning is arbitrary. To be sure, the

---

26 Alasdair MacIntyre, *Whose Justice? Which Rationality?* (Notre Dame, IN: University of Notre Dame Press, 1988), 326–48. Subsequent paginations to be found in the main text.

authority of a community will be found in certain texts and voices. Such an authority may be for a time obeyed without question, but if the community is capable of maintaining itself across time a tradition will develop a need to account for the changes the community cannot avoid (354). The event that often is decisive for necessitating change that may open up new possibilities in a community's tradition is the encounter with another community with a history that challenges some of the assumed givens of the community (355).

Through such developments, inadequacies in a tradition can be revealed in a manner that results in new formulations designed to remedy the discovered limits. In the process, a tradition will reach a stage in which it is possible to ascribe falsity to earlier judgments and beliefs. MacIntyre suggests that on such a basis a correspondence theory of truth can be established, but such a theory in the early stages of a tradition will more likely take the form of a correspondence theory of falsity. Such a process calls into question Cartesian passive conceptions of the mind in favor of the mind as activity. For MacIntyre, to think is possible because the mind can be adequate "to its objects insofar as the expectations which it frames on the basis of these activities are not liable to disappointment" (356).

Crucial for understanding MacIntyre's account of the rationality of tradition is his understanding of what he calls an "epistemological crisis." According to MacIntyre, traditions are to some degree local. They are shaped by the particularity of language and of the peculiar geography that the language reflects. So a tradition will have its peculiar history and often seem to be independent, if not isolated from, other alternative traditions. That such is the case is why some think MacIntyre has no way of avoiding relativism or perspectivism (361).

MacIntyre's first response to the accusation that he cannot avoid relativism and perspectivism is to observe that those alternatives are based on the assumption that something like rationality as such exists (352). More significantly, those alternatives fail to take account of the possibility that a tradition can recognize a fundamental challenge to its presumptions and make constructive responses. The latter often requires fundamental changes, but the changes can be located as a working out of the fundamental convictions of that tradition. The solution to a decisive epistemological crisis, such as the reception of Aristotle's work for Christian theology, may well require the discovery or production of new concepts that makes possible the framing of the challenge in a manner that enables those in the tradition to recognize the continuities as well as the discontinuities with the tradition to that point (361–2).

MacIntyre draws on John Henry Newman to give examples of successful responses to an epistemological crisis. In particular, Newman's exposition of the crisis in the fourth century over the Trinity MacIntyre thinks to be a great achievement. That controversy, a controversy that arose from competing interpretations of Scripture, was given a satisfactory resolution by using philosophical and theological concepts that had come from debates rationally unresolved up to the point of Nicea. Of course those very philosophical and theological concepts occasioned new challenges that continue to inform thinking around the Trinity. But MacIntyre does not regard that as a failure but rather an accomplishment, because a tradition in healthy working order will always be an extended argument (362–3).

MacIntyre also uses examples from science to illumine his account of the significance of epistemological crisis. For example, he calls attention to how the late medieval physics was called into question by Galileo and later by Isaac Newton. They identified the phenomena of nature in such a way that a lack of correspondence between what the impetus theory presumed about motion became obvious. What such an example suggests is that epistemological crisis is not only the result of one alien tradition calling another into question, but an epistemological crisis can be occasioned by internal tensions within a tradition (365).

MacIntyre acknowledges, however, that a tradition may be in an epistemological crisis for centuries. For some, epistemological crisis cannot be resolved, which means a tradition may be discredited rationally by appeal to its own standards. What must be denied, however, is that there is some neutral standing ground that can provide the rational resources for an inquiry independent of all traditions. To position oneself outside all traditions is to assume a position that not only makes one a stranger to all inquiry but ultimately makes one a stranger to oneself (367).

Such persons MacIntyre believes exist. They are post-Enlightenment agents who have responded to the failure of the Enlightenment to provide neutral and impersonal standards by concluding that no set of beliefs proposed for acceptance can be justified. Such persons view the social and political contexts in which they find themselves as falsifying masquerades that hide from us the reality of the nothingness that grips our lives. At best, such people think they are cosmopolitans who are home nowhere other than everywhere.

Ending with a beginning

I trust that the implications of MacIntyre for how theology is understood as a traditioned form of inquiry are obvious. MacIntyre's stress on the importance of a tradition to develop the skills to introduce the young into the tradition is singularly important for Lindbeck's account of doctrine. That is particularly the case given Lindbeck's observation, an observation with which I agree, that Christianity now finds itself in the awkward position of having been culturally established but increasingly disestablished. For Christianity to be so positioned can be seen as an advantage because to be a Christian now requires a formation that has been missing.

Equally important is how MacIntyre's account makes the language we speak as Christians crucial for the sustaining of the tradition. The tendency of liberal Protestants to assume that what we believe as Christians must be put in languages that most people can use has been a determinative mistake. Thus the presumption by liberals that our basic convictions as Christians can be translated into a language that is allegedly anyone's language. Lindbeck saw quite clearly that was a mistake, but MacIntyre provides him with the philosophical reasons why you cannot translate a language in use.

MacIntyre's account, moreover, helps make clear that the arguments Christians continue to have about the Trinity are testimony to the truthfulness of the fundamental Christian convictions. So the tradition of inquiry that is Christianity is integral for any considerations of what it might mean to say what we believe is true. Tradition turns out to be the discovery of the conceptual means to rightly tell the story of Christ and how that story cannot be told without the story of Israel. MacIntyre helps make clear why Williams rightly argued the importance of the past for Christians.

MacIntyre also makes clear why there can be no separation of theology from what might be called "ethics." To be located within the Christian tradition means a training is required for the formation of habits necessary to sustain a distinctive way of life. This is particularly true in social orders that have been shaped by liberal theory.

Finally the political implications of *The Nature of Doctrine* become more pronounced against the background MacIntyre provides. Liberal Protestantism was an accommodationist strategy to make the church at home in the world. If the church is to be a community capable of maintaining the integrity of its speech, that accommodation must come to an end. That is part of the story that must be told. But it is one with ample precedence in the Bible and past Christian history. Those stories make clear that the tradition called Christian can never be finished but must remain open to God's unrelenting desire to have us for his people.

Part II

DIFFERENT INFLECTIONS TO RETRIEVAL: CONFESSIONAL
APPROACHES

Chapter 3

ORTHODOXY

Andrew Louth

It might be thought, both by Orthodox and non-Orthodox, that the term "theology of retrieval" captures well the nature of Orthodox theology, for it suggests that theology is there to be retrieved—in recognized authorities, in the decisions and canons of the councils of the Church, in the collective mind of the Church in some way. There is some truth in that: Orthodox think of their Church as the "Church of the Fathers," or the "Church of the Seven Ecumenical Councils (or Synods)," which suggests a body of doctrine, or doctrinal definitions, there (somewhere) to be retrieved. Such a notion, however, demands more reflection on what is meant by retrieval in this context; at the very least, reflection and clarification is needed about the location of what is often called the "deposit of faith" and what are the means by which the faith "once delivered to the Saints" (Jude 3) is to be retrieved—all of which quickly leads into questions that make clear that the notion of an Orthodox "theology of retrieval" is much less simple than it might at first sight appear.

I want to start by introducing thoughts of St. Silouan, the Athonite monk, by origin a simple Russian muzhik, whose message has been made known through his disciple, Fr. Sophrony, founder of the Orthodox Monastery of St. John the Baptist in Essex. In the first part of this book, there is a section "Concerning Tradition and the Scriptures." Fr. Sophrony sets out the saint's teaching in these words:

> The Staretz's [written before he was canonized] regard for obedience as an essential condition for discovering God's will is closely linked with his attitude towards Sacred Tradition and the Word of God. The living tradition of the Church, continuing down the centuries from generation to generation, is one of the most material and at the same time most subtle facets of her life. When there is any resistance, however slight, on the part of the disciple the thread of pure tradition is broken and the teacher silenced.

> For the Staretz the life of the Church meant life in the Holy Spirit, and Sacred Tradition the unceasing action of the Holy Spirit in her. Sacred Tradition, as the eternal and immutable dwelling of the Holy Spirit in the Church, lies at the very root of her being, and so encompasses her life that even the Scriptures

themselves come to be but one of its forms. Thus, were the Church to be deprived of Tradition she would cease to be what she is, for the ministry of the New Testament is the ministry of the Spirit "written not with ink, but with the Spirit of the living God; not in tables of stone, but in the fleshy tables of the heart" (2 Cor. 3:3).

Suppose that for some reason the Church were to be bereft of all her books, of the Old and the New Testaments, the works of the holy Fathers, the whole body of the Liturgy—what would happen? Sacred Tradition would restore the Scriptures, not word for word perhaps—the verbal form might be different—but in essence the new Scriptures would be the expression of that same "faith once delivered unto the saints" (Jude 3). They would be the expression of the one and only Holy Spirit continuously active in the Church, her foundation and her very substance.[1]

I have quoted this passage at length, for it seems to me that this expresses something that is at the very heart of any Orthodox understanding of what is meant by the transmission of the faith by sacred tradition. Whatever else absolutely indispensably needs to be considered—and, as we shall see, there is much—at the very heart, there is tradition understood as the life of the Holy Spirit in the Church, and this life is experienced, first and foremost, in the prayer of the Church, seen most clearly in those who have devoted their lives to prayer, primarily, but not exclusively, in the monastic state. To think of synods and bishops and creeds, as histories of the Church encourage us to do, is to miss the heart of the matter: the life of the Holy Spirit in the Church, manifest in those who have become prayer, and in prayer become deified. The passage just cited begins by mentioning St. Silouan's "regard for obedience," for the monastic life has at its core the relationship between spiritual father and disciple, a relationship characterized by obedience. In the paragraph that stands immediately before the passage we have quoted, Fr. Sophrony has this to say:

In the vast sea which is the life of the Church the true tradition of the Spirit flows like a thin pure stream, and he who would be in this stream must renounce argument. When anything of self is introduced the waters no longer run clear, for God's supreme wisdom and truth are the opposite of human wisdom and truth. Such renunciation appears intolerable, insane even, to the self-willed, but the man who is not afraid to "become a fool" (1 Cor. 3:18–19) has found true life and true wisdom.[2]

Such a position might seem to rule out the whole gamut of theology as generally understood: learning has no place; what is required is submission to the

---

1 Archimandrite Sophrony, *The Undistorted Image: Staretz Silouan: 1866–1938*, trans. Rosemary Edmonds (London: The Faith Press, 1958), 58–9.
2 Sophrony, *Undistorted Image*, 58.

mysterious, even unaccountable wisdom, of the spiritual father, the starets; and there are certainly strands in Orthodox theology that adopt such a position. There is, however, more to be said, and I shall attempt to outline it in what follows. Nevertheless, the sense that tradition as the life of the Holy Spirit in the Church is something that is to be experienced, and that experience requires ascetic struggle to the point of radical self-denial, seems to me to be fundamentally Orthodox. The great Russian theologian of the beginning of the last century, Fr. Pavel Florensky, who died murdered by the People's Commissariat for Internal Affairs (NKVD) in 1937, put it like this:

> The indefinability of Orthodox ecclesiality . . . is the best proof of its vitality . . . There is no *concept* of ecclesiality, but ecclesiality itself is, and for every living member of the Church, the life of the Church is the most definite and tangible thing he knows. But the life of the Church is assimilated and known only through life—not in the abstract, not in a rational way. If one must nevertheless apply concepts to the life of the Church, the most appropriate concepts would be not juridical and archaeological ones but biological and aesthetic ones. What is ecclesiality? It is a new life, life in the Spirit. What is the criterion of the rightness of this life? Beauty. Yes, there is a special beauty of the spirit, and, ungraspable by logical formulas, it is at the same time the only true path to the definition of what is orthodox and what is not orthodox.
>
> The connoisseurs of this beauty are the spiritual elders, the *startsy*, the masters of the "art of arts," as the holy fathers call asceticism. The *startsy* were adept at assessing the quality of spiritual life. The Orthodox taste, the Orthodox temper, is felt but is not subject to arithmetical calculation. Orthodoxy is shown, not proved. That is why there is only one way to understand Orthodoxy: through direct Orthodox experience . . . [T]o become Orthodox, it is necessary to immerse oneself all at once in the very element of Orthodoxy, to begin living in an Orthodox way. There is no other way.[3]

What then of synods, bishops, creeds? What of the Orthodox Church as the Church of the Fathers? Whatever we say must preserve the sense, affirmed uncompromisingly and eloquently by Fr. Sophrony and Fr. Florensky, of an "Orthodox taste," an "Orthodox temper" that discerns the beauty of the Spirit, the connoisseurs of which are the spiritual elders, the *startsy*. There can be no question of regarding synods of bishops, creeds, and synodical dogmas as external authorities; rather, authority in the Church is the authority of the Holy Spirit, which does not constrain so much as lead to freedom in the Spirit. The dogmas of the Church distill spiritual experience; they are there to prevent us pursuing a wild goose chase, leading further and further from the truth that is found in the One who said, "I am the Truth."

---

3 Pavel Florensky, *The Pillar and Ground of the Truth*, trans. Boris Jakim (Princeton, NJ: Princeton University Press, 1997), 8–9; italics in original.

Nevertheless, such a stress on spiritual experience, on prayer as a touchstone of belief, of dogma, does not mean that dogma and creed can be derived directly from spiritual experience, and certainly not from individual experience, nor does it mean that the dogmatic decisions of the Church, settled in synods of (mostly) bishops, are unimportant. Nor, furthermore, does it mean that there is no place in the Orthodox Church for the work of the theologian, though his or her role is a subordinate one, not a defining one (though more of that later). One way of opening up the question could be to assert that, in making prayer and spiritual experience in some sense a touchstone for belief, what is meant by such experience is the experience of the whole Church, both in space and in time. The so-called Vincentian canon, which makes the criterion of truth in the Church, *quod ubique, quod semper, quod ab omnibus creditum est*—"what is believed everywhere, always, and by everyone"—so easily criticized as unsatisfactory for deciding the contents of the Catholic faith, is perhaps best understood in these terms: the experience of the Church, the tradition of the Holy Spirit in the Church, is to be the experience of the whole Church, wherever it exists (*quod ubique*), and throughout the whole course of its existence (*quod semper*), whether understood as since Pentecost or, as with Hermas and other early Christians, from the beginning, from creation. This can be, as the Vincentian canon is often perceived to be, a self-defining bit of wishful thinking, or it can be, as I think it is regarded in Orthodox theology, a conviction that every response to the Gospel—over the centuries and throughout the world—has a place in ascertaining and fostering the Faith. One way in which this can be seen and verified is in the liturgical poetry of the Orthodox Church, for this liturgical poetry is exceptionally rich, both in imagery and in recalling the sometimes very precise ways in which the dogmas of the Church—first of all, the Trinity and Christology—have been defined.

Already we are beginning to embark on what is meant to be the central subject of this chapter: the way in which theology of retrieval is conceived within the Orthodox Church, for what is asserted in the last paragraph is not something that is obvious, but something that needs demonstration, or at least illustration. As we proceed to unfold this, we shall see that the process of retrieval in the articulation of Orthodox theology is a given, but that the way in which it has come to be seen to be central to any Orthodox theology itself has a history—and not a self-contained history.

"Theologies of retrieval" were very much a feature of the history of theology in the last century; in some contexts it is mostly known by the French word *ressourcement*, perhaps itself a revisiting of the slogan of the Renaissance: *ad fontes*, "to the sources." This is no less true of the history of Orthodox theology in the last century, which has its own peculiarities, mostly because it is bound up with the exile of the Russian intelligentsia from the Soviet state, and the encounter of these thinkers, especially the theologians and philosophers among them, with their Western counterparts, not least in Paris in the 1920s and 1930s.[4] The prevailing

---

4 For some account of all this, set in the broader context of the recent history of Orthodox theology, see my *Modern Orthodox Thinkers: From the* Philokalia *to the Present* (London: SPCK, 2015).

movement among Orthodox theologians who consciously engaged in this theology of retrieval is often called the "Neopatristic movement," called such by Fr. Georges Florovsky and manifest most clearly in the writings of Vladimir Lossky and Fr. Dumitru Stăniloae, as well as, though often forgotten, the woman historian and thinker, also an émigrée in Paris, Myrrha Lot-Borodine.[5] All of these individuals talk about tradition and see the return to the Fathers as making contact with the roots of the authentic Christian, Orthodox tradition. Florovsky in the few short articles on tradition gathered together in the first volume of his collected works fairly closely assimilates the Fathers and tradition: it is the Fathers who preserve and transmit the apostolic teaching of the Church, which comes to us from the apostles and through the Fathers. He makes an attempt to define more clearly what he has in mind:

> *First*, the phrase "the Fathers of the Church" has actually an obvious *restrictive* accent: they were acting not as individuals, but rather as *viri ecclesiastici* (a favourite expression of Origen), on behalf and in the name of the Church. They were spokesmen for the Church, expositors of her faith, keepers of her Tradition, witnesses of truth and faith,—*magistri probabiles*, in the phrase of St Vincent . . . *Secondly*, it was precisely the *consensus patrum* which was authoritative and binding, and not their private opinions or views, although even they should not be hastily dismissed. Again, this *consensus* was much more than just an empirical agreement of individuals. The true and authentic *consensus* was that which reflected the mind of the Catholic and Universal Church—τò ἐκκλησιαστικòν φρόνημα.[6]

Lossky himself reflected on the notion of tradition in an article entitled "Tradition and traditions," written for the book he coauthored with Leonid Ouspensky, *The Meaning of Icons*.[7] This is a profound and subtle essay, and I shall come back to it later, but when it comes to identifying tradition, we find Lossky speaking of an "interdependence between the 'Tradition of the Catholic Church' (= the faculty of knowing the Truth in the Holy Spirit) and the 'teaching of the Fathers' (= the rule of faith kept by the Church),"[8] which is fairly close to what we have just found in Florovsky. The "Fathers" and the concept of tradition are very close to each other: it is in the Fathers that we find the tradition of the Church. It is this, I think, that lies behind any unwillingness to conceive of Orthodox theology

---

5 Much of what follows is based on a lecture by the present author in Greece (and as yet unpublished) in spring 2013. <AQ: Is this a lecture given by you?>

6 Georges Florovsky, *Bible, Church, Tradition: An Eastern Orthodox View* (Belmont, MA: Nordland, 1972), 102–3; italics in original.

7 Leonid Ouspensky and Vladimir Lossky, *The Meaning of Icons* (Boston: Boston Book & Art Shop, 1969; originally published in Bern and Olten, in 1952)

8 Vladimir Lossky, *In the Image and Likeness of God* (Crestwood, NY: St. Vladimir's Seminary Press, 1974), 165.

as going "beyond the Fathers," for this seems to be equivalent to "going beyond tradition," which is unthinkable. And yet we have to go "beyond the Fathers"—on that both Florovsky and Lossky are clear. Simply to *repeat* the Fathers is to fail in the task of the theologian. Florovsky's notion of the "patristic φρόνημα" is an attempt to find a way of creatively developing patristic insights, without being constrained by the thought-forms of their time.

Let us look at this from a somewhat different perspective. The Fathers and tradition become assimilated when we think of tradition in the active, verbal sense—of the process by which the Gospel is passed down through the ages, for it is, it seems, the Fathers who pass on this tradition. Not only that, the Fathers themselves become not just the transmitters of the tradition but also the content of the tradition—used, now, in its passive, nominal sense. The Fathers have passed on the tradition but have themselves become part of that tradition; when we read them we are immersing ourselves in the tradition of the Church. It is not the only way of immersing ourselves in the tradition of the Church: the liturgical services of the Church are also a repository of tradition, but we think of that, too, as patristic. We regard the two principal Eucharistic liturgies as compositions of two of the Fathers, St. John Chrysostom and St. Basil the Great, and very many of the songs and troparia we sing are composed by Fathers of the Church, such as St. John Damascene, and furthermore are composed of passages taken from patristic writings, especially the homilies of St. Gregory the Theologian.[9] The Fathers are those who passed on the tradition, and the works of the Fathers have been handed down through the ages to us by the Church.

There is much truth in that, but it is only partly true. Let me give an example: on occasion I have quoted (and others have, too)—as evidence for the Orthodox tradition—from the *Epistle to Diognetos*, who says of Christians that "though residents at home in their own countries, their behaviour is more like that of resident aliens; they take their full part as citizens, but they also submit to anything and everything as if they were aliens. For them any foreign country is a motherland, and any motherland is a foreign country" (*ad Diog.* 5). It is certainly evidence of how a second-century Christian felt about the relationship of Christians to the Roman society in which they lived, but is this part of the patristic witness, part of the tradition of the Church? For it has not been handed down to us *by* the Church. The history of this text is curious. We know nothing of it from the early centuries. Eusebios, though he clearly makes a serious attempt to survey the literature of the early Church in his *Church History*, makes no mention of it. It was unknown until, round about 1435 in Constantinople, Thomas of Arezzo, a young Italian student, noticed that some ancient codex was being used to wrap fish in the fish market, and bought the codex instead of fish. The "epistle to Diognetos" was the fifth treatise in

---

9 See, for example, my article "St. Gregory the Theologian and Byzantine Theology," in *Re-Reading Gregory of Nazianzus: Essays on History, Theology, and Culture*, ed. Christopher A. Beeley (Washington, DC: Catholic University of America Press, 2012), 252–66, esp. 264–6.

the codex, the four earlier being falsely ascribed to Justin Martyr. It is entitled "The Same, to Diognetos," but like the other treatises it is certainly not by Justin. The manuscript was brought back to the West, and this sole manuscript was the basis of various editions, starting with that published by Henri Estienne (Stephanus) in 1592. The manuscript no longer survives: it was destroyed when the library in Strasbourg was burned down in 1870, a casualty of the Franco-Prussian War. It is not, in any ordinary way, part of the "tradition of the Church": it was saved to be, in the event, a fleeting witness of an unknown moment in the second century by the quick-wittedness of an Italian student in Constantinople. It is a gift of scholarship to the Church, not something the Church saved and prized.

This points, I think, to a more general issue about the place of the Fathers, the place of patristics, in Orthodox theology. In many cases, our awareness of the Fathers, the works of them that we know, even how we categorize them are less part of the tradition of the Church, but rather part of the tradition of scholarship. To take an example that is much the same as the example just discussed of the *Epistle to Diognetos*: the so-called Apostolic Fathers. Their very title suggests an ecclesiastical evaluation: the Fathers who were closest to the apostles. The Fathers, and the works, included in this title are Clement of Rome, Ignatios of Antioch, Polycarp of Smyrna—his letter and the account of his martyrdom, Hermas of Rome, the Epistle of Barnabas, the *Didache*. They are all mentioned by Eusebios in his *Church History*. Despite that, these are not writings that were treasured and preserved by the Church. Though some of them seem to have been popular in the early centuries—an interest reflected in Eusebios's *Church History*—there is scarcely a trace of them from the fourth century until the Renaissance, when gradually the few surviving texts of these writings were (re)discovered—some copied into the final pages of manuscripts of the Scriptures, and conceivably regarded at that time as canonical (e.g., I Clement and a bit of II Clement in Codex Alexandrinus; Barnabas and the Shepherd of Hermas in Codex Sinaiticus). Someone in eleventh-century Byzantium seems to have had an, for then unusual, interest in such early Christian writings and had the epistles of Clement, Barnabas, and the *Didache* copied. The manuscript was discovered in a library belonging to the Patriarchate of Jerusalem in 1873 by Philotheos Bryennios. The letters of Ignatios were known only in an interpolated version until detective work by seventeenth-century scholars discovered first Latin versions and then the sole Greek witness to the authentic text, the text quoted by Eusebius in his *Church History*. So the works of what we know as the Apostolic Fathers are writings discovered by scholars of the Renaissance, supplemented by the discoveries of a nineteenth-century Greek scholar; indeed, it was only in the seventeenth century that they came to be known as the "Apostolic Fathers."

The role of scholarship in our perception of the Fathers can be illustrated in ways that bear more directly on Orthodox theology. Take two of the Fathers most important in much modern Orthodox theology: St. Maximos the Confessor and St. Gregory Palamas. They are the two figures given most prominence in the *Philokalia* of St. Makarios of Corinth and St. Nikodimos of the Holy Mountain (apart from Peter of Damascus, whose "proto-Philokalia" is the longest item in the *Philokalia*). However, they appear there in a very selective light. Maximos is represented almost entirely by centuries, and about half of these centuries were not composed as centuries by Maximos himself: they represent a kind of digest of bits and pieces, mostly from the *Questions to Thalassios* and the scholia that came to be attached to them. Maximos has been reduced to a, not too demanding, mostly devotional writer; little remains of his powerful analytical mind or of the metaphysical vision that he developed. Much the same is true of Palamas as presented in the *Philokalia*: he is represented mostly by devotional texts, save for the *150 Chapters*, which is a bald summary of his position against Gregory Akyndinos, and the Hagioretic Tome, a brief statement of the hesychast position, written by Palamas and endorsed by leading monks of the Holy Mountain. One might say that the *Philokalia* is only intended as a devotional book for monks, and that is true. The fact remains that at the beginning of the last century, neither of these Fathers was at all well known in the Orthodox world: their discovery is a matter of quite recent history. The story of the way they have attained the importance they now assume as resources for Orthodox theology is notable. In the case of Palamas, he came to assume a pivotal role in defining Orthodox theology—both those who espoused the Neopatristic synthesis, and others, such as Bulgakov, who continued the Russian tradition of the nineteenth century—against the position of the Catholic Church, represented by Thomas Aquinas, declared the common doctor of the Catholic Church by Pope Leo XIII in 1879. In the 1930s, theologians such as (later Archbishop) Basil Krivochéine and Fr. Dumitru Stăniloae were working on manuscripts of Palamas—on Athos and in Paris—but recourse to manuscripts for serious work on the Saint was still necessary when Fr. John Meyendorff began to work on Palamas in the 1950s. Alongside his monograph and some articles, Meyendorff edited the *Triads*, perhaps his most important contribution to our understanding of Palamas. Soon after, under Panayiotis Christou's editorship, a complete critical edition began to appear.[10] With Maximos the story is different. Already there was an edition of his works, more or less complete, in Migne, but apart from some Russian scholarship at the turn of the nineteenth/twentieth century, there was little attention paid to him, by the Orthodox or by anyone else; he was mostly known in the histories of dogma as the champion of Orthodoxy against the heresy of monotheletism. This began to change in the interwar period and then, from the 1940s onward, major works by Hans von Balthasar, Polycarp Sherwood, and Lars Thunberg began to reveal the scope and profundity of the teaching of the Confessor. There followed waves of scholarship, in the 1970s and then in the 1990s; beginning in the 1980s, a fine edition of the Confessor's works began to appear in *Corpus Christianorum*.

There are some striking contrasts between these stories of modern scholarly interest in Palamas and Maximos the Confessor. Interest in Palamas has been largely Orthodox: the edition is by Orthodox scholars, though this has been

---

10 Now complete with the publication, as vol. 6 of Christou's edition, of the homilies, edited by V. S. Pseftogkas (Thessaloniki: Ekdotikos Oikos Kyromanos, 2015).

supplemented by (rather better) editions of a few works by non-Orthodox; the bulk of scholarship about Palamas has been Orthodox. It is quite different in the case of Maximos: early interest was largely non-Orthodox (Florovsky's lectures, published in Russian in the 1930s, were at textbook level, though sound, in my view), and that has remained so (the towering figures in the discovery of Maximos's vision, mentioned above, are, two of them Catholic and one a Swedish Lutheran)—only very recently with scholars like Jean-Claude Larchet, Melchisedec Törönen, and Torstein Tollefsen has the Orthodox contribution become significant; the critical editions are almost entirely the work of Western scholars.

For work on the Fathers generally, it is the Maximos story that has been more typical, not the Palamas story: the riches of the patristic tradition have been rediscovered and made available by Western scholars, both Catholic and Protestant, mainly, perhaps, Catholic. What we understand by the patristic tradition nowadays is largely the result of non-Orthodox scholarship, both in terms of critical editions and works of interpretative scholarship. What does this mean for our Orthodox understanding of Tradition and the Fathers?

First of all, I think it forces us to think a little more clearly about what we mean by the Fathers, and the witness of the Fathers. Florovsky was fond of developing his ideas about the patristic witness from the words "following the holy Fathers," which introduced conciliar definitions; their first, and most famous use, was at the Synod of Chalcedon in 451. This phrase does not, however, introduce the Chalcedonian Definition; rather, it only introduces the last paragraph, which has often been taken, wrongly, to be the definition. For the Ὅρος πίστεως begins by recalling Christ's words addressed to his disciples in Jn 14:27—"my peace I give you, my peace I leave you"—and then recites the creed of Nicaea, the creed of Constantinople I, mentions Cyril's letters endorsed by the synod of Ephesos, and the Tome of Leo, sent to Flavian, archbishop of Constantinople, now "among the saints." So "following the holy Fathers" means following Christ and the Apostolic witness to him; more particularly this phrase refers, not to the Fathers in general but to the Fathers of the first three Ecumenical Synods, with Cyril mentioned and Leo added. In seeing a more general reference to the patristic tradition implied in these words, Florovsky was not wrong, for, as he asserts, following the Anglican patristics scholar, G. L. Prestige, "[t]he Fathers were the true inspirers of the Councils,"[11] That would suggest that the "Fathers" whom we are to follow are the Fathers whose doctrinal reflection was enshrined in the Synods of the Church. A few years after the Synod of Ephesos, we find Vincent of Lérins, already mentioned, seeking to define what is the *ecclesiae catholicae traditio*, the tradition of the Catholic Church, in more general terms. His answer was that this tradition that we should adhere to is *quod ubique, quod semper, quod ab omnibus creditum est*—"what has been believed everywhere, always and by all."[12] There have been other, later attempts to identify the Fathers, or a core among them: the Three Great

11 Florovsky, *Bible, Church, Tradition*, 103.

12 Vincent of Lérins, *Commonitorium* 2. 3, ed. R. S. Moxon (Cambridge: Cambridge University Press, 1915), 10.

Hierarchs and Universal Teachers, St. Basil the Great, St. Gregory the Theologian, and St. John Chrysostom, whose feast the Orthodox keep on January 30. All of this suggests that the question of who the Fathers are is not straightforward. Maybe it suggests, too, the "Fathers" are not all equal: there are some who stand out as beacons, and it is their light that clarifies the overall witness of the Fathers. There is another suggestion we could take on board, found in Vincent of Lérins and, very strikingly, in Maximos the Confessor. After a brief discussion of three notes of tradition as being worldwide, constant, and confessed by all, he introduces another characteristic of the tradition of the Church: namely, that it has been defended to the point of suffering and death by confessors and martyrs.[13] We find this again in Maximos, who speaks of the true tradition of the faith as founded on the apostles and their successors, the fathers and the synods where they declared their faith, and that it has been tried in the suffering of their lives, both the suffering of those who endured persecution and martyrdom, and also those who shone forth in the ascetic life.[14]

What difference does the nature of modern scholarship on the Fathers make to our understanding of appeal to the Fathers? I think we shall get a better perspective on this if we remind ourselves of the history of patristic scholarship. We can take this back to the patristic period itself, for from the fourth century onward, Christian theologians begin to appeal to the "Fathers" to buttress their arguments; collections of citations from the Fathers, first of all on questions of Christology, are the main evidence of this appeal to the Fathers.[15] Patristic scholarship, however, emerges in the period of the Renaissance and Reformation to support the appeal to the Fathers made by humanists, and especially Catholics against Protestant and Protestants against Catholics: many of the great monuments of patristic erudition—ranging from editions of texts to clarification of the events of the history of the Church—had, as part of their motivation, polemical aims. Many of the great names familiar to patristic scholars—Le Nain de Tillemont, Muratori, Mabillon, Montfaucon—belong to a history of polemic that has been recently explored to marvelous effect by the lamented Bruno Neveu.[16] Whatever the purpose, however, the result was to make available the Fathers in a way that had never been known before, at least to scholars. This led to interest in the Fathers for their own sake, and attempts to make them available in translation in England and Russia, at least, in the nineteenth century (this is doubtless true elsewhere; I just do not know). The Russian translation project, masterminded by the great Metropolitan of Moscow, St. Philaret (1782–1867) and shared out among the Spiritual Academies of Moscow, St. Petersburg, Kiev, and Kazan was so extensive

---

13 Vincent of Lérins, *Commonitorium* 5.7–8.

14 *Opusc.* 11 (PG 91.140AB).

15 Fundamental here is Thomas Graumann, *Die Kirche der Väter: Vätertheologie und Väterbeweis in den Kirchen des Ostens bis zum Konzil von Ephesus (431)*, Beiträge zur Historischen Theologie, 118 (Tübingen: Mohr Siebeck, 2002).

16 See his *Erudition et religion aux XVIIᵉ et XVIIIᵉ siècles* (Paris: Albin Michel), 1994.

that it has been said of it that "at the end of the 19th century, Russia had at its disposal, in its own language, the best patristic library in Europe."[17] J.-P. Migne produced his series of Latin and Greek Fathers in the nineteenth century—*Patrologia Graeca* and *Patrologia Latina*—which, whatever its faults (very variable quality in the editions used, and accuracy in reproducing them), has provided a standard, and extensive, place of reference for recourse to the works of the Fathers that is still valuable. By the end of the nineteenth century, various scholarly series of the Fathers were being inaugurated, culminating later in the twentieth century in the great series *Corpus Christianorum, Series Latina*, and *Series Graeca*. Alongside these series there were now others, notably, *Corpus Scriptorum Christianorum Orientalium*, with subseries in all, or most, of the Oriental languages: Syriac, Armenian, Coptic, and so on. Perhaps most notable among these series was that founded in 1943 by Henri de Lubac and Jean Daniélou, *Sources Chrétiennes*, which now runs to hundreds of volumes, publishing works in Oriental languages, as well as Latin and Greek, with a French translation.

All this has made the Fathers much more accessible than they have ever been before, and it has changed the nature of recourse to the Fathers. There remains, in some quarters, the polemical use of the Fathers that inspired the recourse to the Fathers in the period of the Renaissance and Reformation, but it is hardly characteristic of modern patristic scholarship. Modern patristic scholarship is an ecumenical venture. The patristic riches on which modern Orthodox theology can, and does, draw have been provided for the most part by Western scholarship, maybe predominantly Catholic, though many of the greatest names in patristic scholarship have been Protestant. This phenomenon is well known and has been the subject of scholarly reflection itself: two volumes of essays testify to this—*Les Pères de l'Église au XXᵉ siècle*, a volume commemorating the fiftieth anniversary of *Sources Chrétiennes*,[18] and, explicitly, the proceedings of a conference held in Constanța, in Romania, to which Catholic and Orthodox scholars contributed, *Patristique et Œcuménisme: thèmes, contextes, personnages*.[19]

This ecumenical dimension has implications for the nature of patristic authority. Traditionally, the Fathers have been used as an arsenal, from which weapons have been drawn to combat one's opponent; from the fourth century, they have been used as authorities to defend positions *against* other positions, held to be in error, as departing from the tradition of the Church. The ecumenical dimension of modern patristic scholarship has largely (though not entirely, especially, alas, among the Orthodox) abandoned such polemical use and found a more fruitful way of using the Fathers: as a treasury, wherein we can find the riches of the Church's

---

17 Olivier Clément, quoted by Fr. Boris Bobrinskoy, in his article "Le Renouveau actuel de la patristique dans l'Orthodoxie," in *Les Pères de l'Église au XXᵉ siècle: histoire— littérature—théologie* (Paris: Cerf, 1997), 437–44, at 440.

18 *Les Pères de l'Église an XXᵉ siècle: histoire—littérature—théologie*, already cited.

19 *Patristique et oecuménisme: thèmes, contextes, personnages*, ed. Cristian Badiliţa (Paris: Beauchesne, 2010).

tradition, handed down from the apostles through the Fathers. This might seem radical, but quite how radical it is will emerge from noting a further point. The last century has made available as never before (even, indeed, to those Christians who valued them) the writings of those condemned as heretics. This is especially true of those traditions in the East that rejected the Synod of Chalcedon, those traditions we are accustomed to call "Nestorian" and "Monophysite." We now have access to works written in Greek but preserved in Syriac, because their authors had been condemned by the imperial Church and its synods: works by Evagrios, Theodore of Mopsuestia, Severos of Antioch. In addition to these, there are those who wrote in Syriac or Armenian, who belonged to the non-Chalcedonian traditions: bishops like Philoxenos of Mabbug, Jacob of Serug; great spiritual fathers such as Isaac of Nineveh, Dadisho, Joseph Hazzaya, John of Dalyatha; great scholars (and poets) such as Gregory of Narek. These are all traditionally regarded as heretics, and some of them are condemned in the hymns of the Orthodox Church.[20] Some of them slipped under the net, as it were, and were preserved in Greek: many of Evagrios's writings survived ascribed to others. Many of the ascetical homilies of Isaac of Nineveh (known as "Isaac the Syrian") were translated into Greek in the ninth century by two monks of the Mar Saba Monastery and became very popular throughout the Orthodox world, though he would have been regarded (had it been known) as a Nestorian. Now, however, they are readily available, and we find a wealth of spiritual wisdom and theological reflection, not to be discarded by being dubbed "heretical." The Monophysite bishop Philoxenos of Mabbug has inspired a remarkable work by a French philosopher.[21]

It seems to me that the labors of patristic scholarship have changed the landscape of the Fathers of the Church. We now know them so much better, or at least we have the resources to acquire such knowledge. Some of the ways in which we have opposed the traditional categories of Orthodox and heretical only make superficial sense; this applies particularly to the divisions that resulted from the fifth-century synods of Ephesos and Chalcedon. Most scholars who have studied the issues believe that differences between Orthodox and "monophysite" over their understanding of Christ had more to do with styles of theology than fundamental differences of belief. What the Orthodox condemn as "monophysite"—a confusion in Christ of the divine and the human—is not something affirmed by those who rejected Chalcedon. This does not mean that "Orthodoxy" is not important: far from it, but it does mean that the ways in which Orthodoxy can be expressed are more diverse that we have been accustomed to think, and might well become

---

20 On this odd, and surely regrettable, phenomenon, see Archimandrite Ephrem (Lash), "Byzantine Hymns of Hate," in *Byzantine Orthodoxies*, ed. Andrew Louth and Augustine Casiday, Society for the Promotion of Byzantine Studies, Publications 12 (Aldershot: Ashgate, 2006), 151–64.

21 Guy Lardreau, *Discours philosophique et discours spiritual: Autour de la philosophie spirituelle de Philoxène de Mabboug*, Collection "L'ordre philosophique" (Paris: Éditions du Seuil, 1985).

more diverse as Christians encounter other traditions than the classical tradition of ancient Greece and Rome. Maybe we can speak too quickly of what Florovsky called "the patristic φρόνημα," something we can adopt for ourselves and apply to our own problems; there is certainly the risk of forcing the "Fathers" into too narrow a straitjacket. I am not sure this charge can be made against Fr. Florovsky: for him acquiring the "patristic φρόνημα" would be "a mysterious way of spiritual labour (*podvig*), a way of secret and silent labour in the acquisition of the Holy Spirit."[22] We need to recognize that there is a wealth of different voices among the Fathers, revealing to us what the Apostle Paul called the πολυποίκιλος σοφία τοῦ θεοῦ—many-variegated wisdom of God. The Fathers introduce us to a fabulously varied treasury, in which we can find endlessly rich implications of God's love for the world and humankind.

To begin to grasp this will involve a revolution in our understanding of theology; it has implications, too, for our understanding of the truth, the truth that is Christ. We are still too defensive in our reflection on God's love for us manifest in the mystery of Christ—too fearful, too afraid of error. We do not very often recall that St. Gregory the Theologian, no less, said that there were subjects—the world, matter, the soul, the good and evil rational natures, the Resurrection and the Passion of Christ—in which "hitting on the truth is not without profit and error is without danger" (Ἐν τούτοις γὰρ καὶ τὸ ἐπιτυγχάνειν οὐκ ἄχρηστον, καὶ τὸ διαμαρτάνειν ἀκίνδυνον).[23]

What does all this mean for the Orthodox, who think of themselves (ourselves) as the Church of the Fathers? First of all, we need to welcome the way in which we can now know more about the Fathers, more about the breadth of their interests and concerns, so that it is not just their contribution to the theological issues that were settled by the Ecumenical Synods that is our primary concern—though that, largely concerned with Trinitarian theology and Christology, remains important. The Fathers' understanding of the nature of the created order, of the nature of humankind and its relationship to God and the cosmos, of the nature of the Church, and our encounter with Christ through the Church and the sacraments: all this adds richness to our understanding of the theology of the Fathers. The fact that much of this has been revealed by non-Orthodox scholars, or that we can gain deeper insights from those who rejected the Orthodox Church of the Ecumenical Synods in their day: all this need not be an occasion for anxiety. It remains the case, however, that the Fathers are special to us Orthodox in a way that is not necessarily the case with non-Orthodox Christians (though there are many non-Orthodox who value the Fathers highly): we regard them as our Fathers, our parents in the faith; we belong to one another; we belong to the same family. How

22 Georges Florovsky, *Ways of Russian Theology*, vol. 2, *The Collected Works of Georges Florovsky*, vol. 6 (Vaduz: Büchervertriebsanstalt, 1987), 308 (translation modified with reference to the Russian text: G. Florovsky, *Puti Russkogo Bogosloviya* (Paris: YMCA Press, 1937/1981), 520).

23 Gregory of Nazianzus, *Or.* 27.10 (PG 36:25A).

do we know this? How do we experience it? Fr. Pavel Florensky spoke, as we have seen, of the "Orthodox taste," a way of perceiving rather than of things perceived— since, for all Christians, what we apprehend as the truth is Christ Himself. Lossky suggested that that entering into the tradition that we discover through the Fathers is a matter of inhabiting the "margin of silence" that surrounds the Scriptures and hearing the stillness of Christ.[24] Both of these ways of trying to characterize what it is to enter the tradition of the Fathers, the tradition of the Church, suggest that it is a matter of what the scientist Michael Polanyi called a "tacit dimension," and I would suggest, as I have before, that this tacit dimension is something we become familiar with through prayer, rather than thought.[25] Furthermore, it is a matter of attitude, an attitude fostered by, more than anything else, the experience of the Divine Liturgy. Experience of the Divine Liturgy seems to me of paramount importance in becoming familiar with the patristic tradition. This is partly because the liturgical texts we sing are so often derived directly from the writings of the Fathers; it is patristic theology as song.[26] More deeply, however, in the worship of the Church, most fundamentally in the Divine Liturgy, we become one with the Fathers of the Church; we come to stand beside them in prayer, prayer that seeks to respond to the love of the Incarnate Christ, who is present with us in the Divine Liturgy; and in that response we raise up to God the concerns of the world to be enfolded in his love.

24 Lossky, *Image and Likeness*, 151. On this see Rowan Williams's reflections in his *A Margin of Silence: The Holy Spirit in Russian Orthodox Theology/Une marge de silence: l'Esprit Saint dans la théologie orthodoxe russe* (Québec: Éditions du Lys Vert, 2008).

25 See the chapter on "Tradition and the Tacit," in *Discerning the Mystery: An Essay on the Nature of Theology* (Oxford: Clarendon Press, 1983), 73–95.

26 I have touched on this elsewhere; see my *St John Damascene: Tradition and Originality in Byzantine Theology* (Oxford: Oxford University Press, 2002), 252–82; and "St. Gregory the Theologian and Byzantine Theology," cited above.

Chapter 4

REFORMED RETRIEVAL

Michael Allen

Imagine two cities. In one city, the ailing find care within their homes, watched over by their family members; the dying are observed from their final breath until burial, never left alone for even a moment; their bodies will be preserved and buried in the ground, and their graves will be a witness and sign to all, located in church graveyards within the center city bounds. In a second city, the gravely sick are moved from their homes to hospitals for care by professionals; the dying are given over to the funeral service upon bodily expiration; their bodies will be burned and their ashes scattered.

Historians have noted changing practices with regard to the care of the sick and dying and the treatment of dead bodies by Christians. By and large, the modern era in the Western world has ceased investing in center city graveyards and traditional Christian burials. Instead, bodies are buried in extreme suburbs or exurbs, well outside the daily commute, or, more likely than not, are cremated. For various reasons, the dead no longer function as a costly presence as they used to when they would not merely geographically be present to daily life but also take up valuable real estate. Moderns continue to remember the dead, of course, but that remembrance comes in personal, individual form and finds little structural support or encouragement.

Protestantism has functioned in parallel form to both cities, theologically speaking, with regard to its concern for the dead. Classical Protestantism has tended to the dead and viewed the testimony of this cloud of witnesses as a costly presence. An individualized or radical Protestantism, however, has reduced the presence of the dead to a cost-less memory, whatever occasions for individual remembrance may arise. The issue of cost is not insignificant: moderns remember the dead, of course, though they do not allocate real estate resources in the same way as classicals did for center city graveyards. Having a geographic allocation of capital focused on the location of the dead signals a priority and ongoing necessity of tending to the witness of the dead, exceeding the whim of nostalgia or of personal remembrance, which may come and go.

This chapter seeks to consider the logic of classical Protestantism, specifically of Reformed Protestantism in its classical confessional forms, regarding the role of retrieval in theology. It wagers that there is a distinctly Reformed basis for retrieval in theology. Before we seek to explain that logic, however, we must consider the nature of retrieval in contemporary theological conversation.

Anthropological and theological forms of retrieval

Retrieval might be conceived as archaeological analysis and deemed prudent in light of realities regarding our embeddedness in social and cultural webs of relationships that predate our conscious or subconscious commitments. If the rise of late modernity or postmodernity has meant anything, it has involved the aggravated sense that all knowledge, experience, and action finds its meaning and shape in a context or a nexus of interrelated contexts. Global telecommunications and the ease of international travel made cognizance of diverse cultures more prominent in the Western world. Then the technological advance of the last thirty years has made the experience of men and women more available and accessible than ever before through the Internet and social media. While humans may be no more diverse or no more dependent on deeply rooted patterns of social habit than before, we can be more aware now of ways in which various customs, mores, practices, and principles have shaped and do shape the lived reality of men and women around the globe today.

In such a schema, retrieval might be proposed and pursued as a diagnostic tool, a means of excavating underneath the current iterations of human culture or, in our case, theological confession. Retrieval might involve the historical assessment of thought patterns, textual practices, philosophical revolutions, ideological formations, and the like, which have clustered together to shape current engagement in the theological task.[1] In such a scheme, theological retrieval would serve as a parallel to investigation of how economic distribution in nineteenth-century England shaped family structures in the late Victorian period. Such an approach is not directive or prescriptive but descriptive and diagnostic. Retrieval in such a guise becomes simply an assessment of the contextualizations of theology and piety in various eras.

An archaeological approach to retrieval stands or falls with its anthropology. Nothing provides ballast or momentum for its efforts other than the sense that human society and its various forms of production (including the intellectual and theological) show a causal coherence that genuinely runs through its diverse and complex history. Feminist theologians have offered such readings by seeking to show how misogynistic patterns of human organization have bred and entrenched gender binaries that degrade women. The viability of such analysis depends, of course, upon the plausibility of causal demonstration, namely, that something more than mere chronology or parallelism can be shown regarding

---

1 For an example of such anthropological analysis outside the theological realm, see Paul Connerton, *How Societies Remember* (Cambridge: Cambridge University Press, 1989).

social precursors or current patterns and their theological confessions. Unless we want to fall into the temptation to simply shout *post hoc, ergo propter hoc*, then we must see deeper evidence of causal influence. Here various genealogies of modernity show not only their vitality but also their severe limits. Consider the many objections to narratives of decline whether portrayed by Radical Orthodoxy or others in similar projects.[2]

While historical assessment has so frequently been pursued with motivation from such archaeological and diagnostic concerns, I wish to propose a markedly different approach to the Christian past. In this chapter retrieval is considered from a theological vantage point, inquiring after theological affirmations that compel a program of retrieval and characterize the posture of retrieval. Because claims are made regarding material principles of the gospel of Jesus Christ, this proposal will no doubt share much and distinguish itself from those proposed by theologians working within the Eastern Orthodox and Roman Catholic traditions.[3]

2 For influential examples of grand narratives, see, for example, Alasdair MacIntyre, *After Virtue: A Study in Moral Theory*, 2nd ed. (Notre Dame, IN: University of Notre Dame Press, 1984); Amos Funkenstein, *Theology and the Scientific Imagination from the Middle Ages to the Seventeenth Century* (Princeton, NJ: Princeton University Press, 1985); Alasdair MacIntyre, *Whose Justice? Which Rationality?* (Notre Dame, IN: University of Notre Dame Press, 1988); Charles Taylor, *Sources of the Self: The Making of Modern Identity* (Cambridge, MA: Harvard University Press, 1989); John Milbank, *Theology and Social Theory: Beyond Secular Reason* (Oxford: Blackwell, 1990); J. B. Schneewind, *The Invention of Autonomy: A History of Modern Moral Philosophy* (Cambridge: Cambridge University Press, 1998); Charles Taylor, *A Secular Age* (Cambridge, MA: Belknap, 2007); Jean Bethke Elstain, *Sovereignty: God, State, and Self* (New York: Basic, 2008); Michael Allen Gillespie, *The Theological Origins of Modernity* (Chicago: University of Chicago Press, 2009); and Brad S. Gregory, *The Unintended Reformation: How a Religious Revolution Secularized Society* (Cambridge, MA: Belknap, 2012). For an example of objections to such narratives, see the essays in Lawrence Paul Hemming, ed., *Radical Orthodoxy—A Catholic Enquiry?* (Aldershot: Ashgate, 2000).

3 For survey of commonalities across ecumenical traditions with regard to recent retrieval or *ressourcement*, see John Webster, "Theologies of Retrieval," in *The Oxford Handbook of Systematic Theology*, ed. John Webster, Kathryn Tanner, and Iain Torrance (New York: Oxford University Press, 2007), 583–99. For an example of Webster's own judgments regarding how ecumenical differences do affect one's retrieval of the theological tradition, see his "Purity and Plenitude: Evangelical Reflections on Congar's Tradition and Traditions," *International Journal of Systematic Theology* 7 (2005), 399–413; and "Ressourcement Theology and Protestantism," in *Ressourcement: A Movement for Renewal in Twentieth Century Catholic Theology*, ed. Gabriel Flynn and Paul Murray (New York:Oxford University Press, 2012), 482–94.

A brief dogmatics for retrieval

A theology of retrieval follows from a host of more basic theological beliefs about matters intrinsic to the gospel of Jesus Christ. In short, retrieval—or a program and posture with which one stands in regard to the past—must be related to basic metaphysical, soteriological, and ethical claims that compose the Christian confession.

Doctrine of God

The prompt for a theology of retrieval may be seen in the prologue to John's Apocalypse: "Grace to you and peace from him who is and who was and who is to come" (Rev. 1:4). Grace and peace are granted unto his servant as the gift of God, and God is identified by this expansion of the tetragrammaton. "I am the Alpha and the Omega," says the Lord God, "who is and who was and who is to come, the Almighty" (Rv 1:8). With this repetition of the three tenses prompted by the divine name ("I am"), the link between the burning bush and this searing apocalypse becomes more than apparent.

"Fear not, I am the first and the last, and the living one" (Rv 1:17–18). Beginning and end. Alpha and Omega. First and last. With these pairings, the steady possession of time comes to confession. God is the living one, Almighty with respect to limits of time. God does not grow or fulfill himself through time, nor does the Almighty suffer any change of diminution throughout time's lapse. God possesses life in and of his triune self—just so, he is the "living one." God holds eternity in his repose. God enjoys the fullness of life in his own self-sufficient movement internal to the Godhead as Father, Son, and Holy Spirit. The internal processions of the Trinity bespeak of origin and end, possessed eternally and perfectly, without any need or loss.

God's eternity does not undermine or denigrate time. Rather, time finds its reference point, amidst its own intrinsic dynamics and shiftiness, in God's constancy and faithfulness. And any attempt to connect the confession of the past with present or future attestation must first attend to the consistent identity and character of the God of this confession. The words of our speaking Savior should grip us: "Fear not." We need not fear the lapse of time for God has not evolved. We need not fear the passing of generations for death has no power over the living one. We need not fear the vanquishing of leading lights theologically for, in the land of God's limitless freedom, their witness continues.

Doctrine of humanity

The infinite fullness of the divine life does not serve as a bound to the story of the gospel. Rather, God's perfection functions as a baseline and ballast unto the good news that this perfect life is made common or shared with others. In creation, the God who has all life and fullness in himself calls other life into being, summoning dependence, contingency, and finitude into his presence and calling them good.

Having made them, God placed them in Eden. Not only does this action manifest God's superabundant goodness in granting paradise but it also witnesses to humanity's limits: they were in one place; they were in one time. They are bounded not by God's grandiose majesty but by their given nature as finite and ordered.

A remarkable dignity is conveyed upon the human creature in the scriptures of the prophets and apostles. Psalm 8 attests the grandeur and scope of creation (long before telescopes could plumb the massive character of deep space on a far greater scale) and attests "what is man that you are mindful of him?" God is mindful of this limited and ordered being, this creature who comes from the will of another and lives by the provision of that which is outside him, whether in the form of oxygen to breathe, of food and water to nourish, or of God's providence to sustain.[4]

Humanity continues to live on borrowed breath and in dependence upon those who go before them. Nothing so sharply substantiates this neediness as the abject and complete dependence of infants upon their parents: for protection, for provision, for cleanliness for instruction, for love. Life returns at its end to such a state, more often than not, as the elderly again require care from their descendants. Again, basic needs of food, sanitation, medical care, and the like signal the interconnected and interdependent nature of human life. The fifth commandment calls for honoring one's father and mother. In ancient Israel, this involved not only heeding their authority but also providing for their livelihood in old age. It was a costly gift, not a cheap grace.

Generational interdependence goes hand in hand with the finite limits of any and every human being. And these realities have much to say about the nature and activity of knowing the one true God. Any individual man or woman faces severe limits in this regard owing to their weak and bounded mind, their unique perspective and experience, their own giftings and lack thereof. Any individual man or woman, however, ought to be trained in the nurture and admonition of the Lord by those who go before them, whether from biological or spiritual family.

Doctrine of sin

Knowing God occurs in a conflicted time and space, for those called to such knowledge have turned stubbornly and pridefully from their God to their own wisdom. In sin, humans have run from the light and made their home in the darkness.

---

4 Regarding the nature of this providence, I assume something along the lines of the Augustinian tradition herein as later developed in Thomistic and Reformed approaches. Thomas is instructive: "During the whole of a thing's existence, God must be present to it, and present in a way in keeping with the way in which the thing possesses its existence" (Thomas Aquinas, *Summa Theologiae*, 1a.8.1, reply). The Thomist-influenced Reformed theologian John Owen agrees: "The Holy Spirit so worketh in us as that he worketh by us, and what he doth in us is done by us." See his *Pneumatologia, or A Discourse Concerning the Holy Spirit*, Works of John Owen (Edinburgh: Banner of Truth Trust, 1965), 204.

The effects of sin magnify the limits of created finitude and, by implication, cause a situation to fester in which maturing in the knowledge of God occurs in a doubly constrained context. Not only individual limits but now also human immorality besmirches our efforts to gaze at the light: to discern the truth, to ponder the good, and to behold the beautiful.[5]

Sin operates at multiple levels. The apostle Paul attests to multiple facets of sinful causality: "And you were dead in the trespasses and sins in which you once walked, following the course of this world, following the prince of the power of the air, the spirit that is now at work in the sons of disobedience—among whom we all once lived in the passions of our flesh, carrying out the desires of the body and the mind, and were by nature children of wrath, like the rest of mankind" (Eph 2:1–3). This thick description of sin's influence takes in the distortion of human nature ("by nature children of wrath"), the diabolical efforts of spiritual forces ("the prince of the power of the air, the spirit that is now at work"), the disorder of human desire and passion ("in the passions of our flesh, carrying out the desires of the body and the mind"), and the social malformations of society ("following the course of this world").

Given the malformations of social groupings, any closed set finds itself more limited and endangered than an open set. While there may be generational progress in certain areas, it is invariably offset by other moral and social losses. For example, recent decades in the United States have managed to include both an increasing awareness and appreciation of equality across racial lines (since the civil rights movement of the 1960s) and a decreasing concern for spiritual matters, that is, of transcendent significance (and even polling data that shows the continuing religiosity in the United States also exemplifies the naturalizing of those religions, as in what sociologist Christian Smith has termed "moral therapeutic deism").[6] While a narrow frame of reference may not harm racial reconciliation, it is only through expanding that frame of reference to a wider conversation with others of an earlier era and through a more transcendent hope that the secularizing of religion might be offset. Blind spots can be systemic precisely because of our social interrelationships.

Doctrine of grace

The reparative work of the gospel brings grace and peace into a wasteland of history. Sin has cut off men and women from their origin, as they have been sent

---

5 More than ignorance or misdirection affects the individual in this regard, contrary to the claims of Eduardo Echeverria, *Berkouwer and Catholicism: Disputed Questions*, Studies in Reformed Theology (Leiden: Brill, 2013), 212–19. While Echeverria rightly notes the limits of knowledge acknowledged by Thomas, he does not demonstrate that these limits parallel those sketched by Berkouwer's confessional tradition.

6 Christian Smith with Melina Lundquist Denton, *Soul Searching: The Religious and Spiritual Lives of American Teenagers* (New York: Oxford University Press, 2009).

out from the paradisal presence of God. Sin has also severed their grasp upon their end, for which they have been rendered incompetent. To that distance and disorder, the gospel offers a promise of reprieve. The old is made new again in Jesus Christ.

First, grace brings the restoration of humanity's relation to its past in the person and life of Jesus of Nazareth. In this one, through the sanctifying work of the Holy Spirit, a posture of resolute and personal agreement with the faithful of the past and the testimony of God's self-revelation finds its ultimate expression. As "author and perfector of faith" (Heb. 12:2), Jesus exemplifies human excellence in embracing his Father's care through the vicissitudes of history, even embodying his calling as "man of sorrows," by remembering the testimony of faithful confession from centuries past. By faith, he proclaims deliverance with the prophetic call of Isaiah 61. By faith, he laments with the words of Psalm 22. And he not only reverences the scriptural heritage of Israel's law and prophets but also embraces the formation found in the liturgical patterns of God's people. He savors time in the Lord's house in holy season (Lk 2:49). He sets his eye so regularly and determinatively upon Jerusalem (Lk 9:51).

Second, grace brings the renewal of humanity's relation to its past in Christ's body, the communion of those made holy in him. While sin takes the form of many things, either an attempted manipulation of others by way of the path of social and even religious conformity or by means of auto-creativity and self-stylization, grace brings peace again between the self and human nature and Christian society. In Christ, humanity finds reconciliation with God as well as restoration of its disordered nature. John Calvin referred to this as the "twofold grace" (*duplex gratia*) of the gospel, meaning to keep us alert to its relational and moral facets without allowing them to be reduced one to the other.

In terms of restoring the knowledge of God, that is, of the theological task, we can speak with the traditional language of the principles of theology and in so doing mark the ways that our minds are restored to their intended function. The triune God is the ontological principle of theology. The Holy Scriptures are the external cognitive principle of theology. The regenerated heart and illumined mind are the internal cognitive principle of theology. We do well to consider each principle in turn.

First, the triune God is the ontological principle of theology. That is, God is not only the content but also the context for the practice of theology. Theology focuses upon knowing God and, in so doing, it is beholden to God: to divine self-disclosure, to divine gift, to divine presence. God is not approached as a postulate or as a hypothesis. Theology is a realist enterprise premised on tracing the presence of God in the divine economy. Thus, theology is an a posteriori discipline and eschews any a priori temptations.

Second, the Holy Scriptures are the external cognitive principle of theology. God's gracious self-disclosure has taken place in Christ, in covenant with Israel and now the whole church of Jews and Gentiles, and in various episodes of the divine economy. However, the revelatory provisions of the divine economy repeatedly culminate, epoch after epoch, with a prophetic or apostolic word delivered not only to God's people but also in written form. Thus, the self-disclosing presence of God, which alone gives light and wisdom, has been made available from generation unto generation with the promise of God's presence therein. The Scriptures are not merely a repository of ancient religious reflection (though they do contain evidence of ancient faith and practice). They are a living Word, active with the communicative and spiritual power of the triune God (Heb 4:12–13).

Third, the regenerated heart and illumined mind are the internal cognitive principle of theology. A Word from God results in many things. In the parable of the soils, Jesus points to four possible results, only one of which proves life giving and beneficial in the long run (Mk 4:3–9 and 13–20). One fundamental observation from this episode relates to the need for not only an external self-revelation from God, that is, a real or objective communication outside of us, but also for an internal renewal from God, that is, a real or subjective reception of that communication within us. Unless the word be received in faith, it does not bless the hearer.

The traditional exposition of divine revelation by means of the principles of theology has been meant to highlight grace as not only the cherished content of theology but also the essential context for its practice. By bringing together the doctrines of God, of Holy Scripture, and of sanctification, these principles seek to locate growth in theological knowledge within the gospel.

Doctrine of church

In our recent manifesto regarding the promise of retrieval for renewing theology today, Scott Swain and I suggest a fourth theological principle to pair with the ontological and cognitive principles mentioned above. We argue that tradition is the elicitive principle (*principium elicitivum*), that is, the temporally extended, socially mediated activity of renewed reason.[7] Our concern remains the same as that behind the other three principles, namely, to locate theological knowledge within the gospel and to attend to the particular ways in which the news of God's life-giving work in Christ takes hold of human reality this side of the Fall. We believe that another facet must be considered—the ecclesial—if we are to appreciate the nature and necessity of the gospel for knowing God. Before we can consider this fourth principle, we must attend to matters ecclesiastical in their own terms.

"Jesus Christ is Lord of the Church." These are the first words of Reformed polity, as illustrated in the various books of church order in the Presbyterian tradition. The claim is not genealogical: Jesus as creator of the church. The claim is also not metaphysical: Jesus as God over the church. The claim includes but subsumes such matters under its functional, present-tense focus: Jesus as the chief shepherd, the king, the warrior, the teacher, the great high priest of the church. The heavenly session of the risen Lord finds extensive exposition in the Reformed

---

7 Michael Allen and Scott R. Swain, *Reformed Catholicity: The Promise of Retrieval for Theology and Biblical Interpretation* (Grand Rapids, MI: Baker Academic, 2015), 36.

tradition, inasmuch as Christ is viewed as being as personally involved in applying his salvation to his people as he was in accomplishing that salvation in his own person.

The ongoing agency of the risen Christ means that grace continues to be given to the church generation after generation.[8] This grace no longer takes the form of discrete new revelation. The canon for the covenant of grace has now been closed. But this grace takes the form of lordly address through those Holy Scriptures to ever-new situations of need. And with that grace comes not only illumination and insight but also wisdom and confession. The church has been brought to hear and to attest the gospel, and even to order its thinking around that gospel, by the lordly exercise of Christ's kingly office.

The church does not experience this refreshing without remainder, however, for indwelling sin persists in her members and her society. The distinction between the invisible and the visible church has been intended through the reformed confessions to make plain the eschatological tension experienced as the church has already heard the gospel afresh by Christ's life-giving grace, though she has not yet fully heard the gospel with clarity and comprehension. That gap between promise and reality marks the church not only in that some of her members are nominal Christians (and will prove to be like unto the second and third soils in Jesus's parable) but also that all members are shy of glory at this point. The imagery of the pilgrimage has been definitive for the Reformed tradition at this point, locating the church on the way to glory and no longer mired in sin. But her present location in grace continues to experience the tug and pull of both that past in sin and that promised hope in glory.

A reformed ethic of retrieval

This irregular dogmatics (to use Karl Barth's term) has sought to locate retrieval within the orbit of the Christian confession, asking what significance the Christian past might have within the lived drama of the present. Without decrying archaeological or anthropological accounts of attending to the past, we have sought to inquire after what gospel hope might be offered specifically to Christian retrieval of the heritage of the saints. Diagnostic analysis of the agonies and exigencies of human social formation may or may not prove fruitful, case by case, based on little more than the availability of causal evidence in each circumstance. But we have sought to ask whether fundamental claims about the oneness and constancy of the

---

8 Mark Bowald has helpfully traced the "Deistic" turn in modern biblical criticism owing to a metaphysics noninclusive of divine missions in his *Rendering the Word in Theological Hermeneutics: Mapping Divine and Human Agency* (Aldershot: Ashgate, 2007), 173; see Herman Bavinck, *Reformed Dogmatics*, vol. 1, Prolegomena, ed. John Bolt (Grand Rapids, MI: Baker Academic, 2003), 384–5. A similar argument could be made regarding the deistic analysis of much modern ecclesiology (especially that influenced by so-called postliberalism).

triune God, the character of humanity created after his image, and the nature of
the economy of grace in response to human sin do not leave us with good news for
historical retrieval regarding the confession of the gospel.

Specifically, we have sought to explain how Reformed theological method is
itself shaped by the material content of the gospel. Knowing God flows completely
from God's own action on our behalf, or it occurs not at all. Whereas the classic
threefold distinction of the principles of theology was meant to attest this reality
that grace is not only the content but also the context of theology, we have tried to
affirm and amplify that confession by noting its ecclesiastical implications. Thus,
we return to our fourth principle, namely, that tradition is the elicitive principle of
theology (*principium elicitivum*). In so doing, we must comment on tradition itself
(as an eliciting principle) and upon the posture of retrieval (as a corresponding
ethical principle).

First, tradition represents the temporally extended, socially mediated activity
of renewed reason within the communion of the saints. Tradition may take the
form of many social activities, whether they be creeds or confessions, treatises or
catechisms, rubrics for worship or sacramental practice, disciplines for daily piety
and spiritual exercise, authority structures, musical accompaniments to personal
or corporate worship, architectural or artistic structures that mark the space of
Christian practice, and so forth.

And yet tradition is the result not only of the accumulation of human social formation in its intellectual, liturgical, educational, and other forms. Tradition is, first
and foremost, the result of the risen Christ's continued lordship over and through
his church. The fundamental basis for tradition is Christological: "Jesus Christ is
the same yesterday, today, and forever" (Heb 13:8). But the Christological claim is
not only regarding identity but also office: he is now also "the great shepherd of the
sheep" (Heb 13:20). That the risen one continues to exist and to minister faithfully
undergirds a "great cloud of witnesses" (Heb 12:1) as well as the value of imitating
the faith of his undershepherds whose life outcomes we have discerned (Heb 13:7;
notice that the famous Christological teaching of 13:8 follows as an explanatory
basis for this practice of imitating church leaders, evidencing a link between Christ
and his body).[9]

---

9 The most fundamental matter shaping the ecclesiology of Hebrews is
Christological: "Jesus Christ is the same yesterday, today, and forever" (Heb 13:8); see Ceslas
Spicq, *L'Epitre aux Hébreux II—Commentaire* (Paris: Gabalda, 1953), 2; George Hunsinger,
"The Same Only Different: Karl Barth's Interpretation of Hebrews 13:8," in *Thy Word is
Truth: Barth on Scripture*, ed. George Hunsinger (Grand Rapids, MI: Eerdmans, 2012),
112–24. And this Jesus who is unchanging is a speaker: see Tomasz Lewicki, *"Weist nicht ab
den Sprechenden!": Wort Gottes und Paraklese im Hebräerbrief*, Paderborner Theologische
Studien (Paderborn: Schöningh, 2004), chap. 3; as well as B. F. Westcott, *The Epistle to the
Hebrews: The Greek Text with Notes and Essays*, 3rd ed. (London: Macmillan, 1903), 4.
Surely the insistence that "he upholds all things by his powerful word" (Heb 1:3) applies to
the church as well.

Tradition cannot be defined reductively, then, as the artifacts and accumulations of religious history alone, as if it were simply the relics of spiritual hoarding through the centuries. Tradition must be defined spiritually—as a reality in the divine economy, traced to the life-giving work of the triune God—and perceived by the eyes of faith. In this regard, it is crucial to remember that the ontological principle of theology serves an axiomatic role with respect to the cognitive or elicitive principles. All the other principles are instruments and signs of that triune God's gracious provision for his people's intellectual and theological nurture.

We might elaborate on this priority of the ontological principle over all other epistemological principles by means of Trinitarian theology. Not only Thomas Aquinas but also the Reformed doctrinal tradition has made use of the doctrine of the divine missions of the Son and Spirit here to affirm the link between the God, himself full of grace and truth, who has shed abroad in our hearts the knowledge of his glory and light. "In his light do we see light" (Ps 36:7-9).[10] Theology has hope, precisely because we have an evangel and, more fundamentally, because the God we have been given to know is the God of the Gospel. Though he has all wisdom in and of himself, he has seen fit to share with us that wisdom in creation and again, decisively, in Jesus Christ and with the communion of saints united to him. Tradition has hope, then, for evangelical and Trinitarian reasons.

Second, Christian moral theology seeks to consider the implications of doctrinal claims and to root proverbial, legal, or casuistic reasoning in the theological order of the Gospel. In speaking of a posture of retrieval, we are attesting the necessary ethic of receiving gratefully and humbly from those who have gone before us in the Christian pilgrimage. While this ethic may be identified with obedience to the fifth commandment (honoring one's spiritual parents), it is crucial to note that its logic does not exhaust itself in that legal command. Rather, it fits the warp and woof of Christian anthropology, wherein human experience and human knowledge are located within the divine economy of the Gospel.

A Reformed ethic of retrieval will refuse to locate those who have gone before us as existing in any other strata than that which we now share. In other words, the past is not pristine and bears no more promise for perfection than do we at present. Thus, the task of critical appropriation becomes absolutely necessary, as is made so apparent by the distinction between the visible and the invisible church. We are not called to look elsewhere than the real church or to look only to its spiritual moments. We are, however, summoned to look to the church with the eyes of faith. Calvin reminded us that we confess that we *"believe* one, holy, catholic, and apostolic church" rather than that we "believe *in*" such a church.[11] In so doing, he

---

10 On the Gospel hope for ongoing theology, see Michael Allen, "'In Your Light Do We See Light': The Self-Revealing God and the Future of Theology," in *Theology and the Future: Evangelical Assertions and Explorations*, ed. Trevor Cairney and David Starling (London: T & T Clark, 2014), 13–26.

11 John Calvin, *Institutes of the Christian Religion*, Library of Christian Classics, ed. John T. McNeill (Louisville: Westminster John Knox, 2004), 1013 (IV.i.2); italics added.

reminds us that the church is an instrument of God, not to be confused with God himself. Tradition is not inerrant or indefectible, then, and we do well to view tradition as a reality brought by grace but not yet glorified.

In recent Roman Catholic accounts of tradition, notably those provided by Lewis Ayres and Matthew Levering, tradition finds description in Christological and pneumatological forms. Ayres suggests that we must grasp the economy of God's speech as one "in which the mystery of God is spoken among us, through the interaction of Word and Spirit, word and answering word."[12] And Levering adds that "the way to understand the active place of the Church in divine revelation is to reflect upon the missions of the Son and Spirit."[13] This is very promising. Yet tradition—whether in the form of the history of biblical exegesis (in Ayres) or of liturgy (in Levering)—is described in ideal terms. So Ayres: "we may conceive of these later 'ecclesial' readings of the New Testament as truer, deeper readings of the literal sense."[14] And Levering: "The liturgy is the true home for the reading of Scripture . . . it is in and through the liturgy that revelation is truly proclaimed, interpreted, and enacted for the life of the world."[15]

Reformed retrieval will demur from assuming the ideal or expounding the church only in terms of divine grace. Reformed ecclesiology, and its consideration of tradition as one key element in this broader topic, will also consider the church's tradition in an eschatological hue, graced out of darkness but not yet glorified into undimming light.[16] With Ayres, Reformed retrieval will focus upon church

---

12 Lewis Ayres, "The Word Answering the Word: Opening the Space of Catholic Biblical Interpretation," in *Theological Theology: Essays in Honour of John Webster*, ed. R. David Nelson, Darren Sarisky, and Justin Stratis (London: T & T Clark, 2015), 49. For further reflections on Scripture and tradition and a posture of critically receptive theology as a way forward for modern Roman Catholic theology, see also Lewis Ayres, *Nicaea and Its Legacy: An Approach to Fourth Century Trinitarian Theology* (New York: Oxford University Press, 2004), 384–429.

13 Matthew Levering, *Engaging the Doctrine of Revelation: The Mediation of the Gospel through Church and Scripture* (Grand Rapids, MI: Baker Academic, 2014), 56. For further reflection upon the missions of Son and Spirit and a graced participation of human mediating figures within those missions, see also Matthew Levering, *Christ and the Catholic Priesthood: Ecclesial Hierarchy and the Pattern of the Trinity* (Chicago: Hillenbrand, 2010); idem, *Participatory Biblical Exegesis: A Theology of Biblical Interpretation* (Notre Dame, IN: University of Notre Dame Press, 2008), esp. 90–140.

14 Ayres, "Word Answering the Word," 46; italics added.

15 Levering, *Engaging the Doctrine of Revelation*, 80.

16 Levering does suggest ways in which the doctrine of the indefectibility of the church might be maintained along with an awareness of errors on nonessential matters (*Engaging the Doctrine of Revelation*, 27). For further Reformed analysis of the indefectibility of the church, see Michael Allen, "'The Church's One Foundation': The Justification of the Ungodly Church," in *Justification and the Gospel: Understanding the Contexts and the Controversies* (Grand Rapids, MI: Baker Academic, 2013), 153–78. Affirming the sinful yet holy character

tradition in its various forms as lineaments of the history of the Word and, thus, of exegetical reasoning. It will do so because such an interrogation of the tradition offers more promising grounds for hearing the Word more faithfully. Other potential interrogations—regarding the political, social, missiological, or philosophical constructions of the church—may offer benefits but do not necessarily put us in conversation with the ultimate source of authority and the promised bearer of life, the prophetic witness of the Holy Scriptures. Even in its retrieval of the tradition, Reformed Christians will remember the axiomatic words of the first thesis of Berne (1528): "The holy, Christian Church, whose only Head is Christ, is born of the Word of God, abides in the same, and does not listen to the voice of a stranger."[17]

And yet retrieval will not take the form of cynicism or of modern progress's sneer toward the past, for the agonistics of indwelling sin continue to plague us as well. We are no more glorified than the saints of days past or the councils of centuries old. Retrieval attests our remembrance of this common location and this shared vocation to know God more fully while on this journey unto the promised glory of Canaan's shore.

---

of the church does not thereby implicate one in claims akin to those of Ephraim Radner, who argues for the pneumatic deprivation of the Western church (so, e.g., *A Brutal Unity: The Spiritual Politics of the Christian Church* (Waco, TX: Baylor University Press, 2012)). While Radner's argument may find fit with certain prophetic texts read figurally, it cannot attend to the breadth of the apostolic witness regarding the nature of the Christian community. Whereas Levering attends too exclusively to texts attending to divine mission in defining the church and her tradition, Radner responds by focusing single-mindedly upon texts of divine abandonment. The key is to note that God has come to the church, but that God continues to come to the church; she is in a state of grace, but not yet in the realm of glory.

17 "The Ten Theses of Berne [1528]," in *Reformed Confessions of the Sixteenth Century*, ed. Arthur C. Cochrane (Louisville: Westminster John Knox, 2003), 49.

Chapter 5

"ONLY WHAT IS ROOTED IS LIVING": *
A ROMAN CATHOLIC THEOLOGY OF *RESSOURCEMENT*

Jennifer Newsome Martin

This chapter supplies a gestalt of Roman Catholic theological retrieval in the twentieth century, offering in its sketch a constructive proposal for what is emblematically Catholic about the varied approaches of figures working in this milieu. The primary focus is on the Francophone Catholic theological renewal, or *"ressourcement,"* movement—which was by no means formally organized—centered around the Jesuits of Lyon-Fourvière and the Dominicans of Le Saulchoir.[1] Perhaps the most prominent Jesuits counted in their ranks are Henri de Lubac (1896–1991) and Jean Daniélou (1905–1974), and among the Dominicans Yves Congar (1904–1995) and Marie-Dominique Chenu (1895–1990). A fuller treatment would, of course, consider many other figures, including Dominique Dubarle (1907–1987), Henri Bouillard (1908–1981), Henri-Marie Féret (1904–1992), Louis Charlier (1898–1981), René Draguet (1896–1980), and Louis Bouyer (1913–2004), not to mention German speakers like Joseph Ratzinger (1927–) and Hans Urs von Balthasar (1905–1988).[2]

---

* Henri de Lubac, *Paradoxes of Faith* (San Francisco: Ignatius Press, 1987), 55. I am enormously grateful to Anne Carpenter, Cyril O' Regan, and Jay Martin for reading and providing incisive comments upon earlier drafts of this chapter.

1 For a marvelous overview of *ressourcement* thought, to which I am indebted, see Gabriel Flynn, "Introduction: The Twentieth-Century Renaissance in Catholic Theology," in *Ressourcement: A Movement for Renewal in Twentieth-Century Catholic Theology*, ed. Gabriel Flynn and Paul D. Murray (Oxford: Oxford University Press, 2012), 1–19. Also see Hans Boersma, "Analogy of Truth: The Sacramental Epistemology of *Nouvelle Théologie*" and Jürgen Mettepenningen, *"Nouvelle Théologie:* Four Historical Stages of Theological Reform Towards *Ressourcement* (1935–1965)," in *Ressourcement: A Movement for Renewal in Twentieth-Century Catholic Theology*, ed. Gabriel Flynn and Paul D. Murray (Oxford: Oxford University Press, 2012), 157–71 and 172–84 respectively.

2 For treatments of Balthasar as a theologian of Catholic retrieval, see Edward T. Oakes, "Balthasar and *Ressourcement*: An Ambiguous Relationship," in *Ressourcement: A Movement*

The contributions of *ressourcement* thought, though controversial in the atmosphere of *Humani Generis* amid the modernist controversy,[3] directly paved the way for the reforms of the Second Vatican Council in the mid-1960s. The history of the reception of *ressourcement* thought in Catholic theology is incredibly complex, as it has been appraised negatively for two exactly contrary reasons. On the one hand, its preconciliar reception—that is, its reception before the Second Vatican Council—was markedly chilly on account of a perceived excessive innovation. On the other hand, what had been deemed innovative and even transgressive before the Council is sometimes dismissed as overly retrograde and conservative after Vatican II, especially when juxtaposed with the notion of *aggiornamento*, a word invoked by Pope John XXIII in a January 1959 speech announcing the forthcoming convocation of the Council and the spirit of openness and modernization that it would adopt. I suggest fundamentally that though Catholic *ressourcement* thought is often mischaracterized as a nostalgic strain, sustained recovery of its poetic and literary forebears—specifically, the notebooks and poetry of Charles Péguy—supplies an interpretive complexity that can foster a more discerning reception of *ressourcement* theology on the whole.

These Catholic retrievalists are sometimes referred to as theologians of or associated with *la nouvelle théologie*, although this appellation was a polemical one that they did not give themselves and from which many, including de Lubac, Chenu, and Congar, wished to distance themselves.[4] The name, as is already well known, originated with the movement's critics, first by Msgr. Pietro Parente and most pointedly by the Dominican Réginald Marie Garrigou-Lagrange, OP, who posed the question "*La nouvelle théologie, où va-t-elle?*" and answered it emphatically by saying it was modernism *redivivus*.[5] This level of suspicion and froideur persisted for years, as those associated were ostracized, removed from their teaching

---

for Renewal in Twentieth-Century Catholic Theology, ed. Gabriel Flynn and Paul D. Murray (Oxford: Oxford University Press, 2012), 278–88, which refers to Balthasar as "the 20th century's premier *ressourcement* theologian" (288); Cyril O'Regan, "Von Balthasar and Thick Retrieval: Post-Chalcedonian Symphonic Theology," *Gregorianum* 77 (1996): 227–60; Adrian J. Walker, "Love Alone: Hans Urs von Balthasar as a Master of Theological Renewal," *Communio* 32 (2005): 1–24.

3 See Joseph A Komonchak, "*Humani Generis* and *Nouvelle Théologie*," in *Ressourcement: A Movement for Renewal in Twentieth-Century Catholic Theology*, ed. Gabriel Flynn and Paul D. Murray (Oxford: Oxford University Press, 2012), 138–56.

4 De Lubac wrote in a letter to theology student Hubert Schnackers that "I do not much like it when people talk of 'new theology,' referring to me; I have never used the expression, and I detest the thing" (*At the Service of the Church: Henri de Lubac Reflects on the Circumstances that Occasioned His Writings*, trans. Anne Elizabeth Englund (San Francisco: Ignatius Press, 1993), 361).

5 Réginald Garrigou-Lagrange, "*La nouvelle théologie, où va-t-elle?*" *Angelicum* 23 (1946): 126–45. See Pietro Parente, "Nouve tendenze teologiche," *L'Osservatore Romano* (February 9–10, 1942) for a critique of le Saulchoir theologians Chenu and Charlier.

positions, and otherwise ecclesiastically disciplined. De Lubac, himself the subject of censure, characterized this era as having a pervasive atmosphere of insularity and suspicion, noting that

> a certain Scholastic conservatism, which claimed in all good faith to be tradition itself, was alarmed at any appearance of novelty. A kind of so-called "Thomist" dictatorship, which was more a matter of government than intellectuality, strove to stifle any effort toward freer thought. A network made up of several professors and their former students, which was spread throughout the world, distrusted anything that came into existence outside itself.[6]

Similarly, Balthasar famously spoke of his formation in the Jesuit scholasticate as a stultifying time of "languishing in the desert."[7] Balthasar even went as far as to offer the humorous confession that he and Daniélou, who shared a desk during this time of study, would often smuggle in texts of the Fathers to read during these "boring" theology lectures.[8]

While not an organized movement, the general sensibility of *ressourcement* thinking was largely oppositional to the ascendency of neo-scholasticism, which prioritized certitude, argument, rationalism, and explication in response to the perceived threats of modernity. Neo-scholasticism was seen as excessively relying on what would otherwise be goods, in its reactionary and myopic restriction of theology to a system of the rational propositions of manual theology that was not representative of the complexity of the tradition. In particular, it obscured the breadth and depth of Thomas Aquinas as earlier commentators had effectively replaced the Angelic Doctor with a kind of ossified catechism, stone for bread, a poor substitute for the originality and capaciousness of his thought. It is important to note that it was this truncated Thomism to which *ressourcement* thinkers objected, and generally not to Thomas himself.[9] In a letter to de Lubac, for example, Étienne Gilson writes,

---

For a helpful secondary account see Gerard Loughlin, *"Nouvelle Théologie:* A Return to Modernism?" in *Ressourcement: A Movement for Renewal in Twentieth-Century Catholic Theology,* ed. Gabriel Flynn and Paul D. Murray (Oxford: Oxford University Press, 2012), 36–50.

6 De Lubac, *Service,* 47.

7 Hans Urs von Balthasar, *My Work in Retrospect,* trans. Joseph Fessio and Michael Waldstein (San Francisco: Ignatius Press, 1993), 89.

8 Hans Urs von Balthasar, preface to Jean Daniélou, *Prayer: The Mission of the Church,* trans. David Louis Schindler (Grand Rapids, MI: William B. Eerdmans, 1996), xi.

9 Some of the criticisms of Thomas that were the most pointed were later corrected; for example, Maurice Blondel recognized that his *Letter on Apologetics* had more issues with the scholastic manuals than Thomas himself (M. Blondel, *Le problem de la philosophie catholique* (Paris: Bloud et Gay, 1932), 47).

Our only salvation lies in a return to Saint Thomas himself, before the Thomism of John of Saint Thomas, before that of Cajetan as well—Cajetan, whose famous commentary is in every respect the consummate example of a *corruptorium Thomae* . . . Salvation lies in returning to the real Saint Thomas, rightly called the Universal Doctor of the Church; accept no substitutes![10]

Along with this impulse to access the original Thomas there was also among the *ressourcement* thinkers a definitive attempt to pluralize the range of magisterially sanctioned thinkers, to recall from their oubliette systematically and massively forgotten voices of the Christian tradition. John Paul II's *Fides et Ratio* (1998) shares this double inheritance insofar as it both affirms Thomas's "enduring originality" (§43–44) and even normativity in continuity with Leo XIII's *Aeterni Patris*, but subsequently includes alongside him not only the Cappadocians, Augustine, Anselm, and Bonaventure but also John Henry Newman, Étienne Gilson, Antonio Rosmini, Jacques Maritain, Edith Stein, Vladimir Soloviev, Pavel Florensky, Petr Chaadaev, and Vladimir Lossky, an enormously ecumenical set of thinkers by any measure that includes theologians as well as speculative philosophers (§74).[11]

Daniélou together with de Lubac made patristic and medieval sources considerably more accessible by their joint editing of *Sources chrétiennes*, a publication that provided good French translations of the Fathers alongside the texts in their original languages.[12] According to de Lubac, *Sources chrétiennes* attempted to "trace Christian doctrine to its sources, in order to find there the truth on which our lives are based."[13] *Sources chrétiennes* was therefore both a stay against forgetfulness as well as a sign of contradiction insofar as it recovered the texts of the Fathers and asserted that the Fathers were not simply to remain shrouded in the past but had abiding relevance to modern readers. Indeed, Daniélou suggested that the series operated under the assumption that the Fathers are even more present than the present, with something to say immediately to contemporary believers.[14]

10 Étienne Gilson, *Letters of E. Gilson to Henri de Lubac*, trans. Mary Emily Hamilton (San Francisco: Ignatius Press, 198), 23–4, dated July 8, 1956. Cf. Marcellino D'Ambrosio, "*Ressourcement* Theology, *Aggiornamento*, and the Hermeneutics of Tradition," *Communio* 18 (1991): 530–55, here, 543. De Lubac similarly expresses a fondness for Thomas, writing that "I in no way scorn the effort of Scholasticism, and in particular that of Saint Thomas, who is the author I have most often read" (*Service*, 361).

11 See Cyril O'Regan, "Ambiguity and Undecidability in *Fides et Ratio*," *International Journal of Systematic Theology* 2 (2000): 319–29.

12 De Lubac acknowledges the often forgotten fact that the original person who conceived and gave birth to the project was Fr. Victor Fontoynont, SJ, who considered the series a step toward ecumenical dialogue with Greek and Russian Orthodoxy (de Lubac, *Service*, 94n24).

13 Henri de Lubac, *Mémoire sur l'occasion de mes écrits* (Namur: Culture et Vérité, 1992), 29.

14 Jean Daniélou, "Les orientations presentes de la pensée religieuse," *Études* 79 (1946): 10. I am grateful to François-Xavier Malartre for his generous assistance with the translation.

In his 1946 *Études* article "Les orientations presentes de la pensée religieuse," which has rightly been called a "manifesto" for *ressourcement*,[15] Daniélou criticizes the inadequate resources of neo-scholasticism to address faith, life, and pastoral care. He finds the disproportionate reaction of neo-scholasticism to the specter of modernism most manifest in its treatment of God as a pure object of intellectual inquiry and its contraction of living thought to "mummified" and "frozen" forms, which had led to an ossification of thought rather than a renewal of theological thinking.[16] For Daniélou the solution was threefold: first, theology ought encounter God as God is, as infinite and infinitely mysterious Subject revealed with perfect freedom to whom human beings ought respond with wonder and adoration; second, theology must be no less responsive to the experiences of the modern person, taking into account developments in culture, including science, history, literature, and philosophy; finally, theology should adopt a posture attentive to the concrete particulars of the whole human being, which does include the spiritual, but also the exigencies of the physical and the political.[17]

In Daniélou's estimation, repeated consistently among other *ressourcement* theologians, the connection of theology to the Scriptures, the Fathers, the church, and the liturgy had grown too tenuous. Moreover, theological science had fragmented into overly autonomous subdisciplines and needed to reclaim its original disciplinary integration of the biblical, dogmatic, spiritual, and speculative: this sense of unity, particularly that between dogmatic theology and spirituality, was represented in spades in the Fathers and was the model toward which *ressourcement* thought aspired.[18] Anticipating Vatican II's *Dei Verbum*, Daniélou simultaneously affirms the value of the historical-critical method of biblical interpretation, but gestures toward its limits as he suggests the primacy of rediscovering the Bible first and foremost as *une Parole de Dieu* addressed to human beings. Furthermore, the recovery of this more expansive mode of reading Scripture was inseparable from reclaiming patristic theology, which Daniélou characterized first and foremost as one "vast commentary on Holy Scripture"[19] that was able to preserve continuities not only between Old Testament and New Testament but also between Scripture, spirituality, and liturgy.[20] For the patristic

---

15 D'Ambrosio, *"Ressourcement* Theology," 534.

16 Daniélou, *"Orientations,"* 6.

17 Daniélou, *"Orientations,"* 7.

18 See Hans Urs von Balthasar, "Theology and Sanctity," *Explorations in Theology*, vol. 1, *The Word Made Flesh* (San Francisco: Ignatius Press, 1989), 181–209.

19 Daniélou, *"Orientations,"* 12.

20 Cf. also Jean Daniélou, *The Bible and the Liturgy*, trans. Michael A. Mathis (Notre Dame, IN: University of Notre Dame Press, 1956). For examples of other *ressourcement* attention to spiritual exegesis, cf. Henri de Lubac's *History and Spirit: The Understanding of Scripture According to Origen* (San Francisco: Ignatius Press, 2007), and the three-volume

writers, especially Irenaeus, Origen, and Gregory of Nyssa, Christian religion was not simply a system of doctrines but fundamentally a history of God's salvific work in the economy, the locus of the saving entrance of the Incarnate Word.[21] Thus, the full complement of theological resources must be recovered precisely as an organic unity.

For the *ressourcement* theologians, however, a retrieval of a unified tradition must be accompanied by a no less serious and coincident awareness of the modern situation. Daniélou provides a compelling picture of the proper task of the Catholic theologian, namely, "to move, like angels on Jacob's ladder, between eternity and time, weaving among them always new connections."[22] According to Daniélou, this weaving requires openness to philosophical and literary developments as the human imagination and experience are expanded by the contributions of such figures as Friedrich Nietzsche, Fyodor Dostoevsky, Søren Kierkegaard, Karl Marx, Charles Darwin, Blaise Pascal, Gabriel Marcel, and Max Scheler, among others.[23] Certainly de Lubac, who published not only in patristics but also in modern atheism, communism, Buddhism, theosophy, the socialism of Pierre-Joseph Proudhon, and Renaissance Platonist Giovanni Pico della Mirandola, can serve as a prime example of this generosity. Influenced profoundly by de Lubac, Balthasar likewise endeavored to bring renewed attention to the Greek Fathers, writing monographs on Gregory of Nyssa and Maximus the Confessor and completing translations of Origen[24] but also approaching these texts and figures in the tradition

---

Medieval Exegesis: The Four Senses of Scripture, Ressourcement: Retrieval and Renewal in Catholic Thought (Grand Rapids, MI: William B. Eerdmans, 1998 (v. 1), 2000 (v. 2), and 2009 (v. 3)). See also Susan K. Wood, *Spiritual Exegesis and the Church in the Theology of Henri de Lubac* (Grand Rapids, MI: William B. Eerdmans, 1998). These texts might serve as counterevidence for George Lindbeck's characterization of *ressourcement* interpretation (whether Protestant or Catholic) as being prone to intellectual elitism and overdetermination by modern historical criticism (George Lindbeck, "Ecumenical Theology," in *The Modern Theologians: An Introduction to Christian Theology in the Twentieth Century*, vol. 2, ed. David Ford (Oxford: Blackwell, 1995), 265). Lindbeck does cite Balthasar and Barth approvingly as examples of what he calls "pre-modern" approaches to Biblical interpretation that recapitulate "the same universe of theological discourse as the fathers" (269).

21 Daniélou, "Orientations," 10. This interest in recovering a thick sense of history as a theological category is shared among many thinkers associated with this movement. See, for instance, Henri de Lubac, *Catholicism: Christ and the Common Destiny of Man*, trans. Lancelot C. Sheppard and Sister Elizabeth Englund, OCD (San Francisco: Ignatius Press, 1988), especially pt. 2; Henri de Lubac, *Theology in History* (San Francisco: Ignatius Press, 1996); Hans Urs von Balthasar, *A Theology of History* (San Francisco: Ignatius Press, 1994); Joseph Ratzinger, *The Theology of History in St. Bonaventure* (Chicago: Franciscan Press, 1971).

22 Daniélou, "Orientations," 13.

23 Daniélou, "Orientations," 13.

24 Original titles include *Parole et Mystère chez Origène* (1957); *Présence et Pensée: Essai sur la Philosophie Religieuse de Grégoire de Nysse* (1942); *Kosmische Liturgie: Höhe und Krise*

anachronistically such that, for instance, Maximus the Confessor could stipulate an answer to the denaturing claims of Hegelian philosophy even before the fact. In this respect, Balthasar is performing the task that Daniélou set out for the Catholic theologian, traversing up and down Jacob's ladder, weaving together strands of the eternal with the temporal to make a durable cloth marked always by a temporal strangeness and density, drawing together the modern situation and the "treasures of revelation . . . [which are] bound as much to the past as to the future."[25]

Although the patristic era is privileged to a certain extent because, as de Lubac suggests, it is a time in which "the Christian tradition is expressed with a particular intensity,"[26] it would, however, be a mistake—indeed, *the* mistake of neo-scholasticism—to invest too heavily in the claim that one figure or era is the only sanctioned expression of Christian tradition. Surely, an important commitment of the Catholic *ressourcement* theologians was critically to rehabilitate both major and minor figures, and these across the temporal and geographical wideness and complexity of the tradition. In particular, it was de Lubac and Balthasar whose efforts likely bore the most fruit on this front.[27] This "pied beauty" of the Christian tradition—a tradition that is not above critique—is underscored in Balthasar's somewhat neglected but programmatic 1939 essay, "Patristik, Scholastik, und wir," that is, "The Fathers, the Scholastics, and Ourselves."[28] The stated purpose of this essay is to discern among all the expressive forms of Christianity through the different epochs of the tradition "that living wellspring that lies behind all these cultural forms of expression."[29] The temptation in such a project would be, as Balthasar knows, to blame the most recent iterations of Christian expressive

---

des griechischen Weltbilds bei Maximus Confessor (1941). On Balthasar's named debts to de Lubac, see *My Work*, 11, 47, and 89; cf. Hans Urs von Balthasar, "In Retrospect," *The Analogy of Beauty*, ed. John Riches (Edinburgh: T & T Clark, 1986), 195.

　25　Balthasar, "In Retrospect," 202.

　26　Henri de Lubac, *Mémoire sur l'occasion de mes écrits* (Namar: Cultrue et vérité, 1989), 94; quoted in D'Ambrosia, 532n9.

　27　Balthasar, for instance, drew from all quarters; in his retrospective account of his career, he notes efforts to treat or translate "Irenaeus, Origen, Gregory of Nyssa, Denys the Areopagite, Maximus the Confessor, Augustine, Anselm, William of St. Thierry, the two Mechthilds, Julian of Norwich, The Cloud of Unknowing, Hilton, Jeanne D'Arc, Catherine of Siena, John of the Cross, Lallemant, Surin, Peter Faber, Ignatius, Angelus Silesius, Görres, and, from our day, Therese of Lisieux, Maurice Blondel, and Divo Barsotti" ("In Retrospect," 207). Elsewhere, Balthasar suggests approvingly that de Lubac "made himself the defender of misunderstood and unappreciated themes and currents in . . . theology" (*Theology of Henri de Lubac*, 91). One of the best examples here is probably de Lubac's interest in Pierre Teilhard de Chardin.

　28　Balthasar, "Patristik, Scholastik, und wir," *Theologie der Zeit* 3 (1939): 65–109, translated as "The Fathers, the Scholastics, and Ourselves," in *Communio: International Catholic Review* 24 (1997): 347–96.

　29　Balthasar, "The Fathers, the Scholastics, and Ourselves," 348.

forms for denaturing or distorting the simple power of the originary or oldest forms. Balthasar facetiously details an exaggerated version of the received narrative: that the expressive forms of later eras in the church (whether Renaissance, baroque, scholastic, or modern) were deadening departures from the essential living core of Christianity, which can be found only in some lost Edenic paradise of patrology.[30] Such a project, however, would be manifestly Harnackian but never Balthasarian: he is unwavering in his claim that *no* past era can be repristinated. He moves systematically through the patristic, the scholastic, and the modern periods of Christian history, identifying in each what he calls an "innermost structural law" (*Gesetz*), a pattern that structures its particular contribution in time and history; Balthasar adjudicates the contributions of each epoch by the measure of what he calls the "fundamental law" or "essence" of Christianity. This essence is not an abstraction but, here relying upon the thought of the Catholic Tübingen School, "expresses itself in the level of history in ever-new forms without our being able thereby to call any one of these forms the absolute one."[31] Balthasar's tendency is to pluralize styles rather than reify privileged ones.

According to this essay, the patristics had the benefit of the radiance of youth, a "greatness, depth, boldness, flexibility, certainty and a flaming love" in which "life and doctrine are immediately one,"[32] but may have capitulated in certain ways to an overspiritualizing Platonism that would tend to flee nature. For Balthasar—which may be surprising given his well-documented resistance to manual theology—it is actually *scholasticism* that provides a corrective to patristic thought in its resolute opposition to emanentism and its grounded accent on nature. Certain forms of scholasticism, though, may have overemphasized natural *ratio* and Aristotelian logical categorization at the expense of supernatural mystery.[33] Balthasar here gestures in an interrogative rather than a declarative manner:

> But does not this Aristotelian worldview hide the reverse danger in itself? Namely, in place of supernaturalism, naturalism; instead of spiritualistic mysticism, a collapse into rationalism? Isn't Scholasticism soon liable to the danger of overvaluing the natural *ratio* and its capacities? We do not wish to deny this lurking danger, still less the partial distortion of late Scholasticism into a rationalistic subtilization of the content of revelation. But what we must first realize is that the great scholastics strove to fashion neither pure philosophy nor

---

30   Balthasar, "The Fathers, the Scholastics, and Ourselves," 350.

31   Balthasar, "The Fathers, the Scholastics, and Ourselves," 352.

32   Balthasar, "The Fathers, the Scholastics, and Ourselves," 371.

33   Balthasar, "The Fathers, the Scholastics, and Ourselves," 382–3. See Oakes's claim in "Balthasar and *Ressourcement*" that Balthasar does not romanticize the patristic era, 284–5. He made a similar case in Edward T. Oakes, *Pattern of Redemption: The Theology of Hans Urs von Balthasar* (New York: Continuum, 1994), 102–30. Cyril O' Regan suggests that Oakes's presentation of Balthasar's critique of the Fathers might be somewhat overstated ("Balthasar and Thick Retrieval," 228n1).

pure theology but rather a total view of the world that emerged from nature and supernature.[34]

These commitments are only heightened in Balthasar's 1951 book on Karl Barth, which suggests that expressions of Christian truth must be multiple, admitting an array of expressive forms or styles. Truth, as Balthasar understands it, is "profuse" and, as expressed in nearly infinitely variable historical contexts, also expressed "kinetically" in time and in history.[35] With respect to the Christian theological tradition, this profuseness and kineticism means at the very least that the process of conservation and retrieval must be a creative effort that accounts for multiple concrete approaches and byways to truth—Aristotle, Plato, the Stoics, Plotinus, Aquinas, and so on—all of whom presuppose the others in their responses and own articulations of the truth. Balthasar makes a distinction between revelation and the philosophical or finite forms or expressions of it. "No matter," Balthasar says, "how definitive and irrevocable an ecclesial definition is, its object is still revelation alone and not the philosophic system from which it borrows a concept or a term to give more appropriate expression to its meaning," [36] suggesting that the expressions of theological truths have a certain degree of malleability. When new contexts arise, a dialectical process must take place to ensure the suppleness of tradition such that the "forms" themselves are not simply repeated without consideration for new contexts.

Nostalgic pining for a time long past is naïve and impossible, not to mention weak pneumatology: here nostalgia is prohibited by Balthasar's confidence in the unfailingly consistent presence in Christian history of the Holy Spirit, who is the guarantor of the tradition's unity and veracity but also supple enough (Jn 3:8) to speak to different situations differently. Likewise, according to de Lubac, the theologian who refuses to recognize this evolution of Christian tradition relinquishes the very power of a living faith; the claim "to abide once and for all by such and such a stage in the expression of faith—whether his preference retains him in the fifth, the twelfth, or the nineteenth century—that man, ceasing to believe and think with the living Church, not only forgoes new gradations of new degrees of precision, he loses reality, the very substance of faith."[37] Thus, for the *ressourcement* thinkers, theologians must on the one hand attend seriously and concurrently to "the signs of the times," to borrow the language of Vatican II.[38] On the other hand,

---

34 Balthasar, "The Fathers, the Scholastics, and Ourselves," 382.

35 Hans Urs von Balthasar, *The Theology of Karl Barth: Exposition and Interpretation*, trans. Edward T. Oakes, SJ (San Francisco: Ignatius Press, 1992), 251.

36 Balthasar, *The Theology of Karl Barth*, 253.

37 De Lubac, *Paradoxes*, 100.

38 For warnings about uncritical repristination of the past, see "The Fathers, the Scholastics, and Ourselves," 370. On the pneumatological point, see "The Fathers, the Scholastics, and Ourselves," 350, and Hans Urs von Balthasar, "The Place of Theology," in *Explorations in Theology*, vol. 1, *The Word Made Flesh* (San Francisco: Ignatius Press, 1989),

the renewal required cannot simply be, in Daniélou's words, merely "au goût du jour."[39] What renewal means is not an overthrowing or an annulling of the past by the new but rather a creative appropriation of the past that simultaneously enlivens the present. However counterintuitive, the work necessary for renewal is archaeological at the very same time that it is innovative, and vice versa. Balthasar expresses well the concurrence of these theological modes as he describes the position of both himself and his like-minded colleagues:

> Indeed, it was not as though we were unaware that with an opening to the world, an *aggiornamento*, a broadening of the horizons, a translation of the Christian message into a language understandable by the modern world, only half is done. The other half—of at least equal importance—is a reflection on the specifically Christian element itself, a purification, a deepening, a centring of its idea, which alone renders us capable of representing it, radiating it, translating it believably in the world.[40]

In short, in the concept of *ressourcement* renewal and retrieval are always concomitant realities: this point is absolutely crucial for understanding the distinctive quality of Catholic retrieval, and is, as I shall argue, deeply indebted to French poet Charles Péguy (1873–1914),[41] whom Balthasar names consummately, in the disposition of *Gaudium et Spes*, as "*the* representative of the contemporary Church in dialogue with the world."[42]

Péguy is certainly not the sole influence on French *ressourcement* theology. Other genealogies could also begin with figures like Johann Adam Möhler and Johann Sebastian von Drey of the Tübingen school, especially with respect to their privileging of metaphors of organicity for the church, interest in history, and willingness to engage secular culture and philosophy; John Henry Newman on the development of doctrine; Maurice Blondel's Christologically aspirated philosophy of action and call for a rediscovery of authentic Catholic tradition as simultaneously progressive and conservative;[43] or Pierre Rousselot and Joseph Maréchal's

---

159–60. For similar statements from de Lubac that suggest that an overconcern with purity and religious scrupulosity vis-à-vis the tradition is not only misguided but also destructive to the faith, see de Lubac, *Paradoxes*, 20.

39   Daniélou, "*Orientations*," 5.

40   Balthasar, "In Retrospect," 196.

41   This connection between Péguy and *ressourcement* thought is often overlooked. D'Ambrosio's splendid article "*Ressourcement* Theology," to which I am indebted, does make it much more explicit than most (530–1, 537, 545, and 551). Readers may also wish to consult John Milbank's chapter in this volume entitled, "There's Always One Day Which Isn't the Same as the Day Before': Christianity and History in the Writings of Charles Péguy."

42   Balthasar, "In Retrospect," 214–15; italics added.

43   For an overview treatment of Blondel and the *ressourcement* movement, see Michael A. Conway, "Maurice Blondel and *Ressourcement*," in *Ressourcement: A Movement for*

accent on sacramental epistemology. The other relevant poet, and one particularly important to de Lubac, is Paul Claudel, whose work along with Péguy's gently suffused the thinking of a critical mass of *ressourcement* thinkers and writers and those sympathetic to them, including Georges Bernanos, Romano Guardini, de Lubac, Congar, and Balthasar, among others.[44]

Péguy remains, however, the most significant of these influences for understanding Catholic retrieval. First, he is credited with articulating the language of *ressourcement* itself; indeed, his connection of *ressourcement* with the idiom of revolution reveals a nuanced, temporally complex mode of retrieval that is simultaneous with renewal and that does not exclude but rather contextualizes political action; next, his peculiar poetic rhythm of nonidentical repetition serves as a model of how Catholic retrieval ought to operate; finally, the striking image of the living fountain in *Le porche du mystère de la deuxième virtu* provides a compelling picture of—if not the direct inspiration for—a more expansive concept of "source" as an ever-renewing wellspring to which the *ressourcement* thinkers regularly recur.

First, it is significant that, as Congar noted, it was Péguy rather than any of the theologians who actually coined the term *"ressourcement."*[45] In the ninth notebook in the fourteenth series of *Argent*, in an entry dated April 27, 1913, Péguy uses the language of *ressourcement* albeit with a more political inflection:

Nothing is so poignant, I know, as the sight of an entire people raising itself up, which wills and pursues its recovery. And nothing is so poignant as the sight

Renewal in Twentieth-Century Catholic Theology, ed. Gabriel Flynn and Paul D. Murray (Oxford: Oxford University Press, 2012), 65–82.

44 Henri de Lubac, along with Jean Bastaire, wrote *Claudel et Péguy* (Paris: Aubier, 1974). De Lubac also quotes Péguy in *Paradoxes* (32 and 36) and mentions Péguy positively in *Catholicism: Christ and the Common Destiny of Man*, trans. Lancelot C. Sheppard and Sister Elizabeth Englund, OCD (San Francisco: Ignatius Press, 1988) at least five times (31, 144, 321, 321, and 347), especially with respect to his political action (321). Also see Yves Congar, "Le prophéte Péguy, *Témoignage Chrétien*, August 26, 1949, 1. Péguy is likewise a—if not *the*—major presence in Congar's *True and False Reform in the Church*, trans. Paul Philibert (Collegeville, MN: Liturgical Press, 2011), a translation of *Vraie et fausse réforme dans l'Église*, rev. ed. (Paris: Les Éditions du Cerf, 1968). cf. Yves Congar, *The Meaning of Tradition*, trans. A. N. Woodrow (San Francisco: Ignatius Press, 2004), 11. Balthasar acknowledges both poets in his retrospective look over his career ("In Retrospect," trans. by Kenneth Batinovich, and "Another Ten Years," trans. by John Saward, in *The Analogy of Beauty*, ed. John Riches (Edinburgh: T & T Clark, 1986), 210–11 and 233), also devoting a lengthy essay to Péguy in *The Glory of the Lord*, vol. 3, and translating Claudel's *The Satin Slipper*.

45 See Congar, *True and False Reform*.> 39n35. Congar also notes similar formulations in Erasmus ("ex fontibus praedicare Christum"), Pius X ("redire ad fontes"), Blondel, and Pius XII, in *Humani Generis*. Congar does not necessarily claim that Péguy is a direct source for his theological thinking, but does describe these following formulations as expressing his ideas "with an unequaled evocative gift" (369). Elsewhere, in an homage piece to Chenu, Congar reiterates their shared commitment to Péguy's particular vision of

of a youth in revolt. I know this. If I do not mention this more often, it is that I recoil from all that is exuberant, and all that is romanticism and an enthusiasm that is unconstrained. But ultimately it is allowable to speak of it, provided one speaks of it in a disciplined way. Nothing is so intensely beautiful as the sight of a people which raises itself up by an interior impulse, from a profound return to the origins [*ressourcement*] of its ancient pride and from a springing forth [*rejaillissement*] of the instincts of their race.[46]

Elsewhere, Péguy speaks to this process of gathering up "sources" in the surprising idiom of revolution:

> What creates the strength of a fully traditional situation is that it is anchored in the present; it gathers together in present action and in current life the entirely of its past humanity, an entire antiquity of life and action, of thought, of feeling, of passion, and of history; against this there is nothing, absolutely nothing, that can measure up except a full revolutionary action, that is to say, not an arbitrary reversal, not a superficial turning, not a political, parliamentary, intellectual or literary reversion, but on the contrary, an interior summons, a deeper summons to other human forces, to more profound human characteristics, *a new and deeper probe to ancient, inexhaustible and common cultural resources.*
>
> Against a fully traditional situation, against the fullness of a traditional situation, nothing, absolutely nothing can measure up except a full revolutionary action, that is to say, not a full situation of transformation or overthrowing of authority that is arbitrary and literary in inspiration, but fundamentally what we need is a summons to a deeper tradition. *A revolution is a summons from a less perfect tradition to a more perfect one, a summons from a less profound tradition to a more profound one; it is a movement of return to a more ancient tradition, a surpassing in depth: namely, a search for the deepest origins. In the literal sense of the word, a "resource."*[47]

In his contesting of a purely political concept of revolution that would connote merely an upending of the past by something new, Péguy springs the notion of revolution from its modernist, nonmetaphysical captivity of hyperpraxis. Revolution is thus not merely an isolated political act where the future and the

---

ressourcement, which "was then at the heart of our efforts. It was not a matter either of mechanically replacing some theses by other theses or of creating a 'revolution' but of appealing, as Péguy did, from one tradition less profound to another more profound" (Yves Congar, "The Brother I Have Known," trans. Boniface Ramsey, OP, *The Thomist* 49 (1985): 499).

46 Charles Péguy, *L'Argent suite, Cahiers XIV*, IX (April 27, 1913), *Oeuvres en prose complètes III* (Paris: Gallimard, 1992), 987. I am grateful to my colleague Alain P. Toumayan for checking my French translations.

47 Charles Péguy, *Cahiers, V, XI* (March 1, 1904), *Oeuvres en prose complètes I* (Paris: Gallimard, 1987), 1305; italics added. Congar refers to this passage directly in *True and False Reform*, 369–70.

novel are uncritically hegemonic vis-à-vis the past simply by virtue of temporal proximity, but it sends its roots deeper into that which is more ancient, disrupting a merely linear account of time that would uncritically privilege whatever happens to be the most recent.

Péguy's close pairing of the language of *ressourcement* and "revolution" is predicated on a Catholic, thoroughly Trinitarian worldview that makes profound assumptions about the relationship between eternity and temporality, about the structures of world and time and history and how human beings relate to it and to God. This implicit way of seeing the world and its history within the encircling horizon of the Trinity, with Christ as the fullest expression of this coincidence, conjoins the eternal and the temporal. The Catholic sacramental theologies of history in de Lubac or Balthasar, or, for that matter, Irenaeus, Origen, Bonaventure, or Augustine are likewise committed to maintaining a permeable border between temporal and eternal, a boundary that is also a crossing, and that resists the sense that history and tradition can proceed only linearly.

This coincidence allows for the strong claim that excavation of traditional sources is not a retrograde antiquarianism but is ever new. It also allows for such seemingly paradoxical statements as these: from de Lubac, "To get away from old things passing themselves off as tradition it is necessary to go back to the farthest past—which will reveal itself to be the nearest present";[48] or from Gilson, "If theological progress is sometimes necessary, it is never possible unless you go back to the beginning and start over";[49] or again from de Lubac, "of eternal life itself, we are ever going from 'beginnings to beginnings.'"[50] In a sense, then, Péguy's model of "revolution" could be likened to the revolution of the Earth upon its axis through the duration of a day, an orbital motion that simultaneously returns to its starting point but also accumulates new experiences through the passage of time. On this model of the Catholic tradition, progress is not tantamount to innovation that requires the absolute displacement of older expressive forms in revelation; though they do evolve, nothing is ever lost.[51] Further, this temporally dense mode of reading the tradition prevents it from being read merely as a relic of history. As Balthasar put it, theologians "have to make our way, loaded up with the whole positive legacy of the past, toward the future."[52]

Péguy not only informed the theology of French Catholic *ressourcement* by lending it a language imbued with temporal and even topographic complexity,

48 De Lubac, *Paradoxes*, 20.

49 *Letters of E. Gilson to Henri de Lubac*, trans. Mary Emily Hamilton (San Francisco: Ignatius Press, 198), 179.

50 De Lubac, *Paradoxes*, 10.

51 This idea evokes an image from Péguy's *Portal of the Mystery of Hope*, in which a person walking "eternally leaves/Intact the imprints of all those/Who came before him. Who have passed since the first hour" (Charles Péguy, *The Portal of the Mystery of Hope; Ressourcement: Retrieval and Renewal in Catholic Thought*, trans. David L. Schindler Jr. (Grand Rapids, MI: William B. Eerdmans, 1996), 121).

52 Balthasar, "The Fathers, the Scholastics, and Ourselves," 385.

in which the nature of revolution is orbital rather than linear. A further mode in which Péguy might be thought to provide a model for Catholic retrieval is latent even in the form of his poetry, which makes abundant use of nonidentical repetition as he weaves together the old and the new such that the seams are often no longer visible. At the center of the triptych between *The Mystery of the Charity of Joan of Arc* (1910) and *The Mystery of the Holy Innocents* (1912), Péguy's luminously plain poem *The Portal of the Mystery of Hope* (1911) requires of its readers the practice of the ascesis of its meditative and quite repetitive rhythm. A turn of phrase or an image—whether it be Night, gardens, good and poor soil, pilgrimage, living water, the audacity and freshness of childhood, the lost things from the Lukan parables of hope, or the opening salvo of that Gospel pericope: "*A man had two sons*,"—that surfaces in the beginning of the text continually resurfaces again and again throughout it. The pattern, however, is fugal. It presses forward always, and the repetitions are never exact but circle back with subtle changes overlaid carefully with elements from the intervening material. Péguy's poetic repetition is far from rote: while the original image is instantly recognizable in its later iterations, the language grows more and more supple and variegated as it takes into account the new images and contexts. Analogously, "revolutionary" *ressourcement* functions somewhat recursively insofar as it is a procedure that can repeat itself indefinitely but nonidentically in a sequence by changing the previous term. We might surmise, then, that not only is development observable within the tradition but also in the very operation of engagement the act of retrieval itself can lead to fructification.[53]

This repetitive form accentuates the content of the poem, which reveals ultimately that the repetition of days, bread, suffering, sacraments, grace, and so on are not displaced or erased but rather "added to the eternal treasury."[54] Recalling what appears from a finite perspective to be the identical repetition of ordinary days, Péguy writes,

> On earth, according to human wisdom, those are twenty times
> > of increasing difficulty
> Of repetition, of the same thing
> Twenty times in vain, right on top of each other
> Because they all went by the same road
> To the same place, because it was the same route.
> > But for God's wisdom
> Nothing is ever nothing. All is new. All is other.
> All is different.
> In God's sight nothing repeats itself.[55]

---

53 A. N. Williams, "The Future of the Past: The Contemporary Significance of the *Nouvelle Théologie*," *International Journal of Systematic Theology* 7 (2005): 347–61, here 351.

54 Péguy, *Portal*, 120.

55 Péguy, *Portal*, 118–19.

Congar has praised Péguy's poetry for stipulating a "phenomenology" of the tendency of the freshness of *vivre* to become fossilized by structures or systems that choke its originary vitality and that require continual return to the wellspring of life.[56] The resistance to an ossification of doctrines, institutions, and structures does not mean, however, that the careful work of "archeology" of those same doctrines, institutions, and structures can be passed over. As de Lubac suggested by recurring to the exodus and the Israelites wandering in the wilderness, there is for the Catholic theologian no shortage of effort required: "It took forty years in the desert to enter into the Promised Land. It sometimes takes a lot of arid archeology to make the fountains of living water well forth anew."[57]

Theologians of *ressourcement* were certainly attuned to the perils of an identical repetition of the Catholic tradition, the kind of lifeless "bad infinity" that they found in the tedious propositionalism characteristic of certain forms of neoscholasticism. Catholic *ressourcement* must bear within it a sense of revolution, a newness of interpretation. De Lubac, for example, warns, "repetition of formulas does not assure the transmission of thought . . . intelligence must play a part in its conservation, rediscovering it, so to speak, in the process."[58] Likewise, Balthasar pointedly conjures an image of the menial work of an assembly line passing bricks from person to person in order to suggest that transmitting the goods of the tradition can never come without new interpretive efforts.[59] Balthasar could not be clearer when he writes that past theology—even that dogmatically defined in creeds and councils—is

> never a pillow for future thought to rest on. Definitions are not so much an end as a beginning. Nothing that is the fruit of hard struggle is ever lost to the Church, but this does not mean that the theologian is spared further work. Whatever is merely put in storage, handed down without any fresh efforts being made on one's own part (and *ab ovo*, the very source of revelation) putrefies, like the manna did. And the longer the living tradition has been broken through purely mechanical repetition, they more difficult it may become to renew it.[60]

De Lubac presses this point home consistently, arguing in *Catholicism* that imitation of the patristics or the medievals alone is insufficient. Because Christian history is always evolving in response to various cultural situations, retrieval requires the recognition of the keen differences existing between us and them, and thus "an assimilation which is at the same time a transformation" such that "a return to the sources of antiquity will be the very opposite of an escape into a dead past."[61]

56 Congar, *True and False Reform*, 135.
57 De Lubac, *Paradoxes*, 57–8.
58 De Lubac, *Paradoxes*, 23.
59 Balthasar, "Place of Theology," 160.
60 Balthasar, "Place of Theology," 157.
61 Henri de Lubac, *Catholicism*, 322. Cf. *The Splendor of the Church*, trans. Michael Mason (London: Sheed & Ward, 1956), 11.

The third contribution of Péguy for contextualizing *ressourcement* thought is his striking image of the living fountain in *Le porche du mystère de la deuxième virtu*. Here Péguy—perhaps for the first time—pairs the words *ressourcement* and *rejaillissment* (splashing or springing forth), exactly as they were paired in his notebook entry from 1913. It is my claim that this juxtaposition of these words condenses into a trope for the Catholic tradition as a whole for how retrieval should operate within it. This close pairing of *ressourcement* and *rejaillissment* suggests that the "sources" in Péguy's articulation of Catholic *ressourcement* cannot be considered in the indigent sense of texts simply as artifacts—which might be suggested by the English connotations of "source"—but should be interpreted more in accordance with its association with *fontes* in French or in Latin.[62]

In *Portal*, Péguy invokes the image of a living fountain of water that is renewing itself constantly but also the origins of which are unrecoverable: "There is, in that which begins, a spring; roots that never return."[63] This poetic image of that mysterious and mysteriously Christological and Trinitarian wellspring is an emblem deeply resonant with the *ressourcement* theologians' commitment to interpreting "source" as a vivifying font always in excess of whichever finite forms contain it. The image functions as poetic shorthand for the strange logic of Catholic retrieval. First, return to a "source" in the barest sense is not only impossible insofar as the origins cannot be accessed by simply reversing the wheel of history but also counterproductive. Second, and more important, this mysterious font is an infinitely reviving and revivifying fountain that, like the one who sits on the throne in the Apocalypse, makes all things new (Rv 21:5). The font cannot ever run dry: thus, a retrieval of traditional sources is much different from a retrieval of bare *re*-sources. This image of source as dynamic wellspring reoccurs consistently in the writings of the French Catholic *ressourcement* figures. In their response to the criticisms of Michel Labourdette, OP, the Fourvière theologians refer to the Fathers as "sources, not in the restricted sense in which literary history understands the term, but in the sense of wellsprings which are always springing up to overflowing."[64]

The primary goal of Catholic retrieval, then, is fundamentally nonforensic, insofar as it does not and cannot presuppose the lapsed mortality of its subject. Rather, to return to the source is to drink deeply at an eternal font of the ever-new and the ever-living, which Péguy in his poem (audaciously) has God himself describe:

> But, wonderfully, it's this very water that they collect and which does
>   not hinder them in the least.

---

62 Cf. A. N. Williams, 350 and 353, and D'Ambrosio, "*Ressourcement* Theology," 537–8.

63 Péguy, *Portal*, 23.

64 Fourvière theologians, "La théologie et ses sources: réponse aux etudes critiques de la *Revue Thomiste* (mai-août, 1946)," *Recherches de Science Religieuse* 33 (1946): 395; quoted in D'Ambrosio, "*Ressourcement* Theology," 540.

Because, wonderfully, it's from this very water that they create the spring
(*source*).
It's this water; it's the same water that runs along the meadows.
It's the same healthy water that flows in the stalks of wheat for the
    Bread.
It's the same healthy water that flows in the vines for the Wine.
It's the same healthy water that flows in both buds, in both shoots.
In both Laws.
It's the same collected water, it's the same water, healthy, purified, that
    flows around the world.
That returns, that reappears, having flowed around my whole creation.
It's the same collected water that bursts forth, that springs forth.
From the new fountain, from the young wellspring.
From the spring and resurgence [*ressourcement*] of hope.[65]

Suffusing the discrete categories of retrieval, whether scriptural, traditional, or liturgical, is the infinite and infinitely mysterious and lively Word of God who exceeds always the bounds of finite text and which gives fundamental unity to these discrete expressive forms of revelation.[66] Therefore, for Catholic retrieval, a robust Christology is indispensable insofar as it is Christ the Word, the perfect coincidence of finite and infinite and the expression of the mysterious and cosmically encompassing horizon of Trinitarian reality, who is, to invoke Augustine, "O Beauty, ever ancient, ever new." De Lubac in particular was fond of this association between the figure of Christ and absolute newness, often quoting Irenaeus on this point ("Omnem novitatem attulit semetipsum afferens, qui fuerat annuntiatus").[67] So retrieval is not in the first instance an academic enterprise concerned with recovering parts of something, but is fundamentally a recovery of something structurally whole, of Being as luminously appearing in the concrete manifestations. This "according to the whole" (*kath-olic*) is literally catholic, and Christ is in this sense "the Catholic One," able to integrate parts of wholes that have come disconnected and to make pliable absolute categories that have become ossified.[68]

One site of such disconnection is the perception of a breach in the postconciliar era between *ressourcement* and *aggiornamento* ("a bringing up to date"), which belies a misreading of both terms. It seems clear, for example, in his essay "Ecumenical

65 Péguy, *Portal*, 100–1.

66 Cf. de Lubac, *Paradoxes*, 109, on the rich "infinity" of the hermeneutic loop between text and commentary.

67 Saint Irenaeus, *Adversus Haereses*, IV, 34, 1. This line is the inscription of de Lubac's *Theology in History*: "He has brought total newness by bringing himself, who had been announced." Cf. Balthasar, *The Theology of Henri de Lubac*, 61.

68 Balthasar, "Another Ten Years," 228–31. Cf. D. C. Schindler, "Reason as Catholic," *The Catholicity of Reason* (*Ressourcement: Retrieval and Renewal in Catholic Thought*), 3–32. Elsewhere, Balthasar suggests that a failure to adopt this kind of catholic standpoint is

Theology" that George Lindbeck sees *ressourcement* and *aggiornamento* as mutually exclusive approaches within Catholic theology. He notes a marked "shift" in the
theological climate with ascendency of the latter (what he sees as a turn "to the needs
of the world") characterizing the post–Vatican II era: "However one evaluates it," he
writes, "a pervasive change in theological orientation has taken place."[69] He explains
the turn by asserting that the originators of the *ressourcement* movement—whom
he describes as "formidably learned theological elites"—had superior grounding in
the sources and equal facility with modern scholarship; their epigones, on the other
hand, did not.[70] On Lindbeck's account, which stipulates mutual exclusivity, certain
Catholics were compelled by *ressourcement*

> even when their primary desire, *unbeknownst to themselves*, was to update the
> Christian message *rather than* to return to its roots. These fellow travelers of the-
> ologies of renewal discovered what they really wanted only in the post-conciliar
> period when newer outlooks began developing whose starting-point was not the
> sources, but rather the urgent issues of modernity.[71]

Lindbeck suggests, moreover, that the *ressourcement* theologians' "primary concern was faithfulness to the total catholic heritage and only secondarily adjustment
to the contemporary situation,"[72] but to dis-integrate these commitments from one
another falls short of the Catholic hermeneutic in which recovery and discovery
must function integrally.

While it is certainly true that *ressourcement* thinkers privilege tradition and
even find a particular vitality in the patristic era, there is no possibility of pure
sourcing because the Fathers, responding in their own time and for the first time
to the cultural matrix of the secular—are always already demonstrating what it is
to "throw open the windows" to the outside culture. *Ressourcement* is fundamentally grammatical insofar as it returns to this inaugural utterance of the Gospel
into the classical world, retrieving the moment when the church first spoke audaciously to the world as such with the expectation that the Gospel not only could
resonate through it but also that the world had been implicitly prepared for it
by the Holy Spirit. If *ressourcement* is grammatical, *aggiornamento* is procedural,
indicating a reciprocity between the terms of Christian kerygma and the ends to
which it is directed. The grammar of *ressourcement* provides the terms for adju-
dicating the procedure of cultural capaciousness. But with apologies to Immanuel
Kant, a grammar without the procedure is mute, and the procedure without the
grammar is blind.

"always" the reason for "the evident as well as the hidden catastrophes . . . in the ecclesial-
theological domain" (*The Theology of Henri de Lubac*, 29–30).
  69 Lindbeck, "Ecumenical Theology," 260. Cf. 255 and 258.
  70 Lindbeck, "Ecumenical Theology," 264.
  71 Lindbeck, "Ecumenical Theology," 264; italics added.
  72 Lindbeck, "Ecumenical Theology," 258.

As our thick description of Catholic *ressourcement* in tandem with the clarifications offered by Péguy's more poetic use of the term have suggested, it was not by accident but rather by design that *ressourcement* paved the way for the reforms of Vatican II.[73] To suppose a separation a priori, as in Lindbeck's position, is already a stipulation upon the terms of *aggiornamento*, namely, to assert that the only way the church can be updated is by merely accommodating to the new. Here a reductive constriction of *aggiornamento* to the political or the social is an equally destructive mistaking of the part for the whole. This represents a counterfeiting of the genuine force of *aggiornamento*, "the one whose roots are at the basis of the promulgated texts, the one that is accomplished at first in depth, in a renewed faith—not the foam that is splashing around all over."[74] De Lubac says elsewhere that paradoxes "attack only the counterfeits,"[75] those parts that presume to stand in for the whole. He assumes, of course, that Christianity must be expressed temporally, in the world and in action, for spirit to inform matter in the strongest way possible. Evoking but not invoking Dostoevsky's Grand Inquisitor, de Lubac aphoristically asserts, however, that "a wish to 'incarnate' Christianity sometimes really leads to disincarnating it, emptying it of its substance. It becomes lost, buried in politics or in sociology or, at best, in morality."[76] It would be a grave poverty indeed to mistake the overspray for the living fountain itself. Péguy's nuanced notion of revolution as *ressourcement*, as "appeal . . . to a deeper tradition, *a search for the deepest origins*" can serve as a corrective for this reduction.

The irony of Lindbeck's narrative of a reduction of a genuinely catholic and deeply complex methodology of the whole (which included within itself already the terms of retrieval and of updating) to a catechetical catalogue of ecclesial, political, or social positions—a reduction in which the theology of a deeply complex theological figure (or in this case, set of figures) is flattened out interpretively by a later generation to a set of propositions (or in this case, political positions)—cannot possibly escape us, since it is in effect a recapitulation of neoscholasticism. Thus it may be time in Catholic thought for a *ressourcement* of *ressourcement*. If we take Lindbeck's account to be an accurate description of contemporary Catholic thought, where *ressourcement* and *aggiornamento* have somehow divorced and become antagonistic to one another, then Catholic theologians must not only engage in a retrieval of tradition, Scripture, liturgy, ecclesiology, and the like but also find a way of going back to the sources of this particular crack in the edifice, to perceive and receive in good faith the unity of *ressourcement* and

---

73 De Lubac claims as much, writing, "*aggiornamento* was made possible by the patristic renewal of the last fifty years" (*Service*, 319). Moreover, de Lubac's engagement with Buddhism and modern atheism clearly resurfaces, respectively, in *Nostra Aetate* and *Gaudium et Spes*. On de Lubac's connection with *Gaudium et Spes*, cf. Balthasar, *The Theology of de Lubac*, 47.

74 De Lubac, *Service*, 319.

75 De Lubac, *Paradoxes*, 63.

76 De Lubac, *Paradoxes*, 64.

aggiornamento connected at the root, growing together under the earth. If these impulses are separated from one another, the twin temptation is a contraction of memory: for *ressourcement* it is to forget its font of living water and to wilt into dead traditionalism, neglecting the new for the dry bones of rote repetition; for *aggiornamento* alone, the corollary temptation is to forget the depth of its roots growing old in the earth, and built on sand alone the good fruits of its renewal might die on the vine. Catholic *ressourcement* itself ought not be considered simply a trend in the history of Catholic thought but as an approach with abiding theological viability insofar as it recovers an originary unity between *ressourcement* and *aggiornamento* as the church continues to interpret and implement Vatican II fifty years after the Council.

Part III

TWENTIETH-CENTURY FIGURES

Chapter 6

GEORGES FLOROVSKY

Paul Gavrilyuk

Georges Florovsky's neopatristic synthesis is an authoritative presentation of Orthodox theology and a paradigm case of a theology of retrieval. How did Florovsky understand such a retrieval? What were his polemical motivations, methodological assumptions, and constructive aspirations? What is Florovsky's place in Russian religious thought? What impact did he have on the development of Orthodox theology? How does his neopatristics compare to non-Orthodox theologies of retrieval, especially the *ressourcement*? This chapter addresses these questions in order to bring out the distinctiveness of Florovsky's theological vision.

Georges Florovsky (1893–1979) is commonly associated with a "return to the Church Fathers" in twentieth-century Orthodox theology. The image of a "return" implies that the relationship between the patristic theological heritage on the one hand and modern Orthodox theology on the other hand has not been that of untroubled continuity. Florovsky's call for a "return to the Church Fathers" implies a digression from, a distortion of, or even an abandonment of Orthodox theology's patristic moorings. In his magnum opus *The Ways of Russian Theology* (1937), Florovsky argues that Orthodox theology from the sixteenth century onward has been held captive by various forms of Western religious thought, from Latin scholasticism to German idealism. According to Florovsky, this Western captivity led to pseudo-morphoses, or distorting transformations, which brought about a chasm between Orthodox worship, which remained essentially unchanged, and academic theology, which fell prey to various Western influences. As Florovsky wrote in the preface to *The Ways of Russian Theology*,

> The study of the Russian past has convinced me that an Orthodox theologian today can find the true norm and the living spring of creative inspiration only in the heritage of the Holy Fathers. I am convinced that the intellectual separation from patristics and Byzantinism was the main cause of all interruptions and spiritual failures in Russian development. A history of these failures is narrated in this book.[1]

---

1 Georges Florovsky, *Puti russkogo bogosloviia* (Paris: YMCA Press, 1937/1983), xv. Cf.

For Florovsky, a particularly telling example of such failures was the dependence of Russian sophiology on German idealism and Western forms of mysticism. Florovsky engaged with several prominent representatives of Russian sophiology, especially Vladimir Solovyov, Pavel Florensky, and Sergius Bulgakov. In his Russian period (1893–1920), Florovsky was religiously "awakened" by Solovyov and his followers, but in the first decade of his European period (1920–1948), he came to a more critical evaluation of Solovyov's influence on Russian religious thought. As Florovsky came to emphasize, Solovyov's theology was overly dependent on gnosticism, Jacob Boehme, and German idealism, and fell prey to syncretistic forms of religious experience. Florovsky regarded the pantheistic and monistic tendencies of Solovyov's philosophy of all-unity as jeopardizing the central patristic "intuition of creaturehood," which postulated an ontological divide between the uncreated God and creatures. For Florovsky, Russian sophiology was a species of Origenism, with its "cosmism" (a tendency to eternalize the world), "organicism" (an assumption that the agency of groups of people could be seen according to the development of a biological organism), and a tendency toward determinism. On Florovsky's reading, Bulgakov's theological system, despite its problematization of pantheism, nevertheless belonged to the intellectual trajectory connecting pagan Hellenism, Origenism, German idealism, and Russian sophiology, with all the attendant difficulties. In contrast to this trajectory, which he regarded as a theological dead end, Florovsky proposed neopatristic theology as a corrective to the Western distortions of Orthodox theology.

It is generally recognized that Florovsky did not complete his neopatristic synthesis, preferring to treat the subject in a "rhapsodic" rather than systematic manner.[2] In my monograph, *Georges Florovsky and the Russian Religious Renaissance*,[3] I distinguish between a "return to the Fathers" as a polemical stance, a research project, a hermeneutical strategy, a theological program, and a synthesis proper.

As a polemical stance, a "return to the Fathers" was opposed to the modernism of Russian sophiologists on the one hand and to the "theology of repetition" propounded by Orthodox traditionalists on the other hand. On the modernist front, Florovsky's neopatristic vision was articulated in conversation with and in opposition to the Russian religious renaissance, particularly the ideas of Florensky, Bulgakov, and Nicholas Berdyaev. Florovsky was positively influenced by Florensky's account of corporate religious experience and his treatment

Dmitry Chizhevsky, *Narysy z istorii filosofii na Ukraïni* [A sketch of the history of philosophy in Ukraine] (Prague: Ukraïns'kyi hromads'kyi vydavnychyi fond, 1931), 9: "The history of philosophy is a history of errors of human spirit."

2 See G. H. Williams, "The Neo-Patristic Synthesis of Georges Florovsky," in *Georges Florovsky: Russian Intellectual, Orthodox Churchman*, ed. Andrew Blane (Crestwood, NY: St. Vladimir's Seminary Press, 1993), 287–340.

3 *Georges Florovsky and the Russian Religious Renaissance* (Oxford: Oxford University Press, 2013).

of the doctrine of creation out of nothing. Without admitting the matter directly, Florovsky was influenced by Berdyaev's existentialism and his emphasis on freedom as a defining characteristic of divine and human agency, although he took exception to Berdyaev's bold claim that freedom was the uncreated ground of divine being. The influence of Bulgakov on Florovsky went even deeper, since Bulgakov was for more than two decades his senior colleague at the Orthodox Institute of St. Sergius in Paris. Florovsky criticized Florensky and other leaders of the Russian religious renaissance for failing to accord a focal character to Christology in their speculative theology. Partly for this reason, Christology became the focus of his own historical research.

As a research project, a "return to the Fathers" primarily involved the study of patristic texts. Important forays into the study of the church fathers were made in Russian and Ukrainian Orthodox scholarship in the nineteenth century. The project included the introduction of the discipline of patristics into the curricula of the main seminaries in the 1840s and the translations of a considerable corpus of patristic texts. It must be emphasized, however, that prerevolutionary Russian patristic scholarship remained largely historical and did not have tangible impact on constructive theology. In this regard, it would be a mistake to view the nineteenth-century achievements of Russian and Ukrainian patristic scholarship as instances of *neo*patristics. While Florovsky undoubtedly benefited from these developments and was familiar with the relevant scholarly works, what differentiated his project was an impulse to challenge the theological vision of his contemporaries, particularly their philosophical and ecclesiological presuppositions. Florovsky brought together historical and systematic theology in a manner that was novel in Orthodox scholarship of his time.

Florovsky began to study the church fathers in earnest when he started teaching at the Orthodox Institute of St. Sergius in 1926. In the early 1930s, he published his lectures on patristics under the titles *The Eastern Fathers of the Fourth Century* (1931) and *The Byzantine Fathers of the Fifth–Eighth Centuries* (1933). His lectures possessed two features that were often present in similar historical surveys: an emphasis on the history of ideas and the dedication of chapters to individual patristic authors. Florovsky's treatment of patristic theology tended to emphasize the continuity and unity of patristic thought, while glossing over important differences in the individual authors. Given this tendency, it is not surprising that Florovsky's account of patristic theology gives a prominent place to the concept of *consensus patrum*, that is, a broad informal consensus of patristic writers over a vast body of doctrine on which no dogmatic definitions were produced. Florovsky's reliance on *consensus patrum* and his insistence on the ecclesiological grounding of theological knowledge differentiated him from the thinkers of the Russian religious renaissance.

Undergirding his commitment to *consensus patrum* was a hermeneutical strategy of "acquiring the mind of the Fathers" through empathy (*Einfühlung*) and incorporation into the life and worship of the church. Empathy was a concept that entered Russian philosophy of history from German romanticism through the work of Mikhail Gershenzon. Empathetic understanding consists in entering imaginatively the inner world of a particular historical figure in order to discover the values and motivations that guide her thinking. Florovsky explains, "An *Einfühlung* into the witnesses is an obvious prerequisite of understanding . . . No understanding is possible without some measure of 'congeniality,' of intellectual or spiritual sympathy, without a real meeting of minds."[4] *Einfühlung* allowed entering emotional attitudes and volitional dispositions that were the driving forces of theories put forth by prominent past thinkers. Florovsky treated the realm of ideas and the realm of emotion-driven motivations as two inseparable parts of one psychointellectual whole.[5] Following Gershenzon, Florovsky was more focused on the prelogical impulses stimulating the emergence of ideas than on the unfolding of ideas into comprehensive theological systems.

The purpose of empathetic historical knowledge does not consist in mere representation of the past. Florovsky underscores that "cognizing the past is richer than 'the past itself,' since such cognition consists in a fresh reliving of the past as a viable tradition and its appropriating and clarifying interpretation."[6] Emphasizing an active role of the historical inquirer, Florovsky speaks of the prominent role that the historian's presuppositions and personal judgments play in the selection and arrangement of source material:

> One should not forget that all acts of understanding are, strictly speaking, personal, and only in this capacity of *personal acts* can they have any existential relevance and value. One has to check, severely and strictly, one's prejudices and presuppositions, but one should never try to empty one's mind of *all* presuppositions. Such an attempt would be a suicide of mind and can only issue in total mental sterility.[7]

Florovsky views historical inquiry as a balancing act between the objective aspect of the source material and the subjective presuppositions of the historian, between the scholar's receptivity and empathetic imagination. In other words, Florovsky's account of historical knowledge involves a range of complex and nonrule-governed mental acts, ranging from the passive reception of data to

---

4 Georges Florovsky, "The Predicament of the Christian Historian," in *The Collected Works of Georges Florovsky*, ed. Richard S. Haugh, 14 vols. (Belmont, MA: Nordland, 1972–1989), 2:39 and 40 (hereafter *CW*).

5 Georges Florovsky, "Michael Gerschensohn," *Slavonic Review* 5 (December 1926): 315–31, at 320.

6 Georges Florovsky, "O tipakh istoricheskogo istolkovaniia" [On the types of historical interpretation], in *Sbornik v chest' na Vasil N. Zlatarski po sluchai na 30-godishnata mu nauchna i profesorska deinost'* (Sofia: Drzhavna pechatnitsa, 1925), 521–41, at 528. Florovsky refers with approval to a theory of "imaginative complementation" of the gap in historical evidence advanced by Benedetto Croce (1866–1952).

7 Georges Florovsky, "The Predicament of the Christian Historian," *CW* 2:42, italics in original.

active imaginative reconstruction and selection leading to a "historical synthesis." According to Florovsky, the acquisition of the mind of the fathers allowed a theologian to go beyond deploying patristic writings as authoritative sources and to internalize patristic modes of theological thinking, and by doing so to correct and renew contemporary Orthodox theology. The impulse toward renewal found its expression in various aspects of Florovsky's theological program.

As a theological program, the "return to the Fathers" included the following building blocks: intuition of creaturehood, Chalcedonian Christology, historical revelation, ecclesial experience, personalism, and antideterminism. Perhaps the most important characteristic of Florovsky's neopatristic theology is its strong focus on the Christological vision of Chalcedon. Florovsky opposed Russian sophiology's tendency to convert the Chalcedonian dogma into an extrahistorical metaphysical principle of Godmanhood and emphasized instead the historical embeddedness of divine revelation and of theological reasoning, especially as exemplified by the doctrine of the incarnation.[8] While insisting that theological reasoning happens in history, Florovsky distanced himself from historicizing relativism by insisting on the permanent theological value of the "Christian Hellenism" of the church fathers. In practice this meant that Florovsky resisted the "translation" of patristic theological and philosophical categories into various discourses of modern philosophy. The patristic categories had an abiding significance because they accurately captured the truths of divine revelation and ecclesial experience.

The category of ecclesial experience occupies an important place in Florovsky's religious epistemology. Florovsky's earliest engagement of the category of experience was occasioned by his reading of Florensky. At the beginning of his major theological work, *The Pillar and Ground of the Truth* (1914), Florensky wrote, " 'Living religious experience as the only legitimate way of understanding dogmas'—this is how I would express the general aspiration of my book."[9] In his ecclesiological debut, "The Father's House," Florovsky drew on Florensky by asserting that "all Christian teaching is a description of ecclesial experience."[10] More precisely, "all fullness of knowledge is originally given in the experience and consciousness of the Church and only needs to be *recognized* as such."[11]

8 Matthew Baker, "'Theology Reasons'—in History: Neo-Patristic Synthesis and the Renewal of Theological Rationality," *Theologia* 81 (2010): 81–118.

9 Georges Florensky, *Stolp i utverzhdenie istiny*, 2 vols. (Moscow: Pravda, 1990), 1:3. For a discussion of this passage, see Avril Pyman, *Pavel Florensky: A Quiet Genius* (London: Continuum, 2010), 72.

10 Georges Florovsky, "Dom Otchii" (1925–1927), in *Izbrannye bogoslovskie stat'i* (Moscow: Probel, 2000), 9–36, at 10. Cf. J. A. Möhler, *Unity in the Church or the Principle of Catholicism: Presented in the Spirit of the Church Fathers of the First Three Centuries* (Washington, DC: Catholic University of America Press, 1996), 87.

11 Georges Florovsky, "Problematika khristianskogo vossoedineniia" (January 1933), in *Izbrannye bogoslovskie stat'i* (Moscow: Probel, 2000), 175; italics in original. In *Puti russkogo bogosloviia*, 274, he credited a similar point to A. S. Khomiakov.

To theologize is to draw on the reservoir of revealed knowledge received by the church.

Following the nineteenth-century Russian lay theologian Alexei Khomiakov, Florovsky held that in her catholic fullness the church is infallible: "The Church alone possesses the force and the capacity for true and catholic synthesis. Therein lies her *potestas magisterii*, the gift and unction of infallibility."[12] Florovsky located infallibility in the church's ability to offer a catholic synthesis based on the shared experience of believers throughout the ages. He contrasted the "living experience of the Church" with the "subjective religious experience" and "solitary mystical consciousness" for which he criticized the representatives of the Russian religious renaissance.[13]

The "living experience of the Church," as Florovsky uses the expression, is not a separate source of the knowledge of God but rather a set of historical practices that reliably mediate the content of divine revelation, enshrined in Scripture and tradition. Scripture is a fruit of the church's reception of divine revelation. As such, the church holds a chronological, hermeneutical, and epistemological priority over Scripture. Chronologically, the Gospels are "records of church experience and faith."[14] Florovsky was especially fond of repeating Tertullian's assertion in *De praescriptione hereticorum* that outside the church there could be no Scripture, properly speaking.[15] The biblical teaching could be correctly understood, interpreted, and transmitted only within the community that brought it about, namely, the church.[16]

Hermeneutically, Scripture is a part of the tradition of the church. As such, the tradition is not a second source of Christian doctrine, the authority of which can be variously calibrated in relation to Scripture. The core of the apostolic

---

12 Florovsky, *Puti russkogo bogosloviia*, 507; cf. Florovsky, "The Authority of the Ancient Councils and the Tradition of the Fathers," *CW* 1:103. On the infallibility of the church, see also A. S. Khomiakov, "Tserkov' odna" (1864), in *Sochineniia bogoslovskie* (St. Petersburg: Nauka, 1995), 40; Sergius Bulgakov, *The Orthodox Church* (Dobbs Ferry, NY: American Review of Eastern Orthodoxy, 1935), 79; Möhler, *Unity in the Church*, 106. In nineteenth-century Orthodox theology, "The Encyclical of the Eastern Patriarchs" (1848) asserted the infallibility of the church in reaction to the Roman Catholic claims of papal infallibility.

13 Florovsky, "Catholicity of the Church," *CW* 1:49.

14 Florovsky, "Revelation and Interpretation," *CW* 1:25; cf. Florovsky, "Bogoslovskie otryvki," *Izbrannye bogoslovskie stat'i* (Moscow: Probel, 2000), 127.

15 Tertullian, *De praescriptione haereticorum*, xxxvii. Florovsky first developed this point independently in "Dom Otchii," 28, and later supported it with other patristic proof texts, probably drawn from Möhler, *Unity in the Church*, 97. See Florovsky, "The Function of Tradition in the Ancient Church," *CW* 1:73–92.

16 Florovsky, "Bogoslovskie otryvki," 127; "The Authority of the Ancient Councils and the Tradition of the Fathers," *CW* 1:98; *Puti russkogo bogosloviia*, 177 and 274–5; cf. A. S. Khomiakov, "Tserkov' odna," 42.

tradition is summarized in the ancient rules of faith, which served as a basis for the ancient Christian baptismal instruction and preaching. Drawing on the work of a distinguished Anglican historical theologian, Henry Ernest William Turner (1907–1995), Florovsky held that the rule of faith served as an ancient hermeneutical principle of Scripture.[17] The rule of faith safeguarded the integrity of Scripture against the attacks of heretics. By receiving and interiorizing the rule of faith within the church, believers were able to grasp the overarching plan and the intent of Scripture. Thus, the rule of faith was not an externally imposed criterion. Both Scripture and the rule of faith originated in the ecclesial experience of the reception, appropriation, and transmission of divine revelation.[18]

As a carrier of ecclesial experience, tradition is not merely a collection of ancient artifacts but rather "the inner, charismatic or mystical memory of the Church."[19] In opposition to the leaders of the "new religious consciousness," such as Dmitry Merezhkovsky and Vasily Rozanov, who criticized the "historical Church" for quenching the Spirit and awaited God's more powerful revelation in the future, Florovsky located the work of the Holy Spirit squarely within the "historical Church" and saw the tradition itself as charismatic, mystical, and liberating. On occasion, Florovsky expressed himself boldly, in language reminiscent of Bulgakov and Vasily Zenkovsky: "[L]oyalty to tradition means not only concord with the past but in a certain sense freedom from the past. Tradition is not only a protective, conservative principle, it is primarily the principle of growth and regeneration . . . Tradition is the constant abiding of the Spirit, and not only the memory of words. Tradition is a charismatic, not an historical principle."[20] Some Renaissance theologians, including Bulgakov, also stressed the pneumatological and dynamic character of tradition. Yet Florovsky departed from modernist Russian theologians by insisting that the retrieval of patristic theology was itself creatively liberating. In Florovsky's mind, twentieth-century Orthodox theology first had to emancipate itself from its intellectual captivity to the philosophical paradigms of the West and expand its intellectual horizon beyond the possibilities of the nineteenth century.

---

17 Florovsky, "The Function of Tradition in the Ancient Church," *CW* 1:82 and 124n11, referring to H. E. W. Turner, *The Pattern of Christian Truth* (London: Mowbray, 1954), 193–4.

18 I develop this point in "Scripture and *Regula Fidei*: Two Interlocking Components of the Canonical Heritage," in *Canonical Theism: A Proposal for Theology and the Church*, ed. William J. Abraham, Jason E. Vickers, and Natalie B. Van Kirk (Grand Rapids, MI: Eerdmans, 2008), 27–42.

19 Florovsky, "Revelation, Philosophy and Theology," *CW* 3:36. Cf. Sergius Bulgakov, *The Orthodox Church* (Crestwood, NY: St. Vladimir's Seminary Press, 1988), 19: "Tradition is the living memory of the Church."

20 Florovsky, "Catholicity of the Church," *CW* 1:47. On this passage, see Aidan Nichols, *Light from the East: Authors and Themes in Orthodox Theology* (London: Sheed & Ward, 1995), 141–2.

By "returning to the Fathers" Orthodox theology was engaged in the task of endless patristics.[21]

The catholicity of ecclesial experience safeguards the unity and continuity of the Christian teaching. To participate in ecclesial experience is to overcome the subjectivity of private religious experience: "It is precisely through the 'common mind' of the Church that the Holy Spirit speaks to the believers."[22] By offering access to the "mystical memory of the Church" tradition could be said to conquer time. Florovsky explains that "time-conquering unity is manifested and revealed in the experience of the Church, especially in its Eucharistic experience."[23]

Florovsky emphasizes a vital connection between the *lex orandi* and the *lex credendi* in patristic theology. As he contends in *The Ways of Russian Theology*, this connection has been lost in modern Orthodox theology. But the "worshipping Church," unlike "school theology," has not lost its patristic moorings. In Florovsky's judgment, "one can be best initiated into the spirit of the Fathers by attending the offices of the Eastern Church, especially in Lent and up to Trinity Sunday."[24] More generally, for Florovsky, "true theology can spring only out of a deep liturgical experience,"[25] an observation that connected him to Bulgakov, who according to his own admission "drank his theology from the bottom of the Eucharistic chalice."[26] While Florovsky himself did not elaborate on this point, the reconnection of liturgical practice with dogmatic theology was systematically undertaken by Florovsky's follower Alexander Schmemann.[27]

Another constructive move that characterizes Florovsky's theological program is his claim that the articulation of the theological significance of human personhood is one of the central achievements of patristic theology. While originally inspired by Western and Russian personalist philosophies, including existentialism, Florovsky later came to credit the idea more directly to the church

---

21 The expression is attributed to Sergei Khoruzhy.

22 Florovsky, "The Lamb of God," *Scottish Journal of Theology* 4 (1951): 13–28, at 16. Cf. "The Catholicity of the Church," *CW* 1:49: "We put forward no subjective religious experience, no solitary mystical consciousness, not the experience of separate believers, but the integral, living experience of the Catholic Church, catholic experience, and Church life."

23 Florovsky, "Catholicity of the Church," *CW* 1:45; cf. "Revelation, Philosophy and Theology," *CW* 3:39.

24 Florovsky, "*In Ligno Crucis. The Patristic Doctrine of the Atonement*," unpublished typescript, Georges Florovsky Papers, 1916–1979, Princeton University Library, C0586, box 2, folder 1, p. 9. Cf. "The Ethos of the Orthodox Church," *CW* 4:21.

25 Florovsky, "The Legacy and the Task of Orthodox Theology," *Anglican Theological Review* 31 (1949): 65–71, at 70.

26 Sergius Bulgakov, *Evkharistiia* (Moscow: Russkii Put', 2005).

27 Florovsky, "Catholicity of the Church," *CW* 1:50. See, for example, A. Schmemann, *Introduction to Liturgical Theology* (Crestwood, NY: St. Vladimir's Seminary Press, 1966); and *Of Water and the Spirit: A Liturgical Study of Baptism* (1974) (Crestwood, NY: St. Vladimir's Seminary Press, 1997).

fathers: "The idea of personality itself was probably the greatest Christian contribution to philosophy."[28] Following Sergei Trubetskoy and Alexei Losev, Florovsky maintained that pre-Christian Greek philosophy offered limited philosophical tools for articulating the metaphysics of personhood. In patristic theology, in contrast, the grappling with the mystery of the three persons in the Godhead and with the divine-human person of Christ gave a strong impetus to the development of personalist metaphysics.[29] These insights were later developed in different and controversial ways by Vladimir Lossky and John Zizioulas.[30]

As a personalist, Florovsky resisted deterministic and organicist tendencies of German idealism and Russian sophiology. He held that "history is a realm of personal agency, hence a realm of creativity and freedom. Person is the true subject of history."[31] This construal of historical agency was sharply opposed to a tendency in Hegelian and Marxist historiographies to ascribe causal significance to corporate entities, including states, nations, and cultures. Russian sophiology was equally dominated by abstract quasi-organic corporate entities, such as "divine humanity," "world soul," and the like. In Florovsky's judgment, such categories threatened to undermine the indeterministic character of individual human agency and genuine human freedom. The antinomic character of theological thinking was underscored by Florensky in *The Pillar and Ground of the Truth*. Florovsky tended to resolve the fundamental antinomy of the transcendent and immanent in the direction of emphasizing divine otherness at the expense of divine immanence, whereas Bulgakov, and Russian sophiology more generally, tended to emphasize divine indwelling of all things and interpreted everything from the perspective of eschatological fulfillment, of the divine "all in all." It would be misleading to credit Florovsky's stance as being more faithful to the patristic tradition than Bulgakov's one. Both views represent important aspects of the patristic tradition, Florovsky

---

28   Georges Florovsky, "Eschatology in the Patristic Age," *Studia Patristica* 2 (1957): 235–50, at 249. The essay was published while Florovsky was teaching at Harvard University. American personalism also had important exponents, including Harvard professor Ernest Hocking (1873–1966) and the so-called Boston personalist school, founded by B. P. Bowne (1847–1910) and continued in Florovsky's time by R. T. Flewelling (1871–1960), among others.

29   For an illuminating constructive engagement of the Trinitarian ontology of personhood, see Philip Rolnick, *Person, Grace, and God* (Grand Rapids, MI: Eerdmans, 2007).

30   Vladimir Lossky, *In the Image and Likeness of God* (Crestwood, NY: St. Vladimir's Seminary Press, 1997); J. Zizioulas, *Being as Communion* (Crestwood, NY: St. Vladimir's Seminary Press, 1997). For an illuminating comparative analysis of both theologians, see Aristotle Papanikolaou, *Being with God: Trinity, Apophaticism, and Divine-Human Communion* (Notre Dame, IN: University of Notre Dame Press, 2006).

31   Georges Florovsky, "Evoliutsiia i epigenez," *Vera i kul'tura* (St. Petersburg: Izdatel'stvo Russkogo Khristianskogo gumanitarnogo instituta, 2002), 424–40, at 439. Originally published in a German translation as "Evolution und Epigenesis (Zur Problematik der Geschichte)," *Der russische Gedanke* 1 (1930): 240–52.

drawing more heavily on Irenaeus and Athanasius, Bulgakov perhaps aligning himself more closely with Origen and Maximus the Confessor.[32] It should be noted that unlike Bulgakov, Florovsky never attempted to develop his theological program into a comprehensive theological system. Florovsky's neopatristics retains its open-ended texture and resists systematization.

In terms of its theological focus and methodology, it would be helpful to distinguish Florovsky's neopatristics from the patristically saturated theology of his younger contemporary, Lossky. In constructing his theological synthesis, Lossky kept the apophatic theology of Pseudo-Dionysius the Areopagite at the center. He subsequently drew a connection between Dionysius's participatory metaphysics and Gregory Palamas's theory of divine energies. On these grounds, Lossky referred to his work as a "Palamite" synthesis. While Florovsky acknowledged that Lossky's synthesis authentically represented the Orthodox tradition, his own theological accents belonged elsewhere. For Florovsky, the organizing principle of neopatristic theology was Chalcedonian Christology, not apophaticism. According to Florovsky, Lossky's neopatristic theology lacked a sufficient Christological emphasis.[33] In his more constructive works, Florovsky tended to dwell more on the early church fathers, and less on the Byzantine theologians. More generally, it would be wrong to lump Florovsky's neopatristic theology together with the retrieval of Palamite theology in the works of Basil Krivocheine, Vladimir Lossky, John Meyendorff, and other twentieth-century Orthodox scholars. The Palamite distinction between the unknowable essence of God and the uncreated divine energies did not play a noticeable role in Florovsky's theological program.

Finally, as a synthesis proper, a "return to the Fathers" was meant to draw together patristic research, a hermeneutical strategy, a theological program, and a polemical stance in a comprehensive, yet open way. Florovsky had recourse to all of the above-mentioned aspects of a "return to the Fathers," without always clearly differentiating between them himself.

One of the main difficulties in understanding Florovsky's neopatristic theology is that he rarely inquires into the operation of a synthesis with methodological precision. Nevertheless, Florovsky's nonsystematic reflections on the nature of the synthesis make it possible to distinguish four major types: religious, historical, patristic, and neopatristic. A "religious synthesis" is obtained when theological knowledge is integrated with other knowledge domains. Florovsky's

---

32 See my article "Georges Florovsky's Reading of Maximus: Anti-Bulgakov or Pro-Bulgakov?" in *Knowing the Purpose of Creation through the Resurrection: Proceedings of the Symposium on St. Maximus the Confessor*, ed. Maxim Vasiljević (Alhambra, CA: Sebastian Press and University of Belgrade Press, 2013), 407–15.

33 Georges Florovsky, Letter to S. Sakharov, April 8, 1958, in Sofronii Sakharov, *Perepiska s protoiereem Georgiem Florovskim* (Sergiev Posad: Sviato-Troitskii Predtechenskii monastyr'/Sviato-Troitskaia Sergieva Lavra, 2008), 68. Florovsky also did not share Lossky's claim that human nature is saved by Christ, whereas human personhood is saved by the Holy Spirit.

early essays, published while he was a graduate student in Odessa, rely on the religious philosophy of Solovyov and his concept of integral knowledge in order to develop this form of synthesis. After his disaffection with Solovyov's philosophy in the 1920s, Florovsky lost interest in this type of synthesis. Since his scholarly interests came to be dominated by intellectual history, it was natural for "historical synthesis" to occupy much of his attention.

According to Florovsky, a "historical synthesis" emerges when a historian converts a record of past events and a collection of sources into a judgment-laden intelligible unity. A scholarly inquirer accesses ancient literary sources and non-literary artifacts as signs of the past that need to be rendered intelligible in the present. Florovsky insists that such a synthesis involves personal judgment and empathetic imagination. As we mentioned earlier, historical knowledge is not exclusively bound up with the past; on the contrary, history becomes known always from the standpoint of the present. Understood in this way, "no ultimate synthesis is possible in history but still there is a measure of integration for every age."[34] In the closing sentence of *The Ways of Russian Theology*, Florovsky wrote, "A genuine historical synthesis is not so much *an interpretation of the past* as a *creative fulfillment of the future*."[35] Such a synthesis can operate both on the microlevel of individual human achievement and on the macrolevel of large-scale historical transformations.

A "patristic synthesis" refers to cases where ancient Christian authorities, whether individually or collectively, expressed a widely held church teaching. Some of Florovsky's examples are the "theological-metaphysical synthesis" of Basil of Caesarea, the "aesthetic synthesis" of Ephraem the Syrian, the "short-lived theocratic synthesis" of Emperor Justinian, and the "ascetic synthesis" of Maximus the Confessor. Florovsky discusses different examples of such a synthesis in his patrology lectures without clarifying how those connect to his search for a "new Christian synthesis," announced in the preface to the book. To clarify this relationship, it is helpful to distinguish between a "patristic synthesis," achieved by ancient Christian authors, and a "*neo*patristic synthesis," sought by contemporary historical theologians.

In his "Theological Testament," composed toward the end of his life, Florovsky defined the neopatristic synthesis in the following way:

> I was led quite early to the idea of what I am calling now "the Neo-Patristic Synthesis." It should be more than just a collection of Patristic sayings or statements. It must be a *synthesis*, a creative reassessment of those insights which were granted to the Holy Men of old. It must be *Patristic*, faithful to the spirit and vision of the Fathers, *ad mentem Patrum*. Yet, it must be also *Neo*-Patristic, since it is to be addressed to the new age, with its own problems and queries.[36]

34 Florovsky, "The Greek and Latin Mind in the Early Ages of the Church," *CW* 14:41.

35 Florovsky, *Puti russkogo bogosloviia*, 520; italics in original.

36 Blane, *Georges Florovsky*, 153–4; italics and capitalization in the original.

This is Florovsky's most explicit statement of what he intended by the neopatristic synthesis. Florovsky contrasted his neopatristic theology with the traditionalist "theology of repetition." As far as he was concerned, such a repetition was both theologically undesirable and hermeneutically impossible. The neopatristic synthesis is a result of applying a "historical synthesis" to different instances of a "patristic synthesis."

In any historical narrative, past events and ideas can never be frozen entirely in the past, but are reinterpreted from the standpoint of the present. But what precisely was involved in such a reinterpretation? Bulgakov and other "modernist" theologians construed such a reinterpretation rather freely—as involving a translation of the ancient dogmatic definitions into the language of contemporary philosophy and as sanctioning a speculative expansion of traditional beliefs. Theoretically, Florovsky was opposed to any expression of the modernist philosophical translation of patristic theological categories, since for him the Christian Hellenism of the church fathers was *philosophia perennis*. But in actual practice he read the insights of modern historicism and personalism back into the patristic sources, crediting the church fathers with the "discovery" of history and personhood. His guiding paradigm of theological inquiry was an ever-deepening interiorization of patristic theology, entering the mind of the Fathers and sharing in their experience of God. He contrasted this paradigm with merely repeating patristic statements (the error of the Orthodox traditionalists and fundamentalists) or, worse still, purporting to go *beyond* the Fathers into the realm of speculation (the alleged error of Bulgakov and other "modernists"). For Florovsky, Orthodox theology cannot be *post*patristic in the sense of rejecting or revising its patristic foundations.[37] His guiding metaphor was that of deepening one's engagement with patristic thought rather than going beyond the tradition.

Three phases may be identified in the Orthodox reception of Florovsky's neopatristics. The first phase is marked by his engagement and conflict with the leaders of the Russian religious renaissance, taking place roughly from the mid-1920s through the 1930s. Of central importance for understanding Florovsky are his youthful fascination with and a more mature critique of Solovyov, his encounter with the thought of Florensky, his collaboration with Berdyaev in the editing of *The Way* journal, his participation in Bulgakov's Brotherhood of St. Sophia, and his later teaching at the St. Sergius Theological Institute in Paris. It was during this period that the seminal ideas of the neopatristic synthesis were formulated in the discussions with the leaders of the Russian religious renaissance.

The second phase is characterized by a general acceptance of Florovsky's program by his younger contemporaries and the next generation of theologians, lasting approximately from the postwar period until the end of the twentieth century.

---

37 Andrew Louth, "The Authority of the Fathers in 'Post-Patristic Orthodox Theology,'" paper presented at the international conference "Neo-Patristic Synthesis or Post-Patristic Theology: Can Orthodox Theology Be Contextual?," Volos Academy of Theological Studies, Volos, Greece, June 3–6, 2010.

Florovsky's call for a "return to the Fathers" was answered by Lossky, who took Pseudo-Dionysius's mystical theology and Palamite theology of the divine energies as his patristic foci; by Leonid Ouspensky, who lamented the Westernization of iconography and called for a neo-Byzantine revival in Orthodox religious art; by Alexander Schmemann, who connected dogmatic theology and liturgical practice; and by Christos Yannaras, who applied Florovsky's historiography of the Western pseudomorphosis to the history of modern Greek theology.

In the twenty-first century, the third phase is gradually emerging, punctuated by the criticism and revision of Florovsky's theological vision. One group of Florovsky's critics consists of Orthodox scholars who work within a broadly defined neopatristic paradigm but call for a refinement of Florovsky's historical methods. The most prominent voices in this group include Andrew Louth, John Behr, John McGuckin, Marcus Plested, and Hilarion Alfeyev. The second group of Florovsky's critics consists of those who have questioned the hegemony of the neopatristic paradigm and are exploring new paradigms under the umbrella term of "contextual theology." The representatives of this group include Pantelis Kalaitzidis, Aristotle Papanikolaou, Radu Preda, Assad Kattan, and Brandon Gallaher. This criticism notwithstanding, Florovsky continues to be widely read and respected by contemporary Orthodox theologians.

Florovsky's neopatristic stance had significant implications for his participation in the ecumenical movement. The study of the church fathers provided a natural common ground for his theological exchange with the Anglican scholars at the meetings of the Society of St. Alban and St. Sergius in Great Britain. Florovsky's recourse to patristic theology was respected and trusted by his non-Orthodox conversation partners, even when he opposed Bulgakov's efforts at intercommunion with the Anglicans. As a participant of the Oxford Patristic Society meetings since its inception in 1951, Florovsky advocated contemporary theological appropriation of the heritage of the church fathers. Florovsky was also a major spokesman for Orthodoxy in the World Council of Churches at a time when the voice of the Christian East was only beginning to be heard in this important international forum.

The movement that was most congenial to Florovsky's neopatristics was *ressourcement*, which was animated by the same impulse toward a theological renewal by returning to the sources of the patristic tradition, with a special emphasis on the Eastern church fathers.[38] Both movements led to the revival of the historically informed study of the liturgy. *Ressourcement* was a challenge to the ahistorical presentation of neo-Thomism. Neopatristics was a reaction against the scholastic theology of the Orthodox manuals. *Ressourcement* was a more traditionally grounded alternative to Catholic modernism; the neopatristic theologies of

---

38 For the relevant comparison, see Andrew Louth, "The Patristic Revival and Its Protagonists," in *Cambridge Companion to Orthodox Christian Theology*, ed. Mary B. Cunningham and Elizabeth Theokritoff (Cambridge: Cambridge University Press, 2008), 188–202.

Florovsky and Lossky were a response to the modernism of the Russian religious renaissance. While they emerged in neighboring theological circles, Orthodox neopatristics preceded Catholic *ressourcement* by several years. Among the leaders of the *ressourcement*, Florovsky knew Yves Congar and Jean Daniélou personally and engaged with others at the international conferences. It is a tribute to the permanent legacy of the *ressourcement* and neopatristics that the Orthodox–Catholic dialogue in the twenty-first century on issues ranging from the doctrine of the Trinity to papal authority has as its primary frame of reference the theological heritage of the first millennium.

While the recent engagement of the church fathers in Orthodox theology has involved new methods and new challenges, Florovsky's contribution will remain a milestone and a major catalyst of church renewal.

Chapter 7

KARL BARTH

Kenneth Oakes

Introduction

Karl Barth is often taken to be and interpreted as a theologian of retrieval. If such a label is meant to be descriptive of a mode of theology that resources once traditional theological categories, distinctions, judgments, and content for purposes both contemporary and venerable, then it would be difficult to argue against such an interpretation. Taken as an evaluation, however, there have been both positive and negative assessments of Barth's practice of retrieval. On the Protestant side, Barth was sometimes feared to be a "crypto-Catholic" and at times he was praised or pilloried for being "neoorthodox."[1] For instance, his erstwhile comrades in arms Emil Brunner and Rudolf Bultmann quickly judged Barth to be succumbing to an obsolete scholasticism with his return to the Protestant scholastics in the mid-1920s and his flirtation with traditional doctrines, especially Mariology and the Virgin Birth.[2] On the Catholic side, he was at times received as the reembodiment of the fierce and objective Protestantism of Martin Luther, John Calvin, and

---

1   In an interview from 1968, the last year of his life, Barth gave this answer when asked about the label "neoorthodox": "When I hear this term I can only laugh. For what does orthodox mean? And what does neo-orthodox mean? I am acquainted with what is called orthodoxy. In theology it is usually equated with the theology of the 16th and 17th centuries. I respect this. But I am far from being of this school. On the other hand, I am accused of being orthodox because I have found much help in it. Others have usually not even read the older orthodox. I myself was so liberal that I read them and found many good things in them. But 'neo-orthodox'! I just find it comical when people use terms like that." Karl Barth, "Liberal Theology," in idem, *Final Testimonies*, ed. Eberhard Busch (Grand Rapids, MI: Eerdmans, 1977), 33–4. For the original, full interview, see Karl Barth, "45 Interview von A. Blatter, Schweizer Radio und Westdeutscher Rundfunk (24.10.1968)," in idem, *Gespräche 1964–1968*, ed. Eberhard Busch (Zurich: Theologischer Verlag Zürich, 1996).

2   See Emil Brunner, *Truth as Encounter*, trans. T. H. L. Parker (Philadelphia: Westminster, 1964), 42–3; Karl Barth/Rudolf Bultmann, *Letters 1922–1966*, trans. Geoffrey W. Bromiley (Edinburgh: T & T Clark, 1982), 38.

Huldrych Zwingli over and against a nineteenth-century modern Protestantism that was seen as being overly subjective or reductionistic. It is remarkable that many of the Roman Catholic luminaries of the early to mid-twentieth century—Erich Przywara, Gottlieb Söhngen, Hans Küng, Henri Bouillard, and especially Hans Urs von Balthasar—felt compelled to engage Barth's theology both as a worthy combatant and as a source for fruitful conversation.[3] An older Barth was even invited to Rome and enjoyed an hour-long audience with Pope Paul VI.[4] In this light, one guideline for the interpretation and exposition of Barth's theology, which is undoubtedly Reformed and modern, might be that it could attract the attention of Roman Catholics, whether in a critical or appreciative mode.

In addition to resourcing the Protestant scholastics or raising the banner of the Reformation, Barth has also been taken as revitalizing and reemphasizing specific doctrines: the freedom and transcendence of God, the eschatological character of the Christian message, and justification by grace through faith. It has also become a commonplace (usually more stated than shown) that Barth's work, despite its alleged pneumatological deficits, initiated a trinitarian revival within twentieth-century theology after the doctrine had languished in the nineteenth century. He is also sometimes counted among the theologians responsible for the reemergence of the theological interpretation or post-critical exegesis of Scripture in the twentieth century.[5] There is also the sense that Barth's theology offered a return to a positive account of doctrine in general. In contrast to theologies too distracted by apologetic engagement with other discourses, or entirely focused upon criticism of Scripture or traditional doctrine, or reduced to psychology or ethics, Barth understood the task of theology to be a joyous and demanding discipline undertaken as an element of the church's life. Theology is an ecclesial activity whereby the church attempts to test its proclamation (its confession, teaching, worship, service, and mission) against its source and norm, the risen Jesus Christ who speaks to his church in Holy Scripture. Defined in this way, theology necessarily contains a critical moment, which should neither be understated nor overstressed,[6] but the unavoidable criticism of doctrine

---

3 Barth could return the favor, especially later on. In the last year of his life Barth would listen to both Protestant and Catholic services on the radio, and he thought there to be more renewal and vitality in the Petrine church than he did in the Reformation churches. See Karl Barth, "Radio Sermons Catholic and Evangelical," in idem, *Final Testimonies*, 43–9.

4 Eberhard Busch, *Karl Barth: His Life from Letters and Autobiographical Texts*, trans. John Bowden (Philadelphia: Fortress, 1976), 482–4. Barth had also been invited to be an observer at Vatican II but had to decline for health reasons.

5 For one of the earliest accounts of Barth as a postcritical exegete, see Rudolf Smend, "Nachkritische Schriftauslegung," in *Parrhesia: Karl Barth zum achtzigsten Geburtstag* (Zurich: Evangelischer Verlag Zürich, 1966), 215–37.

6 "Dogmatics is a critical science. So it cannot be held, as is sometimes thought, that it is a matter of stating certain old or even new propositions that one can take home in black and white. On the contrary, if there exists a critical science at all, which is constantly having to begin at the beginning, dogmatics is that science." Karl Barth, *Dogmatics in Outline*, trans. G. T. Thomson (New York: Harper and Row, 1959), 12.

is subordinate to the elaboration of the self-revelation of God in Scripture. Finally, Barth also consistently held that theology and ethics are inextricably related and neither is reducible to the other, for theology takes place for the edification and correction of the church's teaching and life.

Given that Barth's theology has rightfully been taken as a species of a theology of retrieval, it might be helpful to identify its particular contours and characteristics. In what follows we first outline Barth's theology more generally as a theology of Reformed and timely retrieval. We then offer a brief account of Barth's practice of retrieval during the early and formative stages of his development, moving from his earliest thought up until the 1924–26 *Göttingen Dogmatics*. We then see how Barth's general practice of retrieval continued in later works, especially the *Church Dogmatics*.

Preliminaries: reformed and timely retrieval

A helpful baseline for Barth's approach to theological retrieval can be found in the fruitful tension between these two remarks: "we cannot possibly think that church history began in 1517, and even as Protestants we have to think in Catholic terms, and we must never lose sight of the 'always, everywhere, and by all' ";[7] "the slogan 'Back to Orthodoxy,' and even the slogan 'Back to the Reformers,' cannot promise us the help that we need today. 'Back to . . .' is never a good slogan."[8] Barth's theology of retrieval stands at the intersection between needing to think "catholically," even as Protestants, and recognizing that one cannot fulfill the tasks of theology merely by repristinating past theologies. As will be shown, Barth's theology is indeed one of retrieval, but it is also irreducibly timely as well as marked by Barth's Reformed background.

The first baseline remark, "we have to think in Catholic terms," comes from the summer of 1924, during Barth's first semester of teaching systematic theology. More specifically, the line appears in a lecture given on July 14, 1924,[9] roughly a short two years after the publication of *Romans* II. "To think in Catholic terms" is an admonition within Barth's discussion of authority and freedom in the church and here means the necessity of thinking along with the whole of the church's tradition and with a view toward the whole range of Christian doctrine. Certainly in practice, Protestants have their own ecclesial authorities, their own church fathers

---

7 Karl Barth, *The Göttingen Dogmatics: Instruction in the Christian Religion*, vol. 1., trans. G. W. Bromiley (Grand Rapids, MI: Eerdmans, 1991), 241 (subsequently *GD*).

8 Karl Barth, *Church Dogmatics* IV/1, trans. G. W. Bromiley (Edinburgh: T & T Clark, 1956), 372. Subsequent references to the *Church Dogmatics* will be given as *CD* along with volume and part number: Karl Barth, *Church Dogmatics*, 4 vols., trans. G. W. Bromiley and T. F. Torrance (Edinburgh: T & T Clark, 1936–77).

9 This is the date for the lecture given in Karl Barth, *Unterricht in der christlichen Religion*, vol. 1, ed. Hannelotte Reiffen (Zurich: Theologischer Verlag Zürich, 1985), 293; Barth, *GD*, 241.

and mothers, but the circle of listening, responsibility to, and authority spreads much wider. Barth advances a variety of arguments at this point: listening to the Word of God in Scripture, believing in the present activity of God, and confessing the Spirit to be a Spirit of peace and unity means that we must listen to what earlier Christians heard in their listening to Scripture, believe that God was no less active and present to his church in the past, and remain concerned for the peace and unity of the churches in their activity of teaching and service.

> We are guilty of an inappropriate arbitrariness if we say that for us . . . the only authority at issue is, of course, that of the Reformation confessions. As though the Reformation churches, no less than the Roman Catholics, did not base their claim to be the Christian church on the fact that they formally presupposed an acknowledgement and confession of the symbols of the first five centuries, and as though for an understanding of Protestant dogmas we could set aside even for a single moment the Nicene doctrine of the Trinity and Chalcedonian christology. No, if in its own sphere and relative sphere there is a category of dogma just as there is a category of doctors of the church, then we cannot possible [*sic*] think that church history began in 1517, and even as Protestants we have to think in Catholic terms, and we must never lose sight of the "always, everywhere, and by all."[10]

Three years after writing *Romans* II, Barth is telling his Protestant students to remember that the church did not begin in 1517 and that they must think in Catholic terms. Barth himself seems to have followed his advice to his students. Indeed, what would Barth's theology have been without Paul and the "new world of the Bible," without Nicaea and Chalcedon, without Anselm and Calvin, without the Reformed and Lutheran Protestants, or even without the Blumhardts? Without all these figures we might have had a sophisticated and admirable extension of the school of Friedrich Schleiermacher, Albrecht Ritschl, and Wilhelm Herrmann, some innovative type of Christocentric, ecclesial, and pious existentialism, but we would not have had the Barth of the *Church Dogmatics*.

The second baseline remark, " 'Back to . . .' is never a good slogan," comes from the other end of Barth's career, from the 1953 *Church Dogmatics* IV/1. Its context is a discussion of the relationship between revelation, Scripture, and the doctrine of sin in seventeenth-century Protestant orthodoxy. Barth sees in its doctrine of sin a subtle transition "from biblical to Biblicist thought," which is not an advance into a more Scriptural theology but actually "the transition to a rationalism— supranaturalistic though it is in content."[11] He thinks that the supreme confidence in reason in some strands of the Enlightenment of the eighteenth century is well presaged in the Protestant scholastics of the seventeenth century. In a short excursus, Barth holds that the will and law of God, and thus the obedience or sin of

---

10 Barth, *GD*, 241.
11 Barth, *CD* IV/1, 368.

humanity, is found in Jesus Christ as attested in Scripture. The Protestant orthodox erred here, Barth alleges, and failed to follow the Reformers by tacitly adding
"another principle, that of reason" to the Scripture principle that they explicitly
endorsed. Seventeenth-century Protestant orthodoxy was thus already sliding
toward a rationalism in the guise of Biblicism, and in doing so placed another
principle alongside its Scripture principle. It is this set of historical and theological
judgments that gives Barth "a further proof that the slogan 'Back to Orthodoxy,'
and even the slogan 'Back to the Reformers,' cannot promise us the help that we
need today. 'Back to . . .' is never a good slogan."[12] What these lines show is that
Barth's theology of retrieval is a timely one, although we might just as well describe
it as creative, revisionist, or modern. The irreducible timeliness of theology means
that Barth's is a theology of retrieval, not one of repristination, restorationism, or
primitivism. As Barth was fond of saying, we must "begin again at the beginning in
every point," meaning at our own beginning in our own time and place.[13]

To these elements of Barth's theology in general, that it is one of timely retrieval,
there must be added a third: Barth's theology, and thus his theology of retrieval, is
Reformed. It is even arguably significant that Barth's theology is Swiss Reformed
in particular. Historically speaking, the theologies of the Reformed churches have
viewed themselves as concerned with the freedom, majesty, and sovereignty of the
triune God; election, covenant, and predestination; law and gospel, justification
and sanctification, and faith and obedience; the primacy of Holy Scripture over
tradition, creeds, and confessions; and they have entertained perpetual worries
regarding different forms of idolatry. All of these traditional Reformed hallmarks
find their place within Barth's theology, and Barth himself took his Reformed
inheritance with the utmost seriousness, despite his occasional and deep criticisms of it. In his 1937–38 Gifford lectures, which consist of a commentary on
the Scots Confession of 1560, Barth speaks of "my calling as a theologian of the
Reformed Church, a calling which I cannot well exchange for any other."[14] Barth's
timely theology of retrieval, with its Reformed atmosphere, habits of judgment,
and conversation partners, will thus be different from the Luther renaissance initiated by Karl Holl and the twentieth-century Roman Catholic *ressourcement* movement, even if there are clear marks of convergence at times. As for the significance
of Barth's theology being Swiss Reformed more specifically, one might note how
the Reformed churches in Switzerland have traditionally been relatively autonomous within their respective cantons, or between the larger cities, which illustrates

12 Barth, *CD* IV/1, 372.

13 Barth, *CD* I/2, 868.

14 Karl Barth, *Knowledge of God and the Service of God According to the Teaching of
the Reformation*, trans. J. L. M. Haire and Ian Henderson (London: Hodder and Stoughton,
1955), 5. This book is perhaps the clearest presentation of what Barth considers to be
the best habits and tendencies within Reformed theology. For Barth more generally as a
Reformed theologian, see John Webster, *Barth's Earlier Theology* (London: T & T Clark,
2005), 57–64.

well the historic plurality of the Reformed confessions even if the Second Helvetic Confession often held a prominent place.[15] Equally, in the nineteenth century the Swiss Reformed cantons and churches dropped mandatory adherence to creeds and confessions while also staunchly remaining state churches until the beginning of the twentieth century.[16] Barth thus grew up in and was a minister to a church tradition that was decidedly relaxed confessionally and that was accustomed to some variety and relative autonomy.

Such are, in broad outlines, the particular characteristics of Barth's theology of retrieval. Indeed, that Barth is engaged in a form of timely, Reformed theology of retrieval seems to hold true of his theology more generally. Certainly there are other elements of his theology: its Scriptural nature, its churchly setting, its realist or "scientific" character, its Christocentrism, and its deeply joyous and kerygmatic tone. Yet even these aspects of his theology are present in a kind of timely and Reformed mode of retrieval, even if one of the three elements seems to come to the foreground at times. We now shift to Barth's early development to illustrate these points and to see how quickly he settled upon this mode of theology.

The early Barth's performance and theology of retrieval

Barth's theological development from roughly 1909 to the mid-1920s can readily be seen and interpreted as a performance of timely and Reformed retrieval, and it is by the mid-1920s that Barth's explicit theology of retrieval is already well formed and in place.

Barth's earliest theology, from roughly 1909 to 1915, has been variously described as "liberal," "predialectical," or "modern." Educated during the twilight of the Ritschlian school, Barth was intellectually closer to his teacher Wilhelm Herrmann than to Ernst Troeltsch. Herrmann and Troeltsch were taken to be the two lead bearers of Ritschl's theology at the time although each differed from Ritschl in profound ways. Herrmann's theology, for instance, was a creative and existentialized mixture of Luther, Schleiermacher, and Immanuel Kant. His Luther was more dialectical than that of Ritschl's, and his understanding of what is "historical" more focused upon a figure's personality and its effects, while Ritschl's account of history is arguably broader and more sophisticated. The young Barth's theology was deeply marked by Herrmann, Martin Rade, Swiss religious socialism, and the exigencies of life as a pastor in a small industrial town. It was experiential, ethical, ecclesial, "positive" rather than speculative, and focused on the personality of Jesus Christ rather than the claims of natural theology or metaphysics. It was concerned with going beyond mere historicism in exegetical or historical work but

---

15 See James I. Good, *History of the Swiss Reformed Church since the Reformation* (Philadelphia: Publication and Sunday School Board of the Reformed Church in the United States, 1913).

16 Good, *History of the Swiss Reformed Church*, 406–8.

also worried about the potential presence of "mechanistic" or "mantic" tendencies in some traditional accounts of Scripture's verbal inspiration. It viewed traditional creeds and Protestant confessions with warm yet cautious appreciation, sought to make the Reformers relevant for contemporary times, and placed great emphasis on the autonomy or "independence" (*Selbstständigkeit*) of religious life and knowing and of theology in turn. Many of these traits, which are simply part and parcel of modern Protestantism, would survive long beyond Barth's "break with liberalism" in the summer of 1915, but they would take on surprising guises at times. It is from this constellation of Protestant thought, which considered itself simultaneously modern and Christian, that Barth would begin his activity of retrieval and continue it throughout his theological work.

The first moment of retrieval in Barth's career is his return to Paul and to Scripture.[17] Following the outbreak of the First World War and his teachers' religious support for Kaiser Wilhelm II's war policy, the disillusioned and shocked Barth and his friend Eduard Thurneysen attempted to rethink their theological inheritances. While struggling and engaging with the religious socialists, meeting with the younger Blumhardt in Bad Boll and reading the works of the elder, Barth and Thurneysen settled on reading Paul's Epistle to the Romans in their search for a "'wholly other' theological foundation."[18] Barth began taking notes during his reading of Paul and eventually began to assemble them into a book. In his reading of Paul and Scripture, Barth encountered the overwhelming reality of the righteous God, "God himself, the real, living God and his love which comes in glory";[19] the unrighteousness of humanity's cultural achievements, ethics, aspirations, and supposed progress and piety; and the righteousness of God at work when God justifies sinners. In short, Barth discovered that "there is a new world in the Bible, the world of God,"[20] and that what this new world "offers us is the glorious, driving, hopeful life of the seed [cf. Mk 4:26–29], a new beginning out of which everything shall become new."[21] "See I make all things new!" (Rv 21:5) is how Barth comes to understand the fundamental message of the New Testament: "Everything that the New Testament affirms about God, humans, and the world is related to this possibility [Rv 21:5] without exception, which in the strictest sense is beyond all consideration. For this reason, it is always at the same time related to the greatest

---

17 As Busch relates, "It was the discovery of the Bible which held his attention. He had now 'gradually become aware of the Bible.' And so expected that the new basis for which he was searching would come from a new attempt to be 'more open towards the Bible and to allow it to tell me what it might have to do with Christianity more directly than before.'" Busch, *Karl Barth*, 98.

18 Busch, *Karl Barth*, 97.

19 Karl Barth, "The Righteousness of God, 1916," in idem, *The Word of God and Theology*, trans. Amy Marga (London: T & T Clark, 2011), 1–14, here 11.

20 Karl Barth, "The New World in the Bible, 1917," in idem, *The Word of God and Theology*, 15–30, here 19.

21 Barth, "The New World," 23.

critical negation that the possibility of a new order unrelentingly presupposes."[22] The "object of the Bible" is the "'Easter message,' which comes to us not only as cognitive content, but as 'movement and truth.'"[23] The message of the Bible is resurrection, which means "the sovereignty of God," eternity, "the new world," "a new embodiment," and "the unique experience of humanity."[24] In addition to a series of breathtaking speeches, the result of Barth's encounter with Paul and Scripture was the first edition of his commentary on Romans, published in 1919, revised into its second edition during the end of 1920 and the fall of 1921, and published in 1922.[25]

The next great moment of Barth's theology of retrieval came soon after his return to Paul and Scripture in the form of close engagement with the theology of the Reformers and their scholastic descendants. In 1921 Barth was appointed an honorary professor of Reformed theology at Göttingen and found himself simultaneously educating his students and himself. Barth had been an assistant pastor and pastor for roughly twelve years, had never completed a PhD, hardly knew the Reformers, and was in awe of the erudition of the other members of the largely Lutheran faculty. The flurry of study Barth undertook in his first years as a second-career professional theologian paid off handsomely, however: "The most intense period of development in Barth's thought coincided with his astonished discovery of the confessional and dogmatic traditions of early Calvinism."[26] Barth's main tasks in his first years at Göttingen were biblical exegesis and the exposition of the Reformed tradition, and in this way Barth was able to continue his study of Paul and Scripture and become more conversant in his own Reformed tradition.

In terms of our theme, what we find in these first lectures at Göttingen is the broadening of Barth's horizons, the sharpening of his intuitions, and a respectful yet judicious engagement with his theological predecessors. In his lectures on Calvin from the summer semester of 1922, for instance, Barth appreciates how the early Reformed were able to combine "the vertical" and "the historical," justification and sanctification, gospel and law, and thus theology and ethics: "the unity of faith and life, dogmatics and ethics, this attempt to answer the question of human striving and willing that Luther's discovery had for a moment pushed into

---

22 Karl Barth, "Biblical Questions, Insights, and Vistas, 1920," in idem, *The Word of God and Theology*, 71–100, here 91. Italics in original removed.

23 Barth, "Biblical Questions," 95.

24 Barth, "Biblical Questions," 95–100.

25 For material on *Romans* I and *Romans* II and the revision process, see Busch, *Karl Barth*, 106–23; Bruce McCormack, *Karl Barth's Critically Realistic Dialectical Theology: Its Genesis and Development 1909–1936* (Oxford: Clarendon Press, 1995), 184–203.

26 John Webster, "Theologies of Retrieval," in *The Oxford Handbook of Systematic Theology*, ed. Kathryn Tanner, John Webster, and Iain Torrance (Oxford: Oxford University Press, 2007), 583–99, here 592.

the background, was distinctive, natural, and original in the Reformed."[27] Barth also tells his students that studying Calvin cannot mean only establishing what Calvin said or did not say, for this "would be to deny the immortal Spirit of God whom Calvin heard speaking through Paul even though Paul was long dead";[28] it also cannot mean "repeating Calvin's words as our own or making his views ours";[29] and it cannot mean forcing Calvin to say what he in fact did not say, for "we must pay our first and very serious attention to him, beginning our thinking with him, if we really have it in view to let ourselves be taught by him."[30] When treating a historical figure or past author there must be "a certain humility on the one side" and on the other "a certain free and understanding humor, presuming the author is probably always right in some sense even when wrong."[31] Barth even defends scholasticism, both Protestant and Catholic, against its detractors. The Protestant scholastics "had the ability to think and they took pleasure in think-ing. They had dialectical courage and consistency. Their academic tradition has had four hundred years of vitality. Once the reformers were no longer present, Protestant theology could do no better than adopt that tradition."[32] As for the Roman Catholic scholastics, "those who do not admire them, those who are not in danger of becoming scholastic themselves, simply have no inner right to pass judgment on them."[33] It is worth remembering that these lectures come from 1922, the same year *Romans* II appeared.

What Barth thinks of his Reformed tradition and the status of its confessions within theological work can be seen in his lectures on the theology of the Reformed confessions from the summer semester of 1923. He notes five characteristics of the Reformed confessions. First, there is their particular or regional character, "as though from one island to another, greetings were exchanged between Geneva and Zurich, Basel and Strassburg, with recurring delight and sometimes disappointment."[34] What the regional as opposed to national or imperial character of the confessions means is that the truth and thus ecumenicity of a Reformed confession can be estab-lished "solely through its connection to Holy Scripture and not through its formal

27 Karl Barth, *The Theology of John Calvin*, trans. Geoffrey W. Bromiley (Grand Rapids, MI: Eerdmans, 1995), 77.

28 Barth, *Theology of John Calvin*, 3.

29 Barth, *Theology of John Calvin*, 4.

30 Barth, *Theology of John Calvin*, 5.

31 Barth, *Theology of John Calvin*, 6. For similar remarks on how to approach figures from the past, see Karl Barth, *Protestant Theology in the Nineteenth Century: Its Background and History*, trans. Brian Cozens (Valley Forge, PA: Judson Press, 1973), 15–29. Cf. also Webster, "'There is no past in the Church, so there is no past in theology': Barth on the History of Modern Protestant Theology," in idem, *Barth's Earlier Theology*, 91–117.

32 Barth, *Theology of John Calvin*, 26.

33 Barth, *Theology of John Calvin*, 26.

34 Karl Barth, *The Theology of the Reformed Confessions*, trans. Darrell L. Guder (Louisville: Westminster John Knox, 2005), 11.

connection to a universal church or a normative exposition of Scripture."[35] In other words, "The legitimate pathway to universality is here the pathway of particularity."[36] Secondly, each confession is a *"singular work*, one next to many others,"[37] meaning that "Reformed confessions, as long as and to the extent that they are Reformed, will always be *many* and not *one*."[38] Thirdly, the Reformed confessions purposely considered themselves "confessions" rather than "symbols," thereby denoting their inferior status to the creeds of the early church, and emphasizing their "humanity and capacity for error."[39] Fourthly, the Reformed confessions were intended to be provisional and subject to improvement upon or even to being replaced. Fifthly, although these confessions were provisional, they were taken with the utmost seriousness and commitment as part of the objective and public nature of Christian faith and life. What unifies the Reformed confessions in all their diversity and particularity is their commitment to the Scripture principle: "the Scripture principle is the only article of faith that has persisted up to today in the doctrinal statements of all Reformed documents."[40] In their Scripture principle the confessions admit that their significance is found in their "essential nonsignificance," their "obvious relativity, humanity, multiplicity, mutability, and transitoriness" before Scripture.[41]

Soon after his arrival to Göttingen, Barth decided to offer lectures in systematic theology. The lectures were to begin in the summer semester of 1924, and so Barth spent that spring reflecting on how to approach the task of dogmatics as well as reading a swath of Patristic authors, Aquinas, and figures from modern Protestantism.[42] It was also during this spring that Barth ran across Heinrich Heppe's sourcebook of Reformed scholasticism (which first appeared in 1861) as well as its Lutheran version, which was edited by Heinrich Schmid (first edition from 1843). These books are essentially collections of longish passages from sixteenth- and seventeenth-century Protestants scholastics arranged by doctrine and that cover the whole of systematic theology, from prolegomena to last things. Positively stated, it is a testament to Barth's immense willingness to learn and listen that he could find so much theological and spiritual depth and inspiration in what are basically books composed entirely of block quotations. The negative corollary, however, might be just how fruitless and empty Barth thought modern Protestant theology to be.

---

35 Barth, *Theology of the Reformed Confessions*, 11.

36 Barth, *Theology of the Reformed Confessions*, 11–12.

37 Barth, *Theology of the Reformed Confessions*, 12; italics in original.

38 Barth, *Theology of the Reformed Confessions*, 16.

39 Barth, *Theology of the Reformed Confessions*, 19.

40 Barth, *Theology of the Reformed Confessions*, 64. Two lectures from this time deal with the same issues: "The Substance and Task of Reformed Doctrine" (1923), in Barth, *The Word of God and Theology*, 199–237; and "The Desirability and Possibility of a Universal Reformed Creed" (1925), in Karl Barth, *Theology and Church: Shorter Writings 1920-1928*, trans. Louise Pettibone Smith (New York and Evanston: Harper and Row), 112–35.

41 Barth, *Theology of the Reformed Confessions*, 38.

42 For background, see McCormack, *Karl Barth's Critically Realistic*, 331–7.

Barth himself related his encounter with Heppe in a preface to a newer edition of the volume.[43] As Barth tells it, in the spring of 1924 he was convinced that Scripture had to be the absolute guide for Protestant dogmatics, disaffected with contemporary theology, and he wanted to learn more from the Reformers. He felt as if he had no guide for reconnecting to the Reformers and through them to Scripture. He was "more terrified of the footprints of modern Biblicism than attracted to them,"[44] and thought that modern Biblicism was too similar to modern Protestantism to combat effectively the latter's deficiencies. Heppe and Schmid then came into his hands, and Barth felt that he had entered into an "atmosphere" in which it was natural to tread "a road by way of the Reformers to H. Scripture,"[45] a road he no longer thought Ritschl and Schleiermacher could pave for him. He discovered a dogmatics with "form and substance," which was oriented to Scripture, inspired by the Reformation, and which attempted to follow in the footsteps of both the doctrinal work of the early church as well as the scholasticism of the medieval church. Heppe and Schmid showed him a style of Protestant dogmatics that was ecclesial and scientific, and they gave him hope that it was perhaps possible to "return to a strict, Churchly and scientific outlook,"[46] The theology contained in these volumes gave Barth "cause for astonishment at its wealth of problems and the sheer beauty of its trains of thought."[47]

Barth is also clear that "a return to this orthodoxy . . . could not be contemplated."[48] He offers three brief reasons for why this was so. First, Protestant orthodoxy adopted the form of its surrounding philosophy to such an extent that its theological substance suffered. Second, the orthodox risked losing a distinctively Reformed account of God, revelation, and salvation in their "justifiable attempt to adopt the Early and Medieval church tradition."[49] Third, Barth detects an impulse to master revelation: "they were too extreme—this is particularly in their doctrine of Scripture—in turning revelation in all its mystery into a handy intellectual principle."[50] Not much else is offered in way of content or context, but the meaning is clear: the orthodox have their own questionable elements and cannot be followed in every regard. The exegesis of Scripture is still best done in the school of the Reformers, but Barth considers it preferable and profitable to study among the orthodox rather than pushing them aside for the sake of a "Biblical-Reformed theology." Interpreting Scripture with the Reformers while ignoring the Protestant scholastics would most likely result in a "new mixture of Enlightenment and

---

43 Karl Barth, "Karl Barth's Foreword," in Heinrich Heppe, *Reformed Dogmatics: Set Out and Illustrated from the Sources* (Grand Rapids, MI: Baker, 1978), v–vii.

44 Barth, "Karl Barth's Foreword," v.

45 Barth, "Karl Barth's Foreword," v.

46 Barth, "Karl Barth's Foreword," vi.

47 Barth, "Karl Barth's Foreword," vi.

48 Barth, "Karl Barth's Foreword," vi.

49 Barth, "Karl Barth's Foreword," vi.

50 Barth, "Karl Barth's Foreword," vi.

Pietism."[51] Thus the Protestant orthodox can neither be followed tout court nor ignored. Instead, "Success can only come if we have previously learned to read the Reformers as the Church's teachers, and with them, Scripture as the document for the Church's existence and nature, and therefrom to ask what Church science may be. That precisely may be learned, nay must be, from the early Orthodox men."[52]

The impact of Heppe and the Protestant scholastics upon Barth's systematic lectures, which were eventually published as the *Göttingen Dogmatics*, can be seen in both their form and content, but it is a constantly negotiated impact. While slightly overstated, these lectures, and thus the *Göttingen Dogmatics*, have been helpfully likened to a commentary on Heppe in the vein of commentaries upon Peter Lombard's *Sentences*.[53] Despite its rather different introductory sections, the structure of the *Göttingen Dogmatics* loosely follows that of Heppe, moving from prolegomena, to the doctrines of God, creation, covenant, sin, Christology, salvation, the church, and last things. The arguments and positions of the Protestant scholastics appear throughout the text and are especially engaged in the doctrines of God, covenant, and election. From these engagements, it is clear that Barth feels free to learn from the scholastics and free to disagree with them.[54]

Just as in the later *Christliche Dogmatik* (1927) and *Church Dogmatics* (1932–61), Barth attempts to thread his course through what he takes to be two "counterbalancing heresies": Roman Catholicism and modern Protestantism.[55] Despite his criticisms of Roman Catholicism, it should be noted that his evaluation of it is not entirely negative. He begins his first lectures with a prayer from Thomas Aquinas,[56] recommends that his students read Bonaventure's *Breviloquium* in addition to reading the Reformers and Protestant scholastics, and even delves into the doctrines of the Virgin Birth and of Mary. Indeed, Barth can even say, as he sometimes would elsewhere, that he would choose Roman Catholicism over modern

---

51 Barth, "Karl Barth's Foreword," vi.

52 Barth, "Karl Barth's Foreword," vi–vii; italics in original. Eberhard Busch relates these autobiographical remarks from Barth regarding the Reformation: "I soon saw that it was also necessary to continue it, to arrange the relationship between law and gospel, nature and grace, election and Christology and even between philosophy and theology more exactly and thus differently from the patterns which I found in the sixteenth century. Since I could not become an orthodox 'Calvinist,' I had even less desire to support a Lutheran confessionalism." Busch, *Karl Barth*, 210–11.

53 McCormack, *Karl Barth's Critically Realistic*, 331–4; Rinse H. Reeling Brouwer, *Karl Barth and Post-Reformation Orthodoxy* (Aldershot and Burlington: Ashgate, 2015), 3–6. This dependence upon Heppe becomes even more striking when it is remembered how the subsequent *Christliche Dogmatik* (1927) and *Church Dogmatics* themselves depend heavily on the *Göttingen Dogmatics*.

54 For a summary of his engagement with the Protestant scholastics, see *GD*, xxxiv–xxxix.

55 Barth, *GD*, 211.

56 Barth, *GD*, 3, 21–2.

Protestantism if forced to decide: "if I had to choose between them I am not sure whether I would not have to prefer the classical heresy to the nonclassical one."[57] Just as with Heppe and Schmid, so the presence of Roman Catholicism is also often mediated through sourcebooks, in this case being the *Patrologiae Graeca* and *Latina*, Heinrich Denzinger's *Enchiridion symbolorum*, and Bernhard Bartmann's *Lehrbuch der Dogmatik*.

In these lectures Barth admits that contemporary Protestant theology is somewhat at a loss regarding issues of normativity and authority within theology, such as how one might combine the Scripture principle with the relativity of confessions, or how to relate Scriptural and ecclesial authority, or what Christian freedom entails if it is not interpreted as caprice or subjectivism. Barth's thoughts here are similar to what we encountered above: Scripture remains the absolute authority alongside the relative authorities of the creeds and confessions of the churches that baptize us. Both "attentiveness" and "respect" should be granted to past theologians,[58] and one cannot neglect the voices of the past even when following the Scripture principle: "We are not simply to think and speak in detachment from them, as though the church began only with us today—not even if we use the Bible. At every point we must at least take note of the way in which the church thought it should understand the witness to revelation at the great crises in its history."[59] Protestant churches have currently resolved the issues of normativity and authority through a mixture of "Conservatism, modernism, and independency, without giving to any the honor that is their due." Such a mixture "honors neither the connection of our faith with what has been believed always, everywhere, and by all, nor the indubitably valid desire for new words for the faith of a new age, nor the commands that we should be truthful in relation to the situation as it now is."[60] The challenge, then, is to find a way to honor "the connection with what has been believed always, everywhere, and by all" and the "valid desire for new words for the faith of a new age" as well as the "commands that truthful in relation to the situation as it now is."[61]

Similar remarks can be found somewhat later in Barth's 1935 *Credo*, the published version of which includes Barth's responses to questions raised by his

---

57 Barth, *GD*, 211. Such a line also appears in Karl Barth, "Roman Catholicism: A Question to the Protestant Church," in idem, *Theology and Church*, 307–33, especially 314.

58 Barth, *GD*, 239–40.

59 Barth, *GD*, 239.

60 Barth, *GD*, 242.

61 Similarly, in an address given in October 1925, Barth responds to Erik Peterson's question regarding dogma and authority within theology in this way: "We must therefore recognize in the concrete authority: the decisions of the Church on the canon and on the canonical text of the Scripture; certain assertions in the Church's message, more or less clearly accepted as fundamental, based on the former and explained by the words of the Fathers; and lastly also that command of the hour (which likewise is to be understood as given to the Church). These three or four elements lie obviously on very different levels

original audience. One such question involved the relationship between dogmatics and tradition, which seem "to have aroused particular displeasure"[62] among his listeners. In response, Barth advances a "Reformation Scripture-principle" that seeks to maintain the necessary distinctions between revelation, Scripture, and tradition, which he thinks have become blurred in Roman Catholicism. Nonetheless, the Reformation's scripture principle does not equal pure Biblicism: "In consonance with the Fathers of the Early Church and the Reformation," "there can never be any question of overleaping the centuries and immediately (each trusting to the sharpness of his eye and the openness of his heart) linking up with the Bible."[63] One cannot "with a lofty gesture" dismiss "Nicænum, Orthodoxy, Scholasticism, Church Fathers, Confessions and cling 'to the Bible alone'!"[64] In practice, Barth alleges, Biblicism has ironically led to a recognizably and essentially modern theology. The biblicists "were no doubt free of Church dogma, but not of their own dogmas and conceptions. Luther and Calvin did not go to work on the Bible in this way. Neither should we. It is in the *Church* that the Bible is read; it is by the *Church* that the Bible is heard."[65] When understood as a practice of the church in response to revelation and to its Lord, the Scripture principle neither unduly elevates tradition nor does it abandon tradition.

This combination of retrieval, timeliness, and the Reformed emphasis upon the Scripture principle is also readily evident in Barth's later 1947 exposition of the Heidelberg Catechism. In his introduction to the catechism, Barth observes that "we live no longer in the sixteenth but in the twentieth century," which means "there is no point in staring spellbound at the sixteenth century and holding on to what was said then and there as unmoveably and unchangeably as possible. Such a procedure would be inconsistent with the Reformation."[66] There should be reverence and gratitude for the fathers and mothers of the church, but it is a misunderstanding of the communion of saints and of the place and role of our fathers and mothers "when their confession is later understood as chains, so that Christian doctrine today could only be a repetition of their confession."[67] In the communion of saints there is also freedom, and reverence and gratitude are also free acts. Such freedom for reverence and gratitude stem from the Scripture principle: "Not to allow and require such freedom would mean that we in the church

and are significant in very different ways. But all these components together—and not dogma alone—constitute the concrete authority to which theology must render concrete obedience." Karl Barth, "Church and Theology," in idem, *Theology and Church*, 286–306, here 291.

62 Karl Barth, *Credo*, trans. J. S. McNab (Eugene, OR: Wipf & Stock, 2005), 179.

63 Barth, *Credo*, 180.

64 Barth, *Credo*, 180.

65 Barth, *Credo*, 181; italics in original.

66 Karl Barth, *Learning Jesus Christ through the Heidelburg Catechism*, trans. Shirley C. Guthrie Jr. (Grand Rapids, MI: Eerdmans, 1964), 21.

67 Barth, *Learning Jesus Christ*, 21.

had returned to a kind of tradition which stands with equal honor alongside Holy Scripture."[68]

Continual retrieval and revision in a reformed key

Moving more broadly into Barth's work, we can see the story of his theological career is one of continual retrieval and revision in this generous Reformed key. The sources mined expand, his descriptive powers increase, his personal contacts and engagements widen, but the intuitions explored above remain in place.

There was, for instance, Barth's move to the University of Münster (1925–30) and his increased interaction with Roman Catholic theology in the mid-to-late 1920s.[69] There was his tête-à-tête with the Jesuit Erich Przywara, the provocative 1928 lecture entitled "Roman Catholicism: A Question to the Protestant Church," and his doctoral seminars on Aquinas in the winter of 1928–29 and on Anselm's *Cur Deus homo* in Bonn in the summer of 1930. The result of the Anselm seminar was the 1931 book *Anselm: Fides Quaerens Intellectum*, in which Barth states that Anselm's *Proslogion* is "a piece of theology that has quite a lot to say to present-day theology, both Protestant and Roman Catholic, which, quite apart from its attitude to its particular form, present-today theology ought to heed."[70] Whether one takes a minimal or a maximal view of Anselm's influence on Barth's theology, it is clear that Barth thought engaging with Anselm's theology would be profitable for both Catholics and Protestants.

When we turn to the unfinished *Church Dogmatics*, there has already been quite an intellectual and biographical journey. That the *Church Dogmatics* performs a theology of retrieval, conversation, and revision can be seen in the small print excursuses interwoven throughout. In these excursuses, Barth explains, will be "reproduced *in extenso* passages adduced from the Bible, the fathers and theologians."[71] While somewhat disorienting or plodding for first-time readers, these

---

68 These lectures were published in English as Karl Barth, *Learning Jesus Christ through the Heidelburg Catechism*, trans. Shirley C. Guthrie Jr. (Grand Rapids, MI: Eerdmans, 1964), 21–2.

69 For a helpful account on this point, see Lidija Matošević, *Lieber katholisch als neu-protestantisch: Karl Barths Rezeption der katholischen Theologie 1921–1930* (Neukirchen-Vluyn: Neukirchener, 2005).

70 Karl Barth, *Anselm: Fides Quarens Intellectum: Anselm's Proof of the Existence of God in the Context of his Theological Scheme*, trans. Ian W. Robinson (London: SCM Press, 1960), 9. Even somewhat later, in *Church Dogmatics* II/1, Barth refers to his work on Anselm as a resource that describes the "fundamental attitude to the problem of the knowledge and existence of God which is adopted in this section." Barth, *CD* II/1, 4. For Barth's reading and appropriation of Anselm, see Martin Westerholm, *The Ordering of the Christian Mind: Karl Barth and Theological Rationality* (Oxford: Oxford University Press, 2015), 179–228.

71 Barth, *CD* I/1, xii.

sections and passages from others are present in case readers do not have access to the originals and so that they may "hear the voices which were in my own ears as I prepared the text, which guided, taught, or stimulated me, and by which I wish to be measured by my readers."[72] He admits that it may seem as if "historically, formally, and materially I am now going the way of scholasticism. It would seem that Church history no longer begins for me in 1517. I can quote Anselm and Thomas with no sign of horror. I obviously regard the doctrine of the early Church as in some sense normative."[73] Such was also already the case in the Göttingen dogmatics lectures. As for the charge of "crypto-Catholicism,"[74] Barth asks, "Shall I excuse myself by pointing out that the connexion between the Reformation and the early church, Trinitarian and christological dogma, and the very concept of dogma and the biblical Canon, are not in the last resort malicious inventions of my own?"[75] He even goes so far as to say that we "can never listen too much to the witness of the primitive and mediaeval church."[76] Nevertheless, "gratitude for previous dogmatic teaching is no constraint on independence."[77] The task of dogmatics will always be undertaken confessionally, but it should also be performed with a view and responsibility to the whole church in an attempt to be "a dogmatics of the ecumenical Church."[78] Just as with his lectures on the Reformed confessions, the pathway to any ecclesial universality or ecumenicism begins with the particular. Finally, the task of systematic theology is always undertaken for the sake of a dogmatics of our own time. Being in constant and necessary contact with the past does not mean that we can speak from another century, pretending to offer a dogmatics "belonging to the 4th or 16th or 17th century" and ignoring the present state of the church.[79] True doctrine from the past is no guarantee of fidelity to the Word of God today: "The ghosts even of the true Church of the past may lead the Church astray and into temptation no less than the spirits of the present." Finally, when pursuing dogmatics it is essential to remember with Luther that we do not hope in ourselves, our theological predecessors, or our theological descendants: "It is not we who can sustain the Church, nor was it our forefathers, nor will it be our

---

72 Barth, *CD* I/1, xii.

73 Barth, *CD* I/1, xiii.

74 Barth, *CD* I/1, xiii.

75 Barth, *CD* I/1, xiv.

76 Barth, *CD* I/2, 614.

77 Barth, *CD* I/2, 769.

78 Barth, *CD* I/2, 823.

79 Barth, *CD* I/2, 842. In the foreword to the English translation of *Evangelical Theology* (1963), Barth states that "what we need on this and the other side of the Atlantic is not Thomism, Lutheranism, Calvinism, orthodoxy, religionism, existentialism, nor is it a return to Harnack and Troeltsch (and least of all is it 'Barthianism'!), but what I somewhat cryptically called in my little final speech at Chicago a 'theology of freedom' that looks ahead and strives forward." Barth, *Evangelical Theology: An Introduction*, trans. Grover Foley (Grand Rapids, MI: Eerdmans, 1963), xii.

descendants. It was and is and will be the One who says: 'I am with you always, even unto the end of the world.' "[80]

Throughout the *Church Dogmatics* we see Barth in steady retrieval in a timely and Reformed key. In his prolegomena Barth uses Heinrich Bullinger's doctrine of the threefold Word of God while also criticizing some perceived problems with the traditional Protestant doctrine of Scripture's verbal inspiration. There is continual reference to the Protestant scholastics in his doctrine of the knowledge and being of God even if he thinks that natural theology was the fundamental error that pervaded their doctrine of God at almost every point.[81] When it comes to his innovative doctrine of election, Barth admits that he is hazarding novelty and error, but that some risk had to be taken to improve the doctrine. His intention, nevertheless, "is to recapture a concern which underlay this particular Reformed tradition."[82] In his doctrine of providence, Barth muses that "I found it possible to keep far more closely to the scheme of the older orthodox dogmatics (*conservatio, concursus, gubernatio*) than I anticipated," even if he must offer a "radical correction" in the form of a Christocentric account of providence.[83] An angelology even makes an appearance in his doctrine of creation. The exquisite architecture and content of Barth's doctrine of reconciliation, which he says came to him in a dream,[84] creatively appropriates and interweaves Christ's threefold office as priest, king, and prophet; his two states of humiliation, exaltation, and their unity; his deity, his humanity, and their unity; sin as pride, sloth, and falsehood with salvation as justification, sanctification, and vocation; and the Holy Spirit's work in the church as the gathering, upbuilding, and sending of the community, and in the believer as the generation of faith, love, and hope. Finally, there is Barth's abandonment of the " 'sacramental' understanding of baptism" and his "opposition to the custom, or abuse, of infant baptism."[85] Barth ventures, however, that such an opposition will in turn provide a better positive account of baptism as the foundation of the Christian life.

Conclusion

Such is, in the broadest of strokes, Barth's Reformed and timely theology of retrieval. At each moment there is much more that could be described, explained,

---

80 Barth, *CD* I/2, xi, referencing Martin Luther, "Die angebliche 'Vorrede D. M. Luthers, vor seinem Abschied gestellet' zum zweiten Band der Wittenberger Gesamtausgabe seiner deutschen Schriften. 1548," in idem, *D. Martin Luthers Werke: Kritische Gesamtausgabe*, vol. 54 (Weimar: Hermann Böhlaus Nachfolger, 1928), 468–77, here 470.

81 Barth, *CD* II/1, 261.

82 Barth, *CD* II/2, 79.

83 Barth, *CD* III/3, xii.

84 See Busch, *Karl Barth*, 377.

85 Barth, *CD* IV/4 *(Fragment)*, x.

or questioned. The hope, nonetheless, is that each of the three moments of deep retrieval, timeliness, or innovation, and the impact of Barth's Reformed inheritance can be intimated and registered in his theology. What can be difficult when interpreting and evaluating Barth's theology is assigning to each moment its appropriate relative weight, which will most likely shift depending on which area of Barth's theology is under examination. I would hesitate to call "dialectical" Barth's combination of authority and freedom, tradition and the Scripture principle, or particularity and ecumenicism. To label these conjunctions "dialectical" would entail that we could only imagine them to be a matter of contrast rather than complexity, and it would also be a tacit reification of their purported opposition. It would be better simply to acknowledge Barth's timely and Reformed theology of retrieval as multilayered, complex, and counterintuitive at times, but it is not overly intricate or difficult to understand even if it might be difficult to perform.

Chapter 8

HENRI DE LUBAC

David Grumett

In this chapter, I first examine the French Jesuit Henri de Lubac's retrieval of patristic and earlier medieval sources, especially in his role as codirector of the *Sources Chrétiennes* series. I suggest that this textual *ressourcement* was motivated by a concern, which was properly theological, to reconceive the human person and human action in their relation to God, but that this theological concern was philosophically motivated by Maurice Blondel. These historical and philosophical currents flowed together into de Lubac's fundamental theology, especially the *Théologie* series, which de Lubac was also instrumental in establishing and to which he contributed several volumes. I conclude by assessing the relative importance and interrelation of these different strands in his retrieval project.

Retrieval, the *Sources Chrétiennes* and Origen

1940 was an inauspicious year to launch a major new project in theological publishing. France was divided into an occupied northern sector, centered on Paris, and a notionally free southern zone, which was governed from the spa town of Vichy in the Auvergne. On both sides of the division, some Jesuits were viewed with suspicion by the state authorities for their protests against anti-Semitism and Jewish registration. Within the church, the standard model for biblical and historical studies was positivist, while in the university theology faculties of the Third Republic new scholarly departures were discouraged. Because of wartime shortages, even the printing paper was of poor quality.[1]

Nevertheless, the obstacles to a major new project also justified its pursuit. The rise of Nazism, the persecution of Jews, and the tumult of war were viewed by many theologians and clergy as symptoms of a national crisis that was fundamentally

---

1 Etienne Fouilloux, *La Collection "Sources chrétiennes": éditer les Pères de l'Eglise au XXe siècle* (Paris: Cerf, 1995). For the contexts of war and anti-Semitism, see also Kevin L. Hughes, "Deep Reasonings: *Sources Chrétiennes, Ressourcement,* and the Logic of Scripture in the Years before—and after—Vatican II," *Modern Theology* 29 (2013): 32–45.

spiritual, and which, being such, required a theological response by the whole church. With this end in view, de Lubac, Pierre Chaillet, and some of their Jesuit confreres in the occupied zone instigated the *Cahiers du Témoignage chrétien*.[2] Printed in secret and circulated via underground networks, this journal exhorted Christians to resist Nazism by providing unredacted texts of papal pronouncements and disseminating extracts from comparable writings by theologians in other European countries, such as Karl Barth.

This effort to shape the attitudes of ordinary Christians, undertaken at tremendous personal risk, needed to be accompanied by a similar project to influence clergy and theologians. In France, there was a strong tradition of publishing patristic and medieval texts, exemplified by the massive editions of the Abbé Jacques-Paul Migne.[3] It was not the case that patristic and earlier medieval texts were unavailable nor that they had not been extensively circulated. The problem was, rather, that such texts had not been deployed to shape constructive theology. Migne's editions were large and uncritical, and omitted any translation from the original Greek or Latin.

The form of the existing texts was not the only obstacle to their theological use. At the time, the dominant theological paradigm in France and other Roman Catholic countries was scholasticism. As Rudolf Voderholzer argues in his assessment of de Lubac's project, this neglected historicity, both through ignoring the impact of contingent events on theological development and by taking revelation to be objectively true independently of its historical context.[4] By bringing new editions of patristic and earlier medieval texts into the theological arena, de Lubac hoped to demonstrate that revelation is historical, with this history being rooted in, and pointing to, Scripture and the action of Christ. David Ford spells out the wide practical import of this project, rightly noting de Lubac's deep involvement in both the church and the world, and that his motivation for immersing himself in the texts and history of the past was a passionate concern for the present.[5]

---

2 *Cahiers et courriers clandestins du Témoignage chrétien: 1941-1944*, ed. Renée Bédarida (Paris: Éditions ouvrières, 1977); edited as *La Résistance spirituelle, 1941-1944: les cahiers clandestins du Témoignage chrétien* (Paris: Albin Michel, 2001). For an overview, see James Bernauer, "A Jesuit Spiritual Insurrection: Resistance to Vichy," in *"The Tragic Couple": Encounters between Jews and Jesuits*, ed. James Bernauer and Robert A. Maryks (Leiden: Brill, 2014), 203–15; and generally, W. D. Halls, *Politics, Society and Christianity in Vichy France* (Oxford: Berg, 1995), 95–147.

3 *Patrologiae Graecae Cursus Completus*, 166 vols. (Paris: Migne, 1857–66); *Patrologiae Latinae Cursus Completus*, 217 vols. (Paris: Migne, 1844–55). For wider context, see Émile Poulat, "Le renouveau des études patristiques en France et la crise moderniste," in *Patristique et Antiquité tardive en Allemagne et en France de 1870 à 1930*, ed. Jacques Fontaine, Reinhart Herzog, and Karla Pollmann (Paris: Institut d'études augustiniennes, 1993), 20–9.

4 Rudolf Voderholzer, "Dogma and History: Henri de Lubac and the Retrieval of Historicity," *Communio (US)* 28 (2001): 648–68.

5 David F. Ford, *The Future of Christian Theology* (Oxford: Wiley-Blackwell, 2011), 12–21.

The new series, which de Lubac was instrumental in founding, became known as the *Sources Chrétiennes*. Notably, it was a cooperative venture between Jesuit editors and the new Dominican publishing house Éditions du Cerf, which had been established in 1929 at the behest of Pope Pius XI with the aim of reviving Christian spirituality by returning it to its historic sources.[6] The efforts of Cerf in the northern zone, and especially of its editor, Thomas-Georges Chifflot, were complemented by those of its imprint in the southern zone, Éditions de l'Abeille. The images of the stag (*le cerf*) and the bee (*l'abeille*) suitably indicated the complementary endeavors that the project would demand as well as the results it would achieve.[7] While the stag majestically traverses the hills in quest of the flowing streams of truth springing out of the rock, the bee works unseen to collect and produce a sweet and sustaining substance.

In his memoir, de Lubac recounts in detail the inception of the *Sources*, attributing the original idea to Victor Fontoynont, who was prefect of the Jesuit scholasticate at Fourvière in Lyons and whose role in nurturing the work of de Lubac and his confreres is generally underacknowledged. Fontoynont, de Lubac states, had intended the series to promote ecumenical links between the Roman Catholic and Orthodox Churches.[8] This accounts for its Greek focus in the early years: only after six years was the first volume published from a Latin author, Hilary of Poitiers.[9] Moreover, Fontoynont believed that his church needed to recover its roots in Greek theology in order to redress an excessive dependence on Ambrose, Augustine, and Jerome. However, Fontoynont was himself too old to assume the demands of directing such a large enterprise. Chaillet and Pierre Rondet were each approached, but were indisposed due to war mobilization and academic administration respectively. At this point, de Lubac was invited to assume responsibility and accepted. In conjunction with his Parisian confrere Jean Daniélou, he proposed translations of classic Greek and Latin texts that would include a substantial introduction by the translator. Not all of the early translations had the original text in parallel; however, those that did not were republished, with this arrangement soon becoming the norm.

De Lubac intended that the patristic and earlier medieval *Sources* would broaden conservative scholasticism, which employed the methodology of later medieval theology, but also call into question modern liberal approaches that

---

6 Étienne Foullioux, "Autour de l'histoire des 'Sources Chrétiennes,'" in *Fe i teologia en la història: estudis en honor del Prof. Dr. Evangelista Vilanova*, ed. Joan Busquets and Maria Martinell (Barcelona: Facultat de Teologia de Catalunya, 1997), 519–35.

7 Albert Fandos, "Le cerf et l'abeille: méditation allégorique," at gregoiredenysse.com, http://www.gregoiredenysse.com/?page_id=285 (accessed April 25, 2016).

8 Henri de Lubac, *At the Service of the Church: Henri de Lubac Reflects on the Circumstances that Occasioned his Writings*, trans. Anne Englund Nash (San Francisco: Ignatius, 1993), 94–5; Étienne Fouilloux, *Une église en quête de liberté: la pensée catholique française entre modernisme et Vatican II, 1914–62* (Paris: Desclée, 1998), 184.

9 Hilaire de Poitiers, *Traité des mystères*, trans. Jean-Paul Brisson, SC 19 (Paris: Cerf, 1947).

largely ignored historical sources. To these ends, he had already, in a large appen-
dix to his 1938 study *Catholicisme*, published short extracts from texts that would
later comprise some of the *Sources*. He there urged that the renewal of the church
would be promoted by an increased "knowledge of the patristic period, as well as
of the golden age of medieval theology, studied in conjunction with the former."[10]
Among the excerpts were two from Gregory of Nyssa's *On the Making of Man* and
others from the *Shepherd of Hermas*, Ignatius of Antioch's *Letter to the Magnesians*,
Ambrose of Milan's *Exposition of the Gospel of Luke*, a Christmas sermon of St. Leo
the Great, and a treatise by Augustine on the first letter of John.[11] In *Catholicisme*,
de Lubac also lays out some of the theological foundations for the *Sources*, stating
that retrieval cannot employ mere imitation; rather, it demands an "assimilation
which is at the same time a transformation."[12] This, de Lubac continues, is because
of the theological diversity that any genuine recovery of past thought will inevitably uncover. Another reason why retrieval cannot be merely imitative is that
theory depends upon social, intellectual, and cultural factors that exist in a state
of continual flux. For these reasons, de Lubac writes, a "return to the sources of
antiquity will be the very opposite of an escape into a dead past."[13] Rather, in the
present age such a return will require a demanding and delicate combination of
the church's theological heritage with modern secular concerns and critique. What
has arisen within the church's body, he suggests, needs to be brought into constructive engagement with what has emerged outside of that body.

The patristic theologian in whom de Lubac took greatest interest was Origen.
This is indicated by the unusual arrangements for the early volumes of the
Alexandrian biblical exegete. The introductions to the *Sources* were normally pro-
duced by the translator. However, for the first two volumes of Origen, which were
his homilies on Genesis and Exodus, de Lubac wrote the introduction himself.[14]
The Genesis introduction offers several useful indicators of his methodology

---

10 De Lubac, *Catholicisme*, 319–20.

11 Henri de Lubac, *Catholicisme: les aspects sociaux du dogme* (Paris: Cerf, 1947), trans.
Catholicism: Christ and the Common Destiny of Man (San Francisco: Ignatius, 1988), 371–4,
380–1, 414–16, 426–7, and 440–1. See Grégoire de Nysse, *La Création de l'homme*, trans.
Jean Laplace, ed. Jean Daniélou, SC 6 (Paris: Cerf, 1943); Ignace d'Antioche and Polycarpe
de Smyrne, *Lettres: Martyre de Polycarpe*, trans. and ed. Pierre Thomas Camelot, SC 10
(Paris: Cerf, 1945); Léon le Grand, *Sermons*, trans. René Dolle, ed. Jean Leclercq, SC 22, 49,
and 74, 3 vols. (Paris: Cerf, 1947–61); Ambroise, *Traité sur l'Evangile de S. Luc*, trans. and ed.
Gabriel Tissot, SC 45 and 52, 2 vols. (Paris: Cerf, 1956–8); Hermas, *Le Pasteur*, trans. and
ed. Robert Joly, SC 53 (Paris: Cerf, 1958); Augustin d'Hippone, *Commentaire de la Première
Épître de S. Jean*, trans. and ed. Paul Agaësse, SC 75 (Paris: Cerf, 1961).

12 De Lubac, *Catholicisme*, 321.

13 De Lubac, *Catholicisme*, 322.

14 Henri de Lubac, introduction to Origène, *Homélies sur la Genèse*, SC 7, trans.
Louis Doutreleau (Paris: Cerf, 1944), 5–62; idem, introduction to Origène, *Homélies sur
l'Exode*, SC 16, trans. P. [Joseph] Fortier (Paris: Cerf, 1947), 7–75. Although further homily

of retrieval.[15] At the outset, de Lubac states that he does not wish to "defend" Origen but simply to understand him, recognizing the great intellectual and cultural distance that separated the third century from his own. Nevertheless, this quest for understanding includes identifying the accusations that were leveled against Origen—such as the Hellenizing of Christian theology, and departure from Scripture's literal truth—and weighing their merits. De Lubac is alert to how his subject, and his theological commitments, have been viewed by critics as corresponding with contemporary intellectual tendencies and figures, specifically David Strauss and his mythologizing of the literal descriptions of Jesus's Gospel miracles. Nonetheless, he warns against hasty judgment of Origen's project, urging the reader to inhabit his work and sense its rhythm. Making direct reference to modern exegesis, de Lubac likens this to springs welling up in ground rendered arid by rationalism and positivism. Origen, he suggests, can give greater theological confidence to readers of Scripture today.

Some of de Lubac's other methodological commitments are displayed, at least implicitly, in his presentation of Origen the man.[16] He acknowledges Origen's perception of himself as a defender of threatened faith as well as a protector of ordinary believers, recognizing that the questions he honestly addressed about the relation of classical and Christian learning, and how to interpret contradictory or difficult passages of Scripture, were live in the first half of the third century. De Lubac pointedly acknowledges that his subject appeals not to "Orthodoxy," which is so easily misunderstood as a fixed system of unchanging truth, but to tradition, which, although also a single whole, encompasses greater diversity. Then come two further counterintuitive assessments. Origen, de Lubac insists, was wary of the dangers of philosophy, likening it to several biblical images, such as the words of the serpent to Eve, the Israelite captivity in Egypt, offerings to idols, and the words of Solomon's wives, which drew the otherwise faithful king to worship other gods. Finally, de Lubac justifiably contends, Origen closely attended to Scripture's literal sense, using it as the foundation for the spiritual interpretation that was nevertheless compatible with it.

Further methodological points are made in the Exodus introduction.[17] Focusing on Origen's distinction between three senses of Scripture—the historical, the mystical, and the moral/spiritual—de Lubac observes that a single scriptural episode, phrase, or word may have several meanings. For instance, the flight out of Egypt may be read mystically, as an allegory for the passage from the shadows of error

---

volumes followed, Leviticus, to which de Lubac refers, was not in fact published until 1981. The two introductions provided the core material for all eight chapters of his *Histoire et esprit: l'intelligence de l'Écriture d'après Origène* (Paris: Aubier, 1950); *History and Spirit: The Understanding of Scripture according to Origen*, trans. Anne Englund Nash and Juvenal Merriell (San Francisco: Ignatius, 2007).

15 De Lubac, introduction to Origène, *Homélies sur la Genèse*, 6–8 and 62.

16 De Lubac, introduction to Origène, *Homélies sur la Genèse*, 26, 31, 37, and 41.

17 De Lubac, introduction to Origène, *Homélies sur l'Exode*, 7–8, 31–2, 34–42, and 52.

into the light of truth, or morally, as a flight from the current world into the age to come. To take another example, the distinction between the houses of Jacob, constructed out of solid material upon the Promised Land, and the tents of Israel, made from skin and repeatedly pitched and struck in the desert, may be taken as signifying spiritual perfection versus seeking, but equally, in historical terms, as the law in contrast with the prophets, or mystically, as the soul rather than the body. Such an exegetical mode, de Lubac avers, is eclectic, accommodating, and always open. It is further embodied in the principle that, just as the Old Testament provides images and narratives that are completed in the New Testament, so the New Testament offers analogous images and narratives that are consummated only in the age to come. This is different from the typological view of the relation between the Testaments, which would later become standard, based on dualistic supersession, in which the New Testament fully completes and validates what is found in the Old Testament. Origen undermines any notion that the New Testament is self-sufficient or complete. Indeed, de Lubac shows him upholding *three* Testaments, with the New Testament subordinated, in its turn, to a future truth of which it is itself merely an image. This double typology allows an understanding of spiritual perfection as requiring historical and personal time. While accepting that Origen does not conceive of revelation as subject to historical development, de Lubac suggests that he does propose a view of salvation history as both immanently begun and transcendentally completed that has quite different foundations from the large and simplistic immanentist schema of secular developmental theories. Finally, de Lubac draws from Origen a key interpretive principle that, in the 1940s, became his own: there is only one Spirit, which is of Christ, and any other human, historical, or political spirit that is unrelated to Christ is counterfeit.

De Lubac's description of his initial hopes for the *Sources* is illuminating. At the outset, he and his confreres wished to situate particular texts within the wider tradition, nourish the faith of the next generation. and combine ease of use with accessible pricing.[18] The Library of the Fathers series, edited in England by Edward Pusey, John Keble, and Charles Marriott, which theologically sustained the Oxford Movement, served as a model, although de Lubac hoped for volumes with a more acute critical perspective.[19] He envisaged several series, including some devoted to the theological literature of major modern languages, although adds self-deprecatingly that he "was not the Abbé Migne."[20] From the perspectives of both breadth and intended readership, the present-day English

---

18 De Lubac, *At the Service*, 317.

19 *A Library of Fathers of the Holy Catholic Church: Anterior to the Division of the East and West*, 51 vols. (London: Rivington and Oxford: Parker, 1838–81). This series formed the basis for the *Nicene and Post-Nicene Fathers of the Christian Church*, ed. Philip Scaff and Henry Wace, 28 vols. (Edinburgh: T & T Clark; Buffalo: Christian Literature Company, 1886–1900). See the discussion by Roger Pearse at The Tertullian Project, http://www.tertullian.org/fathers/lfc_list.htm (accessed April 13, 2016).

20 De Lubac, *At the Service*, 95n25. The *Sources* in fact came to comprise four series: Greek, Latin, Monastic, and Oriental.

language series that most closely correspond to what de Lubac originally had in mind are Newman Press's Ancient Christian Writers, which commenced in 1946 and was acquired by Paulist in 1962, and Paulist's counterpart Classics of Western Spirituality, which was founded in 1979 and, until 1989, jointly published in the United Kingdom by SPCK. However, the readership of the Sources was ultimately more scholarly, with texts presented in parallel rather than in translation alone.

Philosophical hermeneutics and Maurice Blondel

De Lubac's interest in patristics is well known, and, as has already been shown, has received a good deal of attention over the past two decades, even if Aidan Nichols does well to emphasize that he wished equally to promote earlier medieval theology.[21] Less clearly understood, however, is the contribution that philosophy made to his thought. De Lubac's reading of modern philosophers was extensive, extending to unlikely figures such as the anarchist Pierre-Joseph Proudhon, Karl Marx, and Friedrich Nietzsche. Moreover, in a recent study, Joshua Furnal has demonstrated his debt to Søren Kierkegaard. Examining explicit citations, allusions, turns of phrase, and even the communicative style that de Lubac adopts in *The Drama of Atheist Humanism*, *Paradoxes of Faith*, *The Discovery of God*, and *The Mystery of the Supernatural*, Furnal builds a persuasive case that Kierkegaard significantly shaped de Lubac's theology. Particular instances that Furnal identifies include the use of the category of paradox to capture the complexity of the nature–grace relation; a deep appreciation of inward faith as complementing institutional church belonging; and the taking seriously of existential concerns, such as the possibility that God does not exist. Furnal avers, "Rather than construing *ressourcement* as a purely patristic enterprise, de Lubac's engagement with Kierkegaard shows how the scope of *ressourcement* can be extended to include engagement with modern thought."[22]

De Lubac's project of retrieval undoubtedly extended to modern sources, which sharpen its critical edge. As was seen in the last section, the fact that the *Sources* contained a scholarly introduction indicates that they were recognized as demanding critical contextualization and interpretation. In de Lubac's constructive oeuvre, these are frequently achieved by the cumulative juxtaposition of contrasting sources and concepts from different eras in order to call modern secular assumptions into question, uncovering their genealogies in contestable theological suppositions and methods. For instance, in his work on the supernatural he shows how the modern idea of the subject as an autonomous, freely willing being emerged from the later medieval scholastic supposition that a realm of pure nature

---

21 Aidan Nichols, *Catholic Thought since the Enlightenment: A Survey* (Leominster: Gracewing, 1998), 137.

22 Joshua Furnal, *Catholic Theology after Kierkegaard* (Oxford: Oxford University Press, 2015), 104–43, here 105.

exists independently of divine grace, which was, in turn, grounded in a denial of the Augustinian acknowledgment that grace is needful even for purportedly purely natural human activities.[23] Similarly, in his study of Joachim of Fiore, de Lubac views the modern conception of history as developmental and as culminating in age of material satisfaction as an outworking of the Calabrian monk's belief that history would be consummated in a third age of the Spirit, which, by separating the work and reign of the Spirit from the reigns of the Father and the Son, amounted to a corruption of true Trinitarian doctrine.[24] By tracing genealogies such as these, de Lubac wished to demonstrate that classic Christian theology does not denigrate humans nor their communities, but, when correctly understood, contests the secular anthropologies, philosophies, and sociologies that themselves fail to cognize human dignity.

Returning to Kierkegaard, some twentieth-century Christian theologians have taken him as an ally. Nevertheless, his individualistic perspective on faith was, for de Lubac, ultimately unsatisfactory, even if it corrected excessively collectivist and objectivist approaches to belief. The philosopher who exerted the greatest positive influence on de Lubac was Maurice Blondel, whose philosophy of action shaped the content and method of de Lubac's theological hermeneutics of retrieval. De Lubac espoused Blondel's view, which the latter systematically expounded in his paradigm-shifting study *L'Action*, that philosophy has a unique negative role to play in preparing the mind for theology by demonstrating the falsity of premature resolutions of speculative problems. This negative philosophy leads the mind through an intellectual ascent in which the speculative problem in question—which was, in Blondel's case, the nature of human action—is set within a series of progressively wider concrete contexts that include family, country, and humanity. Eventually, however, even the universality of humanity is seen to provide an inadequate context because it supposes a merely immanent order of being. Philosophy thereby leads the mind to a threshold at which it recognizes the inevitable transcendence of the solution to speculative problems. At this point, theology assumes the leading role in offering resolutions, which draw on its distinctive sources of Scripture, tradition, and church teaching, to the problems that philosophical speculation has posed but has been unable to resolve.

How this progression works in practice may be seen with closer reference to the presenting problem of action. In considering this, Blondel distinguishes the willing will (*la volonté voulante*) from the willed will (*la volonté voulue*).[25] Expressing this more simply, there is a difference between what I will in the abstract and how I in fact exercise my will in concrete situations. This double willing cannot

---

23 Henri de Lubac, *Surnaturel: études historiques* (Paris: Aubier, 1946).

24 Henri de Lubac, *La Postérité spirituelle de Joachim de Flore*, 2 vols. (Paris: Lethielleux, 1979–81).

25 Maurice Blondel, *Action: Essay on a Critique of Life and a Science of Practice*, trans. Oliva Blanchette (Notre Dame, IN: University of Notre Dame Press, 1984), §§ 19, 42, 132; 32, 53, and 134–5.

be synthesized, Blondel argues, by the unaided effort of the actor. The conflict between the willing will and the willed will may be resolved, he contends, only by the activity of an absolute principle, which appears as the "forced presence of a new affirmation in consciousness."[26] This necessary presence orients action to the transcendent, thereby bringing together the human will and the divine will in what Blondel strikingly describes as a "secret nuptial."[27] In a person's action, a principle operating from outside of them is thereby at work within them, unifying their divided will. Blondel describes this principle as the "absolute," which is known and possessed in action through its reconciling power.[28]

That de Lubac's theology was philosophically impelled is suggested by the ordering of his posthumous *Oeuvres complètes* by Cerf, which follows that adopted by Jaca for his *Opera Omnia* in Italian translation, which began during his lifetime and about which he was consulted.[29] The opening volume is not a tome of patristic or early medieval exegesis but his frequently overlooked study *Sur les chemins de Dieu*, which was originally published in 1956 as an expanded version of a study that had first appeared in 1945.[30] Translated as *The Discovery of God*, this fundamentally Blondelian work reflects the Roman Catholic lay philosopher's deep and wide influence on French Jesuits of de Lubac's generation—including key figures in the *Sources* and *Théologie* series such as Fontoynont, Gaston Fessard, and Henri Bouillard—that continued during the years leading up to Blondel's death in 1949 and beyond.[31] Close to the opening of the book's second chapter, on the affirmation of God, which is pivotal for the book as a whole, de Lubac writes,

> Every human act, whether it is an act of knowledge or an act of the will, rests secretly upon God, by attributing meaning and solidity to the real upon which it is exercised. For God is the Absolute; and nothing can be thought without positing the Absolute in relating it to that Absolute; nothing can be willed

26 Blondel, *Action*, § 339, 314.

27 Blondel, *Action*, § 371, 342.

28 Blondel, *Action*, §§ 117, 378, 420; 122, 348, and 385.

29 Henri de Lubac, *Oeuvres completes*, 50 vols. (Paris: Cerf, 1999–); idem, *Opera Omnia*, 32 vols. (Milan: Jaca, 1975–2009).

30 Henri de Lubac, *Sur les chemins de Dieu* (Paris: Aubier, 1956); idem, *De la connaissance de Dieu* (Paris: Editions du Témoignage chrétien, 1945).

31 Peter Henrici, "La descendance blondelienne parmi les jesuites francais," in *Blondel et la philosophie française*, ed. Emmanuel Gabellieri and Pierre de Cointet (Paris: Parole et silence, 2007), 305–22; Fouilloux, *Une église*, 174–81; Jacques Guillet, "Courants théologiques dans la compagnie de Jésus en France" (1930–1939), in *Spiritualité, théologie et résistance: Yves de Montcheuil, théologien au macquis de Vercors*, ed. Pierre Bolle and Jean Godel (Grenoble: Presses universitaires de Grenoble, 1987), 35–41. For an overview, covering the period up to Pope John Paul II, William L. Portier, "Twentieth-Century Catholic Theology and the Triumph of Maurice Blondel," *Communio* 38 (2011): 103–37.

without tending towards the Absolute, nor valued unless weighed in terms of the Absolute.[32]

This description of human action could have been composed by Blondel: the absolute, who is God, is a transcendent presence at the heart of reality and provides the basis for human knowledge of that reality.[33]

The impact on de Lubac of Blondel's demonstration that natural human affirmation and action must be sustained by divine power has been justifiably stressed in French, German, and Italian scholarship.[34] In a letter of April 3, 1932, composed fourteen years before he was to publish *Surnaturel*, de Lubac wrote to Blondel about the hypothesis of a state of pure nature, which is the idea that a realm of being may, in principle, exist independently of divine grace.[35] De Lubac concurs with Blondel's contestation of the notion that any such realm may exist in reality, although on notably different grounds. Whereas Blondel had sought to demonstrate, from the standpoint of the philosopher, the insufficiency of any purely natural philosophy, de Lubac wished to prosecute Blondel's project from the side of theology. In a second letter to Blondel, he writes,

> If I let myself dream before you about the elaboration of a theology of the Supernatural, it was with the idea, not at all that you should do it, but that it could now be done because your philosophical work had paved the way . . . Although incompetent in pure philosophy, my ambition would be to demonstrate that one day, on the level of the most positive theology. The completion and implementation of the already voluminous file I have gradually put together awaits only a renewal of strength that Providence will perhaps not grant me.[36]

The open acknowledgment that Blondel's work "paved the way" for his own, several decades before it appeared, suggests that, at the least, the philosophical reorientation of scholasticism was the necessary prolegomenon to de Lubac's project of theological retrieval. Nevertheless, Blondel's philosophy also exerted an influence upon the content of de Lubac's theological retrieval, informing his broadly humanistic selection and interpretation of patristic and earlier

---

32 Henri de Lubac, *The Discovery of God* (Grand Rapids, MI: Eerdmans, 1996), 36.

33 Also de Lubac, *The Discovery*, 64–5, 85, 94, 106, and 134.

34 Jean-Pierre Wagner, *Henri de Lubac* (Paris: Cerf, 2001), 33–7; Antonio Russo, *Henri de Lubac: teologia e dogma nella storia: l'influsso di Blondel* (Rome: Studium, 1990), 275–317; Rudolf Voderholzer, *Meet Henri de Lubac: His Life and Work*, trans. Michael J. Miller (San Francisco: Ignatius, 1988), 122–8; Hans Urs von Balthasar and Georges Chantraine, *Le Cardinal de Lubac: l'homme et son oeuvre* (Paris: Lethielleux, 1983), 108–9. Recently, see also Francesca Aran Murphy, "The Influence of Maurice Blondel," in *T & T Clark Companion to Henri de Lubac*, ed. Jordan Hillebert (London: T & T Clark, 2017).

35 De Lubac, letter to Maurice Blondel of April 3, 1932, in *At the Service*, 183–5.

36 De Lubac, letter to Blondel of April 8, 1932, in *At the Service*, 187–8.

medieval theologians as refuting a theological anthropology based on the idea of pure nature with a view of humans as illumined and given their full dignity by God. Indeed, de Lubac goes so far as to identify Blondel's conception of Christian philosophy—"the synthesis of all knowledge, operating in the light of faith"—with that espoused by the Fathers of the church, contrasting this with Jacques Maritain's belief that philosophy could operate largely independently of faith as well as with Étienne Gilson's view of reason as generated solely by revelation.[37]

Returning to *The Discovery of God*, numerous uses of patristic texts are identifiable that give theological content to Blondel's philosophical thesis that the Absolute is implicit in all human acts of knowing and willing. To take just one example, de Lubac refers to Clement of Alexandria's notion of *prolepsis*, or anticipation, which he develops in book 2 of his *Stromateis*, as the confident faith upon which the life of the Spirit rests. Clement, who was a Greek convert to Christianity, concurred with his Gnostic opponents, Basilides and Valentinus, that philosophy is essential in the quest for true knowledge. However, he did not accept that philosophy could ever be the purely natural exercise of human ingenuity. Rather, the divine power is always present, and due to wisdom the "foreign philosophy we follow is in actual fact complete and true." There is no knowledge (apprehension) without an act of faith (preconception), which is the "spring of action, being the foundation of an act of choice based on thought . . . in a preliminary and actual demonstration."[38] De Lubac also deploys Clement in his critique of Nazism and communism, when he quotes an extended passage in which faith is presented not as destroying humanity but as exalting and completing it. He cites Clement's statement that the "sun of righteousness," "having snatched man out of the jaws of destruction raised him to the sky, transplanting corruption to the soil of incorruption, and transforming earth into heaven," thereby "granting to us the Father's truly great, divine and inalienable portion, making men divine by heavenly doctrine." Clement continues,

> Now the heavenly and truly divine love comes to men in this way, whenever somewhere in the soul itself the spark of true nobility, kindled afresh by the divine Word, is able to shine out; and, greatest thing of all, salvation itself runs side by side with sincere desire for it, will and life being, as we may say, yoked together.[39]

---

37 Henri de Lubac, "On Christian Philosophy," trans. Sharon Mollerus and Susan Clements, *Communio (US)* 19 (1992): 478–506, here 496–7.

38 Clement of Alexandria, *Stromateis* 2.2–4, trans. John Ferguson (Washington, DC: Catholic University of America Press, 1991), 160–8; see de Lubac, *Discovery*, 46–7.

39 Clement of Alexandria, *The Exhortation to the Greeks* 11 (Cambridge, MA: Harvard University Press, 1919), 248–51; also trans. as *Le Protreptique* by Claude Mondésert, SC 2 (Paris: Cerf, 1943); see Henri de Lubac, *The Drama of Atheist Humanism* (San Francisco: Ignatius, 1995), 23.

It is clear that, for de Lubac, the Gnostic confidence in the abilities of human reason unaided by faith evoked the confidence of the secularizing political ideologues of his own day. In contrast, the Christian Hellenism represented by Clement helped inspire his own cooperative understanding of the faith–reason relation.

An alternative narrative of the impact of Blondelian philosophy on de Lubac has been adopted by several Anglo-American commentators, who have tended to emphasize Blondel's theory of tradition with reference to his scriptural exegesis.[40] In broad terms, his view of tradition as mediating history and dogma may offer a middle path between an entirely historicist approach to Scripture, according to which its claims have no authority in the present day, and the extrinsicist view that Scripture comprises literal truths that may be directly, systematically, and unproblematically applied to current life. In opening the third and final section of his *History and Dogma*, which was published in 1904, Blondel presents tradition as a vitalizing power. Similarly to his concept of the absolute in *L'Action*, tradition must have an "original force, and a foundation of its own."[41] This immediately indicates that what he has in mind is more than a mere community of practice or reading that derives its consistency from internal relationships. Neither, however, is tradition reducible to the transmission of custom, or the spoken word, or written texts, or a system. Rather, tradition is primarily a lived reality, in Blondel's words an "experience always in act which enables it to remain in some respects master of the texts instead of being strictly subservient to them."[42]

Blondel does not, of course, offer any detailed prescriptions for reading Scripture: for these, it is necessary to turn to de Lubac's *Medieval Exegesis*. Within this, Blondel is cited only in general terms as offering, in the face of modern scientific exegesis, a reconception of the relation between history, dogma, and criticism analogous to that required in the face of the literalizing Victorine exegesis of the twelfth century, which anticipated it.[43] Nonetheless, his philosophy of action

---

40 William M. Wright, "Patristic Exegetical Theory and Practice in De Lubac and Congar," *New Blackfriars* 96 (2014): 61–73; Bryan C. Hollon, *Everything Is Sacred: Spiritual Exegesis in the Political Theology of Henri de Lubac* (Eugene, OR: Cascade, 2009), 97–100; Kevin L. Hughes, "The 'Fourfold Sense': De Lubac, Blondel and Contemporary Theology," *The Heythrop Journal* 42 (2001): 451–62; Susan K. Wood, *Spiritual Exegesis and the Church in the Theology of Henri de Lubac* (Edinburgh: T & T Clark, 1998), 18–21; also Marcellino D'Ambrosio, "Henri de Lubac and the Critique of Scientific Exegesis," *Communio* 19 (1992): 365–88.

41 Maurice Blondel, *The Letter on Apologetics, and History and Dogma*, trans. Alexander Dru (Grand Rapids, MI: Eerdmans, 1994), 264.

42 Blondel, *History*, 267.

43 Henri de Lubac, *Medieval Exegesis*, 4 vols. (Grand Rapids, MI: Eerdmans, 2000–), 3:646. For de Lubac's appraisal of Victorine exegesis, see Ryan McDermott, "Henri de Lubac's Genealogy of Modern Exegesis and Nicholas of Lyra's Literal Sense of Scripture," *Modern Theology* 29 (2013): 124–56.

endorses the tropological possibilities that de Lubac would elucidate in detail else-where, according to which Scripture impels the reader literally to turn away from the text to moral practice in the world.[44] Proving his passionate concern for mate-rial reality, Blondel writes that

> in obeying the precept we make the eminent truth which it expresses come down into us. That is true; but we also transform and raise into that truth the act it prescribes. The literal precept is, so to speak, more living and more spiritual than the spirit it takes hold of. We absorb it into ourselves, and it is the one that absorbs us into it.
>
> The true letter, then, is the very reality of the spirit. It manifests its inaccessible life to us in its depth; it communicates it to us so that we may engender it and make it live in ourselves.[45]

Blondel's description serves as a reminder that the spiritual, polyphonic exegesis that de Lubac excavates in no way absolves the reader from paying close attention to the literal sense. Neither does the spiritual reading of Scripture authorize the reader to ignore its moral implications. On the contrary, spiritual and literal read-ings engender each other. Only in literal and moral practice may spiritual readings of Scripture concerned with doctrine or eschatology become rooted in the mate-rial reality of life. Conversely, only by living out the word of Scripture may read-ers be assimilated into the truths to which Scripture points, thereby themselves becoming active exegetes of Scripture in the world.

Théologie: sources in fundamental theology

As de Lubac's extended introductions to the Origen volumes demonstrate, his pro-ject of retrieval extended beyond the presentation and translation of texts into their constructive engagement and deployment. He pursued these objectives through a total of eleven volumes in a book series. Named *Théologie*, this was founded by the Jesuit scholasticate at Fourvière, in tandem with the *Sources* and also under the direction of its rector, Fontoynont. A review of the initial volumes shows that some focused on specific aspects of patristic theologians or approaches, such as Clement of Alexandria and Gregory of Nyssa.[46] Published in the same year, however, was an historical study of Thomas Aquinas; an assessment, from the perspective of

---

44 De Lubac, *Medieval Exegesis*, 2:127–77.

45 Blondel, *Action*, § 420, 385–6.

46 Jean Daniélou, *Platonisme et théologie mystique: essai sur la doctrine spirituelle de saint Grégoire de Nysse*, Théologie 2 (Paris: Aubier, 1944); Claude Mondésert, *Clément d'Alexandrie: introduction à l'étude de sa pensée religieuse à partir de l'Ecriture*, Théologie 4 (Paris: Aubier, 1944).

fundamental theology, of the contemporary political and social situation; and de Lubac's own diachronic survey of the Eucharist, *Corpus Mysticum*.[47]

Ultimately, de Lubac would publish ten further volumes in the *Théologie* series. This was a greater number than any other author and illustrates his centrality to the series, even if he was not strictly among its editors. These volumes included his three studies, separated by a period of twenty years, on the relation of grace and nature. These were grounded in an essentially Augustinian view of the continued dependence of nature on God, although he contested the pessimistic Jansenistic construal of this relation, which had been theologically pervasive in France during the eighteenth and nineteenth centuries and arguably continued to shape much pastoral practice in de Lubac's own day.[48] In the early 1950s, there appeared de Lubac's collection of posthumous theological writings by his confrere Yves de Montcheuil, who had been shot by the Gestapo after being apprehended on a pastoral visit to members of the resistance; his study of the church, which was enriched with copious patristic imagery; and, very differently, the first of his volumes on Buddhism.[49] Also included were his study of Origen, which was based on the two *Sources* introductions, and three further volumes on patristic and medieval biblical exegesis.[50]

With the exception of the two-decade translation of Hans Urs von Balthasar's massive *Herrlichkeit*, which was completed only in 1983, the *Théologie* series ended in 1971 with a translated study of Paul Tillich.[51] De Lubac comments on the polymorphous character of the series, reporting that it was originally conceived by the fundamental theologian Henri Bouillard in partnership with the Lyons representative of the publishing house Éditions Spes. Bouillard indeed produced the opening volume of the series as well as served as its first secretary.[52] However, on learning of the venture, the management of Éditions Spes, who were located on the other side of the partition in Paris, raised objections. As a result, *Théologie* was merged with a series on patristics, which Daniélou had been

---

47 Henri Bouillard, *Conversion et grâce chez S. Thomas d'Aquin: étude historique*, Théologie 1 (Paris: Aubier, 1944); Gaston Fessard, *Autorité et bien commun*, Théologie 5 (Paris: Aubier, 1944); Henri de Lubac, *Corpus mysticum: l'eucharistie et l'Église au Moyen-Âge: étude historique*, Théologie 3 (Paris: Aubier, 1944).

48 *Surnaturel: études historiques*, Théologie 8 (1946); *Augustinisme et théologie moderne*, Théologie 63 (1965); *Le Mystère du surnaturel*, Théologie 64 (1965).

49 *Yves de Montcheuil: mélanges théologiques*, Théologie 9 (1951); *La Rencontre du bouddhisme et de l'Occident*, Théologie 24 (1952); *Méditation sur l'Église*, Théologie 27 (1953).

50 *Histoire et esprit: l'intelligence de l'Écriture d'après Origène*, Théologie 16 (1950); *Exégèse médiévale: les quatre sens de l'écriture*, Théologie 41, 42, 59 (1959–63).

51 Carl J. Armbruster, *La Vision de Paul Tillich*, Théologie 80 (Paris: Aubier, 1971); Hans Urs von Balthasar, *La Gloire et la croix: les aspects esthétiques de la Révélation*, trans. Robert Givord, Hélène Bourboulon, and Henri Engelmann, Théologie 61, 74, 81–6, 8 vols. (Paris: Aubier, 1965–83).

52 De Lubac, *At the Service*, 30–1.

planning in conjunction with Aubier. Daniélou thus provided the second volume of the expanded series. De Lubac recalls with approval Bouillard's description of the "twofold aspiration" behind their enterprise: to "go to the sources of Christian doctrine" and to "find in it the truth of our life." Theology, de Lubac continues, while properly immersed in the divine Word, needs to take account of the "movement of human thought."

Despite noting the "honourable course" of the series, de Lubac writes that, "at a later time, when it might have played a fortunate and efficacious role in the renewal of the Church . . . diverse influences, about which I prefer to remain silent, came to condemn it to a slow death. A wind of destruction had blown."[53] What were the influences to which de Lubac refers? He delivered his most candid public assessment of these in 1969, four years after the conclusion of the Second Vatican Council, in an address at the University of Saint Louis. Alluding to the student unrest that had peaked the previous year, he states that it is no surprise that the crisis of the church is also a university crisis. In both the church and the academy, he protests, past achievements and traditions, as well as the institutions themselves, are misrepresented, with a spirit of confrontation and criticism prevailing. Tradition is felt to be a "weight to be carried" rather than a "living, actualizing force."[54] To combat this, de Lubac continues, what is required is not novelty but renewal. The idea of renewal has, he protests, been variously misused to justify a failure to preach the Gospel in deference to a religious pluralism, to inaugurate hasty ecumenical projects that disrespect ecclesial distinctiveness, to evacuate the liturgy of its mystery, and to denigrate the vowed religious life. True renewal instead requires a reengagement with historical sources. Strikingly, de Lubac implicitly presents his own project of retrieval as part of this necessary response. "I see these reflections," he writes, "as a pressing invitation to carry through a vast program of research which, despite an incredible mass of work too little known and poorly popularized among the faithful, has not yet attained all the fullness or the hardiness desired."[55]

By bringing together the projects of Bouillard and Daniélou, the *Théologie* series combined fundamental theology and patristics. De Lubac himself evidently approved of this method, and many of the earlier volumes first published within the series have become classics. However, its wide breadth of coverage led to difficulties in ensuring a consistent approach to the integration of historical sources with constructive perspectives. Even de Lubac's own contributions to the series ranged from his Origen volume, which was built around material previously published in the *Sources*, to a study of a non-Christian religion. However, notwithstanding

---

53 De Lubac, *At the Service*, 31. Also Georges Chantraine and Marie-Gabrielle Lemaire, *Henri de Lubac*, 4 vols. (Paris: Cerf, 2007–), 4:211–19.

54 Henri de Lubac, "The Church in Crisis," *Theology Digest* 17 (1969): 312–25, here 315.

55 De Lubac, "The Church," 323. See also his critiques of both the French bishops and the French Jesuits in Chantraine and Lemaire, *Henri de Lubac*, 4:438–9, 490–2, 509, 513, and 518–25.

his own assessment of the series, its breadth points to a shifting conception of the historical boundaries and hermeneutical methods of retrieval.

Conclusion: texts, philosophy and theology

In his letter to Blondel quoted earlier, de Lubac rightly stated that his "voluminous file" of medieval and patristic texts comprised but one element of his retrieval project. Blondel's philosophy, as de Lubac himself admitted to the philosopher of Aix, "paved the way" for his own theology and, as has been shown, formed a continuing thread within it. Moreover, as de Lubac also here made clear, his was indeed a properly theological project: the concept of the supernatural did not emerge fully formed from historic texts.

Étienne Fouilloux suggests that, among de Lubac and his confreres at Fourvière, the Greek Fathers served as a foil for the promotion of a Blondelian theological anthropology.[56] It is certainly true that, in *The Discovery of God*, for reasons of expedience Blondel is cited as much via allusion as by explicit reference. However, de Lubac himself states,

> Every time, in our West, that Christian renewal has flourished, in the order of thought as in that of life (and the two orders are always connected), it has flourished under the sign of the Fathers . . . In a very large part, in all the sectors touched by the Council, this *aggiornamento* was made possible by the patristic renewal of the last fifty years.[57]

De Lubac himself had a lifelong passion for patristic texts, and it seems difficult to maintain that their value to him was merely instrumental. Rather, as has been argued in the course of this chapter, Blondel provided the philosophical hermeneutic that enabled de Lubac and his confreres to recover a conception of the relation between self, God, and world that modern theology had lost. This prepared fertile ground for a philosophically inflected patristic theology.

In an address delivered during an ecumenical visit to Athens and Crete in 1969, in the later period of his work, de Lubac recognized that retrieval comes in waves. His own efforts followed the Latin appropriation of the Greeks, the Carolingian recasting of both, the so-called twelfth-century renaissance, Aquinas's synthesis of previous sacred and secular thought, the humanist movement, the Catholic Reform in France (in which the theology of Augustine was prominent), the Tübingen School, and the Oxford Movement.[58] Nevertheless, successive generations draw out of the tradition sources and interpretive foci for constructive theology in their

---

56 Fouilloux, *Une église*, 187 and 189–90.

57 De Lubac, *At the Service*, 317–18 and 319.

58 Henri de Lubac, "L'actualité des Pères de l'Église," in *Paradoxe et mystère de l'Église* (Paris: Cerf, 2010), 385–93.

own context. In his address, de Lubac identifies three theological topics to which the patristic retrieval could make a positive contribution: scriptural interpretation, doctrine, and ecumenism. In expounding the last of these, he sees as key the doctrines of the Eucharist, and of eucharistic ecclesiology, especially with regard to Roman Catholic–Orthodox relations. In language that resonates with scholarship today, de Lubac argues for the theological commonality of the Latin and Greek traditions. "The Latins," he wrote, "were enriched by the Greeks. But this enrichment was not without consequences. When one examines the Latin tradition a little more closely, as it continues into the Middle Ages, one sees that it is far closer to the Greek tradition on key points than common opinion supposes."[59]

The most bruising critiques of de Lubac and his confreres focused not on their retrieval project as such but upon the theological methodology that was presumed to follow from it, as presented in the *Théologie* series.[60] Michel Labourdette praised many aspects of the *Sources*, even if desiring a scientific rigor that was not always present in the early volumes. However, he contended that the departure of the series from scholasticism was inexcusable, because that alone "represents Christian thought in its truly *scientific* state."[61] Contesting what he regarded as incursions of subjectivism and relativism into this systematically ordered domain, he argued that theological progress would instead be made by further developing and promoting the scholastic synthesis, including by treating God as an object of knowledge rather than as a divine subject. Another Dominican, Réginald Garrigou-Lagrange, critically addressed what he presumed to be a new, Blondelian conception of truth as conformity not to speculative objects of the understanding but to mental reality and life.[62] The Thomist philosophy of being had, he claimed, been replaced by phenomenology and the philosophy of action, with the doctrines of original sin and transubstantiation profoundly undermined in consequence, because the categories on which they depended were thought to have lost their validity. The overall result, Garrigou-Lagrange suggested, was the return to a modernist understanding of theology as no more than a function of religious experience.

These critiques now seem excessive, and for good reasons. Patristic and earlier medieval sources are rightly viewed as connecting theology to its historical roots and doctrinal topics in ways that, nevertheless, are not dissociated from

---

59 De Lubac, "L'actualité," 392–3. For a recent correlate, see Lewis Ayres, *Augustine and the Trinity* (Cambridge: Cambridge University Press, 2010).

60 For an excellent discussion of the context of these critiques, which draws on archival materials, Jürgen Mettepenningen, *Nouvelle théologie—New Theology: Inheritor of Modernism, Precursor of Vatican II* (London: T & T Clark, 2010), 101–14; also Brian Daley, "The *Nouvelle Théologie* and the Patristic Revival: Sources, Symbols and the Science of Theology," *International Journal of Systematic Theology* 7 (2005): 362–82.

61 M. Michel Labourdette, "La théologie et ses sources," *Revue Thomiste* 46 (1946): 353–71; italics in original.

62 Réginald Garrigou-Lagrange, "La nouvelle théologie où va-t-elle?," *Angelicum* 23 (1946): 126–45, which the *Revue Thomiste* had declined to publish owing to its severity.

experience. Diverse portions of de Lubac's vast corpus certainly find different balances of ecclesial and personal concerns. In particular, his studies of the church and of the Eucharist support specifically Roman Catholic claims, whereas his work on faith and reason speaks to an ecumenical audience and even beyond church boundaries. In either case, however, few would question de Lubac's positive impact on the theology of recent decades. The scholasticate at Fourvière closed in 1974, with its theological teaching activity relocated to the Centre Sèvres in Paris. Two years later, the Lyons province of the Jesuits itself ceased to exist, with the creation of a single province encompassing the whole of France. However, the *Sources Chrétiennes* now comprise 600 volumes, with the theological importance of this ongoing collaborative achievement surpassing even that of de Lubac's own constructive corpus. There is currently greater interest in his theology of retrieval than ever before.

Part IV

THEOLOGICAL SOURCES

Chapter 9

SCRIPTURE: THREE MODES OF RETRIEVAL

Michael C. Legaspi

Among the many tasks facing theologies of retrieval, the rehabilitation of scriptural interpretation is surely one of the most essential. Many biblical scholars have begun in recent years to disengage their work from familiar frameworks like those used in historical reconstruction, literary analysis, and critical theory and to orient their efforts, instead, toward theology. After a long estrangement from dogmatics, biblical interpreters enacting a "theological turn" have begun to study the Bible as a profoundly theological work.[1] Many scholars have not only come to recognize the limitations of historical criticism but also, more importantly, to measure its exegetical results against those arising from newer, more compelling articulations of the Bible's coherence as a theological witness. The discipline of biblical studies now includes a growing cadre of "exegetes and historians" who, according to one prominent retrievalist, "often prove more congenial and valuable neighbours than critical philosophers."[2] My aim in this chapter is to consider how biblical scholars and theologians in recent years have approached the task of theological reading. In what sense have they become, as John Webster says, good "neighbours" to the retrievalist enterprise? And, relatedly, what are the prospects for a mode of biblical scholarship decoupled from critical orthodoxies and directed toward an authentic Christian understanding of reality? In what follows, I discuss theological exegesis of the Bible under three headings: biblical theology, theological interpretation, and metacritical interpretation. The first two correspond to loose affiliations of scholars working more or less within shared paradigms, animated by common concerns, and engaged in work that is intended in various ways to serve Christian churches and communities. The third is a rather unsatisfactory name that I have applied to the interpretive program advocated by Joseph Ratzinger in various writings,

---

1 On a "theological turn" in biblical studies, see, for example, Craig Bartholomew, introduction to *"Behind" the Text: History and Biblical Interpretation*, ed. Craig Bartholomew C. Stephen Evans, Mary Healy, and Murray Rae (Grand Rapids, MI: Zondervan: 2003), 10–12.

2 John Webster, "Theologies of Retrieval," in *The Oxford Handbook of Systematic Theology*, ed. Kathryn Tanner, John Webster, and Iain Torrance (Oxford: Oxford University Press, 2007), 596.

most notably his well-known 1988 lecture on the crisis of biblical interpretation.[3] It would be odd (and difficult) to ignore the first two, that is, to discuss modes of scriptural retrieval without considering the work of scholars identifiable either with biblical theology or theological interpretation. Both groups have yielded valuable accounts and examples of theological reading, and, taken together, they afford an indispensable view of where things stand. I include here a discussion of Ratzinger, not because his proposal has spawned new approaches with numerous adherents[4] but because it offers a distinctive way to address what seems to me an essential task: to produce a model of theological reading that acknowledges the legacy of the Enlightenment without capitulating to it.

The title of this chapter mirrors the title of a 1999 essay by George Lindbeck, which also refers to "three modes of retrieval."[5] In this piece, Lindbeck offers a theoretical critique of work done by "scriptural scholars engaged in the post-critical retrieval of classic scriptural hermeneutics."[6] By "classical" hermeneutics, Lindbeck means interpretation that is based on an understanding of the Bible as a single book with a coherent "realistic" story, one whose meaning, though adumbrated in the Old Testament, is fully manifest in the "identity and character of Jesus and Jesus's God." So understood, the scriptural story becomes a framework, a total way of understanding things, a text that absorbs the world.[7] Lindbeck identifies three models by which to retrieve the classical hermeneutic, which are based on formal, second-order hermeneutical goals or interpretive keys. The first model interprets for witness, seeking to understand the testimony of the biblical canon to divine reality (Brevard Childs). The second is concerned, ultimately, with explicating the narrationally structured symbolic world of the Bible (Richard Hays). And the third approaches the Bible as divine discourse (Nicholas Wolterstorff). With characteristic insight and clarity, Lindbeck reviews what he sees as the strengths and weaknesses of each model, arguing that "all three are needed and that when taken in isolation, as is done by Childs and others, they wrongly appear mutually exclusive and contradictory."[8]

---

3 Joseph Cardinal Ratzinger, "Biblical Interpretation in Crisis: On the Question of the Foundations and Approaches of Exegesis Today," in *Biblical Interpretation in Crisis: The Ratzinger Conference on Bible and Church*, ed. Richard John Neuhaus (Grand Rapids, MI: Eerdmans, 1989), 1–23.

4 For examples of works inspired by Ratzinger's call to produce a "criticism of criticism," see Scott W. Hahn and Benjamin Wiker, *Politicizing the Bible: The Roots of Historical Criticism and the Secularization of Scripture* (New York: Crossroad, 2013); Jeffrey Morrow, "The Politics of Biblical Interpretation: A Criticism of Criticism," *New Blackfriars* 91 (2010): 528–45.

5 George Lindbeck, "Postcritical Canonical Interpretation: Three Modes of Retrieval," in *Theological Exegesis: Essays in Honor of Brevard S. Childs*, ed. Christopher Seitz and Kathryn Greene-McCreight (Grand Rapids, MI: Eerdmans, 1999).

6 Lindbeck, "Postcritical Canonical Interpretation, 26.

7 Lindbeck, "Postcritical Canonical Interpretation, 29–30.

8 Lindbeck, "Postcritical Canonical Interpretation, 26.

Despite the conciliatory note struck here, Lindbeck concedes that agreement among retrievalists on the fruitfulness of premodern strategies and the substance of the tradition (Christological, Trinitarian, anti-Marcionite) is matched by the level of *disagreement* concerning how, specifically, to derive theological judgments from Scripture. The unfortunate result, notes Lindbeck, is a "methodological chaos" that "shifts authority, contrary to the intentions of ecclesially oriented interpreters, from the Bible to private preference."[9] An important question, then, is how to adjudicate the methodological debate and avoid fragmentation and, ultimately, solipsism. This is where Lindbeck's third model, presented by the philosopher Wolterstorff, comes in.[10] In describing a different set of three models, however, I do not intend to stake out disparate methodologies and adjudicate among them. The goals here are more modest: to mark an emerging distinction (or division) between biblical theology and theological interpretation, which has become more salient and significant in recent years, and to hear what is, in my view, an appropriate note of caution for the retrievalist enterprise.

Biblical theology

To the strictures placed on biblical interpretation by the canons of modern criticism, theologies of retrieval do not so much offer hearty resistance as semicordial indifference. What energy might have been used to justify a professional interest in theology is used, instead, to get on with the task of reading the Bible for the church. For *biblical scholars* who have embraced this task, however, the question of methodological warrant remains crucial. The legacies of the Enlightenment and nineteenth-century versions of historicism continue to exercise a profound influence. Among such legacies, mandates to root specific interpretations of the Bible in analyses of its textual (as opposed to merely verbal) character and to reconcile them with what scientific reconstructions disclose about the ancient contexts of the Bible are the most obvious. It should be noted that historical criticism in this

---

9 Lindbeck, "Postcritical Canonical Interpretation, 40.

10 Lindbeck commends as a possible solution the proposal of Wolterstorff as presented in his *Divine Discourse: Philosophical Reflections on the Claim that God Speaks* (Cambridge and New York: Cambridge University Press, 1995). For both the "witness" and the "symbolic world" model, "choices between alternative patterns of canonical construal are intratextually arbitrary; one must exit the text in order to find grounds for decision; and as to how one does that they seem to have no hermeneutically usable answers" (Lindbeck, "Postcritical Canonical Interpretation," 44). By understanding Scripture as a set of writings appropriated by God in accord with a communicative purpose (divine authorial intent), the interpreter is able to decide "what speech acts are being performed by the locutions (the utterances of texts)" (48). Lindbeck does not elaborate on the practical reflexes of interpreting for divine discourse.

period was, in its way, a form of retrieval, a way of rescuing the Bible from theological obscurantism and recovering it as a witness to a vital human past. The goal was to receive the Bible once again as an enlivening foundation for modern culture. Biblical theology, while reckoning with the theological and historical character of the Bible, aimed at just such a recovery. The term "biblical theology" predates the Enlightenment, but it was in the late eighteenth century that it received definitive formulation as a critical, historical subdiscipline of biblical studies.[11] It is customary to cite Johann Philipp Gabler (1753–1826) and his 1787 inaugural address at Altdorf as the classic statement of, if not the point of origin for, the distinction between biblical theology and systematic theology, by which the former furnishes historical materials to the latter.[12] As Krister Stendahl later summarized the Gablerian division of labor: systematic theologians are concerned with what the Bible *means*, biblical theologians with what it *meant*.[13] Beginning in its formative period—the generation of Anton Friedrich Büsching (1724–1793) and Johann Salomo Semler (1725–1791)—biblical theology has been distinguished principally by two things: the historical quest to describe accurately *theology contained within the Bible* and the conviction that this descriptive effort differs in important respects from the conceptual, normative work of systematic theologians.

Biblical theology has been defined, then, as much by what it is as by what it is not, by what it does as by what it does not do. In a rather pointed synthesis, Gerhard Ebeling describes the adversarial relationship that has long characterized biblical theology and systematics, especially in the German context. In staking out their independence, biblical theologians defined their scientific, historical work over against the hapless speculations of dogmatic theologians. According to Ebeling, their discipline derived "its vitality from its detachment from dogmatics." Biblical theologians, closer to the text and therefore to the "real, original, and pure source of theological knowledge," insisted that dogmatics "bow to the results of historical study of the Bible" and "answer for its use of scripture" at the bar of historical criticism.[14] Meanwhile, Biblical theology evinced its own "strong dogmatic interest" as practitioners worked under the guidance of submerged theological frameworks ranging from the search for timeless truths among the ruins of history (rationalism) to the search within history itself for patterns of meaning (historicism), and options in between.[15] A key feature of biblical theology in this

---

11 For a review of this history, see Gerhard Ebeling, "The Meaning of 'Biblical Theology,'" in Gerhard Ebeling, *Word and Faith*, trans. James W. Leitch (Philadelphia: Fortress, 1963), 81–91. The essay first appeared in *Journal of Theological Studies* 6 (1955): 210–25.

12 Johann Philipp Gabler, "De justo discrimine theologiae biblicae et dogmaticae regundisque recte utriusque finibus," in J. P. Gabler, *Kleinere theologische Schriften*, ed. Theodor August Gabler and Johann Gottfried Gabler (Ulm: Stettin, 1831), 179–98.

13 Krister Stendahl, "Biblical Theology, Contemporary," in *Interpreter's Dictionary of the Bible*, ed. G. A. Buttrick, 4 vols. (New York: Abingdon, 1961), 1:418–32.

14 Ebeling, "Meaning," 89.

15 Ebeling, "Meaning," 89–90.

historical, analytical mode was to problematize the theological unity of the Bible and, indeed, the internal unity of both the Old and the New Testament. Inasmuch as biblical theology seeks to produce accounts of theology contained within the Bible, it attends to the voices of discrete books, figures, and texts in a way that renders the theological unity of larger canonical units (e.g., the Pentateuch or the Gospels) obscure, tenuous, or epiphenomenal to varying degrees. To this observation, Ebeling adds two more. If the interest of the interpreter lies principally in the religious–historical background of theological statements, then material outside the canon may be more useful in particular exegetical cases than material within the Bible. Moreover, the mistaken belief that ancient authors were interested in conveying revealed truths in propositional form is, like belief in the sacredness of the canon, also seen as unhelpful: "what the Bible testifies to and strives for is not theology, but something that happens to man in God's dealings with the world."[16] Instead of searching within the canon, the critical biblical theologian turns to the ancient world. Instead of constructing theology (classically understood), he or she describes the conditions of religious experience.

Given the historic aversion of biblical theology to features of the classical position—explicit normativity, the theological unity of the Bible, the boundaries of the canon, and even the concept of theology—it would seem that biblical theology has little to offer a theological retrieval of Scripture. Ebeling, for his part, is convinced that it does. He concludes his incisive discussion of biblical theology with a somewhat surprising commendation of historical criticism as a form of loyal opposition to dogmatics, a necessary irritant that serves to clarify the "hermeneutic problem" at the heart of Christian faith ("inquiring into the inner unity of the manifold testimony of the Old or New Testament") and to set up the "task of theology" as the Reformers understood it.[17] Fifteen years after Ebeling's essay first appeared in print, Childs stepped forward with a different (though in some ways sympathetic) program for biblical theology in his groundbreaking *Biblical Theology in Crisis*.[18] The book is not a direct response to Ebeling or the German critical tradition with which Ebeling is largely concerned.[19] A step removed from this tradition, *Biblical Theology in Crisis* considers instead the postwar American biblical theology movement, which had aimed to overcome the liberal–conservative stalemate that resulted from unresolved conflicts originating in the fundamentalist–modernist controversies of the 1910s and 1920s. In an effort to demonstrate the relevance of the Bible to "modern man," proponents of the American biblical theology movement engaged churches and seminaries; shed the older, critical aversion to theology; and championed the recovery of the

---

16 Ebeling, "Meaning," 93.

17 Ebeling, "Meaning," 95.

18 Brevard S. Childs, *Biblical Theology in Crisis* (Philadelphia: Westminster Press, 1970).

19 Childs, however, does respond directly to Ebeling's essay in his *Biblical Theology of the Old and New Testaments: Theological Reflection of the Christian Bible* (Minneapolis: Fortress, 1992), 6–9.

Bible's unity. Lest the movement be seen as a return to the fundamentalist position, however, proponents emphasized the value of historical criticism. They argued that historical criticism was useful, indeed indispensable, in discerning God's self-revelation. As revelation takes place, above all, in concrete historical events, archaeology, philology, and comparative history are necessary to understand more clearly the *magnalia dei* and the distinctiveness of Israel. The synthesis of historical criticism and orthodox theological language, however, would not hold. Childs chronicles the gradual erosion of the movement's key tenets in the 1950s, coordinating its final demise to definitive critiques by Langdon Gilkey (1961) and James Barr (1963).[20]

In *Biblical Theology in Crisis*, Childs begins with a postmortem on a dying American movement and ends with a radically new proposal for doing biblical theology, one centered on the biblical canon. More specifically, Childs takes the canon as the context within which to discern the dialectical relationship between the Old and New Testaments. To speak of canon is not only to affirm the church's judgment that the two, taken together, constitute sacred Scripture. It is also to exclude from the exegetical task conceptual frameworks that are imported from elsewhere to decide what, in Scripture, is normative. For Childs, "the appeal to canon understands Scripture as a vehicle of divine reality, which indeed encountered an ancient people in the historical past, but which continues to confront the church through the pages of Scripture."[21] In order to understand the Bible rightly as Christian Scripture, it is essential, then, that one read it in the authoritative form recognized by the church, in light of the theological dynamics that arise, specifically, from attention to canonical form. It is unhelpful, therefore, to seek to extract "theological data" from the Bible by recognizing some "form of positivity behind the text, such as *Heilsgeschichte*, language phenomenology, or in a mode of consciousness illustrated by the text, such as authentic existence or the like."[22] The slight tone of exasperation in Childs's list of examples here suggests that, in his view, the liberal strategy of theological correlation, failing to arrive at a satisfying solution, has only yielded a string of proposals destined to follow one another in a futile, indefinite succession. Older, critical approaches, in avoiding the necessary and obvious context for reading Scripture, have produced an exotic menagerie of methods only to fall short of the simple truth. Daniel Driver, in his excellent study of Childs, summarizes Childs's "career thesis"

---

20 Childs, *Crisis*, 51–87; on Gilkey and Barr, see 64–66. Both Gilkey and Barr targeted the movement's use of history as a theological category. Gilkey ("Cosmology, Ontology, and the Travail of Biblical Language," *Journal of Religion* 41 (1961): 194–205) demonstrated the incoherence of language used to describe historical events—at one level orthodox and theological but, at another, denuded and naturalistic. Barr ("Revelation through History in the Old Testament and in Modern Theology," *Princeton Seminary Bulletin* 56 (1963): 4–14) argued that the revelatory history touted by the movement was an abstraction ill-suited to much, if not most, of the biblical text.

21 Childs, *Crisis*, 100.

22 Childs, *Crisis*, 102.

as follows: "the historically shaped canon of scripture, in its two discrete witnesses, is a christological rule of faith that in the church, by the action of the Holy Spirit, accrues textual authority."[23] The canon, though singular, is manifestly dual. Neither Testament stands alone; neither subsumes the other. As discrete parts of the canon, they invite interpretations that do justice to the dialectic witness of Scripture to Christ. This, in turn, requires that the integrity of both Testaments be respected: the Old Testament "must be heard on its own terms," and the New Testament understood not just as "an extension of the Old, nor a last chapter in an epic tale" but as that which "bears its totally new witness in terms of the old, and thereby transforms" it.[24] In practice, this means that historical criticism has an important, though qualified, role to play: "There is the full necessity for taking seriously the original context of every biblical passage."[25] Interpretation cannot rest here, however, as the reality of the canon demands theological integration.

A description of the full development and reception of Childs's biblical theology lies beyond the scope this chapter. The point here is that Childs, both as heir to and proponent of biblical scholarship in its Continental and Anglophone modes,[26] succeeded in formulating an influential program for biblical theology that establishes continuity between "theological forces" at work in the composition of the Bible and the "theological context in which the tradition continues to function authoritatively for today."[27] To the consternation of figures like James Barr, Childs dispensed with the old Gablerian division of labor.[28] Partly for this reason, and partly because Childs directs attention to the "inner logic of the faith" and divine realities to which the Scriptures bear witness, the biblical theology of Childs offers a promising mode of retrieval.[29] It would be wrong, of course, to identify biblical theology solely with the work of Childs, but I believe he deserves a prominent (if not preeminent) place in the discussion because of the way he has helped others follow the logic of historical method to its inescapable theological conclusion: namely, that the Bible, ultimately, is what it is by virtue of its shaping and transmission within and by communities of faith.[30] The judgment is

---

23 Daniel R. Driver, *Brevard Childs, Biblical Theologian: For the Church's One Bible* (Tübingen: Mohr Siebeck, 2010), 4.

24 Childs, *Biblical Theology*, 78.

25 Childs, *Crisis*, 112–13.

26 On the place of Childs within the German and Anglo-Saxon contexts, see Driver, *Childs*, 35–79.

27 Childs, *Biblical Theology*, 71.

28 James Barr, *The Concept of Biblical Theology: An Old Testament Perspective* (Minneapolis: Fortress, 1999), 37–9, 47–51, and 378–438.

29 Lindbeck, "Three Modes," 32.

30 In different but compatible ways (not necessarily indebted to Childs, however), James Kugel and Jon Levenson have demonstrated that this is the case mutatis mutandis in Judaism. Kugel makes the point programmatically in "The Bible in the University," in *The Hebrew Bible and Its Interpreters*, ed. William Henry Propp, Baruch Halpern,

borne out by biblical scholars who articulate the coherence of Scripture through other strategies. Without the same explicit attention to canon, Richard Hays, for example, demonstrates how a rehabilitated understanding of narrative (in the wake of Hans Frei) can serve the cause of theological integration by allowing exegetes attuned to biblical intratextuality to heed and synthesize the distinctive voices of discrete writers and texts. In a slightly different vein, N. T. Wright finds in the explication of historically grounded worldviews reflected in the Bible the resources necessary to clarify the grand story that unifies Scripture.[31] Attention to the symbolic world of the Bible—whether reflected in canonical shaping, intratextual narrativity, or historically grounded worldviews—lies at the heart of retrieval in a biblical–theological mode.

Theological interpretation

If the chief impediment to scriptural retrieval among academic interpreters has been the obscuring effects of modern criticism, then it remains to ask whether biblical theology, for all of its efforts at theological integration, still (in a manner of speaking) leaves the fox in the henhouse. That is, to what extent does biblical theology reflect the habits and outlook of a scholarly mode still captive to critical philosophy and its "comprehensive metaphysical and epistemological framework?"[32] Just as the last two decades have seen the development of biblical theologies that

and David Noel Freedman Eisenbrauns (Winona Lake, IN: Eisenbrauns, 1990): 143–65, and in the conclusion to his *How to Read the Bible: A Guide to Scripture, Then and Now* (New York: Free Press, 2007), 662–89. Levenson writes in his famous essay ("Why Jews Are Not Interested in Biblical Theology," in *The Hebrew Bible, the Old Testament, and Historical Criticism: Jews and Christians in Biblical Studies*, ed. Jon Levenson (Louisville: Westminster John Knox, 1993), 33–61) that "[o]ne pursues either Jewish biblical theology or Christian biblical theology, but not both, for the term 'biblical' has a different reference for the Jew and the Christian" (38). The significance of the pressures exerted on exegesis by differing Jewish and Christian Bibles is a theme amply demonstrated in Levenson's works, for example: *The Death and Resurrection of the Beloved Son* (New Haven, CT: Yale University Press, 1993) and *Resurrection and Restoration of Israel: The Ultimate Victory of the God of Life* (New Haven, CT: Yale University Press, 2006).

31   For a helpful summation of the views of Hays, Wright, and others, see Edward W. Klink III and Darian R. Lockett, *Understanding Biblical Theology* (Grand Rapids, MI: Zondervan, 2012). Looking at the extent to which these approaches emphasize "history" or "theology" as controlling categories, Klink and Lockett place "BT 1: Historical Description" (James Barr) on one end and "BT 5: Theological Construction" (Francis Watson) on the other. In the middle are three additional types: "BT 2: History of Redemption" (D. A. Carson), "BT 3: Worldview-Story" (Hays and Wright), and "BT 4: Canonical Approach" (Childs). I recommend the survey for its incisive commentary and helpful taxonomy.

32   Webster, "Theologies of Retrieval," 585.

are more congenial to the retrievalist enterprise, they have also witnessed the rise of a movement distinct from biblical theology, one oriented quite differently toward the task of theological reading: theological interpretation. While overlaps and areas of agreement between biblical theology and theological interpretation are significant—for example, dissatisfaction with historical criticism as tradition-ally practiced, an affirming attitude toward the Christian theological tradition, and a desire to produce work that is useful to Christian churches—disagreements between the two have brought important considerations to the fore. The most obvious one (though, perhaps, the least interesting) is the role that reconstruc-tions of history or original historical context are given to play in understanding the Bible theologically. It is true, of course, that biblical theology, with its roots in the modern discipline of biblical studies, is characterized by a robust interest in what philology, textual criticism, and different modes of historical analysis reveal about various parts of the Bible. A common thread uniting scholars from Gabler to Childs and Hays is doing justice to distinctive or discrete voices within the Bible. For instance, a biblical theologian will not merely be concerned with the New Testament but also, in particular, with (say) the Gospels, and not just the Gospels but, at a more refined level, with the literary–historical personality of Luke-Acts in comparison with those of Matthew, Mark, or the Johannine litera-ture. And so mutatis mutandis for Old Testament voices as well. But as the work of Childs shows, attention to backgrounds and formative processes need not entail a denigration of the classic Christian theological synthesis or an indiffer-ence to contemporary ecclesial theology. Indeed, it may direct attention to them in new and insightful ways. By way of contrast, theological interpretation has no real stake in the regulation or deregulation of historical contextualization per se. What matters is the separable assumption that historical difference can only be overcome by recourse to some *tertium quid* furnished by philosophical hermen-eutics or social theory. This assumption is one that theological interpreters and many biblical theologians reject.

The deeper criticisms of biblical theology offered by theological interpreters have to do with theology not history. As Stephen Fowl writes in his landmark work, *Engaging Scripture: A Model for Theological Interpretation*, biblical theology "is unable to account for the *theological* concerns that must generate and under-write Christian interpretation of scripture."[33] According to Fowl, one of the things that prevents it from being able to account for theological concerns is the notion that the purpose of biblical interpretation is to fix or establish the meaning of the text. In the modern critical milieu, the implicit, scholarly understanding of inter-pretation as the assignment or discovery of a text's meaning is so basic, so deep-seated, that Fowl's criticism must be described as radical. In *Engaging Scripture*, postliberal theory helps Fowl step outside the conceptual framework of modern biblical criticism and mark a contrast between its essential drive to fix meaning

---

33 Stephen E. Fowl, *Engaging Scripture: A Model for Theological Interpretation* (Oxford: Blackwell, 1998), 28; italics added.

("determinate interpretation") and a deconstructive mode by which textual meaning is systematically undermined ("anti-determinate interpretation"). In doing so, Fowl characterizes both as ill-suited to the nature and purposes of Christian theology. Determinate interpretation falsely assumes that meaning is a property inherent in texts and therefore seeks in vain to locate the coherence of Christian faith "in the text of the Bible interpreted in isolation from Christian doctrines and ecclesial practices."[34] Antideterminate interpretation fosters awareness of the textual "other" and invites "interpretive plurality," but rests, in the end, on a metaphysics of textuality—what Fowl nicely calls "a metaphysics without people"—that is at odds with Christian ethics, even as it calls for interpretive practices likely to yield "paralysis and instability" instead of useful moral guidance.[35] What Fowl commends instead is a third option: "underdetermined interpretation." Instead of being preoccupied with fixing objective meanings for biblical texts, this mode is concerned with understanding "textual meaning in terms of varied and diverse interpretive aims, interests, and practices."[36] The issue, then, is not what is argued but who is making the argument, for what reason, and in what context. Fowl's alternative is attractive because it corresponds in an important way to the shape and function of Christian theology. Scripture understood theologically addresses people at the level of their "aims, interests, and practices," not at the level of their ability to overcome exegetical puzzlement by assigning satisfactory meanings to texts in cold blood. Theological interpretation, rather than standing alone, takes its place in an order that is intelligible "within a set of doctrinal, moral, ecclesial, and communal concerns," one that is "continuous with the practice of faithful Christians from past generations."[37] Context, then, is everything. Within the context of the Christian life, communities interpret Scripture in ways befitting Christian identity and practice, consulting biblical scholarship only in an ad hoc way.[38]

Like Fowl, R. R. Reno sees biblical theology as an enterprise seriously impaired by modern intellectual tendencies. As series editor for the *Brazos Theological Commentary on the Bible*, Reno has both criticized and offered an alternative to the work of biblical theologians. A central issue for Reno is the tendency of many theologically minded biblical scholars to retreat into formalities and abstractions, to prescind (ironically) from the particularity of the biblical text.[39] At one level, biblical theology is deeply invested in textual particularity, especially the kind clarified by historical analysis. Yet, as interpreters move from exegesis to theological affirmation, they often resort to generalities that are neither here nor there, vague nostrums in

---

34 Fowl, *Engaging Scripture*, 40.

35 Fowl, *Engaging Scripture*, 5–56.

36 Fowl, *Engaging Scripture*, 58.

37 Fowl, *Engaging Scripture*, 59.

38 Fowl, *Engaging Scripture*, 183.

39 R. R. Reno, "Biblical Theology and Theological Exegesis," in *Out of Egypt: Biblical Theology and Biblical Interpretation*, ed. Craig Bartholomew, Mary Healy, Karl Möller, and Robin Parry (London: Paternoster, 2004), 385–408.

a no-man's-land between actual doctrine and a pretheological literal sense. Fearing anachronism, modern commentators avoid reading biblical texts in light of developed Christian doctrines and opt instead for "sterilized" versions of Christian ideas "at a remove from the specificity of the text" such that the text becomes merely *"evidence* for a 'theology of x.'"[40] But for figures like Irenaeus, Gregory of Nyssa, and John Chrysostom, Reno argues, "theology is a practice of reading" not "a conclusion drawn from reading."[41] Though they presuppose certain dogmas, they do not superimpose them on the texts; rather, their theological exegesis consists in creating a dense "network of associations and allusions" that draw the reader *into*, rather than away from, the particularity of the text. Confident that the Bible is the "privileged key to understanding a natural-historical order that is shaped by God," they understood theological reading to be a kind of arranging or drawing together of Scripture's myriad pieces "in such a way that Jesus Christ is evident as the unifying hypothesis."[42] To read Scripture theologically, then, is to remain firmly within this order, not to move beyond it to some higher level of abstraction. Many modern interpreters, for instance, feel that they have succeeded once they have arrived at the appropriate idea behind or above the text and thus come to recognize "a conceptual artifact resident in a domain of propositions independent of the specific literal world of scripture," a theological "realm" populated by the results of interpretation.[43] According to Reno, even a biblical theologian as respectful of the text as Childs identifies theology with a second-order operation ("theological reflection") that takes place once one has carried out the descriptive task and accounted for the text's discrete voices. Once one has attended to the biblical witnesses (*signa*), one is then able to move on to the theological substance (*res*). In putting the matter this way, Childs "treats theological reflection as concerning the divine *res*, not the scriptural *signa*, and thus understood, the combination 'theological exegesis' is oxymoronic"; Childs finds himself in the awkward position of having to "discipline theological reflection with exegesis conducted by some other means."[44]

A useful example of theological interpretation may be taken from among the commentaries published in the Brazos series for which Reno serves as general editor. In keeping with editorial design, most of the authors in the series are not professional biblical scholars (or, if they are, not experts on the books for which they write commentaries). In writing on Song of Songs, Roman Catholic theologian Paul Griffiths defends the unusual step of basing his commentary not on the original Hebrew but on the (New) Vulgate, an instantiation of what he calls the "Latin Song" (in contrast to the "Hebrew Song," "Greek Song," and so on). Song of Songs and other parts of Scripture have come down to us through what he terms "confection," a cooperative process with many steps, through which something is

---

40 Reno, "Biblical Theology," 390; italics in original.
41 Reno, "Biblical Theology," 403.
42 Reno, "Biblical Theology," 401.
43 Reno, "Biblical Theology," 399 and 400.
44 Reno, "Biblical Theology," 398.

made "sweet and beautiful by judicious mixing of ingredients."[45] This has important implications:

> For Christians, the process of confecting a scriptural book does not yield a single, authoritative original text from which all others are derived and upon which they are parasitic. There is, textually speaking, no real thing: there are only versions, all of them confected, some involving translation from one natural language into another and some not. Affirming the possibility and desirability of translation, which Christians have almost always done, strongly supports this conclusion . . . Hearing the Song in English is not second best to hearing it in Hebrew: both are confected versions, and each is fully the word of the Lord.[46]

Especially relevant here is Griffiths's understanding of what a scriptural text is and what the interpretive task involves. There is a certain similarity between Griffiths's confectionary view of Scripture and a notion of canonical shaping by which the Scriptures, after a long process, come into a stable, final form. But Griffiths is unwilling to assign theological priority to any particular moment in the process or to any version of Scripture (even those considered "originary"), because Scripture cannot be reduced to a single text. Its form and substance are recognized and experienced within particular, in-house confectionary processes, in which Christians are addressed by "the word of the Lord." For Griffiths, no one language (Hebrew, Greek, and Aramaic *not* excepted), even when employed according to the "intentions and understandings of the authors and compilers of the works that now constitute the canon of scripture," is able to "exhaust or contain what the Lord says to his people by way of those works."[47] Yet this does not entail a universalism that flattens or minimizes individual traditional-linguistic confections. To affirm the inexhaustibility of Scripture in this way is rather to heighten the importance of particular traditions, for they are the contexts within which theological reading takes place. In order to read the Song as Scripture, then, Griffiths self-consciously situates himself within the (Latin) theological tradition and (Roman Catholic) ecclesial communion by which the word of the Lord is mediated to him. He takes pains, for example, to square his preference for the Latin Song with the higher authority accorded to the original Hebrew text by Pope Pius XII in *Divino Afflante Spiritu*.[48] He points to the importance of the New Vulgate for ongoing revisions of liturgical texts in the Catholic Church and expresses his hope that the commentary will be of use to those efforts.[49] Most significantly, he describes the writing of a commentary as an effort to respond to God's loving initiative, to receive the Lord's verbal "kiss" in Scripture and join his theological forebears (Jerome and others) in

---

45 Paul J. Griffiths, *Song of Songs* (Grand Rapids, MI: Brazos, 2011), xxiii.
46 Griffiths, *Song of Songs*, xxvi–xxvii.
47 Griffiths, *Song of Songs*, xxxi.
48 Griffiths, *Song of Songs*, xxix–xxxii.
49 Griffiths, *Song of Songs*, xxxiii–xxxiv.

returning the kiss. For him to do so, to respond to the Lord's kiss in a way that adds to the scriptural confection, he "must comment on a version lineally related to and intimate with the one they also commented on."[50]

Griffiths's commentary demonstrates how an academic interpreter who is not constrained by familiar critical mandates (e.g., to prioritize the original language of the biblical text) might approach the task of theological interpretation. His work is not aimed at establishing, once and for all, the meaning of the Song or particular words and passages within it. It offers, in Fowl's sense, an underdetermined reading that is regulated not by scientific goals but by Griffiths's "aims and interests" as a churchly interpreter. His preference for the Latin Song, for example, is not established on "neutral" grounds but rather articulated within a particular set of theological concerns. Neither is Griffiths's commentary the basis for some higher conceptuality (e.g., a "theology of love" or similar). By moving freely from the Song to other biblical texts and by inhabiting the figural traditions developed by earlier interpreters, Griffiths keeps his explication of the Song within what Reno called "the specific literal world of scripture." As a genre of interpretation, the commentary allows Griffiths to work associatively and to carry out the work of "arranging" and "drawing together" that characterized so much early Christian interpretation. Griffiths's interpretation, then, has historical depth, but without a sense of historical rupture. To take but one example, Griffiths dwells on an image from the Song, that of the lover who "lingers" between the breasts of the beloved (1:13). Breasts, he points out, refer to female beauty and sexual attractiveness in Scripture, but also come, by "figural extension," to refer to nourishment.[51] The restored Jerusalem offers her "consoling breast" (Is 66:11) to God's people, and the nourishing breasts of Mary are spoken of as "blessed" in the Gospel of Luke (Lk 11:27). Accordingly, Griffiths develops a double reading of the breasts "as figuring Israel-church's provision of nourishment to the Lord's lovers, and as figuring Mary's provision of nourishment to the Lord." There is no need to choose between the two; both can be affirmed "because both respond to the resonances of the Song's text with the text of Scripture, and both are consonant with the grammar of faith."[52] The verse in the Song, then, points to the mutuality of love and desire that bonds Christ and the church. The impression one gains from Griffiths' treatment of the Song is that his work, though oriented toward the past and the long process of scriptural confection, is not concerned with analyzing a tradition but rather with participating in one.

Metacritical interpretation

The dialogue between biblical theology and theological interpretation is ongoing. In a recent study, Mark Elliott shines a rather unflattering light on a great deal of

---

50 Griffiths, *Song of Songs*, xxxiii.
51 Griffiths, *Song of Songs*, 39.
52 Griffiths, *Song of Songs*, 40.

work that has been done in the name of theological interpretation.[53] In seeking to overcome the limitations of a biblical theology still influenced by certain critical assumptions, theological interpreters, according to Elliott, have largely failed to produce a compelling alternative. Elliott is sympathetic to the aims of theological interpreters and so directs his criticism mainly at particular problems rather than fundamental issues. The former include a misunderstanding of the "Rule of Faith," by which one (wrongly) feels compelled to impose a creedal grid onto his or her interpretation of Scripture.[54] Elliott parodies the tendency to conflate spiritual reading with exegesis, suggesting that theological interpreters are often hasty and shallow in their attempt to replace biblical theology. He imagines them saying, "if we cannot manage to salvage biblical theology, let us at least form a Christian hermeneutic and practice *lectio divina.*"[55] There is also the danger that theological interpreters will stick to well-known texts, ignoring parts of the canon and treating Scripture as a collection of discrete oracles rather than a coherent whole.[56] Elliott's comments about the general tenor of contemporary theological interpretation are the most telling. More a worry than an argument, Elliott writes that "[t]here seems something odd about reading the Bible as virtuous people who want to be more virtuous. It's all about 'us', and we are not all that interesting."[57] If the objectivity of Scripture—its integrity as something distinct from the reader—can be overdone, then perhaps objectivity is also something that can be neglected or underappreciated.[58] Reading the Bible in an "extremely hermeneutical" climate, within "communities of the like-minded," may shift attention unduly to interpreters' efforts and concerns (what Elliott calls "the danger of semi-Pelagianism") and lead to "myopia in what is produced."[59] What Elliott calls for is not a simple return to biblical theology but rather a biblical theology shaped and informed by deep knowledge of the history of biblical interpretation. To the extent that theological reading can or does become a provincial, sectarian affair—a conversation "all about us"—it is necessary to seek correctives. Elliott sees such a corrective in awareness of history—not critical history that reinforces a sense of rupture but one that connects us to the past and works against narrowness of vision. To know this history is to protect the integrity of theology from modishness, to relativize methodological

53 Mark W. Elliott, *The Heart of Biblical Theology: Providence Experienced* (Farnham, Surrey, UK: Ashgate, 2012).

54 Elliott, *Heart of Biblical Theology*, 3–7.

55 Elliott, *Heart of Biblical Theology*, 83.

56 Elliott, *Heart of Biblical Theology*, 23 and 25.

57 Elliott, *Heart of Biblical Theology*, 33.

58 Elliott does indeed identify theological interpretation with postmodern attacks on objectivity: "Theological interpretation acts like 'hit and run' guerilla warfare on the modernist biblical studies project, but it is the mirror image of the shift towards cultural studies in many many university departments" (35).

59 Elliott, *Heart of Biblical Theology*, 35.

questions in appropriate ways, and to understand our place in an "ongoing story of interpretation."[60]

The last point recalls the well-known lecture by Ratzinger on the crisis of modern biblical interpretation. There Ratzinger undertakes to explain the theological sterility of critical biblical scholarship. Despite its impressive gains, critical scholarship has left the theological reader stranded, leaving him or her to ask, "Once the methodology has picked history to death by its dissection, who can reawaken it so that it can live and speak to me?"[61] The sense that historical–critical methodology has become morbid is shared by biblical theologians and theological interpreters alike. What makes Ratzinger's approach distinctive, though, is the perspective he adopts toward it. For him, the history of criticism is not merely a chronological catalogue of findings coordinated to theories or schools of thought. Instead, "it appears much more as a history of subjectively reconstructed interrelationships *whose approaches correspond exactly to the developments of spiritual history*. In turn, these developments are reflected in particular interpretations of texts."[62] The phrase "spiritual history" is conspicuous.[63] Seen in the light of "spiritual history," the development of scholarship is not simply a sequence of disengaged intellectual arguments that stretch across the history of a discipline, a protracted version of an academic debate that spans decades or centuries rather than hours. Scholarship instead participates in the human condition and reflects the life orientation of individuals, societies, and cultures, either toward or away from God. It thus occupies and reflects a particular moment in the relation of God to humanity. In a way, this seems obvious. Theological interpreters are familiar with the concept and quite practiced in discerning the significance of "spiritual history," especially for understanding the positions and perspectives of their academic subjects (biblical figures, early Christian interpreters, and so forth).[64] The difficulty comes in acknowledging that we, too, are embedded. The "now" in which we speak hopefully of retrieval or integration is in fact a moment in a larger history, one affected by conditions that circumscribe our perception of truth. Without adopting the more extreme forms of historicism, it is

60 Elliott, *Heart of Biblical Theology*, 80–1. Fowl, for his part, is certainly right to point out that the vigilance needed to avoid sinful interpretations, including myopic and self-centered ones, is not a function of interpretive method but, ultimately, of the interpreters themselves, specifically their willingness to recognize their own sinfulness and practice forgiveness, repentance, and reconciliation. See Fowl, *Engaging Scripture*, 62–96. But, of course, the relation between Elliott's proposal and Fowl's is not binary. It is not an either-or.

61 Ratzinger, "Crisis," 4.

62 Ratzinger, "Crisis," 8; italics added.

63 I doubt very much that the phrase as intended by Ratzinger has Hegelian overtones. He makes no mention of Hegel in the essay, and the criticisms he directs to Kant would only apply *a fortiori* to Hegelian historicism.

64 Two excellent, recent examples come to mind. Ian Christopher Levy (*Holy Scripture and the Quest for Authority at the End of the Middle Ages* (Notre Dame, IN: University of Notre Dame Press, 2012)) carefully documents the significance of political and ecclesial

nevertheless possible to acknowledge our own contingency, both as an inescapable feature of creatureliness and as a reason to approach retrieval with a sober attitude. As Aquinas, drawing on the ancients, said, the thing known is in the knower according to the mode of the knower.[65] What is true of human beings naturally constrained to reason partially and discursively is also true of human beings as historical creatures: the quality of their knowledge depends more on who and where they are than on the nature of the thing they seek to know. This point must not be confused with Kantian idealism. Ratzinger, in fact, sees Immanuel Kant as the "philosophic turning point" by which moderns came wrongly to believe that the divine realm is intellectually inaccessible, that "the voice of being-in-itself cannot be heard by human beings," and that man "must limit himself to the realm of categories."[66] The point is rather that we come to the Scripture at particular moments in "spiritual history," bringing culturally conditioned assumptions and philosophical frameworks to bear on our understanding of the truth. These need not be theologically fatal. They do, however, require constant reexamination, what Ratzinger calls a criticism of criticism.[67]

As Ratzinger observed in his lecture, the influential biblical scholarship produced by Martin Dibelius and Rudolf Bultmann reflected the spirit of their age: not just the legacy of Kantian idealism but also the growing prestige of the natural sciences and, one might add, the spiritual tumults of the World Wars as reflected in the philosophy of someone like Martin Heidegger. One can scarcely imagine the work of Bultmann developing as it did at some other point in history. By itself, this observation is banal. Put constructively, though, it may afford a useful observation. Exegesis cannot be conceptualized as method and isolated from life. Nor can it be reduced to the individual genius or conscious activity of notable interpreters. Exegesis must be understood, at a more profound level, as the fruit of a culture. To shine a critical light on criticism itself, as Ratzinger advocates, is not a way of transcending this predicament, a means by which to arrive at some higher critical vantage point, to end all previous debates, and finally to close the book on two centuries of fruitless theorizing. As he says, this kind of metacritical approach does not amount to criticism "pulling itself by its own bootstraps"; it is instead a "process of self-limitation" and an attempt on the part of criticism to mark out "for itself its own proper place."[68] For this reason, no one person can accomplish it: "[a]t least the work of a whole generation is necessary to achieve such a thing."[69]

---

contexts for theorizing scriptural interpretation. Peter W. Martens (*Origen and Scripture: The Contours of the Exegetical Life* (Oxford: Oxford University Press, 2012)) demonstrates the dense interpenetration of social, pedagogical, and scholarly concerns in Origen's exegetical enterprise.

65 *Summa Theologica* II.II.1.2.

66 Ratzinger, "Crisis," 15.

67 Ratzinger, "Crisis," 6.

68 Ratzinger, "Crisis," 8.

69 Ratzinger, "Crisis," 6.

Unlike Kant, who saw himself as a philosophical Copernicus, Ratzinger has no revolutionary aspirations. For him, there can be no total repudiation of the past. In the preface to his 2007 work on the life of Christ, Ratzinger points to the modern critical tradition and its prevalence in Catholic exegesis since the issuing of *Divino Afflante Spiritu* in 1943. In keeping with this, he emphasizes that historical-critical method is "an indispensable tool."[70] In endorsing what many theological interpreters see as a dead end, Ratzinger appears, perhaps, to be disappointingly conservative. Yet, in my view, it is appropriate to acknowledge the extent to which our own work still reflects the legacy of a culture indebted to the legacies of critical philosophy. Modern criticism remains a starting point for those who are modern. This need not be celebrated, but neither should it be ignored.

Ratzinger's "metacritical" retrieval resembles theological interpretation in its emphasis on the purposes, interests, and ecclesial situation of the exegete. But self-awareness here has less to do with articulating the aims of one's interpretation than with coming to terms with limitations inherent in the set of presuppositions one brings to the act of interpretation itself. Metacritical retrieval resembles biblical theology in its favorable stance toward historical criticism, its willingness to make use of existing scholarly methods and procedures. But, for reasons already discussed, there can be no attempt at theological formulation that does not account, first of all, for one's place in "spiritual history." It hardly needs to be said that retrieval in a Ratzingerian mode is both guided and bounded by the theological tradition broadly construed as well as the specific formulations of the Roman Catholic magisterium.[71] As utterances of the church, encyclicals and conciliar documents connect the interpreter to the Bible, specifically, as a book of the church. Yet they do so not simply by commanding assent but rather by imparting the "fruit of a long struggle" to understand Scripture and by challenging us to take account of "the magnitude of the Word spoken to us and of the limits of our capabilities."[72] The heart of the encounter with Scripture, though, lies not with the tradition as such but rather with the capacity of the Word both to inhabit and transcend its historical point of origin, its power to address us in our own "living historical moment."[73] Retrieval in this mode begins with disciplined attention to the literal sense and an awareness of one's hermeneutical position. But, placing the interpreter within the church's historical relationship to Scripture, it culminates in exegesis that remains true to us as moderns and true, at the same time, to the

---

70 Joseph Ratzinger/Pope Benedict XVI, *Jesus of Nazareth: From the Baptism in the Jordan to the Transfiguration*, trans. Adrian J. Walker (New York: Doubleday, 2007), xiv and xvi.

71 See, for example, Joseph Cardinal Ratzinger, "Exegesis and the Magisterium of the Church," trans. Adrian Walker, in *Opening Up the Scriptures: Joseph Ratzinger and the Foundations of Biblical Interpretation*, ed. José Granados, Carlos Granados, and Luis Sánchez-Navarro (Grand Rapids, MI: Eerdmans, 2008), 126–36.

72 Ratzinger, "Exegesis," 136.

73 Ratzinger, *Jesus of Nazareth*, xx.

fact that modern exegesis is necessarily incomplete. Ratzinger, for his part, holds out the hope that a chastened attention to history may yet allow criticism, in time, to move beyond itself, to repudiate the critical dogmatism of the past, and "in some sense catch the sounds of a higher dimension through the human word."[74] It is the Word, not the interpreter, who transcends the present historical situation. The hope, then, is that richer forms of life and a renewal of Christian intellectual culture will, over the course of spiritual history, yield better hearers and readers of Scripture.

Conclusion

The growth of biblical theology and theological interpretation in the last two decades suggest that the realization of Ratzinger's modest hope may not be far off. Seen against the backdrop of the larger history of modern criticism, it is clear that what unites the two is far more significant than what divides them. With its interest in recovering the distinctive voices within Scripture, biblical theology manifests a greater continuity with critical scholarship than its counterpart. Though it seeks theological integration, it accepts the model of two-stage exegesis by which descriptive analysis prepares the way for second-order theological reflection. Theological interpreters adopt a more critical stance toward biblical scholarship. In refusing to assign primacy to historical–critical or literary–historical contextualizations, they seek warrants for exegetical work both in the theological nature of Scripture and in the interests, aims, and concerns of the churches and communities of faith for whom their work is ultimately intended. Yet, for both, scriptural interpretation must work with and *within* the classic theological tradition at the roots of Christian faith and practice. In this way, they seek to deepen rather than problematize the contemporary theological relevance of Scripture. To describe this recovery of scriptural profundity as a "retrieval," however, is to prompt an additional question: who are the retrievers? What does their mode of knowing allow them to know? Or, as Ratzinger might put it, at what point in spiritual history are we positioned? It may be well to remember, in the end, that the Lord's question to one as wise and pious as Job focused on identity rather than method: "Who is this that darkens counsel by words without knowledge?" (Jb 38:2). Self-criticism demands that we ask this of ourselves before it is asked of us by another.

---

74 Ratzinger, *Jesus of Nazareth*, xvii.

Chapter 10

TRADITION I: INSIGHTS FROM *RESSOURCEMENT* FOR THE CONTEMPORARY CHRISTIAN CHURCH

Gabriel Flynn[1]

This chapter offers insights for a contemporary theology of tradition from, among others, the two most renowned exponents of *ressourcement*: Yves Congar and Henri de Lubac. *Ressourcement* has received significant attention from scholars in the wake of the fiftieth anniversary of the Second Vatican Council (1962–65).[2] The question of tradition bears further analysis. The challenge for Roman Catholic systematic theologians is to formulate a theology of tradition that is sufficiently robust to facilitate a mutually beneficial engagement of church and society, and to respond to the ever-changing vicissitudes of faith and worship, service and ministry. In order to be effective, therefore, a retrieval of the ancient tradition should enable a renewed engagement with Vatican II, so as to contribute to the present program of reform and renewal spearheaded by Pope Francis (Pope: 2013–). I begin with a précis of the genesis and evolution of *ressourcement* in order to illustrate how tradition stands at the heart of that enterprise.

The origins of French *ressourcement* theology

The distinguished generation of *ressourcement* theologians who influenced French culture and thought in the period 1930 to 1960, and beyond, inspired a

1 My thanks to Oxford University Press for permission to use material from my chapter "The Twentieth-Century Renaissance in Catholic Theology," in *Ressourcement: A Movement for Renewal in Twentieth-Century Catholic Theology*, ed. Gabriel Flynn and Paul D. Murray (Oxford: Oxford University, 2014), 1–19. I have also drawn on material from my *Yves Congar's Vision of the Church in a World of Unbelief* (Oxford: Routledge, 2004), 146–211, used with permission from Taylor & Francis.

2 See *Ressourcement: A Movement for Renewal in Twentieth-Century Catholic Theology*; Jürgen Mettepenningen, *Nouvelle Théologie—New Theology: Inheritor of Modernism, Precursor of Vatican II* (London: Continuum, 2010); Hans Boersma, *Nouvelle Théologie and Sacramental Ontology: A Return to Mystery* (Oxford: Oxford University Press, 2009); Jennifer Newsome Martin, "A Roman Catholic Theology of *Ressourcement*," in the present volume.

renaissance in twentieth-century Catholic theology and initiated a movement for renewal that made a decisive contribution to the reforms of the Second Vatican Council (1962–65). The *ressourcement* passed through various stages of development.[3] The biblical renewal, which began in Germany in the course of the interwar period, spread progressively to the rest of the Catholic world and even to what may be considered the less progressive countries. The liturgical renewal is older and, although known in France from before the First World War (1914–18), its first intense period of activity was linked with the name of Dom Lambert Beauduin (1873–1960), the Belgian liturgist and founder of Chevetogne. But it was in Germany during the interwar period that the liturgical renewal blossomed. The biblical renewal and the liturgical movement were completed by a patristic rejuvenation.[4]

The foremost exponents of *ressourcement* were principally leading French Dominicans and Jesuits of the faculties of Le Saulchoir (Paris) and Lyon-Fourvière, respectively. They included the Dominicans Marie-Dominique Chenu (1895–1990), Yves Congar (1904–1995), Dominique Dubarle (1907–1987), and Henri-Marie Féret (1904–1992), and the Jesuits Jean Daniélou (1905–1974), Henri de Lubac (1896–1991), Henri Bouillard (1908–1981), and Hans Urs von Balthasar (1905–1988), who left the Society of Jesus in 1950. The movement also encompassed Belgium and Germany and included such scholars as Louis Charlier (1898–1981), who taught at the Catholic University of Louvain; René Draguet (1896–1980); Karl Rahner (1904–1984); Joseph Ratzinger (1927–); Benedict XVI (Pope: 2005–13); and the Dutch Dominican Edward Schillebeeckx (1914–2009).[5]

De Lubac and Daniélou were the leading practitioners of *ressourcement*. Their books often seem like a rich, intricately woven tapestry of texts from the tradition. Congar and Chenu, without diminution or denial of the return to the sources, represent a strongly historical theology, what their neo-Thomist confreres would doubtless call a "historicist" approach to theology, including the theology of St. Thomas. What distinguishes the *ressourcement* theologians from the *nouveaux*

---

3 See Yves Congar, "Tendances actuelles de la pensée religieuse," *Cahiers du monde nouveau* 4 (1948): 33–50; Jean Daniélou, "Les orientations présentes de la pensée religieuse," *Études* 249 (1946): 5–21; Roger Aubert, *La Théologie Catholique au milieu du XXᵉ siècle* (Tournai: Casterman, 1954).

4 See Louis Bouyer, "Le Renouveau des études patristiques," *La Vie intellectuelle* 15 (1947): 6–25; Louis Bouyer, *Life and Liturgy*, 3rd ed. (London: Sheed & Ward, 1965).

5 See Mettepenningen, *Nouvelle Théologie—New Theology*, chap. 3; Jürgen Mettepenningen and Ward de Pril, "Thomism and the Renewal of Theology: Chenu, Charlier, and Their *Ressourcement*," *Horizons* 39 (2012): 50–68; Jürgen Mettepenningen, "L'Essai de Louis Charlier (1938): Une contribution à la *nouvelle théologie*," *Revue théologique de Louvain* 39 (2008): 211–32; Jürgen Mettepenningen, "Edward Schillebeeckx: Heredero y promotor de la *nouvelle théologie*," *Mayéutica* 78 (2008): 285–302; Marcellino D'Ambrosio, "*Ressourcement* Theology, *aggiornamento*, and the Hermeneutics of Tradition," *Communio* 18 (1991): 530–55.

théologiens is that the former were also *nouveaux théologiens*, while the latter were not always committed to *ressourcement*. Rahner's approach sets him apart from other *nouveaux théologiens*; his "supernatural existential" is an attempt to rethink the supernatural—one of the preoccupations of the *nouveaux théologiens*. In his later writings, however, he does not tend to refer explicitly to the fathers or to cite them. What unites these overlapping elements is a certain *froideur* toward Thomism, or what they insist on calling neo-Thomism. Étienne Fouilloux contends that Congar became, with Chenu, de Lubac, and Daniélou "the incarnation of a "new theology," French style, less concerned with conformity to scholasticism as with the return to the sources of Christianity and to a dialogue with the great prevailing currents of thought."[6]

It is important to note that while de Lubac did not see himself as an original thinker, still less did he view his work as mere systematization or naive hankering after the glories of a lost past. His aim was to make the tradition known, loved, and efficacious for the present. His description of the methodology of *ressourcement* is apposite since it forges an indispensable nexus between tradition and the return to the sources:

> Without claiming to open up new avenues of thought, I have sought rather, without any antiquarianism, to make known some of the great common areas of Catholic tradition. I wanted to make it loved, to show its ever-present fruitfulness.... So I have never been tempted by any kind of "return to the sources" that would scorn later developments and represent the history of Christian thought as a stream of decadences.[7]

Among the great precursors of *ressourcement*, Maurice Blondel (1861–1949), the acclaimed "philosopher of action," is preeminent. Reference must also be made to Joseph Maréchal (1878–1944), Pierre Rousselot (1878–1915), and Étienne Gilson (1884–1978).[8] Blondel's doctoral thesis, published in Paris in 1893 as *L'Action: Essai d'une critique de la vie et d'une science de la pratique*, was read by the leading figures of the *ressourcement* generation. As de Lubac remarks, "During my years of philosophy (1920–1923) on Jersey, I had read with enthusiasm Maurice Blondel's *Action*, *Lettre* (on apologetics) and various other studies."[9] Congar

---

6 Yves Congar, *Journal d'un théologien (1946–1956)*, ed. Étienne Fouilloux et al., 2nd ed. (Paris: Cerf, 2001), 1 and 2.

7 Henri de Lubac, *At the Service of the Church: Henri de Lubac Reflects on the Circumstances that Occasioned His Writings*, trans. Anne Elizabeth Englund (San Francisco: Ignatius, 1993), 143–4; ET of *Mémoire sur l'occasion de mes écrits*, ed. Georges Chantraine, *Œuvres completes* (Paris: Cerf, 2006), 147.

8 See Michael A. Conway, "Maurice Blondel and *Ressourcement*," in Flynn and Murray, eds., *Ressourcement*, 65–82; and in the same volume, Francesca Aran Murphy, "Gilson and the *Ressourcement*," 51–64.

9 De Lubac, *At the Service of the Church*, 18–19; ET of *Mémoire*, 15.

also came under the spell of Blondel through his mentors Chenu and Ambroise Gardeil (1859–1931). Although Congar began his study of Blondel relatively late, he admits that the more he read, the more he appreciated his thought.[10]

A vast array of new initiatives emerged in the French Church during and after the Second World War (1939–45). This included the movement for the reform of the liturgy, Centre de Pastorale Liturgique; the return to the biblical and patristic sources, exemplified especially in the foundation of the *Sources chrétiennes* series; the renewal of ecclesiology, demonstrated by the establishment of the *Unam Sanctam* series; and the realization of the church's missionary task. De Lubac refers to the spirit of hope, creativity, and originality that pervaded this period in the history of the French church, with the Chantiers de Jeunesse and the *Cahiers du Témoignage chrétien* producing a rich harvest. As he comments, "Both in 1940–1942 and under the total occupation in 1942–1944, Lyons was quite different. Just as earlier, in the sixteenth century, it had been the 'intellectual capital' of France, it became in 1940, the 'capital of the Resistance,'"[11] It should be noted that *nouvelle théologie* is a complex historical movement that emerged from the wider political, cultural, and intellectual milieux of twentieth-century France.[12]

In September 1946, Pius XII (Pope: 1939–58) expressed his concerns regarding the *nouvelle théologie* to representatives of both the Dominicans and the Jesuits, warning against an attack on the fundamental tenets of Roman Catholic doctrine. In an atmosphere of suspicion and controversy, *Humani Generis* was published on August 12, 1950.[13] As the clouds began to gather over the church in France in the wake of the controversial encyclical, it is hardly surprising that both Congar and de Lubac, astute political analysts, rejected the term *nouvelle théologie*. At his own suggestion, Congar went into exile in Jerusalem. Then, in November 1954, he was assigned to Blackfriars, Cambridge. De Lubac was permanently removed from all lecturing duties at Fourvière. *Humani Generis* had effectively signaled the end of his academic career, while his books were withdrawn from Jesuit libraries.[14] In the wake of the encyclical, de Lubac points out that Pius XII wrote to him, through the kind offices of Cardinal Augustin Bea (1881–1968), to thank him for his work

10 Jean Puyo, ed., *Jean Puyo interroge le Père Congar: "Une vie pour la vérité,"* Les Interviews (Paris: Centurion, 1975), 72.

11 See de Lubac, *At the Service of the Church*, 45 and 48; ET of *Mémoire*, 44–5 and 47.

12 See Darrell Jodock, ed., *Catholicism Contending with Modernity: Roman Catholic Modernism and Anti-Modernism in Historical Context* (Cambridge: Cambridge University Press, 2000), 308–36.

13 Pius XII, *Humani Generis*. Encyclical Letter concerning some False Opinions Threatening to Undermine the Foundations of Catholic Doctrine, *Acta Apostolici Sedis* 42 (1950): 561–78; ET, *False Trends in Modern Teaching: Encyclical Letter (Humani Generis)*, trans. Ronald A. Knox, rev. ed. (London: Catholic Truth Society, 1959); Robert Guelluy, "Les Antécédents de l'encyclique 'Humani Generis' dans les sanctions Romaines de 1942: Chenu, Charlier, Draguet," *Revue d'histoire ecclésiastique* 81 (1986): 421–97.

14 De Lubac, *At the Service of the Church*, 71 and 74; ET of *Mémoire*, 72 and 75.

and to encourage him to undertake a future study that would enrich the life of the Church.[15]

Congar's most significant contribution to *ressourcement* is undoubtedly the Unam Sanctam series launched by *La Vie intellectuelle* in November 1935, which became a highly influential ecclesiological and ecumenical library of Éditions du Cerf, running to some seventy-seven volumes. Congar acknowledges that Unam Sanctam prepared the way for Vatican II. De Lubac's prodigious theological program impacted directly on the documents of Vatican II.[16] As Ratzinger states, "In all its comments about the Church [Vatican II] was moving precisely in the direction of de Lubac's thought."[17] Congar adopted *ressourcement* as the standard for Church reform understood as an urgent appeal "from a less profound tradition to a deeper tradition, a search for the deepest sources."[18] The *ressourcement* project was severely criticized by M.-Michel Labourdette as well as by Réginald Garrigou-Lagrange, who seems to have borrowed the phrase *la nouvelle théologie* to describe it.[19] The view of tradition proposed by the *nouvelle théologie*, far from being traditionalist, in the sense of a repetition of the recent past, is concerned rather with the unity of the ever-living tradition, which was precisely Congar's position.[20]

Ressourcement *and Vatican II*

Vatican II provided a historic opportunity for the *ressourcement* intellectuals to influence the Christian churches and modern society. Gerald O'Collins depicts the impact of *ressourcement* on the conciliar texts with acuity: "Those who scour the sixteen documents of Vatican II for *explicit* reference to *ressourcement*, or the return to the sources, will find something to report."[21] He points to the Decree

---

15 De Lubac, *Entretiens autour de Vatican II: Souvenirs et Réflexions*, Théologies, 2nd ed. (Paris: France Catholique/Cerf, 1985), 14.

16 See de Lubac, *Carnets du Concile*, ed. Löic Figoureux, 2 vols. (Paris: Cerf, 2007), i, 421–5 (November 30, 1962).

17 Joseph Ratzinger, *Principles of Catholic Theology: Building Stones for a Fundamental Theology*, trans. Mary Frances McCarthy (San Francisco: Ignatius, 1987), 50.

18 Congar, *True and False Reform in the Church*, trans. Paul Philiber (Collegeville, MN: Liturgical, 2011), 370; ET of *Vraie et fausse réforme dans l'Église*, Unam Sanctam (Paris: Cerf, 1950), 601–2.

19 Réginald Garrigou-Lagrange, "La nouvelle théologie où va-t-elle," *Angelicum* 23 (1946): 126–45; see M.-Michel Labourdette, "La Théologie et ses sources," *La Revue Thomiste* 46 (1946) : 353–71; M.-Michel Labourdette, "La Théologie, intelligence de la foi," *La Revue Thomiste* 46 (1946) : 5–44; Roger Aubert, *La Théologie Catholique au milieu du XXᵉ siècle* (Tournai: Casterman, 1954), 84–6.

20 Yves Congar, *Tradition and the Life of the Church*, trans. A. N. Woodrow, Faith and Fact Books (London: Burns & Oates, 1964), 146; ET of *La tradition et la vie de l'Église*, 2nd ed., Traditions chrétiennes (Paris: Cerf, 1984), 118–19.

21 Gerald O'Collins, *The Second Vatican Council: Message and Meaning* (Collegeville, MN: Liturgical Press, 2014).

on the Appropriate Renewal of Religious Life (*Perfectatae Caritatis*, October 28, 1965) as "the clearest endorsement of *ressourcement.*" In like manner, the Decree on the Training of Priests (*Optatam Totius*), promulgated on the same day as *Perfectatae Caritatis* (October 28, 1965), with its provision for study of the biblical languages, provided access to the sources (§ 13). The Dogmatic Constitution on Divine Revelation (*Dei Verbum*, November 18, 1965) called on all Christians to be "nourished and ruled by Sacred Scripture," "the pure and perennial source of spiritual life" (§§ 21, 25), while the Decree on the Ministry and Life of Priests (*Presbyterorum Ordinis*, December 7, 1965) exhorted clergy to read and meditate on the Scriptures. The Constitution on the Sacred Liturgy (*Sacrosanctum Concilium*, December 4, 1963) and the Decree on Ecumenism (*Unitatis Redintegratio*, November 21, 1964) also contained innovative ideas for a recovery of the ancient tradition.

On July 20, 1960, John XXIII (Pope: 1958–63) nominated de Lubac and Congar as consultants to the Preparatory Theological Commission. De Lubac later commented poignantly on the historical significance of the Pope's nominees: "These were two symbolic names. John XXIII had undoubtedly wanted to make everyone understand that the difficulties that had ---occurred under the previous pontificate between Rome and the Jesuit and Dominican orders in France were to be forgotten."[22] Among the experts (*periti*) at Vatican II, de Lubac was "one of the best-known and most outstanding from the very beginning."[23] His influence on *Lumen gentium* and *Gaudium et spes* has been carefully delineated by scholars. The following elements of *Lumen gentium* are attributed to him: (i) the duty of the Church to proclaim the Gospel to all peoples, as explained in *Le fondement théologique des missions*; (ii) the idea of Mary as a type of the Church; and (iii) the use of the term "the mystery of the Church"; both (ii) and (iii) are expounded in his *Méditation sur l'Eglise.*[24] De Lubac's influence at Vatican II was also evident on the question of the relation of the Church to non-Christian religions, drawing on *Catholicisme* and his works on Buddhism. He wrote a commentary on the preamble and first chapter of *Dei Verbum* in 1966 and again in a larger work published in 1968. He considered this text the most important of Vatican II. De Lubac was a member of the subcommission that produced the first chapter of *Gaudium et spes* that reflects his vision of the place of the Church in the modern world, as outlined in *Catholicisme*. He was also invited to write an introduction to *Gaudium et spes*. Further, de Lubac exercised a profound influence on the treatment of atheism in the Pastoral Constitution through his work *Le Drame de l'Humanisme athée*. Turning to the contribution of Congar, the far-reaching program of ecclesial

22 De Lubac, *At the Service of the Church*, 116; ET of *Mémoire*, 117–18.

23 Karl H. Neufeld, "In the Service of the Council: Bishops and Theologians at the Second Vatican Council," in *Vatican II: Assessment and Perspectives Twenty-Five Years after (1962–1987)*, ed. René Latourelle, 3 vols. (New York: Paulist, 1988), 1:74–105, here 88.

24 See de Lubac, *Le fondement théologique des missions* (Paris: Seuil, 1946); see also Neufeld, "In the Service of the Council," 94.

reform executed at the Council is the de facto consummation of his whole previous theological oeuvre. Congar describes his role in the drafting of texts in *Mon journal du Concile*, where he inserted a useful note, *sont de moi*, to indicate precisely his part in the genesis of the Council's documents.[25] It is to Congar, among others, that credit must also be given for one of the most important achievements of the Council, namely, the transition from a predominantly juridical conception to a more eschatological vision of the Church as the People of God.

Tradition and the challenge of change in the contemporary Christian Church

It is incontrovertible that the Roman Catholic Church is in the midst of a period of tumultuous change as opposing agendas for reform compete for dominance. In the wake of such upheaval, I wish to consider the contribution to the theology of tradition articulated by Congar and de Lubac, the indisputable giants of *ressourcement*, in whom many Catholics recognize an echo of their own hopes. I begin with a consideration of Congar's contribution to tradition that cannot be correctly understood except by reference to his highly developed theory of reform.

Reform and tradition in Congar's vision of the Church

The view of reform that Congar proposes is defined with reference to a constant search of the deepest sources.[26] This approach facilitates openness to change and development while exercising fidelity to the tradition. Reform and tradition cannot, then, be considered in isolation.[27] The predominant concern of Congar's vision of the Church is the preservation and restoration of unity.[28] Unity depends on the realization of an ideal of integration of all the Church's principles of identity, what Trent calls the *sensus Ecclesiae*, or the constant belief of the Church.[29] Congar's reformist program, by presenting an ideal for the Church in its origins

---

25 Yves Congar, *My Journal of the Council*, trans. Mary John Ronayne, OP, and Mary Cecily Boulding, OP (Collegeville, MN: Liturgical, 2012), 871; ET of *Mon journal du Concile*, ed. Éric Mahieu, 2 vols. (Paris: Cerf. 2002), 2:511.

26 Congar, *True and False Reform in the Church*, 602; ET of *Vraie et fausse réforme dans l'Église*, 370; see also Yves Congar, "Vraie et fausse contestation dans l'Église," *Spiritus* 38 (1969): 125–32, here 128.

27 Yves Congar, *Challenge to the Church: The Case of Archbishop Lefebvre* (London: Collins; Dublin: Veritas, 1976), 66–7; ET of *La Crise dans l'Église et Mgr Lefebvre* (Paris: Cerf, 1976), 80–2.

28 See Yves Congar, *The Church Peaceful* (Dublin: Veritas, 1977), 13; ET of *Au milieu des orages: l'Église affronte aujourd'hui son avenir* (Paris: Cerf, 1969), 13–14.

29 Yves Congar, *Tradition and Traditions: An Historical and a Theological Essay*, trans. Michael Naseby and Thomas Rainborough (London: Burns & Oates, 1966), 315–16; ET of

and with regard to eschatology, manifests a concern for the needs of the young and thus displays pastoral sensitivity, which, by virtue of its sources, is unique:

> The young are for a Jesus Christ who is a "man for other men." The only "Church" they will have is the collectivity of those who live the Gospel as a message of liberation and human brotherhood. Theologically, a reformist programme derives from the ideal imposed on the Church, either in regard to its origins, or in regard to what it is called to become throughout history in the direction of eschatology. In both cases, in fact, one can and ought to criticise its present historical *forms* in order to make them conform more (and therefore reform them) to what is required by a more demanding form of faithfulness.[30]

The postwar period in France was also characterized by a new concern for the poor and an urgent need to define the relationship between the Church and the modern world. In the introduction to *Vraie et fausse réforme dans l'Église*, Congar identifies this relationship as a key priority for the Church: "The pastoral activities of the Church no longer had much meaning for the majority of people, especially the more radical and dynamic among them."[31] Congar responds to the demands of the world and of believers, who will only accept the Gospel from a pure and irreproachable Church, by proposing a reform of the Church.[32] He acknowledges the duality that stands as the origin of all reform movements: "There is no ecclesiology which does not have to assume as a statutory fact the irreducible duality of that which exists in fact and that which ought to exist."[33] Based on a reformist current present in French Catholicism since the 1930s, Congar articulates in critical, reflective language a self-critique for the Church.[34] He refers to Chenu, who shows that a successful evangelical reform in the Church requires a radical questioning

La Tradition et les traditions: essai théologique (Paris: Fayard, 1963), 82; see Yves Congar, "Norms of Christian Allegiance and Identity in the History of the Church," *Concilium* 3 (1973): 24; *Enchiridion symbolorum: definitionum et declarationum de rebus fidei et morum*, ed. Henricus Denzinger and Adolfus Schönmetzer, 36th ed. (Freiburg: Herder, 1976), pars. 1532 and 1686.

30 Yves Congar, "Renewal of the Spirit and Reform of the Institution," *Concilium* 3 (1972): 39–49 (47); ET of Congar, "Renouvellement de l'esprit et réforme de l'institution," *Concilium* 3 (1972): 37–45, here 43; italics in original.

31 Congar, *True and False Reform in the Church*, 24; ET of *Vraie et fausse réforme dans l'Église*, 25.

32 Congar, *True and False Reform in the Church*, 48–9; ET of *Vraie et fausse réforme dans l'Église*, 54.

33 Congar, "Renewal of the Spirit and Reform of the Institution," 40; ET of "Renouvellement de l'esprit et réforme de l'institution," 38; see Marie-Dominique Chenu, "The New Awareness of the Trinitarian Basis of the Church," *Concilium* 146 (1981): 14–21, here 14.

34 See Jean-Pierre Jossua, "La Vie de l'Église-Introduction," in *Cardinal Yves Congar, O.P.: écrits réformateurs*, ed. Jossua (Paris: Cerf, 1995), 171–2.

of the social structures and a full return to the sources.[35] Further, Congar insists on recourse to the deep, ever-living tradition of the Church motivated by fervent faith and an impatience for apostolic outreach.[36] He acknowledges that too often, concerns about tradition practically extinguish a consideration of the most authentic improvements and urgent pastoral adaptations.[37] He shows that a successful reform movement necessitates a renewal of the ideas of the Church, and of the sense of the Church, while also providing an important place for the laity. This is seen as the fruit of *Action Catholique* and of the call addressed by Pius XII to the laity to take their place in the apostolic mission to the world.[38]

In a paper published in 1967, concerned principally with the identification of conditions under which it is possible to initiate reform, Congar asserts that the Catholic Church cannot be its own norm or rule of faith because this would be to absolutize its history and to equate the c with divine revelation, thereby robbing God of his sovereignty. What is required, in fact, is a norm that precedes and transcends the Church while judging it. This can only be found in the Word of God.[39]

The conditions for a true reform without schism

In *Vraie et fausse réforme dans l'Église*, Congar describes the conditions for a reform of the Church without schism, which he says can be reduced to four principles as follows:

(i) "The primacy of charity and of the pastoral"

While recognizing a real need for its purification, Congar upholds the integrity of the Church that cannot be called into question by reformers.[40] This situation can be resolved by his principle of dual fidelity whose overriding concern is the preservation of the unity of the Church without prohibiting necessary internal change.

---

35 Congar, *True and False Reform in the Church*, 49; ET of *Vraie et fausse réforme dans l'Église*, 54.

36 Congar, *True and False Reform in the Church*, 50; ET of *Vraie et fausse réforme dans l'Église*, 58.

37 See Congar, *True and False Reform in the Church*, 38; ET of *Vraie et fausse réforme dans l'Église*, 41.

38 Congar, *True and False Reform in the Church*, 39; ET of *Vraie et fausse réforme dans l'Église*, 42. See Pius XII, "Address to the Newly Created Cardinals," Acta Apostolicae Sedis 38 (1946): 141–51, here 149.

39 Yves Congar, "Church Reform and Luther's Reformation, 1517–1967," *Lutheran World* 14 (1967): 351–9, here 354.

40 Congar, *True and False Reform in the Church*, 218; ET of *Vraie et fausse réforme dans l'Église*, 252.

(ii) "To remain within the communion of all"

The concern for communion with the whole, so brilliantly articulated by St. Augustine in his controversies with the Donatists, is indispensable for a true reform. When he asserts that it is only within the communion of the entire body of the Church that total truth may be found, Congar, besides showing that the fullness of Christian revelation lies beyond the grasp of individuals or groups isolated from the Church, also forges a creative link between unity and truth.

(iii) "Patience; respect for delays"

In a proposal that uniquely combines patience, loyalty to the Church, and an ability to struggle for genuine reform without recourse to force, Congar puts in place important elements of a practical vision for reform. Aware of the risks and dangers involved in the matter of reform, he concludes his presentation on patience with a finely balanced statement offering a modus vivendi for reformers and leaders in the Church: "We can only insist that reformers not be too impatient if we ask the overseers of the tradition not to be too patient! We must ask the overseers to be aware of the pressure of the people's demands, which threaten to explode some day because they have been held in check for too long."[41]

(iv) "A true renewal by a return to the principle of the Tradition"

A true Catholic and Christian reform must be based on the authentic principles given in the Gospel and tradition. In an expression of his concern for the unity and Catholicity of the Church, Congar proposes an examination of the tradition, a return to the sources, as the cardinal rule for reform: "A Catholic reform movement therefore will be obliged to begin with a return to the fundamental principles of Catholicism. It will be necessary first of all to consult the tradition and to become immersed in it."[42]

We may now consider Congar's major studies on tradition since neither his specific proposals for reform nor his programme of renewal can be successful or even fully assimilated without a clear appreciation of the role he accords to tradition.

Congar's formulation of tradition provides a "new synthesis" of issues at once complex and controversial in Catholic theology.[43] The precise relationship between tradition, the Church, and the renewal movement based on a return to the biblical

---

41 Congar, *True and False Reform in the Church*, 289; ET of *Vraie et fausse réforme dans l'Église*, 332.

42 Congar, *True and False Reform in the Church*, 48–9; ET of *Vraie et fausse réforme dans l'Église*, 335–6.

43 Walter Kasper, "The Dialogue with Protestant Theology," *Concilium* 4 (1965): 76–87, here 84.

and patristic sources is described in *La Tradition et la vie de l'Église* (1963), the most synthetic of his three studies on tradition. As he writes, "We have also been witnessing, for some time, beginning in about 1937–38, a widespread renewal of patristic studies and a powerful biblical movement. All of this is bound to lead to a greater comprehension of tradition and of its relationship with the Church and with Scripture: three inseparable realities which a truly Catholic theology succeeds precisely in uniting and linking together."[44] Congar situates tradition at the heart of the *ressourcement*. "It's here that tradition (*Tradition*) is located; it's here that the Fathers have pride of place."[45] In contrast to the disciples of the late Archbishop Marcel Lefebvre (1905–1991) of Ecône, Switzerland, who emphasized a particular part of the tradition, Congar, by recourse to a rich metaphor of nature, presents a capacious view of tradition: "[T]he great river of tradition is wider than a straight canal with cemented parapets. The tradition of the Fathers is richer than the tradition whose content was fixed in the face of the Reformation by the 'Holy Council of Trent.'"[46] Congar proposes a dialectical model that links tradition and reform. In this framework, tradition is viewed in its totality while the Holy Spirit is presented as the guarantor of fidelity.[47]

Turning briefly to Congar's influence on the notion of tradition propounded in the *Dogmatic Constitution on Divine Revelation, Dei verbum*, it is important to acknowledge that the French philosopher Maurice Blondel (1861–1949) exercised a decisive influence on Congar's formulation of tradition.[48] It is thanks to Congar that Blondel's personalistic theory of tradition gained entry to the teaching of Vatican II.[49] There is general agreement among theologians concerning the issue of Congar's impact on *Dei verbum*.[50] This matter has already been documented

44 Congar, *Tradition and the Life of the Church*, 150; ET of *La tradition et la vie de l'Église*, 121.

45 Congar, *Challenge to the Church*, 66; ET of *La Crise dans l'Église et Mgr Lefebvre*, 81.

46 Congar, *Challenge to the Church*, 48–9; ET of *La Crise dans l'Église et Mgr Lefebvre*, 57–8; see Yves Congar, "Tradition in Theology," in "A Symposium on Tradition," reprinted from Robert M. Hutchins and Mortimer J. Adler, eds., *The Great Ideas Today 1974* (Chicago: Encyclopaedia Britannica, 1974), 4–20, here 19; Yves Congar, "Archbishop Lefebvre, Champion of 'Tradition'?" *Concilium* 119 (1978): 102, here 119; George H. Tavard, *Holy Writ or Holy Church: The Crisis of the Reformation* (London: Burns & Oates, 1959), 131–50 and 244–7.

47 Congar, *Tradition and the Life of the Church*, 146; ET of *La tradition et la vie de l'Église*, 118–19.

48 Congar, *Tradition and Traditions*, 367–8; ET of *La Tradition et les traditions: essai théologique*, 129.

49 Congar, *Tradition and Traditions*, 363 and 368; ET of *La Tradition et les traditions: essai théologique*, 125 and 129–30; see John J. McNeill, *The Blondelian Synthesis* (Leiden: Brill, 1966), 295–8.

50 See Frederick M. Jelly, "Tradition as the Development of Dogma according to Yves Congar," in *The Quadrilog: Tradition and the Future of Ecumenism*, ed. Kenneth Hagen (Collegeville, MN: Liturgical, 1994), 189–207, here 199.

elsewhere.[51] I want, nonetheless, to refer to an important observation made by Ratzinger in which he outlines Congar's role in the formulation of tradition adopted by the Council:

> **Article 8** appears for the first time in Text E under the heading: *De sacra Traditione* and is an attempt to meet the widely expressed need for a clear and positive account of what is meant by tradition. It is not difficult (as in the additions in which Article 7 goes beyond Trent) to recognise the pen of Y. Congar in the text and to see behind it the influence of the Catholic Tübingen school of the nineteenth century with, in particular, its dynamic and organic idea of tradition, which in turn was strongly impregnated by the spirit of German Romanticism.[52]

Congar acknowledges that even in its restricted dogmatic sense, "tradition" designates a reality that is too large, a concept too dense, to be formulable in a concise definition. Indeed, tradition, being concerned with the most profound realities, is something that can only be articulated in gestures. In the early fathers, tradition (*traditio*) refers to something "handed over" and not something "handed down."[53] Congar points to two senses of tradition. First, in an essential reference to its origin, tradition is viewed as the transmission or communication of faith across space and time. Second, "tradition is development as well as transmission."[54] In this second sense, he introduces the idea that tradition develops in history precisely through the use of new resources in response to new questions and new conditions. It may be said that the ecclesiastical tradition carries on the apostolic tradition and presents it to the Church of today. Thus Congar asserts that while these two senses must be distinguished, they must not be separated.[55]

The classic distinction in Catholic theology, which Congar makes his own, is between Tradition and traditions:

---

51 See Avery Dulles, *The Reshaping of Catholicism: Current Challenges in the Theology of Church* (San Francisco: Harper & Row, 1988), 75–92.

52 Joseph Ratzinger, "The Transmission of Divine Revelation," in *Commentary on the Documents of Vatican II*, ed. Herbert Vorgrimler (New York: Herder and Herder; London: Burns & Oates, 1969), 3:181–98, here 184; bold in original.

53 Congar, *Tradition and Traditions*, 244; ET of *La Tradition et les traditions: essai théologique*, 22.

54 Congar, *Tradition and Traditions*, 266; ET of *La Tradition et les traditions: essai théologique*, 40.

55 Yves Congar, "Tradition in Theology," in "A Symposium on Tradition," reprinted from Hutchins and Adler, eds., *The Great Ideas Today 1974*, 12. The theme of reception is, in Congar's view, of major importance for a wholly traditional Catholic ecclesiology and for ecumenism. See Yves Congar, "La 'Réception' comme réalité ecclésiologique," *Revue des sciences philosophiques et théologiques* 56 (1972): 369; *La Réception de Vatican II*, ed. G. Alberigo and J.-P. Jossua, Cogitatio Fidei (Paris: Cerf, 1985).

Our study has been located within the Catholicism of east and west, so that we have been understanding by "tradition" the continuity of the great doctrinal current that issued from Apostolic Jerusalem and was enriched through centuries in which it traversed many different socio-historical-cultural conditions. What we have called "the traditions" belong rather to the practical order: customs, local rites, devotions, particular forms of discipline and observance.[56]

Without seeking to reconstruct Congar's *Essai historique*, which outlines how the problem of tradition has been examined, it should, nonetheless, be remembered that his history of tradition forms a necessary foundation for the *Essai théologique*. It was as a result of the Reformation that tradition became a major issue in theology. Congar asserts that the reformers were heirs to an unhealthy separation of Scripture, Church, and tradition bequeathed by the fourteenth and fifteenth centuries.[57] This gave rise to a false option between the primacy of Scripture and the primacy of the Church that became for the reformers a choice between submission to God or submission to some human bidding.[58] It is thanks to the ecumenical movement that the old battle cries "Scripture alone," "faith alone," "Church alone" have, for the most part, receded from theological and ecclesial parlance. Congar's appeal to tradition as a principle of Church reform is not uncontroversial. We turn now to the predominant issues raised in his account of tradition.

It is appropriate to begin with the question of the role of Scripture and its relation to tradition. The essential place of Scripture as a norm that transcends and judges the Church is accepted as an established part of Congar's ecclesiology.[59] Scripture is the rule of faith and of truth that, according to the fathers, contains everything necessary to the conduct of our lives.[60] Difficulties arise, however, with regard to the manner in which Scripture is read. Congar is critical of Protestantism for the continued presence therein of some vestiges of a tendency to link the Christian life to the Bible rather than to the living Christ.[61] In order to preserve its full and authentic meaning, Scripture must, in Congar's view, be seen within tradition.[62]

56 Yves Congar, "Tradition in Theology," in "A Symposium on Tradition," reprinted from Hutchins and Adler, eds., *The Great Ideas Today 1974*, 14.

57 Congar, *Tradition and Traditions*, 473; ET of *La Tradition et les traditions: essai théologique*, 226.

58 Congar, *Tradition and Traditions*, 142; ET of *La Tradition et les traditions: essai historique*, 185–6.

59 Congar, "Church Reform," 354.

60 Congar, *Tradition and Traditions*, 381; ET of *La Tradition et les traditions: essai théologique*, 141–2.

61 Congar, *Tradition and Traditions*, 405; ET of *La Tradition et les traditions: essai théologique*, 162.

62 Congar, *Tradition and Traditions*, 414; ET of *La Tradition et les traditions: essai théologique*, 169–70.

As Scripture is not sufficient in itself, it must be viewed in relation to tradition. Nonetheless, tradition cannot be seen as being on the same plane as Scripture.

> In this respect, however, Scripture and Tradition are not on the same level. Scripture has an absolute sovereignty; it is of divine origin, even in its literary form; it governs Tradition and the Church, whereas it is not governed by Tradition or by the Church. Moreover, Scripture is fixed: it contains evidence from human witnesses who have now disappeared in the form in which they gave it. It is thus superlatively qualified to act as the unalterable "witness," and in this respect both the Church and Tradition are seen to be subject to it.[63]

Congar's contribution, clearly reflected in *Dei verbum*, is to situate exclusive authority neither in "Scripture alone" nor "tradition alone" nor "Church alone."[64] Revelation, in fact, flows through Scripture, tradition, and the Church. Congar, whose judgment on this matter resonates with that of the fathers, argues that these terms should neither be separated nor opposed to each other.

> These three realities are thus insufficient, even inconsistent, when separated one from another for they entail one another, beneath the causality of the Holy Spirit which is common to all three. . . . The balance and strength of the Catholic position, as shown in particular in the work and discussions which preceded or accompanied the definitions of the Immaculate Conception and the Assumption, consist in the joint and complementary affirmation of these three realities.[65]

There is a second point that can be alluded to briefly. I want to bring out some implications of the controversy over the sources of Revelation. The view of Scripture and tradition as two distinct sources of Revelation is rejected by Congar as inadequate since, in his view, "there is not a single dogma held by the Church on scriptural grounds alone and not a single one held on the strength of Tradition alone (*Tradition seule*)."[66] The debate in the 1960s concerning the correct interpretation of the decrees of Trent and whether to speak of one or two sources of Revelation seems remote from the problems of contemporary Catholicism.[67]

---

63 Congar, *Tradition and Traditions*, 422; ET of *La Tradition et les traditions: essai théologique*, 177–8.

64 "Dogmatic Constitution on Divine Revelation: *Dei Verbum*, 18 November 1965," in *Vatican Council II: The Conciliar and Post Conciliar Documents*, ed. Austin Flannery, 7th ed., 2 vols. (New York: Costello, 1984), 1: paras. 8–10.

65 Congar, *Tradition and Traditions*, 423–4; ET of *La Tradition et les traditions: essai théologique*, 179.

66 Yves Congar, *Called to Life* (Slough: St. Paul; New York: Crossroad Publishing, 1988), 35; ET of *Appelés à la vie* (Paris: Cerf, 1985), 43.

67 See "Decretum de libris sacris et de traditionibus recipiendis," April 8, 1546, in *Denzinger*, pars. 1501–1505 (para. 1501); see Joseph-Rupert Geiselmann, *The Meaning of Tradition*, trans. W. J. O'Hara (London: Burns & Oates, 1966).

Nonetheless, the Second Vatican Council's rejection of the expression "two sources of Revelation" is of considerable importance for ecumenism.[68] Congar's works on tradition helped overcome the bitter inter-Christian polemics in which Scripture and tradition sometimes appeared as if they were not quite on speaking terms, as rivals rather than partners.[69] As he remarks,

> Both Scripture and Tradition are necessary to arrive at a full knowledge of the saving deposit; they are two means by which the latter reaches us. However, the expression *two sources* should be avoided because it demands subtle explanation and would risk confining the theology of Tradition within a debatable position whose narrowness we are precisely trying to overcome.[70]

By stressing the authority of the word of God found in Scripture and tradition, Congar also helps show that a purely biblical Christianity threatens or omits the community dimension, particularly the liturgical community, seen as an essential element in the economy of salvation.[71] Congar, who views liturgy as "the holy ark containing sacred Tradition at its most intense," points to its indispensable role in the preservation and transmission of the Church's entire tradition.[72] As he writes, "The liturgy, even when it was neither understood nor carried into practice, preserved and transmitted intact to us the totality of the treasure of the Tradition, which we can today rediscover in its entirety."[73]

Now before leaving the question of liturgy, there is an area of difficulty that can only be approached in a direct manner. Congar argues that if all the decrees of Vatican II were really followed, there would be no crisis such as that precipitated by Archbishop Lefebvre.[74] Nonetheless, Congar admits that the liturgical reforms of Vatican II were the most criticized and the most rejected,[75] and that despite

---

68 Congar, *Tradition and the Life of the Church*, 155; ET of *La tradition et la vie de l'Église*, 125.

69 Congar, *Tradition and Traditions*, 414; ET of *La tradition et les traditions: essai théologique*, 170.

70 Congar, *Tradition and the Life of the Church*, 155; ET of *La tradition et la vie de l'Église*, 125; italics in original.

71 Congar, *Tradition and the Life of the Church*, 128; ET of *La tradition et la vie de l'Église*, 103; see J. P. Mackey, "Father Congar on Tradition," *Irish Theological Quarterly* 32 (1965): 53–9, here 58–9.

72 Congar, *Tradition and the Life of the Church*, 132; ET of *La tradition et la vie de l'Église*, 106; see *Dei Verbum*, 8.

73 Congar, "Institutionalised Religion," in *The Word in History: The St. Xavier Symposium*, ed. T. Patrick Burke (London: Collins, 1968), 133–53, here 138; ET of "Religion et institution," in *Théologie d'aujourd'hui et de demain*, ed. Burke (Paris: Cerf, 1967), 81–97, here 86.

74 Congar, *Challenge to the Church*, 50; ET of *La Crise dans l'Église et Mgr Lefebvre*, 59.

75 Congar, *Challenge to the Church*, 37; ET of *La Crise dans l'Église et Mgr Lefebvre*, 42.

the conciliatory language of the Council, the liturgical innovations were, at least in some cases, implemented in an autocratic manner.[76] Thus, to argue forcefully that the Council was in no way responsible for a crisis in the liturgy is to assume a position that is rather difficult to sustain,[77] and one that is certainly not supported by other scholars.[78]

Finally, then, one must also take into account the role Congar gives to the Holy Spirit in his exposition of tradition. In his *Essai théologique*, he acknowledges that a more satisfactory doctrine of the Spirit's activity in the Church is necessary for a more adequate theology of tradition.[79] He regards Christianity as being, by definition, something given and received; otherwise, it is a merely human invention. The guiding principle of this whole process of transmission and reception is the Holy Spirit. As Congar puts it, "The Holy Spirit who is the soul of the Tradition and renews all things is the principle of this continuity."[80] The treatment of tradition in Congar's works evinces a marked shift of emphasis from a Christological to a more pneumatic approach on the Church. While his earlier works are not unconcerned with the role of the Spirit,[81] the main emphasis is Christological. Congar, in point of fact, accedes to a clear evolution in his thought: "When I look back at the route that I have followed, I think that it corresponds very well with that of the Creed: From God through Christ and in the Holy Spirit."[82] It could be argued that Congar's particular juxtaposition of tradition and reform introduces a kind of antinomy that effectively renders a substantive reform in the Church virtually impossible.

Sources Chrétiennes: the living tradition in de Lubac's thought

De Lubac, like Congar, had a dynamic view of tradition: "What I have more than once regretted in highly regarded theologians, experienced guardians, was less, as others have made out, their lack of openness to the problems and currents of contemporary thought than their lack of a truly traditional mind (the two things are moreover connected)."[83] De Lubac was instrumental, with others, in the foundation

---

76   Congar, *Challenge to the Church*, 70; ET of *La Crise dans l'Église et Mgr Lefebvre*, 85.

77   Congar, *Challenge to the Church*, 50; ET of *La Crise dans l'Église et Mgr Lefebvre*, 59.

78   See John W. O'Malley, *Tradition and Transition: Historical Perspectives on Vatican II* (Wilmington, DE: Glazier, 1989), 115.

79   Congar, *Tradition and Traditions*, 493; ET of *La Tradition et les traditions: essai théologique*, 243.

80   Yves Congar, "L'héritage reçu dans l'Église," *Cahiers Saint Dominique* 145 (1974): 229–42, here 242.

81   See Yves Congar, "La Pneumatologie dans la théologie catholique," *Revue des sciences philosophiques et théologiques* 51 (1967): 250–8.

82   See Yves Congar, preface to Charles MacDonald, *Church and World in the Plan of God: Aspects of History and Eschatology in the Thought of Père Yves Congar O.P.* (Frankfurt: Lang, 1982), vii–x, here ix.

83   De Lubac, *At the Service of the Church*, 145; ET of *Mémoire*, 148.

of the *Théologie* series, a project of the Fourvière Jesuits, dedicated to the "renewal of the Church." He launched the series before the end of the Second World War with Henri Bouillard, who became the project's first secretary. Bouillard said that the twofold objective of the project was "to go to the sources of Christian doctrine, to find in it the truth of our life."[84] But it was *Sources chrétiennes*, a bilingual collection published by Éditions du Cerf, under the general editorship of de Lubac and Daniélou, which was the crowning glory of the Fourvière Jesuits, as well as their greatest and most enduring contribution to *ressourcement*.[85] The series was destined to become a living stream of tradition for the Francophone world. As de Lubac remarks, "Each time, in our West, that Christian renewal has flourished, in the order of thought as in that of life (and the two are always connected), it has flourished under the sign of the Fathers."[86] The editors provide an introduction to each work in the series that attempts to situate it "in its own intellectual and spiritual world." This project was thought up and elaborated between 1932 and 1937 by Victor Fontoynont, SJ (†1958), who was the true founder of the collection, as de Lubac acknowledged in his *Mémoire sur l'occasion de mes écrits*.[87] Credit must also be given to other theologians of the period for their contribution to patristic theology, namely, Daniélou, Yves de Montcheuil (1900–1944), and Louis Bouyer (1913–2004). Perhaps the most eloquent testimony to the relevance and success of this venture, the principal aim of which was to provide high-quality translations of the fathers in contemporary French, is the publication to date of over five hundred volumes of Greek, Latin, and occasionally Syriac and Aramaic authors.

The critical goal of making the fathers accessible to successive generations is directly dependent upon the availability of the patristic texts in high-quality translation alongside the original language. Careful study of the fathers has contributed to advances in key areas of theology and ecclesial life, including those of interreligious dialogue, ecumenism, Christology, and Eucharistic theology.[88] Indeed, Fouilloux notes that one of the aims of *Sources chrétiennes*, from its beginnings, was a rapprochement between separated Christians of East and West.[89] The perennial problem of course is to get students of theology as well as bishops, priests, and laity to incorporate the fathers of the Church into their schedule of daily reading, so as to discover how the treasures of the past illuminate the complexities of the present, a point de Lubac was at pains to make in the course of his long career.

84 See de Lubac, *At the Service of the Church*, 31; ET of *Mémoire*, 29.

85 See Étienne Fouilloux, *"Sources chrétiennes": éditer les Pères de l'Église au XXᵉ siècle* (Paris: Cerf, 1995), 219. Fouilloux notes that one of the aims of *Sources chrétiennes*, from its beginnings, was a rapprochement between separated Christians of East and West; see further Aubert, *La Théologie Catholique*, 84–6.

86 De Lubac, *At the Service of the Church*, 95–6; ET of *Mémoire*, 96.

87 De Lubac, *At the Service of the Church*, 94; ET of *Mémoire*, 95.

88 See Michel Fédou, "Sources Chrétiennes: Patristique et renaissance de la théologie," *Gregorianum* 92 (2011): 781–96, here 790–5.

89 Fouilloux, *La Collection "Sources chrétiennes,"* 219; see also Roger Aubert, *La Théologie Catholique au milieu du XXᵉ siècle*, 84–6; de Lubac, *At the Service of the Church*, 95–6; ET of *Mémoire*, 96.

The fathers: "Masters of the Spiritual Life"

John Courtney Murray, the acclaimed American Jesuit and champion of liberty at Vatican II, shows a profound awareness of the implications of *Sources Chrétiennes* in a review of the new series published in *Theological Studies*.[90] First, he points out that the series serves to bridge the gap that had been created between theology and spirituality. As he writes, "The Fathers of the Church are not only teachers of Christian doctrine but masters of the spiritual life; not only do their works give guidance to the mind in its search for the truth of God, but they also afford inspiration to the whole soul in its search for God." This is a point of utmost importance. At the present time, when spirituality is often divorced from the living tradition, theology, and ecclesiology, with resultant deleterious consequences, recourse to the fathers provides access to the riches of the faith and is the only adequate response to the "permanent restlessness" of the human person. The church fathers are, in this regard, models of Christian witness as well as of intellectual courage. Second, the series successfully recreates the "climate of opinion" within which it was conceived. "In the patristic climate of opinion the uninitiated rather tends to gasp for breath. It is to this problem and its solution that *Sources Chrétiennes* directly addresses itself, with altogether remarkable success."[91] De Lubac was a faithful witness to the past and his work on medieval exegesis must also be acknowledged in the context of the present analysis.[92]

In view of the misrepresentation of religion and of serious misunderstandings of the foundational tenets of the faith in influential segments of contemporary society, it is evident that a new reception of the foundational pillars of *ressourcement* is necessary. This would facilitate a reciprocal enrichment of theology and spirituality for the enhancement of the ministries and pastoral practices of the Christian churches. Further, such a renewed engagement with *ressourcement* would in turn help meet the present expectations of Christians for spiritual enlightenment and nourishment for the soul, one of the original aims of *Sources Chrétiennes*.

Tradition, Ressourcement, *and the "new image of the church"*

The question of continuity with the ancient tradition is important; it engenders confidence and fosters growth within the Christian Church. Each new patristic *ressourcement* contributes fresh vitality to the Church and in turn to society and

---

90 John Courtney Murray, "*Sources Chrétiennes*," *Theological Studies* 9 (1948): 250–5.

91 John Courtney Murray, "Current Theology: Source Chrétiennes," *Theological Studies* 9 (1948): 251.

92 See Susan K. Wood, *Spiritual Exegesis and the Church in the Theology of Henri de Lubac* (Grand Rapids, MI: Eerdmans, 1998); see also Fergus Kerr, *Twentieth-Century Catholic Theologians: From Neoscholasticism to Nuptial Mysticism* (Oxford: Blackwell, 2007), 85.

the world. In this regard, Rahner poses a pertinent question: "What is it that makes the properly historical studies like those of de Lubac or de la Taille so stimulating and to the point?" In his response, he lauds de Lubac's acuity and perceptiveness. "Surely it is the art of reading texts in such a way that they become not just votes cast in favour of or against our current positions (positions taken up long ago), but say something to us which we in our time have not considered at all or not closely enough, about reality itself."[93] Vatican II was a council about the Church and for the Church. The success of its work and its reception depended in no small measure on the intellectual capacity, the diplomacy, and the sensibility of the leading *ressourcement* intellectuals who successfully presented a new image of the Church to the world. Today, in the face of grave difficulties in the Church and in the world, as well as the rich opportunities emanating from each successive generation of young people, surely the ongoing success of the Church's mission will be assured by closer adherence to the sacred text and by a successful engagement of tradition and modernity.

93 Karl Rahner, "The Prospects for Dogmatic Theology," in *Theological Investigations* I, trans. Cornelius Ernst (London: Darton, Longman & Todd, 1961), 1–209, here 10.

Chapter 11

TRADITION II: THINKING WITH HISTORICAL TEXTS— REFLECTIONS ON THEOLOGIES OF RETRIEVAL

Darren Sarisky

I.

Theologies of retrieval come in several different varieties.[1] There are different confessional approaches to retrieval: Protestants, Roman Catholics, and Orthodox Christians have their own characteristic ways of drawing upon and appropriating the past for the purpose of using it within constructive theological proposals.[2] A theologian's confessional location shapes both the specific sources to which she gravitates and the manner in which she engages with them. Another source of variety is that some theologies of retrieval are especially alert or sensitive to concerns about race and gender, lest these theologies seem to be simply an effort to "make theology great again" in the way that Donald Trump's campaign for president of the United States attempted the same, that is, by using racist and sexist rhetoric.[3] For some, theologies of retrieval appear to be "a type of protective ideology for affluent bourgeois societies that, confronted everywhere by increasingly insistent demands and challenges, refuse to alter their priorities and look to religion as a supposedly reliable and time-tested accomplice in their efforts to safeguard the status quo."[4] To protect against this danger, theologies especially focused on race and gender are often more critical of the sources they appropriate, with a view toward highlighting how they marginalize certain voices. Yet another factor that conditions theologies of retrieval, generating differences among them, is the

---

1 I very much appreciate the incisive and quite helpful comments I received from Pui Ip on a draft of this essay.

2 See the essays in Part 2 of this volume.

3 See the essay on race in this volume by Brian Bantum and the essay on gender by Ruth Jackson.

4 Johann Baptist Metz, "Productive Noncontemporaneity," in *Observations on "The Spiritual Situation of the Age": Contemporary German Perspectives*, ed. Jürgen Habermas, Studies in Contemporary German Social Thought (Cambridge, MA: MIT Press, 1984), 170.

disciplinary location from which they emerge. Works by historians may venture normative theological views that grow out of intensive exegesis of historical texts, while the overall organization of such works is still defined by period or figure.[5] In contrast, works by systematic theologians may be more conceptual, while delving deeply into historical sources and making interpretation of them crucial to mapping out how issues ought to be understood.[6] It would be possible to continue enumerating reasons for the diversity within this broad type of theology, but even this brief sketch suffices to demonstrate that works of retrieval do not constitute an undifferentiated monolith.

If theologies of retrieval are variegated, what holds these approaches together? In what way is retrieval even a meaningful category? What sort of family resemblance is there between the different theologies of retrieval? By investing deeply in historical investigation, and by not seeking to understand the past for its own sake but utilizing historical understanding within constructive work, these theologies might well be understood as works of "creative archaeology."[7] As Rowan Williams says of Vladimir Lossky and his study of the fourth-century church fathers, "He is claiming that they do, as a matter of fact, move the theological discussion on and allow things to be said that could not be said before."[8] In this way, historical sources open up new perspectives and provide a stimulus to reflection that allows theological conversations to move forward; they enable theologians to map out a territory by means of resources from the tradition of Christian thought. Yet thinking of retrieval as "creative archaeology" is tantalizing and, of course, paradoxical. Archaeology is a matter of finding something in the past, creativity of spontaneous production. How do these two elements relate to one another? What is the relationship between unearthing a moment from history, one rich in meaning and therefore worth ruminating upon and deferring to, and the freer "creative" reflection upon this moment that makes this a mode of *theology*, a matter of thinking that aims to "reapply the lessons to current social and ecclesiastical concerns"[9]? This essay explores the question of what theologies of retrieval are by differentiating these theologies from related approaches, by setting out a collection of theses that characterize theologies of retrieval, and by defending such theologies against a pressing objection. The criticism to which the final section responds is that the

---

5 Khaled Anatolios, *Retrieving Nicaea: The Development and Meaning of Trinitarian Doctrine* (Grand Rapids, MI: Baker, 2011); Lewis Ayres, *Nicaea and Its Legacy: An Approach to Fourth-Century Trinitarian Theology* (Oxford: Oxford University Press, 2004).

6 See, for instance, Sarah Coakley, *God, Sexuality, and the Self: An Essay "On the Trinity"* (Cambridge: Cambridge University Press, 2013); Rowan Williams, *On Christian Theology* (Oxford: Blackwell, 2000); John B. Webster, *Word and Church: Essays in Christian Dogmatics* (Edinburgh: T & T Clark, 2001).

7 Rowan Williams, *Why Study the Past?: The Quest for the Historical Church* (London: Darton, Longman and Todd, 2005), 100.

8 Williams, *Why Study the Past?* 100.

9 Coakley, *God, Sexuality, and the Self*, 11.

supposedly archaeological aspect of works in the mode of retrieval is more apparent than real, for efforts to leverage the past for the sake of the present occlude history itself from view.

II.

It will be illuminating to begin by distinguishing theologies of retrieval from two other ways of engaging with past tracts of theological teaching. First, theology of retrieval is not historical theology. Any theology of retrieval will take part in significant dialogue with history because of the need to understand the past, and so it is closely connected to historical theology, but historical theology's interest in the past is not what defines theology of retrieval. The impulse that stands behind historical theology is to understand portions of the past for their own sake.[10] This requires that the historian "goes native."[11] To understand a written text that originated in a past context, the historian views that text against the background of its circumstances of origin, reading it in its original language and considering the questions the text was designed to address on their own terms. Going native entails that questions of the text's relevance—important as they may be for other purposes—cannot be allowed to distract the historian from pursuing his own queries. In addition to going native, the historian interprets the text, which means explaining the work in language and categories that make sense to a modern audience. It is inevitable that the historian will, thus, understand the past from the point of view of the present, at least to some extent. But what the historian qua historian does not do is attempt to correct views emerging from the past or make normative judgments about the issues that arise from historical study.[12] Historians do not offer explicit normative judgments about the material

---

10 David C. Steinmetz, "Taking the Long View," in *Taking the Long View: Christian Theology in Historical Perspective* (Oxford: Oxford University Press, 2011), 148–9.

11 Steinmetz, "Taking the Long View," 149.

12 Constraints of space allow for discussion only of a mode of historical theology that aspires to be value-free. For a more nuanced consideration of how value judgments factor into historical work, albeit in a limited way where they hover in the background, see Bernard Lonergan, *Method in Theology*, 2nd ed. (London: Darton, Longman and Todd, 1973), 224–33. For a detailed consideration of academic trajectories that contributed to the formation of today's historical theology, which highlights the variety of stances that practitioners had on the role of values and the historian's presuppositions, see Johannes Zachhuber, *Theology as Science in Nineteenth-Century Germany: From F. C. Baur to Ernst Troeltsch*, Changing Paradigms in Historical and Systematic Theology (Oxford: Oxford University Press, 2013). Pertinent reflections are also to be found in Morwenna Ludlow, *Gregory of Nyssa: Ancient and (Post)Modern* (Oxford: Oxford University Press, 2007), 279–92, which offers the test case of Gregory of Nyssa and sheds light on the way in which his interpretation by theologians and others is tied up with the wider commitments of such interpreters.

they study; they also strive not to allow their own views to color the narrative they offer about the past. When history is done well, historians present views they oppose with just as much enthusiasm as they do views they favor. Because one of the defining characteristics of historical theology is holding back verdicts on the past,[13] historical theology differs from theology of retrieval in that the latter has as its purpose offering theological proposals that arise from detailed historical work. Any theology of retrieval will build upon historical theology, but that is not what theology of retrieval is.

Second, neither is theology of retrieval correlationist theology. Theologies of retrieval seek to speak into the present so as to engage a contemporary audience, but they lack the correlationist's in-principle commitment to bring into dialogue the Christian tradition and the religious undercurrent of common human experience and language as sources with equal prominence and weight within the theological task.[14] For a correlationist such as David Tracy, theology draws together these two sources in a mutually critical dialogue, to which both contribute and in which neither is privileged, such that it can set the terms of the discussion. From his point of view, important insights regarding ultimate questions emerge from phenomenological reflection upon scientific investigation, human moral struggles, and even everyday life. The theological value of these sources does not differ in kind from that of the Christian tradition's major texts, which receive greater stress within any approach to theology that emphasizes retrieval enough to qualify legitimately as a form of theology of retrieval. Tracy thus balances a hermeneutical investigation of the texts of the tradition with a phenomenological inquiry into common experience and language. A further factor that relativizes retrieval in his appropriation of classic texts is that suspicion of material from the tradition is a counterweight to deferential reception of it.[15] There are similarities

---

13 For the necessary split between subject and object in historical study, see Martin Rumscheidt, *Revelation and Theology: An Analysis of the Barth-Harnack Correspondence of 1923*, Monograph Supplements to the Scottish Journal of Theology (Cambridge: Cambridge University Press, 1972), 52–3. Also worth consulting is James Barr, *The Concept of Biblical Theology: An Old Testament Perspective* (Minneapolis: Fortress, 1999), 209–12.

14 David Tracy, *Blessed Rage for Order: The New Pluralism in Theology* (Chicago: University of Chicago Press, 1996), 47–8.

15 David Tracy, *Plurality and Ambiguity: Hermeneutics, Religion, Hope* (Chicago: University of Chicago Press, 1994), 100. Tracy speaks passionately about what he sees as the danger of giving retrieval too much prominence, making theology too simple, and thus warping attempts to speak theologically. He says, "Believers, to be sure, have their own reductionistic temptations: the claim, for example, that only a hermeneutics of confessionalist retrieval can be allowed to count. In that case, reductionism has a heyday. Under this banner, we can apparently retrieve anything—however repressive or nonsensical. Dogmas are always right; mystery is always present; retrievability is always in order. These are the temptations of any hermeneutic of pure retrieval." Tracy's own position betrays influence from Paul Ricoeur, *Freud and Philosophy: An Essay on Interpretation*, The Terry Lectures (New Haven, CT: Yale University Press, 1970), 28–36, which calls for an interplay between

between correlationism's stress on a hermeneutic of suspicion and the more critically oriented versions of retrieval, and perhaps the difference between the two
in this respect is merely a matter of degree. But the more basic difference still
obtains: even theologies of retrieval that give greater relative weight to critique of
their sources lack an essential commitment to integrate generic experience into
the theological task as a second independent source of equal standing with established texts. Theologies of retrieval that are deeply moved by considerations of
race and gender still center on *readings* (broadly construed) of sources by groups
that are often relegated to the margins; they do not focus simple on the religious
dimension of the experience of people in general or of specific groups of people,
without any close connection between those people and a set of sources to which
the default orientation is deference.[16] For all theologies of retrieval, classics do not
have a basic parity with other sources of insight[17]; rather, "classics come first."[18]

III.

In the previous section, it was argued that theologies of retrieval exist in contradistinction to two other approaches to the Christian tradition: historical theology,
whose aim is to reconstruct the past without reference to the value it might have
now or to the problems in past formulations, and correlationism, which distinguishes itself as a mode of theological discourse by relating contemporary experience to texts from the tradition. Theologies of retrieval generally have a more
congenial relationship with historical theology than with a rival approach to the
task of systematic theology, though, as will become clear in the final part of this
chapter, the main objection to theologies of retrieval with which this chapter wrestles is inspired by worries that certain historians have about any approach that
engages with the past for the sake of "using" it in some way. The present section
aims to sketch out with a set of expository theses the areas of major overlap among

recollection and suspicion. There is a useful summary of Tracy's thinking, and especially his
early work, in Ian Markham, "Revisionism," in *The Oxford Handbook of Systematic Theology*,
ed. John Webster, Kathryn Tanner, and Iain R. Torrance (Oxford: Oxford University Press,
2009), 601–5. For an interaction with more recent developments in his thought, see the
essay by William Myatt in this volume.

16 For a proposal on race that might well be considered a work of retrieval because of
the stress on engagement with texts, see J. Kameron Carter, *Race: A Theological Account*
(Oxford: Oxford University Press, 2008). There seems to be some development in Carter's
more recent thinking, where perhaps the category of retrieval fits less well.

17 There are, of course, other versions of correlationism than simply Tracy's. See, for
instance, John Macquarrie, *Principles of Christian Theology*, rev. ed. (London: SCM, 2003);
Paul Tillich, *Systematic Theology*, 3 vols. (Chicago: University of Chicago Press, 1951–1963).

18 John Webster, "Theologies of Retrieval," in *The Oxford Handbook of Systematic
Theology*, ed. John Webster, Kathryn Tanner, and Iain R. Torrance (Oxford: Oxford
University Press, 2007), 590.

theologies of retrieval. It begins with two negative theses—ones that indicate assumptions that theologies of retrieval do not hold and intellectual operations that are not part of retrieval—before proceeding to positive claims that specify further what binds together approaches emphasizing retrieval.

(1) Theologies of retrieval do not subscribe to a linear, progressive view of history in which ideas developed in the past are dismissed as obsolete and outmoded, having been superseded by the offerings of the present. Such a belief would render the act of retrieval nonsensical, for a premise of this approach is that there is indeed something valuable to be found within the tradition, a contribution that it still has to make to the life and thought of the church.[19] To hold that theology makes steady, incremental advances that accumulate over time, perhaps on the assumption that scientific understanding does this and that other fields of inquiry ought to model themselves upon natural science, is to commit theology to playing a perpetual game of catch-up, in which theology continually sheds elements from its past and replaces them with whatever is most contemporary.[20] Consider, for instance, an example of how this catch-up mentality could manifest itself in the domain of biblical exegesis. In the conclusion to his substantial study of Origen's hermeneutic, Henri de Lubac articulates this sentiment only to reject it categorically: "Faced with the exegetical constructions of someone like Origen, we could indeed exclaim: This was a great and beautiful dream, but criticism has dispelled it and faith easily passes it by; let the historian allow it a retrospective admiration, today's Christian has nothing more to do with it."[21] Theologies of retrieval proceed on the basis that there is something in the work of major figures from the tradition worth being faithful to, even in a set of circumstances that differ in many respects from those in which works such as Origen's had their first life.

When it is assumed, contra theologies of retrieval, that theological works become obsolete in time, then it follows that the only way they can be read is as past acts of communication, rather than as living voices that engage readers in the present. G. W. F. Hegel comments penetratingly on the commitments that underpin the stipulation that the sole way of interpreting classic texts is to situate them in their original context:

> The most important sign that these positive dogmas have lost much of their importance is that in the main these doctrines are treated *historically*. As far as this historical procedure is concerned, it deals with thoughts and representations that were had, introduced, and fought over by others, with convictions that belong to others, with histories that do not take place within our spirit, do not engage the needs of our spirit. What is of interest is rather how these things have come about in the case of others, the contingent way in which they were formed.

---

19 See the comments on the "simple progressivist myth which allows you to say that we know more of Christ than any earlier age": Williams, *Why Study the Past?* 28.

20 Metz, "Productive Noncontemporaneity," 172–3.

21 Henri de Lubac, *History and Spirit: The Understanding of Scripture According to Origen* (San Francisco: Ignatius, 2007), 429.

The absolute way in which these doctrines were formed—out of the depths of spirit—is forgotten, and so their necessity and truth is forgotten, too, and the question what one holds as one's own conviction meets with astonishment.[22]

What drives an exclusively historical engagement, here, is a conviction that the material content of the text in question has lost its grip on the minds of those living centuries later. Modern readers may investigate these writings out of interest in the past, but not out of a motivation to explore for themselves the questions that animated the prior discussion. By contrast, theologies of retrieval see older texts as ones whose claims might still be considered, and as works that are worth making recourse to well after their date of genesis.

(2) Though theologies of retrieval do not presume that history no longer has value in the present, neither do they operate according to the polar opposite assumption, that the task of constructive theology is simply to conform itself in every detail to commanding figures of the past by repeating exactly what they have said. That is, they neither sneer at history nor simply parrot back the words of acknowledged classics. Faithfulness to key texts within the tradition does not entail reiterating them without considering their claims critically or recontextualizing their insights.[23] Constructive theological work, even by theologians with the deepest reverence for the tradition in which they stand, requires adapting what one says to the particular contingent circumstances one is addressing. Just as those who do constructive work today tailor what they say to their audience, so also past

---

22 G. W. F. Hegel, *Lectures on the Philosophy of Religion*, vol. 1, *Introduction and the Concept of Religion* (Berkeley: University of California Press, 1984), 158–9; italics in original.

23 A review by Peter Leithart of Khaled Anatolios's work *Retrieving Nicaea* portrays the book as offering an organized collection of insights from Athanasius, Gregory of Nyssa, and Augustine as essentially the final word on Trinitarian theology. Leithart concludes, "But I am left wondering: having retrieved, now what? Has he left the rest of us—us systematicians, or perhaps us Protestants—anything more to do?" Peter J. Leithart, "Review of *Retrieving Nicaea: The Development and Meaning of Trinitarian Doctrine*, by Khaled Anatolios," *International Journal of Systematic Theology* 16 (2014): 356. It is true that Anatolios's work has as its purpose commending certain theological ideas that were developed in the Nicene context. It is clear, however, that he conceives of his text as contributing to a larger project of retrieval, rather than constituting all aspects of that task. He makes plain that he sees himself as presenting what ought to be appropriated, rather than as doing the whole work of appropriation. Anatolios writes, describing the task of his concluding chapter, "The following is an attempt to sketch some themes delineating the systematic scope of Nicene theology that can be valuable in informing a contemporary experience of trinitarian faith. . . . They demand further elaboration, nuance, and qualification that cannot be adequately provided here. The present task is simply to recommend these themes as worthy of further reflection both in their original setting and in our contemporary context as evocative of the systematic scope of trinitarian doctrine." Anatolios, *Retrieving Nicaea*, 281.

theologians have done the same. Good reading of historical texts involves seeing how much the theological content within the texts is dependent upon a particular social, intellectual, and cultural setting that is not identical with that of the present moment.[24] Furthermore, even if simple repetition were possible, identifying which voices to follow is not a simple matter. There is a great diversity of theological theories that have been developed in the course of Christian history,[25] even during crucially formative periods for the tradition. Theologies of retrieval must therefore reflectively sort through this variety in the process of deliberating on what to say now. For these reasons, a theology of repetition is a dead end. Retrieval operates differently, through "an assimilation which is at the same time a transformation."[26]

This brings the discussion to the positive propositions that characterize retrieval and how it operates. (3) The single most important positive thesis about theologies of retrieval—the great significance of which derives from the way it summarizes the goal of retrieval—is that they aim to think *with* rather than *about* historical texts. Understanding the past is indispensable for these theologies; they cannot bypass listening to what classical texts actually say. But the main impetus of retrieval, and the reason they make recourse to the past in the first place, is to understand classic texts for the sake of mapping out a particular theological domain by means of the ideas contained within them. It is, in this way, a mode of systematic theology, rather than historical theology, though it positions the two disciplines such that they are in close dialogue.[27] Theological works of retrieval turn expectantly to past tracts of teaching, in the hope that it is possible to receive something from them that will shed light on a certain theological issues. As Jean-Luc Marion says, "It is not so much a matter of explicating authors as it is of asking them to explicate the situation in which we find ourselves."[28] For this reason, theologies of retrieval relate to historical texts as those that speak with a living voice, that did speak in their original circumstances, and that continue to address similar issues that have reemerged in later situations. When they are most deferential to particularly rich texts from the history of the church, these theologies assume a

---

24 Henri de Lubac, *Catholicism: A Study of Dogma in Relation to the Corporate Destiny of Mankind* (London: Burns & Oates, 1958), 172.

25 De Lubac, *Catholicism*, 172.

26 De Lubac, *Catholicism*, 172.

27 See Anatolios, *Retrieving Nicaea*, 12, who says that his work involves "some creative selection" from within the writings of key theologians. He continues to describe his goal: "The present work purports to be a creative systematic retrieval of systematizing elements within the historical development of trinitarian doctrine." This necessarily links up theology and history as disciplines, and unsettles firm divisions between them because history is seen as feeding insights into systematic theology, and the needs of systematic theology at least contribute to deciding which historical figures can serve as helpful interlocutors within contemporary theology.

28 Jean-Luc Marion, *The Idol and Distance: Five Studies*, Perspectives in Continental Philosophy (New York: Fordham University Press, 2001), 22.

commentarial form, commending a synthetic, thematically organized reiteration of theological material as a way to think about God and all things in relation to him.[29] T. F. Torrance's work on the Trinity is an example of this in that it draws upon theological work that fed into the formation of the Nicene Creed and proposes to think with this historical material about the locus of theology proper and the way in which God makes himself known.[30]

In some cases, theologies of retrieval might be described aptly with the terminology of *thinking with and beyond* particular classic texts in order to underscore how historical material is either supplemented by other content or significantly tailored for the sake of its reapplication to a new context.[31] All thinking with goes beyond in some ways, but in these cases the extension is so prominent that it deserves to be highlighted. Historical material remains a tool with which to think, rather than an object of interest per se. But the way in which it undergoes change as it combines with other ideas and is recontextualized can mean that the simpler label of *thinking with* may not be sufficient to depict accurately all that is happening in these cases of retrieval. The expanded rubric, including the term *beyond*, can be called for in cases such as that of Dietrich Bonhoeffer, who was clearly a very significant theologian

---

29 This same dynamic can be seen within disciplines other than theology in which authors utilize particularly stimulating texts to consider issues and solve problems. Philosophy provides illustrations of this. Consider how Saul Kripke characterizes his stance toward Ludwig Wittgenstein: "I suspect . . . that to attempt to present Wittgenstein's argument precisely is to some extent to falsify it. Probably many of my formulations and recastings of the argument are done in a way Wittgenstein would not himself approve. So the present paper should be thought of as expounding neither 'Wittgenstein's' argument nor 'Kripke's': rather Wittgenstein's argument as it struck Kripke, as it presented a problem for him." Saul A. Kripke, *Wittgenstein on Rules and Private Language: An Elementary Exposition* (Cambridge, MA: Harvard University Press, 1982), 5. I owe this quotation to a conversation with Paul Griffiths. Quite similar is Jay Rosenberg's stance toward Immanuel Kant. For a "Dionysian" reading of Kant (as opposed to an "Apollonian" or more straightforwardly historical one), a practicing philosopher construes Kant as a "philosopher who is much smarter than most of us and consequently capable of teaching us a great number of interesting things. The working premise of this approach is that Kant is intelligently and creatively responding to a problem-space which transcends its historical setting." Jay F. Rosenberg, *Accessing Kant: A Relaxed Introduction to the Critique of Pure Reason* (Oxford: Oxford University Press, 2005), 2.

30 See Thomas F. Torrance, *The Trinitarian Faith: The Evangelical Theology of the Ancient Catholic Church* (Edinburgh: T & T Clark, 1988).

31 I owe this language to John W. De Gruchy, "With Bonhoeffer, beyond Bonhoeffer: Transmitting Bonhoeffer's Legacy," in *Dietrich Bonhoeffers Theologie heute: Ein Weg zwischen Fundamentalismus und Säkularismus?* [Dietrich Bonhoeffer's theology today: A way between fundamentalism and secularism], ed. John W. De Gruchy, Stephen Plant, and Christiane Tietz (Gütersloh: Gütersloher Verlagshaus, 2009), 403–16.

but had his life cut tragically short, with the result that his extant works signal important ideas that he did not receive the opportunity to develop fully. In this situation, others can step in and extend a promising line of thought in ways that Bonhoeffer could not. Here, incompleteness prompts going beyond. But significant recontextualization might prompt going beyond as well insofar as what it is really doing is exploring an analogy between a present situation and the one addressed by the older theologian. For instance, theologians in South Africa have gone beyond Bonhoeffer by extending his reflections to those of native Africans in apartheid South Africa.[32]

What is the rationale for allowing historical works to contribute substantially to the material content of theological proposals? Operating in the mode of retrieval expands the theologian's set of dialogue partners beyond what the current scene offers. It opens up a whole new set of possibilities, expanding the horizons within which a theologian can reflect on a set of issues.[33] It moves beyond the state of the present and what is commonplace within contemporary thinking by reconnecting with the legacies of the Christian tradition, thereby seeking to renew the present via accessing insights that lie outside its scope. In the past quarter-century, there has been a notable uptick in theologies that operate in this way.[34] Systematic theology has received a boost from the surge of interest in theologies of retrieval. Granted that opening up new vistas has value, why turn to the *past* for this purpose? Why not achieve the same result by considering material from another geographical location or cultural milieu?[35] There is nothing standing in the way of theologies of retrieval engaging more fully and deeply with forms of Christianity that are developing in parts of the world other than where Christianity has been an established force for many centuries. Yet theologies of retrieval usually assume that the past contains a set of witnesses to the divine who are privileged, nodes within a conversation that extends into the present, and to which some have made especially notable contributions. It is therefore impossible for contemporary theologians to give a complete account of an issue without making reference to their

---

32 De Gruchy, "With Bonhoeffer, beyond Bonhoeffer," 412–15.

33 Karl Barth, *Protestant Theology in the Nineteenth Century: Its Background & History* (London: SCM Press, 1972), 24; Webster, "Theologies of Retrieval," 590.

34 Kathryn Tanner, "Shifts in Theology over the Last Quarter Century," *Modern Theology* 26 (2010): 42–3.

35 A challenge that theologies of retrieval will have to face in coming years is to consider more deeply than they have so far how to engage with the theologies that are emerging from so-called majority world versions of Christianity. On this challenge, see Andrew F. Walls, "The Gospel as Prisoner and Liberator of Culture," in *The Missionary Movement in Christian History: Studies in the Transmission of Faith* (Maryknoll, NY: Orbis, 1996), 9–10. There is a risk, however, in the way that Walls frames this challenge: it would be better to see the "majority world" as entering the theological conversation as a now indispensable dialogue partner, supplementing resources from the West with new insights, rather than displacing the West, as seems to be how Walls sees things.

forebears, to whom they owe a debt of gratitude.[36] There is thus a parallel between theologies of retrieval and what Friedrich Nietzsche calls monumental history: "a history given to reestablishing the high points of historical development and their maintenance in a perpetual presence, given to the recovery of works, actions, and creations through the monogram of their personal essence."[37]

There is also a second half to the rationale for retrieval, which has already been suggested but should now be made explicit. The working assumption is not just that certain high points do in fact exist in the past but also that present thought should expose itself to them and be unsettled by them. Historical work can demonstrate that things are not the way they are by some sort of natural law, for the present came to exist by the confluence of certain forces; the present is a creation of these factors and is not the way that things have simply always been.[38] The way that historical studies highlight the contingency of the present can free up the imagination to envision new paths that might be traveled now and in the future. For theologies of retrieval, the impact of history is not to provide an account of an ideal set of circumstances to which to return, a sort of theological golden age, all differences from which automatically count as declensions.[39] Even theologians who claim to believe that a fall took place at a certain point offer constructive theological proposals that are a complex synthesis of material from the past and the present.[40] The critical force of history is, thus, not to establish a standard

---

36 See Williams, *Why Study the Past?* 26–7.

37 This is Michel Foucault's gloss on "monumental history." See Michel Foucault, "Nietzsche, Genealogy, History," in *The Foucault Reader*, ed. Paul Rabinow (New York: Penguin, 1984), 94. For Nietzsche's own exposition and evaluation of monumental history, see Friedrich Nietzsche, "On the Uses and Disadvantages of History for Life," in *Untimely Meditations*, Cambridge Texts in the History of Philosophy (Cambridge: Cambridge University Press, 1997), 67–72. Nietzsche's concept is not specifically theological, though he does consider how the different sorts of applied histories he expounds can be brought to bear on religion generally and Christianity specifically. See Nietzsche, "On the Uses and Disadvantages of History for Life," 95–7.

38 Williams, *Why Study the Past?* 24–5.

39 Williams, *Why Study the Past?* 105.

40 See, for instance, how Paul Gavrilyuk explains the approach of Georges Florovsky, who saw the patristic era as a golden age, but whose own theological practice combined patristic and modern ideas far more than his own self-description would indicate: "In any historical narrative, the past events and ideas can never be frozen entirely in the past, but are reinterpreted from the standpoint of the present. But what precisely was involved in such a reinterpretation? Bulgakov and other 'modernist' theologians construed such a reinterpretation rather freely—as involving a translation of the ancient dogmatic definitions into the language of contemporary philosophy and as sanctioning a speculative expansion of traditional beliefs. Theoretically, Florovsky was opposed to any expression of the modernist philosophical translation of patristic theological categories, since for him the Christian Hellenism of the Church Fathers was *philosophia perennis*. But in actual practice he read the

that simply needs to be repristinated.[41] On the basis of examinations of previous epochs from the history of the church, some theologies of retrieval do conclude that there are serious problems in the present from which theology needs to extricate itself. For instance, John Milbank judges that what is missing in the present is a participatory metaphysic by which the created realm partakes of grace and points beyond itself and ultimately to God.[42] But even here, it is clear that Radical Orthodoxy is a combination of ideas from prior to a time when supposed problems set in and material that is recognizably postmodern. Or, alternatively, the way in which the past provides critical purchase on the present may take the form of simply insisting that it foreshortens opportunities for reflection to cut theology off from its past; it prematurely shuts down options that ought to remain open.[43] There are, thus, some differences in how theologies of retrieval utilize history as a way to achieve distance from the present, but they all do unsettle the present in some way by means of recourse to history.

(4) Because the act of retrieval involves thinking with historical material, the theologian is a participant in a conversation with a classic text. To retrieve means to engage with the past because one is involved in an inquiry, grappling with a cluster of questions, and committed, at least in a provisional way, to a set of beliefs on the basis of which those questions are intelligible, and out of which they grow. Theological commitments can be reframed as the process of thinking progresses, and especially as the theologian wrestles with texts to which he makes recourse precisely because they have the capacity to broaden his set of operative categories and to change his theological priorities, though beliefs are integral within the process of retrieval. Theologians of retrieval are part of a diachronically extended discussion about God, and are faced with responding in an intelligible way to the same basic reality to which those they are reading responded at a different time and place and perhaps in a different linguistic idiom. "By being aware that we stand alongside theologians of the past in the Church, we are with them, even before we know them more closely, by knowing that in the last resort they are

---

insights of modern historicism and personalism back into the patristic sources, crediting the Church Fathers with the 'discovery' of history and personhood. His guiding paradigm of theological inquiry was an ever-deepening interiorization of patristic theology, entering the mind of the Fathers, and sharing in their experience of God. He contrasted this paradigm with merely repeating patristic statements (the error of the traditionalists) or, worse still, purporting to go beyond the Fathers into the realm of speculation (the alleged error of Bulgakov and others)." Paul L. Gavrilyuk, *Georges Florovsky and the Russian Religious Renaissance*, Changing Paradigms in Historical and Systematic Theology (Oxford: Oxford University Press, 2013), 263. For a convenient summary of this larger volume, see Gavrilyuk's chapter in the present volume.

41 See Rumscheidt, *Revelation and Theology*, 41.

42 See John Milbank, *Being Reconciled: Ontology and Pardon* (London: Routledge, 2003), 111–13. There is a survey of several historical genealogies that feed into works of retrieval, including one that has influenced Milbank, in Webster, "Theologies of Retrieval," 585–9.

43 Williams, *Why Study the Past?* 94.

vitally concerned with the answer to a question which poses itself decisively to them also, a question which is raised for men by the Christian revelation that is the foundation of the Church. They are in search of the answer to a question that concerns us, too."[44] A theologian of retrieval participates in the history she seeks to understand. Participation does not spoil inquiry but helps define its character as a specific sort of theology. It is not that a disengaged reading is the only genuine one, as if "he to whom a moment in the past *means nothing at all* is the proper man to describe it."[45]

(5) That theologians of retrieval are participants in an ongoing conversation, not outside observers of a discussion being had by others, means that the theologian both listens to the historical sources and articulates her own constructive response to them. Because the texts the theologian engages with are genuine high points from within the tradition of the church, the theologian defers to them, though their contents are not simply repeated. Theologians of retrieval relate to classic texts as if they were students before teachers.[46] They read in the first instance to learn, seeing texts as fields of the Spirit's operation, testimonies to God that repay regular reading because of what they disclose. In addition, having listened, theologians of retrieval also speak—or better, even in listening, they speak, for as they draw upon the material they have wrestled with, they articulate it in their own voice and in their own categories, thus inevitably putting their own spin on the theological content that they are appropriating. In an even more significant sense, they speak in another way, as they reflect upon the teaching they have received and give a judgment upon how well it accords with revelation, the ultimate standard in theological construction. As Karl Barth says with reference to John Calvin, "The aim, then, is a dialogue that may end with the taught saying something very different from what Calvin said but that they learned from or, better, through him. . . .We listen, we learn, and then we go our own way and in so doing we give evidence of respect, of doing the teacher justice."[47]

(6) Finally, theologies of retrieval involve selectivity and discrimination. Evaluative judgments about sources that steer the process of engagement with texts are embedded in particular theologies of retrieval in a number of different ways. Theologies of retrieval depend on at least implicit decisions about the value of texts insofar as they call upon certain texts rather than others when considering a given topic. Furthermore, though these texts must be studied in full in order to determine what questions they are designed to answer, theologies of retrieval inevitably fasten onto certain aspects of these texts for appropriation. Finally, judgments about these texts manifest themselves most obviously when they are evaluated: the parts that are retrieved are being commended to contemporary theology as offering material that can chart out how to think about a pressing question

---

44 Barth, *Protestant Theology in the Nineteenth Century*, 27.

45 Nietzsche, "On the Uses and Disadvantages of History for Life," 93; italics in original.

46 Karl Barth, *The Theology of John Calvin* (Grand Rapids, MI: Eerdmans, 1995), 4.

47 Barth, *Theology of John Calvin*, 4–5.

theologians must address. So retrieval is not about reinstituting large swaths of the past, a whole nexus of interconnected elements of meaning, as much as it is *parts* of it that are considered especially worthy of imitation. In this sense, retrieval involves a selective reading of the past—not in a way that simply confirms what one already thought but that gravitates toward especially promising points that might open up new possibilities for theological reflection.[48] It is true that the past by itself does not instruct theologians of retrieval regarding what to say now. Nietzsche protests passionately against the danger inherent in thinking that the past alone can teach: "How much of the past would have to be overlooked if it was to produce that mighty effect, how violently what is individual in it would have to be forced into a universal mould and all its sharp corners and hard outlines broken up in the interest of conformity!"[49] An element of selectivity, and a combination of evaluation as well as observation of the past, is inevitable for theologies of retrieval. To a great degree, assessments of the validity of these theologies depend on what is made of this feature that they exhibit.

IV.

Having expounded these significant similarities between theologies of retrieval, and having indicated what sets them off from alternative ways of engaging the Christian tradition, I turn now to a final task, that is, considering an objection to retrieval. Stated as briefly as possible, the objection is that *retrieval* is a misleading label for a theology marked by the features sketched above. More fully, the critique is as follows. These theologies construe tracts of teaching from the Christian past, not as objects of study but as if they were articulate subjects, works that speak with a living voice and are part of an established conversation that a theologian may join. This way of attending to a text risks failing to achieve "the pure cognition of its object."[50] There seems to be something corrupt about this approach, for in construing the authors of past texts as subjects, and as part of an extended discussion of and response to revelation, the danger is that theologians "of retrieval" assume too much by way of continuity between *their* views of God and all else in relation to him, and whatever it really is that the text in question is propounding. This stance obscures the text's claim in the name of

---

48 See Coakley, *God, Sexuality, and the Self*, 4. But note also that in this very context Coakley is challenging principles of selectivity that are applied in simplistic ways, as approximations of later theological settlements. For an attempt to segregate theological judgment as much as possible from historical narrative, see the way in which the theological postscript to Rowan Williams's treatment of Arius is detached from the main body of his exposition: Rowan Williams, *Arius: Heresy and Tradition*, rev. ed. (Grand Rapids, MI: Eerdmans, 2002), 233–45.

49 Nietzsche, "On the Uses and Disadvantages of History for Life," 69.

50 Rumscheidt, *Revelation and Theology*, 53.

retrieval, while actually amounting to a projection of the views of the theologian onto the historical source, whose authority is used to bolster the credibility of the theologian's views. There is too little investment here in methodological control of the process of interpretation, with the result that subjectivity looms large. The price of all of this is high: this approach does not generate a stance of proper listening, and thus resources that are supposedly being retrieved may well not be—and this by virtue of how particular theological assumptions are built into the whole process.

Several lines of response open up by way of rejoinder to this critical evaluation. First, it does sometimes happen that theologians of retrieval do not attend as closely as they should to the details of texts they are interpreting, having become preoccupied with their agenda to utilize the texts in a certain way in their own contexts. For instance, a critical investigation of Jean-Luc Marion's use of patristic sources rightly faults him for giving varied, lively texts a rather flat reading, taking them as speaking univocally in the service of an agenda to defend orthodoxy.[51] At least some of his interpretations of these early Christian theologians do little to bring out the variegated nature of their theological witness and the distinctive voice in which each of the figures speaks, or of how they reflect their own unique historical circumstances.[52] It is as if the patristic figures each becomes fitted into a single unifying theological construction. This sort of problem *can* happen, but Marion himself does better in some of his other publications; furthermore, other theologians of retrieval are sensitive to this difficulty and show themselves able to offer highly textured, historically dense readings of key thinkers. For instance, as he opens his study of nineteenth-century theology, Barth writes, identifying mistakes he seeks to avoid in his work, "I can think of a whole series of accounts where it is all too evident that the authors are not guiding us in a shared investigation of what the men of the past may be saying to us; rather, the one who has already made his discovery, who has done with listening, directs us with vigorous gestures to the position where he is now standing (not to say, sitting!)."[53] It is certainly not the case that the methodology of historical reading that Barth is following has blinded him to the basic point that it is all too easy to conflate one's own views with those of the sources one is engaging. He sets himself the goal of reading his forebears intensively—announcing that as one of the goals for the success of his own study—and he does an admirable job of fulfilling it in many cases, such as in his interpretation of Kant.[54]

51 Tamsin Jones, *A Genealogy of Marion's Philosophy of Religion: Apparent Darkness*, Indiana Series in the Philosophy of Religion (Bloomington: Indiana University Press, 2011), 42–3.

52 It is arguable that Marion's recent book on selfhood in Augustine is at least much better, if not perfect, in this regard: Jean-Luc Marion, *In the Self's Place: The Approach of Saint Augustine*, Cultural Memory in the Present (Stanford: Stanford University Press, 2012).

53 Barth, *Protestant Theology in the Nineteenth Century*, 20.

54 Barth, *Protestant Theology in the Nineteenth Century*, 266–312.

Second, though theologians of retrieval as such are not engaging with past texts as objects, or not only in that way, when their work is at its best that is in part because they are deeply familiar with the results of such studies. That is to say, they value and make frequent reference to work from the neighboring discipline of historical theology. They do so for the simple reason that they need to learn as precisely as possible what lies in the past, and they benefit from the rounded pictures of past epochs that this discipline produces. That historical theological studies are not selective—or at least less selective by virtue of ruling out focusing on preferred aspects of a particular text or set of texts—means that they can be expected to contribute toward a more comprehensive account of the thinking of key figures from the Christian tradition. Of course, it is still necessary to access multiple historical studies of major texts and thinkers because the substantive views of historians often shine through in the ways that they present the past.[55] Even authors who strive to sideline their own views as a desideratum of their disciplinary location, and to give an account of the past on its own terms, often make those very commitments manifest as they present views with which they do not intend to enter into explicit dialogue.

Finally, and most importantly, this risk or danger is not an inherent difficulty for theologies of retrieval: it is what happens when theologies of retrieval go wrong or are poorly executed, not a problem that arises by virtue of the set of assumptions that mark out theologies of retrieval as such. What results in bad theologies of retrieval is not simply that assumptions are present and drive the selection of material to retrieve. Like all theological beliefs, these presuppositions are provisional and corrigible, not absolutely and permanently fixed. They can be revised if they prove to be problematic. Yet they may, in fact, prove to be just the opposite: they can show themselves to have utility for producing sensitive readings because they generate in those studying the past sympathy with it, a sense that the material is connatural with the interpreter of it, which has the potential to lead to better results than could be attained otherwise. The question is not whether assumptions are present but rather what the content of those assumptions is, and whether they serve or undermine the task of acute investigation of that which is to be retrieved. A theologian may approach a given text on the assumption that there are present within it certain ideas that are not actually there. Perhaps the theologian presumes that certain elements are to be found in the text because her own conception of revelation contains them, and she takes it that the author is responding to the same reality and would of course hold views similar to her own. But if patient investigation of the text does not provide evidence for the presence of these ideas, then the theologian cannot attribute them to the author and must enter into a process of considering what the significance is of the discrepancies between how God is being understood.

Good theology of retrieval is more likely to result when those engaging in it respect and seek to highlight the distinctive contribution of the text being read,

---

55 Cf. Rosenberg, *Accessing Kant*, 2.

rather than assimilating it without remainder to a past or present theological criterion. This involves noting how the item from the past is conditioned by the place and time from which it originated and the particular language in which it was composed. When these guidelines are followed, theologies of retrieval are able to overcome the problems that the objection alleges will necessarily occur; when they are followed, theologies of retrieval can indeed involve listening well to voices that deserve close attention. The objection identifies possible pitfalls for theologies of retrieval, which can be avoided, not logical consequences of their distinguishing features.

V.

What, then, are theologies of retrieval? They vary greatly, but there is a certain family resemblance among them, as has been argued in the pages above. Works of retrieval neither base themselves on the assumption that the march of time always signals progress in theology, nor do they simply isolate a period in the past whose teachings outstrip everything that was said subsequently, such that the truths of this golden age need only to be uttered once more for a treatment of a topic to be satisfying. Retrieval is about working out a middle path between these two problematic extremes. The overarching goal of all theologies of retrieval is to learn about the past for the sake of thinking by means of the resources it offers. When theologians operate in a mode of retrieval, they become participants in a conversation about the subject matter of the texts with which they are engaging. This means that they listen intently to what the texts have to say, understand their material content in their own frame of reference, and articulate a constructive response to the texts' teaching. Theologies of retrieval build upon works of historical theology, though they are necessarily more selective in their orientation, focusing in on what they judge to be especially promising insights contained within the texts they study. This does not, however, lead to efforts at retrieval degenerating into an exercise in projecting a theologian's own views onto texts that offer them little support, for whatever views the theologian brings to the process of interpretation may facilitate it and must, in principle, be verified with reference to the texts under investigation.

Part V

MAJOR DOCTRINES

Chapter 12

BACK TO THE TRINITY

Fred Sanders

The doctrine of the Trinity always seems to be making a comeback. Its most recent return was probably its best publicized and most widely heralded. In the explosion of academic publications on Trinitarian theology in the late twentieth century, participants frequently congratulated each other and themselves for recovering "the Forgotten Trinity."[1] As we will see below, there is ample reason for skepticism about the attendant hype. In light of the present volume's concerns, the main lines of the Trinitarian revival have to be judged so inadequate as retrievals of the doctrine as to be counterproductive; in many cases the main lines of the movement are more about revision than retrieval. Yet the modern movement's note of retrieval rang true, partly because it resonated deeply with something that has always accompanied Trinitarian theology: a retrospective element, a gesture of reaching back, a return to deep sources.

The retrospective tone can be heard in all the classic documents of Trinitarianism. The Nicene Creed itself (that is, the Nicene-Constantinopolitan Creed of 381) was already an exercise in resolutely reclaiming the theological achievement of 325's Council of Nicaea.[2] Even the prologue of John's gospel, so influential for the main lines of patristic thought,[3] framed its teaching not as a sheer novum but as an enriched rereading of Moses, one that found more persons present "in the beginning" than had originally been imagined by readers of Genesis. Trinitarianism appears to be not just a doctrine that is frequently subject to retrieval but also perhaps a dogmatic case of retrieval all the way down. The

---

1 *The Forgotten Trinity: Report of the BCC Study Commission* (London: British Council of Churches, 1989).

2 Lewis Ayres, *Nicaea and Its Legacy: An Approach to Fourth-Century Trinitarian Theology* (New York: Oxford University Press, 2004), chap. 10, "Victory and the Struggle for Definition," 244–69; and Khaled Anatolios, *Retrieving Nicaea: The Development and Meaning of Trinitarian Doctrine* (Grand Rapids, MI: Baker Academic, 2011), "Crisis and Resolution," 20–7.

3 T. E. Pollard, *Johannine Christology and the Early Church* (Cambridge: Cambridge University Press, 1970).

triune God is the fountain of salvation, and *ad fontes* may be the most telling motto for the doctrine of the *fons salutis Trinitas*.[4]

Likewise, this chapter's exposition moves backward, starting with recent theology and peeling off layers of history and historiography from there. We begin with a look at the various mythological accounts of Trinitarianism's fall and recovery, work back through a variety of purported great divides among types of Trinitarianism through history, and finally describe the sort of structural retrospection that is properly inherent to Trinitarian theology itself.

Revival versus retrieval

If the twentieth century witnessed a revolution in Trinitarian projects in systematic theology, it was a revolution followed rapidly by a counterrevolution in historical theology. Almost anywhere that modern systematic theologians claimed to find ancient warrant for the claims they wanted to make, modern historical scholars returned a negative assessment. More was at stake than a mere "strife of faculties," though. Both systematic and historical theologians have a stake in assessing the continuity or discontinuity in what the church has taught in its doctrine of God. Stephen Holmes's 2012 book *The Holy Trinity: Understanding God's Life* provided a helpful summary of the issues involved, with a sharpness that is clarifying. Holmes describes himself as a theologian much influenced by the "new trinitarianism" of the late twentieth century, who eventually had to rethink the movement's own claims, evidences, and conventional wisdom. In *The Holy Trinity*, Holmes argues that "the explosion of theological work claiming to recapture the doctrine of the Trinity that we have witnessed in recent decades in fact misunderstands and distorts the traditional doctrine so badly that it is unrecognizable."[5] What is usually told as a story of exciting discovery and renewal Holmes renarrates as "a catastrophic story of loss."[6] He lists three areas in which the modern Trinitarian revival parted ways with the traditional view: it tended to entangle the being of the Triune God with the world's history; to describe the life of the Trinity as continuous with, or extended into, the life of the church; and to subject Trinitarian terminology to an analytic treatment that closed the analogical interval between creator and creature. In these ways, "the twentieth century renewal of trinitarian theology" depended "in large part on concepts and ideas that cannot be found in patristic, medieval, or Reformation accounts of the doctrine of the Trinity," in fact, on concepts and ideas that were "explicitly and energetically repudiated as erroneous"[7] by the earlier

---

4 "*Fons salutis Trinitas*" is from the last stanza of Venantius Fortunatus's sixth-century hymn "Vexilla regis prodeunt."

5 Stephen Holmes, *The Holy Trinity: Understanding God's Life* (Milton Keynes: Paternoster, 2012), xv.

6 Holmes, *Holy Trinity*, xviii.

7 Holmes, *Holy Trinity*, 2.

consensus. Writing mainly in a historical mode for this project, Holmes reserves judgment about whether the truth about the Trinity is on the side of the ancients or the moderns. His point is simply that the two differ, and that if the moderns are right, "we need to conclude that the majority of the Christian tradition has been wrong in what it has claimed about the eternal life of God."[8] Even allowing for a bit of rhetorical overstatement, we have to acknowledge that Holmes draws a sharp dividing line here, calling into question recent Trinitarianism's appeal to the past. In a perceptive review of Holmes's work, Scott Swain summed up the modern revival of interest in the doctrine of the Trinity as a case of "renewal without retrieval." For twentieth-century theology, in Swain's words, "the path to trinitarian renewal required bypassing rather than retrieving the classical trinitarian consensus."[9]

Holmes's assessment may seem stark, and Swain's summary of "renewal without retrieval" may not sound like the kind of judgment that the participants in the Trinitarian revival would accept as a fair description of what they were undertaking. Certainly there were many motivations and agendas at work across the range of writings on the Trinity in this period. But it is interesting to note how often "renewal without retrieval" actually fits the self-understanding of the movement. Theologians who contributed to the surge of publications on the doctrine of the Trinity in the late twentieth century understood themselves to be participants in a revival of interest in Trinitarianism but not always in a return to the actual content of Trinitarianism. In fact, many of the most vigorous and influential promoters of the new work on the doctrine of the Trinity in the 1990s were quite aggressive in positioning themselves over against a major historical figure, or even against the dominant tradition of classical Trinitarian theology.

Two examples, one Protestant and one Catholic, are illustrative. Colin Gunton's *The Promise of Trinitarian Theology* was published in 1991, and began with the programmatic essay "Trinitarian Theology Today." In that chapter he celebrated the centrality of the doctrine of the Trinity, but lamented "the unfortunate fact" that "the shape of the Western tradition has not always enabled believers to rejoice in the triune being of God."[10] Famously, Gunton identified Augustine as the supreme culprit for the defects of the West's spiritual history, and equally famously, Gunton's historical case has been found wanting.[11] But even if we pardon his rough handling of Augustine and overlook the defects of Gunton as historical theologian

---

8 Holmes, *Holy Trinity*, 2.

9 Scott Swain, "The Quest for the Trinity," review of the *Quest for the Trinity: The Doctrine of God in Scripture, History and Morality*, by Stephen R. Holmes, The Gospel Coalition, January 11, 2013, http://thegospelcoalition.org/book-reviews/review/the_quest_for_the_trinity (accessed December 28, 2016).

10 Colin Gunton, *The Promise of Trinitarian Theology* (Edinburgh: T & T Clark, 1991), 2.

11 A detailed critical examination of Gunton's treatment of Augustine can be found in Brad Green, *Colin Gunton and the Failure of Augustine: The Theology of Colin Gunton in Light of Augustine* (Eugene, OR: Pickwick Publications, 2011).

in order to focus on the benefits of Gunton the constructive systematician, there is a consistent tone of novelty or of fresh discovery in his presentation. He intends to say something about the Trinity that has not been said before, or at least has not been said in Latin or English.[12] Gunton's contagious excitement about the prospect of a refreshed Trinitarianism comes through clearly in this essay: "Because God is triune, we must respond to him in a particular way, or set of ways, corresponding to the richness of his being . . . In turn that means that everything looks—and, indeed, is—different in the light of the Trinity."[13]

Something very similar was found in contemporaneous Roman Catholic theology, such as Catherine Mowry LaCugna's 1993 *God For Us: The Trinity and the Christian Life*. The same tone of new prospects opening up can be heard in its opening pages: "The doctrine of the Trinity is ultimately a practical doctrine with radical consequences for the Christian life. That is the thesis of this book."[14] But as with Gunton, LaCugna's programmatic sense that an important theological project was now underway was dependent on the claim that something had previously gone awry, and that it now had to be set right. But for LaCugna, the problems were not just localized to Augustine, or to Western theology in his wake. She diagnosed the problems as more widespread in the West (unrepaired by Aquinas and other scholastics) and also at work in the East (unresolved by simple appeal to the Cappadocians, whose legacy was also problematic). For LaCugna, the Trinitarian dysfunction had to be stated more broadly as well: the ultimate problem was that the doctrine of the Trinity had become a "nonsoteriological doctrine of God," a merely cognitive statement about God's nature. In contrast, in the new Trinitarianism she championed, "the doctrine of the Trinity is not ultimately a teaching about 'God' but a teaching about God's life with us and our life with each other."[15] The crucial thing for LaCugna's project was that it oriented the doctrine of the Trinity proper toward practice and experience. Her work inspired theologians to articulate Trinitarian theology toward making a difference for the Christian life and church practice.

But as with Gunton's project, the affirmation of something new required the negation of something old; the project's forward thrust was only achieved by kicking off from something traditional. The later reception of the work of both Gunton and LaCugna inevitably posed the question of whether their contributions (everything "looking different in light of the Trinity," a "practical doctrine with radical consequences") could be maintained without the negative judgment

---

12 Gunton does use a rhetoric of retrieval with regard to the Cappadocians, and succeeded in transmitting to many readers an excitement about retrieving their thought. However, his reception of Cappadocian Trinitarianism is fraught, and may be inextricable from an East-versus-West schema, which we discuss below.

13 Gunton, *Promise of Trinitarian Theology*, 4.

14 Catherine Mowry LaCugna, *God for Us: The Trinity and Christian Life* (San Francisco: HarperCollins, 1991), 1.

15 LaCugna, *God for Us*, 228.

about vast tracts of theological tradition.[16] Was the revisionist rhetoric marginal or essential to their constructive task? Was the revival necessarily opposed to retrieval? In many ways, the task of Trinitarian theology in the succeeding years has been to disentangle the remarkable sense of the revival's prospects and projects on the one hand from its countertraditional articulations on the other.

Decontextualized critiques

In journalistic accounts of the Trinitarian revival, it has become conventional to trace its origins to the work of Karl Barth and Karl Rahner. Bibliographically, this origin story has considerable plausibility. The trail of footnotes indeed tends to lead back from current discussions to one Karl or another. But as we attend to the way Barth and Rahner put Trinitarian theology on the twentieth-century agenda, it is worth noting how the particular, local stories both of them told about the doctrine's decline were rapidly appropriated and extended to other contexts. The way these origin stories were stretched to cover new situations reveals much about the motives and preoccupations of the Trinitarian revival.

Barth knew what he was doing when he brandished the doctrine of the Trinity in the opening pages of the *Church Dogmatics*. His primary intention was doctrinal in good earnest, as he had found in Trinitarian theology a way to draw together the form and the content of revealed theology under the sign of God's self-revelation as Lord. But he was also being provocative on purpose, deliberately baiting the leading practitioners of the academic Protestant theology that was enshrined in the universities and divinity schools of a regnant high liberalism. To take recourse to the doctrine of the Trinity was to invite the charge of being positively medieval. "Historically, formally and materially," Barth admitted, "I am now going the way of scholasticism," volunteering for his opponents the easily available evidence: "I obviously regard the doctrine of the early Church as in some sense normative. I deal explicitly with the doctrine of the Trinity."[17] The provocation was as deliberate as it was effective, evoking from Wilhelm Pauck the blustering response, "As if it were really a matter of life and death, that as members of the church of the Twentieth Century—we should accept the dogma of the Trinity!"[18] Pauck considered Barth an inconsistent prophet of a new age for Christian theology, one who kept trying to reach forward to the truly modern, fully existentialist mode of teaching that was appropriate to the twentieth century, but who kept lapsing back into antiquated

---

16 Both authors died in the middle of carrying out their own projects, LaCugna at age forty-four in 1997, and Gunton at age sixty-two in 2003. The fact that they did not live to extend and revise their own lines of thinking adds a poignancy to the question of the ends toward which their ideas were tending.

17 Karl Barth, *Church Dogmatics* I, 1: xiii.

18 Wilhelm Pauck, *Karl Barth: Prophet of a New Christianity?* (New York: Harper, 1931), 189.

modes of thought. For theologians like Pauck, it was clear that the doctrine of the Trinity belonged not to the emerging new age but to the irretrievable dark ages: "We deny that it is necessary that, in our efforts for a new expression of the Christian faith, we occupy ourselves with the Trinity and Christology. We would then commit the same mistake that Barth makes in his *Dogmatics*."[19] Using the terms then current to describe theological trends, we might say that for Pauck, Barth's articulation of neoorthodoxy entailed too much "orthodoxy" and not enough "neo." In recent years, John Webster has observed that a particular combination of the new and the old, with strategic emphasis on the old, was what set Barth apart from his neoorthodox cobelligerents: "What was original to Barth was not his Christological concentration so much as his combination of it with classical conciliar incarnational dogma and Reformed teaching about the hypostatic union."[20] We might say the same about his appeal to the doctrine of the Trinity throughout the entire scope of the *Church Dogmatics*. What is novel, or distinctively modern, in it will fade away sooner than the relatively classical lines on which he developed his Trinitarianism.

Without diminishing Barth's achievement in his own culture and context, we can nevertheless marvel that later thinkers in widely divergent traditions have written as if they, too, were shaking off the scholarly anti-Trinitarianism of high liberalism. Conservative Protestants and Roman Catholics have acted as if Barth's voice led them out of similar dead ends, when in fact Barth's voice was calling German Protestant theology to be, in respect of received dogma at least, more like these other communities. In context, his task was to "bemoan the constantly increasing confusion of modern Protestantism, which, probably along with the Trinity and the Virgin Birth, has lost an entire third dimension . . . which . . . we may describe as mystery."[21] To overcome liberal dismissiveness and reengage academic Protestant theology with Trinitarianism, Barth was willing to risk sounding like some kind of Roman Catholic, or even a fundamentalist evangelical!

Speaking of Roman Catholic theology, Karl Rahner's book *The Trinity* has been so influential that during the Trinitarian revival it seemed de rigueur to begin every essay by quoting his opening laments: that "despite their orthodox confession of the Trinity, Christians are, in their practical life, almost mere 'monotheists,'" and that the situation is so dire that "should the doctrine of the Trinity have to be dropped as false, the major part of religious literature could well remain virtually unchanged."[22] Even for theological reflection on the incarnation, Rahner says, there is almost nothing Trinitarian informing "the catechism of head and heart (as contrasted with the printed catechism."[23] So deep is the "anti-trinitarian timidity"[24] that the doctrine

---

19 Pauck, *Prophet?*, 201.
20 John Webster, "Christology, Theology, Economy," in *God without Measure*, 1:56.
21 Barth, *Church Dogmatics* I, 1:xiii.
22 Rahner, *The Trinity* (New York: Crossroad, 1997), 10–11.
23 Rahner, *The Trinity*, 11.
24 Rahner, *The Trinity*, 13.

has become systemically inert, meaning that "when the treatise is concluded, its subject is never brought up again" in relation to other doctrines. The mystery seems to have been "revealed for its own sake" such that "we make statements about it, but as a reality it has nothing to do with us at all."[25]

These complaints are stinging. But the most curious thing about them is their subsequent usage. They have been cited and echoed in such a vast literature, in provinces so widely different from their context of origin, that they serve as an all-purpose lament against every kind of neglect of the doctrine of the Trinity.[26] In context, what Rahner was railing against was Trinitarian doctrine's isolation in "textbook theology," and in particular in Roman Catholic dogmatics of the neoscholastic period. Whether Rahner was fair or not in his critique of the style, or simply the hegemony, of the neo-Thomism that flourished after 1879's *Aeterni Patris*, his complaints would seem to have been brought against such a specific school of thought that they might not have been transferable.[27] To take one example, when Rahner complained that the treatise *De Deo Uno* ought not to be separated from the treatise *De Deo Trino*, or at least ought not be handled in such a way that it solves in advance all the problems of Trinitarianism and thus renders the second treatise superfluous, he was offering a criticism that could only apply to a very disciplined tradition of inquiry. When that complaint was echoed in theological traditions lacking the kind of formal precision and traditioned structures of neo-Thomism, it made less sense. Consider the parallel warning passed on by students of Bernard Lonergan, who quipped that Thomist Trinitarianism was in danger of being "five notions, four relations, three persons, two processions, one nature, and zero comprehension." The complaint is as stinging as Rahner's. But unlike Rahner's it is so obviously focused on a particular tradition that it is not transferable. Neo-Thomism seemed, for some of its inheritors, to threaten Trinitarian vitality by an overabundance of formal precision. It seems ironic that Rahner's lament against it has been found serviceable in theological traditions with considerably less concern for formal precision or elaborate distinctions in their stated theological positions.

Alongside Barth and Rahner, a third force contributed to the modern Trinitarian revival. That force was the influx of Eastern Orthodox theology, and constructive dialogue with it, in Western centers of theological discourse in the early twentieth century. The literature produced especially by Russian expatriates working in

---

25 Rahner, *The Trinity*, 14.

26 It would be impossible to show how widely diffused Rahner's lament is in Trinitarian literature of the revival period. In retrospect they seem custom designed to be quotable on the opening pages of any book about the Trinity, since they carry with them the justification for writing any book about the Trinity.

27 For a survey of the broader issues at stake in engaging neo-Thomism, including a dispute about "classical theism," see Derrick Peterson, "A Sacred Monster: On the Secret Fears of Some Recent Trinitarianism," *Cultural Encounters* 12:1 (2016), 3–36; especially part 3, on "Rahner's Rule as Historiography."

Paris was vast and vibrant, and the writings of Georges Florovsky, Sergei Bulgakov, and Vladimir Lossky are major contributions to twentieth-century theology at large. But in the doctrine of the Trinity, these theologians and their students frequently adopted an oppositional stance to all things Western. In part this can be accounted for by the revival and extension of polemics against the theology of the filioque, which occupied a key position in distinguishing East from West. One would expect Russians working in Paris to feel the need for a ready answer to the question of what distinguishes the two traditions, and theologians as profound as these would necessarily develop more than an ad hoc answer. But as was the case with Barth and Rahner, the arguments and diagnoses put into circulation by these Orthodox critics of Western Trinitarianism took on a life of their own.[28] Criticisms that made a certain sense as strategic projections in their original setting came to sound increasingly bizarre as young Western theologians adopted them as if they were an accurate self-description of their own traditions. But again, what worked for Russian expatriates writing in Paris in the 1930s made one kind of sense; for Western theologians to accept this projection as their own self-understanding is another matter.

Surely it is an optical illusion when modern evangelical Protestants in the United States, whose actual narrative is one of outgrowing the constrained horizons of fundamentalism, see themselves somehow implicated in Barth's reaction against high liberalism and claim to be recovering the doctrine of the Trinity for reasons similar to his. Surely some unconscious alienation is at work when Presbyterians with Francis Turretin or Herman Bavinck in their intellectual heritage see themselves and their ancestors somehow reflected in the mirror of Rahner's lament that neoscholastic textbook theology has made them "almost mere monotheists." Surely some signals have become crossed when Western theologians in the lineage of Thomas and Bonaventure appropriate as their own self-descriptions the accounts projected onto them by Eastern Orthodox critics, and think of themselves as accidental modalists who have started with the one divine nature and tried in vain to derive the three persons from it. The analyses must ring true, or they would not be so widely redeployed. In some cases, those who retail these criticisms may be using them to draw analogous connections, fully aware of the differences between the situations. There must be some background pressure at work to dislodge these criticisms from their contexts of origin, putting them into circulation throughout the theological world. What capacity for receiving such critiques, apparently any critiques that came along, motivated theologians in such different contexts to apply them to themselves, to their own traditions, to the tradition of Trinitarian theology as a whole?

---

28 See the very helpful survey of waves of reception of the Orthodox argument, and especially to their complex interactions with Rahner's work, in Travis E. Ables, "The Decline and Fall of the West? Debates about the Trinity in Contemporary Christian Theology," *Religion Compass* 6 (2012): 163–73.

The idea of a new Trinitarianism

There is something built into the modern epoch that tends in the direction of a readiness to subject the past to limitless critique. Jaroslav Pelikan, having surveyed the history of dogma from end to end, has said that "the modern period in the history of Christian doctrine may be defined as the time when doctrines that had been assumed more than debated for most of Christian history were themselves called into question: the idea of revelation, the uniqueness of Christ, the authority of Scripture, the expectation of life after death, even the very transcendence of God."[29] It is also the period when old forms and structures were aggressively reinterpreted, or assigned brand new content. Whatever tensions began to be felt by theologians under the conditions of modernism, they apparently rendered the doctrine of the Trinity a uniquely vulnerable field for exploitation.

Friedrich Schleiermacher is a curious case study in this regard. His *Christian Faith* was a remarkable reframing of Christian doctrine in modern categories, consolidating all of theology around the Christian consciousness of the redemption achieved by Jesus Christ. He crafted every doctrine as a presupposition or an implication of that redemption. This method, which sounds so restrictive or even reductive, in fact yields a remarkably full system of Christian doctrine, and certainly one with a striking order and clear connections. But the doctrine of the Trinity fits poorly into the system, partly because it includes a statement about God absolutely in the divine self, which by its nature is not something that can be derived from the Christian consciousness of redemption (a consciousness that is only possible in relation to a God who has stepped out of absolute aseity and crossed over into relation with fallen creatures). As a result, the doctrine of the Trinity, in Schleiermacher's judgment, "is not an immediate utterance concerning the Christian self-consciousness but only a combination of several such utterances."[30] This is the reason the doctrine was assigned a place, notoriously, at the very end of the *Christian Faith,* on the border of what could be said about God within the constraints of the *Glaubenslehre's* logic.

But there is another reason the doctrine of the Trinity fit poorly into Schleiermacher's new account of the Christian faith. The problem with the doctrine is that it had not changed. Schleiermacher begins his account of the doctrine in the *Christian Faith* by saying that the doctrine cannot be considered one of the doctrines that is "finally settled." The reason it cannot be considered settled is that it did not change at the Reformation; it "did not receive any fresh treatment when the Evangelical [Protestant] Church was set up; and so there must still be in store for it a transformation which will go back to its very beginnings."[31] Schleiermacher is

---

29 Jaroslav Pelikan, *Christian Doctrine and Modern Culture (since 1700)* (Chicago: University of Chicago Press, 1989), viii.

30 Friedrich Schleiermacher, *The Christian Faith*, 2nd ed. (Edinburgh: T & T Clark, 1928), 156.

31 Schleiermacher, *Christian Faith*, 747.

not moved here by a mere presupposition that progress or doctrinal development is the only reliable sign of life. Instead, he is so committed to the centrality of redemption, including the Protestant recovery of teaching on it, that he expects that redemption to throw a new light on every aspect of Christian doctrine. It simply follows that any doctrine that did not receive a fresh formulation in the sixteenth century must be destined either for imminent reformulation or oblivion; it either leans toward the future or the past. Schleiermacher himself, as we have seen, did not find a way to reinterpret the doctrine in line with his own principles, at least not in a way that moved it to the center of his concerns. Later in the nineteenth century, theologians working in the *Glaubenslehre* tradition, and theologians attempting to mediate between that method and more traditional ones, would find ways to make the Trinity more central, but its role in Schleiermacher's own carefully articulated system was peripheral. It had all the marks of a doctrine that could wither and fade without affecting the overall scope of Christian doctrine.

The tone set by Schleiermacher has become a pervasive feature of modern theological culture. The notion that the doctrine of the Trinity had fallen into disuse and is ripe for recovery has become such a widespread assumption that it can be found across the spectrum of theological and pastoral writers. Some especially clear phrasing of the attitude can be found in James Morris Whiton, a New England Congregationalist pastor and theologian, who published in 1892 *Gloria Patri: Our Talks about the Trinity*. In the preface he expresses his hope that "sooner or later it must be, that the Church will reap rich harvests of spiritual thought and life from this now weed-grown field, so long left fallow. It cannot be that this fundamental and all comprehending truth of Christianity will always be left in the cloud which barren scholastic controversy has raised about it."[32] The harvest he hopes to reap is to use the Trinitarian form of church confession to teach that "the immanent is one with the transcendent Power; the Filial Stream is one with its Paternal Fount."[33] Whiton juggles with the language of "Filial Stream," exploiting its traditional sound but in fact assigning it a novel meaning. What is filial about the Filial Stream is that it is creation; its oneness with the Paternal Fount signifies that God and creation are one. The eternal Son is replaced by an eternal world, with filial categories covering the switch:

> The Living Father, Maker of heaven and earth, does not live apart from His creation, but lives in it from the beginning, as its Begotten or Filial Life. And this universal Life, whether existing or pre-existing, whether before the world or in the world, through all its myriad ranks from the highest to the lowest, whether in angels or in amoebas, in men or in the Christ, is His coeternal Word, or Son— His utterance, His offspring.[34]

---

32 James Morris Whiton, *Gloria Patri: Our Talks About the Trinity* (New York: Thomas Whittaker, 1892), 4 ("Author's Note").

33 Whiton, *Gloria Patri*, 92.

34 Whiton, *Gloria Patri*, 91.

The world, according to Whiton, slumbers in unconscious sonship except when it wakes in Christ to know itself as being one with the Father. The Spirit, in his scheme, is an even deeper immanence, if that is possible in a system that is all dialectical immanence.

In the down-market Unitarianism represented by Whiton it is easy to recognize earlier forms of thought. Schleiermacher's influence is less evident than certain arguments given currency by David Friedrich Strauss. The replacement of the second person of the Trinity by the created world is a sure sign of left-wing Hegelianism at work, and in Whiton it predictably results in the dogma of an incarnation of God in humanity rather than in one particular human. What is crucial for the story of modern appropriations of Trinitarianism, however, is not whatever content the modern thinker may choose to pour into the inherited forms and terms of Trinitarian doctrine. What is crucial is the whole idea that the doctrine of the Trinity requires new content. Whiton's own doctrines have rarely been revived and taught explicitly, but his revisionist maneuver is strikingly common. Whiton offered this prophecy for the future of the doctrine: "Doubtless, many will move on into the larger Trinitarianism which modern thinking requires. But quite as many will stay within the narrower lines of the past, and will imitate the Greek church in calling themselves 'the orthodox.'" But he was confident that the old view would be utterly replaced by the inevitable logic of the new view: "There is too much of the Holy Spirit now in the church to permit the new Trinitarianism to be again excommunicated by the old."[35] Whiton's phrase "the larger Trinitarianism" did not catch on, but one still hears about a "new Trinitarianism" from time to time.

Trinitarianism since Jane Austen

There have by this time been enough new Trinitarianisms in succession that it might be profitable to construct a typology of their varieties. It would be interesting to see what they have in common with each other and where they differ. But the net result of so many modern theologians adopting the tropes of revival and novelty, of bringing back something old and simultaneously brandishing it as something new, is that the doctrine of the Trinity itself has begun to seem unstable and indeterminate for several generations of theology students and church leaders. There is a constant harassment by bright new ideas, and a relentless production of new schemas by which to distinguish the latest Trinitarianism from the errors that have gone before.

One of the requirements for anybody narrating a revival is to specify some historical coordinates that make the revival a possibility. The main coordinates are a rise and a fall; a time of initial flourishing in the distant past, and a time of deadening at some point thereafter, setting up the revival as the third step in the sequence. There has not been great agreement among the participants

---

35 Whiton, *Gloria Patri*, 128.

in the Trinitarian revival about when these earlier demarcations ought to fall. Some theologians look back to a golden age of Nicene theology followed by an Augustinian fall (Gunton); others think of Nicaea itself as the beginning of fatal missteps (LaCugna). Some might extend the golden age all the way into the Early Middle Ages and find the culprits as late as a sclerotic scholasticism; others could restrict the golden age of Trinitarianism to the early strata of the New Testament itself and find the decline setting in already in those New Testament documents that show greatest signs of acute Hellenization. Wherever the lines are drawn, the revival story will not work unless they are in place.

A related strategy is to subdivide by region. The notion of an Eastern version of Trinitarianism standing in opposition to a Western version of Trinitarianism has become firmly entrenched in the literature of the Trinitarian revival.[36] It is a fairly elaborate schema, typically involving the following cluster of themes:

East and West differ so sharply as to have different theologies of the Trinity

The East is personalistic; the West is essentialist

The East starts with threeness and seeks oneness; the West does the opposite

The East is social Trinitarian; the West is psychological-analogy Trinitarian

Some version of this contrast is operative in a great deal of the literature. Sarah Coakley has lamented that it "has obtained the unfortunate status of a truism in much systematic theological work of the later twentieth century," and that "generations of students have been pedagogically formed by this misleading narrative."[37] Indeed, the present moment is an awkward one for theological instruction. This construal of East and West has been problematized quite effectively by a couple decades worth of historical and descriptive work, especially Michel Barnes's exploration of its surprising genealogy.[38] But the schema was so pervasive for the most productive decades of late twentieth-century Trinitarianism that it is very difficult to assign introductory books that are not infected by it in some way. Students can be counted on to pick up this facile simplification, because its strengths lie precisely in providing a broad organizing category for vast tracts of literature. Nevertheless, it is, as David Bentley Hart points out, self-doomed:

> The notion that, from the patristic period to the present, the Trinitarian theologies of the Eastern and Western catholic traditions have obeyed contrary logics and have in consequence arrived at conclusions inimical each to the other—a particularly tedious, persistent, and pernicious falsehood—will no doubt one day fade away from want of documentary evidence.[39]

36 For some documentation, see Ayres, *Nicaea and Its Legacy*, 385.

37 Sarah Coakley, "Introduction: Disputed Questions in Patristic Trinitarianism," *Harvard Theological Review* 100 (2007): 131.

38 Michel René Barnes, "De Régnon Reconsidered," *Augustinian Studies* 26 (1995): 51–79. For good reporting and analysis, see Ables, "The Decline and Fall of the West?"

39 David B. Hart, "The Mirror of the Infinite: Gregory of Nyssa on the Vestigia Trinitatis," *Modern Theology* 18 (2002): 541.

It is indeed the documentary evidence that will banish this divisive schema, because whatever help it may appear to give in organizing a field of study, it provides no help in navigating any actual primary texts from any period of historical theology. Even as a guide to late polemics about the filioque, the East versus West schema is of limited help. Sarah Coakley likewise looks forward to being able to teach fourth- and fifth-century theology without the distorting paradigm in place: "Once the false wedge between East and West in this early period is removed, certain sorts of polemicizing about the innate superiority of one approach over the other become suspect, and we are returned to the texts themselves with fresh eyes, and—by implication—with fresh possibilities for ecumenical engagement."[40] Just as each chronological period requires more precise definition, if we were to use geograph-ical zones to trace differences in the theological cultures of patristic thought, we would have to zoom in much closer than East and West; we would have to consider actual locations with traditions of inquiry like north Africa, Rome, Palestine, Asia Minor, Constantinople, and Antioch.

One of the ironies of the Trinitarian revival literature is that as it drew much of its energy from attempting to inscribe divisions like this, it actually divided itself from the great, consensual tradition of Trinitarianism, which, with admitted vari-ations of time and place, nevertheless spans Christendom in a striking way. The doctrine of the Trinity simply has not been the site of marked disagreement among the churches, relatively speaking. The modern tendency to draw dividing lines through the history of the doctrine in fact is one of the eccentricities of modern-ism; it marks modern Trinitarianism itself off as being divided from all that went before.

Much is at stake in sorting out falsified historiographies. When C. S. Lewis moved to Cambridge University to occupy a new chair, he took up the title of "Professor of Medieval and Renaissance Literature." In his inaugural lecture for that chair, he argued at length that the "and" in the title was significant, and that what it signified was a real unity: medieval literature and Renaissance literature belonged together as a single field of study. Lewis devoted most of his inaugural lecture, entitled "De Descriptione Temporum," to delegitimizing and relativizing the distinction between the two periods, a distinction that he identifies as "a fig-ment of humanist propaganda."[41] By this he means that the distinction between the periods was calculated by Renaissance scholars to cast the Middle Ages as the Dark Ages (a period of baneful Christian influence) and to congratulate the Renaissance for being a new birth of wisdom. How did Lewis attack this false div-ision between periods? By examining the details of the actual record.

There is a striking parallel to the deconstruction of the East–West paradigm and other bedeviling subdivisions of the field of historical Trinitarianism. What is needed now in systematic theology's appeal to historical theology is the elaboration

---

40 Coakley, "Introduction," 134.

41 C. S. Lewis, "De Descriptione Temporum," in *Selected Literary Essays* (Cambridge: Cambridge University Press, 1969), 2.

of a Trinitarianism that is both Eastern and Western, with the "and" signifying real
unity. Of course there are many differences to mark, and the descriptive tools of
academic historians will always excel at marking those differences. But they are
differences within a striking unity and coherence from the earliest to the latest
period.

Or not quite to the latest. For his part, though he disagreed with the inherited
periodization of his field, Lewis realized he could not simply abolish all periodization. While recognizing the provisional and heuristic character of periodization, he did propose a new way of dividing the times and epochs. Lewis proposed
that we should think of everything from antiquity through the Middle Ages and
the Renaissance as belonging to one major period, and mark the great transition at an idiosyncratic point: Jane Austen. Western literature could be divided
between pre-Jane and post-Jane. No doubt Lewis was being puckish in proposing Austen as the point of division of the ages of Western thought. But the point
is striking, and a similar point needs to be made in the doctrine of the Trinity.
A history of the doctrine of the Trinity that treated everything down to the time
of Jane Austen as one kind of Trinitarianism, and everything after as another
kind, would be instructive.[42] Such a history would run the risk of smoothing
out too many differences and of telling the story of the doctrine's development
without enough dramatic conflict. But for this doctrine, the light of continuity
would be more revealing than the light of discontinuity. Such a history would be
able to make the most of Richard Muller's careful work on the lines of continuity
that connect Protestant thought to the great tradition, and to appreciate Colin
Gunton's perceptive remark that during the times normally considered periods
of decline and neglect by the revivalists, nevertheless "in all periods there have
been competent theologians, Catholic and Protestant alike, who have continued
to work with traditional Trinitarian categories while being aware of the reasons
that have led others to question, modify, or reject traditional orthodoxy."[43]

Retrospection and inherent retrieval

We began this chapter with the claim that Trinitarian theology has something
retrospective built into its deep structure, and suggested that Trinitarianism may
be a doctrinal case of retrieval all the way down. To deliver the doctrine from
movements that claim to revive it but that actually revise it, or at their worst strip

---

42 Jason Vickers, *Invocation and Assent: The Making and the Remaking of Trinitarian
Theology* (Grand Rapids, MI: Eerdmans, 2008) comes very close, putting the dividing line
around the seventeenth century but drawing a lot of the right lessons about how the tor-
sions of early modernism distorted the doctrine.

43 Colin Gunton, "The Trinity in Modern Theology," in *The Companion Encyclopedia
of Theology* (London: Routledge, 1995), 937.

out its essential content and fill its form with something new, it may be helpful to sketch three ways in which Trinitarianism is constituted by retrospection.

First, Trinitarian theology is inherently a matter of retrieval because it has the structure of praise. Biblical praise is a creaturely response to divine initiative and action, offering thanks for something that God has done. But praise does not terminate on the thing that has been done; rather, it aspires to offer praise of the giver as well as the gift. Doxology takes its stand on a divine action in history and thinks back from the action into the being of the actor. Praise is always provoked by a concrete and categorical act of deliverance or blessing, but it is not true to itself unless it reasons its way back to something behind that action. This structure of biblical praise can be seen in the microcosm of every deliverance and in the macrocosm of the entire scope of God's story of keeping covenant with his people. Trinitarian theology is a pan-biblical summarizing doctrine that reads the entire economy of salvation as one integrated act of God for which he is to be praised. As such, it looks back along the lines of salvation history *pro nobis* to who God is *in se*. Trinitarian theology is a confession that in the fullness of time, the Father sent the Son and the Holy Spirit because in the fullness of eternity God is the Father, Son, and Holy Spirit. It retrieves divine identity from the divine economy.

Second, Trinitarian theology is inherently retrieval oriented because at the level of an exegetical undertaking it takes the form of rereading, or of construing the earlier phases of a progressive revelation in light of the later phases. Rereading in light of fuller awareness is a fundamental hermeneutical maneuver, without which the church would never have been able to confess the doctrine of the Trinity at all. The gospels themselves are constructed as inspired rereadings of the life of Jesus Christ in light of his death and resurrection; the retrospective act of understanding more is built into them. The total canon of Scripture is a body of texts to be reread sequentially so that God is disclosed as the one who made promises and then fulfilled them, and his initial, mysterious disclosures lean forward to the future time of greater disclosure. Theological readers of Scripture come to understand God's identity by revisiting prior sites of revelation, hearing with greater clarity the referents of old words, as God who spoke in many ways and many portions long ago speaks at last in his Son.

Third, Trinitarian theology has the character of retrieval because it is a mystery. It is a mystery because it is an articulation of what the entire Biblical witness to the divine economy discloses about God. Scripture is a two-part revelation, with an Old Testament corresponding to a New Testament, and the forward pressure of the Old driving into the greater clarity of the New. Though "mystery" can properly signify many things, and is always associated with the Trinity, in the New Testament the primary meaning of mystery is something that was once kept secret but has now been revealed. Built into the structure of God's self-revelation is a duality in which the second half derives its meaning from revisiting the first half. Knowledge of God comes to us from a biblical act of retrieving God's identity from the first half of the Bible in a way that is faithful to his revelation in the second half of the Bible.

The doctrine of the Trinity thus has a retrospective character built into it, and fruitful work in the field of Trinitarian theology ought to be aligned with that retrograde motion. It ought to be more conspicuously centered on Biblical reflection than it typically has been. But even in the misguided phases of the Trinitarian revival, which so often seemed more like raids on the history of theology or exploitations of the external form of the doctrine, there was frequently some awareness that going back to the Trinity was the right thing to do. We can hope that the way forward in Trinitarian theology will also follow this path back to the deeply retrospective Trinitarianism of Scripture.

Chapter 13

"LOVE IS ALSO A LOVER OF LIFE": *CREATIO EX NIHILO* AND CREATURELY GOODNESS

John Webster

I

Christian teaching about the creation of the world out of nothing is a cardinal doctrine: on this hinge turn all the elements of the second topic of Christian theology, which treats all things with reference to God, their beginning and end, the first topic being God's immanent life. In his work of creation, God inaugurates an order of being other than himself, and this work is presupposed in all subsequent assertions about that order of being, for to create is to bring something into existence, and "God's first effect in things is existence itself, which all other effects presuppose, and on which they are founded."[1] This first effect of God is a radical beginning and precisely as such the establishment of an enduring relation. Other articles of Christian teaching about God's transitive works treat the historical course of the relation so established, but do so on the presupposition that the creaturely term of the relation has been brought into being ex nihilo, and that only as a reality instituted in this manner may its nature and history be understood. Teaching about creation "opens the logical and theological space for other Christian beliefs and mysteries."[2]

Because of this, Christian teaching about the creation of the world out of nothing is also a distributed doctrine, cropping up throughout theology's treatment of the economy with varying degrees of explicitness. Our understanding of creation is amplified and deepened by this frequent recurrence, for its full scope and meaning become apparent in relation to what is said about other divine works of nature, such as preservation and governance, and, most of all, in relation to what is said in the works of grace that culminate in the missions of the Son of God and the Holy Spirit. It is in the works of grace, in which the end of God's act of creation is

---

1 Aquinas, *Compendium of Theology* (Oxford: Oxford University Press, 2009), §68.

2 R. Sokolowski, "Creation and Christian Understanding," in *God and Creation: An Ecumenical Symposium*, ed. D. Burrell and B. McGinn (Notre Dame, IN: University of Notre Dame Press, 1990), 179.

secured, that the natures of God's creatures and of his own benevolence are most fully displayed. Christian beliefs about the character of the Creator and of his creative act are shaped by what can be learned from considering providence and reconciliation, in which the work of creation has its *terminus ad quem* (a point given its most extensive modern exposition in Karl Barth's ordering of creation to covenant). Equally, however, beliefs about providence and reconciliation only make full sense when we attend to their *terminus a quo*, that is, when we bear in mind that the protagonists in the economy are the Creator and his creatures, and that all being and occurrence that is not God is to its very depths ex nihilo.

The Christian doctrine of creation treats three principal topics: the identity of the Creator, the divine act of creating, and the several natures and ends of created things. These topics are materially ordered: teaching about the identity of the Creator governs what is said about his creative act and about what he creates. In early Christian developments of the doctrine of creation out of nothing, much turned on the perception that God's radical perfection requires extensive revisions both of how the act of creation is to be understood (it can have no material cause) and of the natures of the beings created by this act. Of course, the order of inquiry does not necessarily conform to the material order: reflection on the doctrine of creation may take its rise with any one of the topics. But reflection will not reach its term unless the entire range and the order of the matter are brought to mind.

Disarray results from the hypertrophy or atrophy of a given element (as, for example, in theologies that reduce the doctrine of creation to teaching about created things, without adequate consideration of the Creator and his work). Further, misperception or misapplication of this element will deform the whole, whose force depends in part upon the integrity of its constituents. It would be possible to trace how modern theologies of creation have often suffered a series of such misperceptions and misapplications, on the part of proponents as well as despisers. Here I address one such misperception: the anxiety that the pure nonreciprocal gratuity of God's creation of all things out of nothing debases the creature, for a being so radically constituted by another as to be nothing apart from that other is a being evacuated of intrinsic worth. The anxiety is misplaced, sometimes destructively so. Showing why this is the case involves dispute about the elements of the doctrine of creation, that is, exposure of points at which habits of thought are contradicted by faith in God the Creator. This is not, it should be noted, a peculiarly modern task, forced upon theology by hostile circumstances. The doctrine of creation has proved a permanently contrary article of Christian teaching, requiring the release of thought from inhibiting assumptions about God and created things (Lactantius's account in the *Divine Institutes* or Thomas's in the *Summa Contra Gentiles* are classical exercises in extracting the Christian doctrine of creation from inherited misapprehensions). For all that, polemics or elenctics are subsidiary undertakings. The primary theological task in this matter is the dedication of intelligence to devout indication and description of Christian verities, whose goodness, once known and loved, dispels anxiety and draws both intellect and affections to satisfaction.

II

Before treating the matter of creaturely worth directly, we may identify in summary fashion the elements of the doctrine of creation out of nothing.

1. Coming to understand Christian teaching about creation out of nothing is an instance of the special pedagogy by which all the elements of the Christian confession are made objects of intelligent love. The principle parts of this pedagogy are prophecy and reconciliation.

"It is a great and very rare thing for a man, after he has contemplated the whole creation, corporeal and incorporeal, and has discerned its mutability, to pass beyond it, and, by the continued soaring of his mind, to attain to the unchangeable substance of God, and, in that height of contemplation, to learn from God himself that none but he has made all that is not of the divine essence."[3] Why is it that God must be the teacher in this matter? Partly because creation concerns an absolute "beginning," the summoning into being of what is not, and in the nature of the case such a summons cannot be an object of experience. Partly, again, because creation out of nothing is entirely sui generis. It is not an instance of making nor of any causality we might know, and so we may not "inquire by what hands, by what machines, by what levers, by what contrivance [God] made this work of such magnitude."[4] Again, to think about creation out of nothing is not to ponder an event in the history of the world but to come to see that the world, including ourselves as intelligent beings, is not the given reality that we customarily take it to be, but is something that once was not and might not have been at all. We can have this thought, however, only after a conversion of mind that is not within our capacity but rests upon divine instruction. Finally, teaching about creation is teaching about the Creator, and teaching about the Creator is delivered to creatures "under the inspiration of the Holy Spirit."[5] Not without reason, both Ambrose and Basil begin their *Hexamera* by reflecting on Moses, the prophet "who imparts to us what he has learnt from God."[6]

Knowledge of God the Creator and his act of creation, and of the constitutive significance of God and his act for created things, arises not by the spontaneous exercise of intelligence but by the operation of "the Holy Spirit, handing down the discipline of truth."[7] This being so, consideration of the topic of creation out of nothing carries with it the requirement that we be in the process of becoming

---

3 Augustine, *City of God* (Peabody, MA: Hendrickson, 1994), XI.2.

4 Lactantius, *Divine Institutes* (Peabody, MA: Hendrickson, 1994), II.9 (he is criticizing Cicero).

5 Ambrose, *Hexameron* (Washington, DC: Catholic University of America Press, 1993), I.1.2.

6 Basil, *Hexameron* (Peabody, MA: Hendrickson, 1994), I.1.

7 Lombard, *Sentences* (Toronto: PIMS, 2008), II.dist. 1, pt. 1, ch. 3.

certain kinds of persons. This is because being caught up in the Spirit's pedagogy is an aspect of sanctification. Much might be said here: of the need for cleansing prior to divine instruction; of docility and patience; of resistance to curiosity; of acceptance of limits. A good deal of what needs to be said might be gathered under the rubric of "religion" in its deep sense of being bound to God, the one "to whom we ought to be bound as to our unfailing principle."[8] We might also speak of friendship with God as a condition for knowledge of him as Creator and of ourselves as his creatures. In our corrupt state, such friendship is lost to us, for we despise both our creaturely condition and our Creator, and need to be reconciled. Corruption inhibits knowledge. But God the teacher is God the reconciler and overcomes our corruption, establishing the new creaturely nature objectively in the death and resurrection of Jesus Christ and applicatively in the regenerative work of the Spirit. Possessed of this new nature, creatures are being "renewed in knowledge" (Col 3:10), including knowledge of Creator and creature.

The end of consideration of this work of God is faith in God. The core of Christian teaching about creation out of nothing is not cosmology or philosophy of nature or anthropology, but the Holy Trinity's perfection and benevolence. At the beginning of his treatment of creation in the *Summa Contra Gentiles*, Aquinas takes time to spell out how meditation on the transitive works of God enables us "to admire and reflect on his wisdom,"[9] "leads to admiration of God's sublime power, and consequently inspires in men's hearts reverence for God"[10] and "incites the souls of men to the love of God's goodness."[11] In such admiration, reverence, and love of God, the divine pedagogy about creation reaches its term.

2. The primary subject matter of theological treatment of creation out of nothing is God himself; it inquires first, not into the world's beginning but into "who gave it this beginning, and who was the creator."[12] Here I prescind from discussing the Trinitarian dimensions of creation as the work of the three persons of the godhead,[13] in order to concentrate upon creation as the operation of the undivided divine essence, about which a number of lines of reflection need to be followed.

    a. Talk of God as Creator of heaven and earth presupposes the distinction of God's immanent from his transitive operations, that is, the distinction of those works that remain in God and whose term is God's perfect life from those works that have an external object. The importance of this distinction is not simply that it states the difference between the inner

---

8 Aquinas, *Summa Theologiae* (London: Blackfriars, 1964), IIaIIae.81.1 resp.

9 Aquinas, *Summa Contra Gentiles* (Notre Dame, IN: University of Notre Dame Press, 1975), II.2.2.

10 Aquinas, *Summa Contra Gentiles*, II.2.3.

11 Aquinas, *Summa Contra Gentiles*, II.2.4.

12 Basil, *Hexameron*, I.2.

13 On this topic, see J. Webster, "Trinity and Creation," *International Journal of Systematic Theology* 12 (2010): 4–19.

divine processions (generation and spiration) as *actio* from the external work of creation as *factio*.[14] It is also that, by so ordering God's works, it sets before the mind the principle that because God the Creator is perfect in himself, he has no need of creation, acquiring no augmentation from its existence and being deprived of no good by its absence. The nonnecessary character of God's *opera ad extra* is fundamental to understanding all the elements of the doctrine of creation out of nothing: the Creator and his act of creation, the nature of creatures, and the relation that obtains between Creator and created things. The careful specification of this nonnecessity is, moreover, of capital importance for treating anxieties about the debasement of creatures.

b. As Creator, God is "the principle and cause of being to other beings."[15] God is perfect, and his being has no cause, because to be perfect is to be unoriginate, irreducible to some other causal reality. But as this one, God is the "first efficient cause"[16] of all things. God works transitively, and does so first by bringing all things into being as *omnibus causa essendi*. This is the first and most general statement about God as Creator.

c. To be the cause of being of all things is proper to God alone. This, because the Creator is the *first* cause who is himself without cause. "It belongs only to God to be the creator, for creating belongs to the cause that does not presuppose another, more universal, cause . . . but this belongs only to God. Therefore, only he is the creator."[17] As Creator, God is not the most exalted instance of creativity; in its absolute character as that which effects existence tout court, his creating is incommunicable. There can therefore be no instrumental causes in creating, for any such instrument would itself be caused and therefore incapable of being the first cause of being of other things. *Nulla creatura possit creare*;[18] God alone is Creator.

d. God has power to create as "an active and a moving being."[19] Or better: God *is* this power, which is his substance and not some incidental property. Further, God is Creator "through his very self":[20] his creative power is not some capacity that he has in reserve, some underlying principle of his action. The Creator is not simply an immense causal agent, a capitalized Cause or Author; as "first" cause God is not merely possessed of supreme power with greater range than a finite cause. His power is not what he has but what he is.

14 For the distinction of *actio* from *factio*, see Aquinas, *Summa Contra Gentiles*, II.1.4.

15 Aquinas, *Summa Contra Gentiles*, II.6.1.

16 Aquinas, *Summa Contra Gentiles*, II.6.2.

17 Aquinas, *Compendium of Theology* §70.

18 Aquinas, *Summa Theologiae* (London: Blackfriars, 1967), Ia.45.5 ad 3; see also Ia.65.3.

19 Aquinas, *Summa Contra Gentiles* II.7.5.

20 Aquinas, *Summa Contra Gentiles* II.8.6.

e. God is cause of all things by his will, not by natural necessity. His work of creation is not the natural overflow of his self-diffusive being but of intentional, personal action. Creation is spontaneous divine action, not the automatic operation of a "principle of plenitude."[21] And because of this, once again, creation need not have been.

f. In creating, God acts in accordance with his goodness. Here "goodness" is meant not so much in its moral as its metaphysical sense: God's goodness is his entirely realized nature. Of this goodness of his, there can be no supplementation. In creating, therefore, God is not bringing his goodness to realization, for this would make the Creator's goodness depend upon the creature. God's goodness is not the result but the cause of his creating. But divine goodness is, indeed, the source of the being of other things. Divine goodness includes as one of its ends the existence of created goodness, of a further reality that in its own order is good. Divine goodness is creative of likenesses of itself; divine being bestows being. Here metaphysical goodness shades into moral goodness, in that God's work of creation manifests that, precisely because his perfect goodness cannot be expended, he does not begrudge other things their being, but, on the contrary, gives being to other things. "God is good—or rather the source of goodness—and the good has no envy for anything. Thus, because he envies nothing its existence, he made everything from nothing through his own Word, our Lord Jesus Christ."[22]

3. How may the act of creation out of nothing be characterized?

a. The act of creation is ineffable, having no analogues in our experience of causation or agency. Not only does this mean that much of what is said about it consists of negations that draw attention to its sui generis character but it also means that, in dealing with objections to Christian teaching about creation, theology should not be surprised to encounter objections that take for granted certain simplifications that arise when its basic terms are assumed to be univocal. Creation out of nothing is ineffable, not simply because of the grandeur of the agent or the magnitude of the act but because of its incommensurability as "the introduction of being entirely."[23]

b. The divine act of creation is instantaneous, an operation of "incomparable swiftness" devoid of succession.[24] The words "in the beginning," Basil tells

---

21 A. O. Lovejoy, *The Great Chain of Being* (New York: Harper, 1960), 54; for a critique of Lovejoy, see J. F. Wippel, "Thomas Aquinas on God's Freedom to Create or Not," in *Metaphysical Themes in Thomas Aquinas II* (Washington, DC: Catholic University of America Press, 2007), 218–39.

22 Athanasius, *De Incarnatione* in *Contra Gentes* and *De Incarnatione*, ed. and trans. by Robert W. Thomson (Oxford: Oxford University Press, 1971), III.

23 Aquinas, *Summa Theologiae*, Ia.45.1 resp.

24 Robert Grosseteste, *On the Six Days of Creation* (Oxford: Oxford University Press, 1996), I.xi.1.

his readers, indicate "the rapid and imperceptible moment of creation" that is "indivisible and instantaneous . . . at the will of God the world arose in less than an instant."[25] This is said, partly to indicate that the act of creation is not an event in time but that by virtue of which events in time come to be; this act is not a measurable sequence in the world but the world's originating principle. Partly, too, it is said to emphasize that God's work in creation is effortless, without strenuous movement from intention to completion and the relief afforded by cessation from strain. In creating, God "both works and rests simultaneously."[26] Creation is thus more like an inner act of willing than an external act of craftsmanship. "God made all these powers [the physical universe, the nations, and heavenly beings] with such ease that no words can explain it. The mere act of God's will was enough to make them all. An act of the will does not make us tired. Neither did creating so many and such mighty powers weary God . . . Do you not see that not only for creating the things on earth but also for the creation of the powers in heaven the mere act of his will was enough?"[27]

c. The act of creation involves no movement or change in God. Peter Lombard's discussion of this point shows him acutely aware that verbs such as "create," "make," or "do" are predicated of God according to a different "reckoning" from that by which they are predicated of creatures, for "when we say that he makes something, we do not understand that there is any movement in him operating, nor any passion in working, just as there is accustomed to befall us, but we signify that there is some new effect of his sempiternal will, that is, something newly exists by his eternal will."[28] Creatures make by moving and changing, but when God creates "in him nothing new happens, but something new . . . comes to be without any motion or mutation of his own."[29] In the same way that effort has to be stripped out of the conception of the "act" of creation, so, too, do ideas of motion.

d. The act of creation indicates the supereminence of the Creator. God is not simply an immensely resourceful particular agent but "the universal cause of being."[30] Acts of making by a particular agent presuppose something not produced by that agent upon which the agent is at work. Creation is

25 Basil, *Hexameron*, I.6.

26 Augustine, *The Literal Meaning of Genesis*, in *On Genesis* (Hyde Park, NY: New City Press, 2002), IV.24.

27 Chrysostom, *On the Incomprehensible Nature of God* (Washington, DC: Catholic University of America Press, 1984), II.

28 Lombard, *Sentences*, II dist. 1, Pt. 1, ch. 3.

29 Lombard, *Sentences*, II dist. 1, Pt. 1, ch. 3.

30 Aquinas, *Summa Contra Gentiles*, II.16.3.

no such act because it is the crossing of what Aquinas calls the "infinite distance . . . between being and non-being."[31]

e. All this leads to the principal affirmation: God's act of creating is ex nihilo. Creation out of nothing is an extension of teaching about divine perfection: all that is required for the act of creation is God himself, the supreme essence acting "alone and through itself."[32] Because God is such, there is no material cause of creation: no raw material, no antecedent patient entity, nothing which God presupposes, on which he is at work or which he must master. The temptation is to turn the grammatical substantive "nothing" into a metaphysical substance. But "nothing" is not some sort of inchoate stuff to which the act of creation gives form, nor is it potentiality, what Dietrich Bonhoeffer in a careless thought called "obedient nothing . . . that waits on God."[33] Rather, nothing is pure negation, *nihil negativum*. Again, like *nihil*, *ex* can also mesmerize, leading us to think that it refers to the relation of something made to that from which it was made. But *ex* "signifies a sequence not a material cause."[34] "Sequence" here does not refer to a change from nonbeing to being that happens to some constant; rather, the sequence is: there was nothing at all . . . now there is something. Creation ex nihilo is not an act of conversion or modification but one of absolute origination. It is an act of what Norman Kretzmann calls "doubly universal production": distributively universal (God is the cause of being for *all things*) and intrinsically universal (for all things God is out of no preexisting subject the cause of *being*).[35] God is utter plenitude and sufficiency and so the cause of the entire substance of all things.

4. What does creation out of nothing indicate about the nature of created things? Initially, it proposes a negative: the totality of created things is not eternal, necessary, or underived. But this initial negative is preparatory for a positive theological statement that created things have their being in relation to God. Created things do indeed have being. They are not nothing, but participate in the good of being. There is that which is not God, and that which is not God *is*. But the being of created things is had by the divine gift, or *per participationem*.[36] The viability of the idea of "participation" depends upon its not being deployed in such a way as to threaten the distinction

---

31 Aquinas, *Summa Theologiae*, Ia.45.2 obj. 4 and ad 4.

32 Anselm, *Monologion*, in Anselm of Canterbury, *The Major Works* (Oxford: Oxford University Press, 1998), VII.

33 Dietrich Bonhoeffer, *Creation and Fall: A Theological Exposition of Genesis 1–3* (Minneapolis: Fortress, 1997), 34.

34 Aquinas, *Summa Theologiae*, Ia.45.1 ad 3.

35 Norman Kretzmann, *The Metaphysics of Creation: Aquinas's Natural Theology in Summa Contra Gentiles II* (Oxford: Clarendon Press, 1999), 70–100.

36 Aquinas, *Summa Theologiae* (London: Blackfriars, 1975), Ia.104.1 ad 1.

between uncreated and created being that is basic to the concept of creation.[37] Participation does not imply, for example, that the act of creation is simply a natural process of emanation, diffusion or dispersal of divine substance. "Creatures . . . are not born of God [*non de Deo nata*] but made by God out of nothing."[38] Rather, participation is theologically to be understood in terms of the operation of creative benevolence, and so in terms of the *differentiated* sharing of Creator and creature in the good of being, each in their proper order and mode. By the work of divine love, finite things come to share in the universal good of being but only in a finite manner, and only as they stand in relation to the creator God, the source of being. This relation *constitutes* creatures. Every element of creaturely being and action is what it is in "the very dependency of the created act of being upon the principle from which it is produced."[39] There is, therefore, a *depth* to created things. To consider them, we have to understand not only their finite causes but also the first cause, tracing them back to their source, which is God. Creatures have being as *principiata*, as effects of God their *principium*. The movement by which we understand how creatures participate in being is this: "we trace everything that possesses something by sharing, as to its source and cause, to what possesses that thing essentially . . . But . . . God is his very existing. And so existing belongs to him by his essence, and existing belongs to other things by participation. For the essence of everything else is not its existing, since there can be only one existing that is absolutely and intrinsically subsisting . . . Therefore, God necessarily causes existing in everything that exists."[40]

5. What does creation out of nothing indicate about the relation of God and creatures? Creation is an operation of generosity on the part of one who in his inner Trinitarian life is wholly realized, satisfied, and at rest. God gains nothing and loses nothing by the existence or nonexistence of creatures, having "no need for the things he created" since he is "perfectly happy within himself."[41] Without this—seemingly austere but in reality entirely delightful— affirmation, the entire conceptual and spiritual structure of teaching about creation out of nothing collapses. It may be explicated by speaking of the relation of Creator and creature as a mixed relation, real (constitutive) on the side of the creature but not on the side of the Creator. Such entire inequality ought not to be considered a denial of the Creator's relation to created things: God loves, and in providence and reconciliation acts toward that which he causes to be. Rather, a double assertion is being made. First,

---

37 On this, see R. te Velde, *Participation and Substantiality in Thomas Aquinas* (Leiden: Brill, 1995); idem., *Aquinas on God: The "Divine Science" of the Summa Theologiae* (Aldershot: Ashgate, 2006), 123–46.

38 Augustine, *Unfinished Literal Commentary on Genesis*, in *On Genesis*, I.

39 Aquinas, *Summa Contra Gentiles*, II.18.2.

40 Aquinas, *Compendium of Theology*, §68.

41 Aquinas, *Summa Theologiae*, Ia.73.2 resp.

the Creator is radically incomposite. As the cause of finite being, God is not one term or agent in a set of interactions, not a "coeval, co-finite being"[42] but unqualifiedly simple and in himself replete. Second, to deny that God bears a "real" relation to created things is to characterize the *kind* of relation that he has to creatures, one in which God is "in himself his own beatitude . . . all-sufficient to himself and needing not the things he made."[43]

With this, we begin to touch on the anxiety that the relation of created things to the Creator is such that they have no honor.

III

Classical Christian doctrines of creation out of nothing furnished the theological and metaphysical principles for a positive evaluation of created things, an evaluation given material intensification by faith's contemplation of the mysteries of providence and redemption. That absolute creatureliness should be such a good is no longer self-evident to us. In his *System of Christian Doctrine*—which contains what is surely one of the most discerning treatments of the Christian doctrine of creation of the last two centuries—the great mediating dogmatician Izaak Dorner set out an account of God the triune Creator as "the fount of all existence and life," one having "power, in unison with his love which ever tends towards reality, to impart to his ideal creations substantive existence, and make them stand forth in independent being."[44] But the tradition from which Dorner spoke was already well in retreat, its terms having largely lost their suppleness and explanatory power, and its spiritual appeal having waned. What has happened?

In the preface to the *Proslogion*, Anselm spoke of God as "the supreme good needing no other," the one whom "all things have need of for their being and well-being." Such an understanding of the divine nature, extended by teaching about *creatio ex nihilo*, seems to drain created things of value. It does so, first, because it appears to consign creatures to a state of permanent indigence, wholly contingent upon God for origination and continuance; second, because the Creator's perfection is entirely untouched by their existence or nonexistence; third, because no relation exists between Creator and creature save one of radical inequality in which the creature gives, and the Creator receives, nothing. In effect, *creatio ex nihilo* brings with it a metaphysic of privation: to be a creature is to be humiliated, devoid of integrity or power of self-movement or self-subsistence, and so lacking intrinsic worth. To be ex nihilo is to be (almost, apart from the gratuitous act of divine causation) *nihil*.

42 D. Braine, *The Reality of Time and the Existence of God: The Project of Proving God's Existence* (Oxford: Clarendon Press, 1988), 352.

43 Aquinas, *On the Power of God* (London: Burns, Oates and Washbourne, 1933), IV.2 ad 5.

44 Izaak Dorner, *A System of Christian Doctrine* (Edinburgh: T & T Clark, 1881), 2:39.

The objection is at once speculative and practical. In attempting to unravel it, theology has both dogmatic–historical and spiritual–ascetic tasks. The requisite dogmatic–historical work consists in making Christian specifications of the identity of God the Creator, his creative act, and his creatures, deploying these to shed light on the historical course of the objection. Theology asks: at what points in the history of theological, metaphysical, and moral–political thought have exponents of critics of Christian doctrine in some measure missed the rhythm of teaching about creation out of nothing, lost heart about its fruitfulness or wholesomeness, and felt themselves therefore at liberty or obliged to compromise the matter of Christian doctrine? In what ways and with what results has an evangelical metaphysics of creation been harassed or replaced by one owing no allegiance to the Gospel? More particularly: in what ways do mutations in ways in which the natural and human orders are understood, and in which human life is enacted, derive from and reinforce distorted understandings of the Creator? "Errors about creatures," Aquinas remarks, "sometimes lead one astray from the truth of faith, so far as the errors are inconsistent with true knowledge of God."[45] Illuminating such "errors" is the dogmatic–historical task of theology.

The second, spiritual–ascetic, task consists in theology's occupancy and promotion of a spiritual climate in which the force of the objection can be diminished and the persuasiveness of Gospel teaching commended. Intelligence follows love, and love is nourished by habits of life by which goods are sought out and made matters of delight. When love is faint, it must be kindled, and one of the tasks of theology—not its only task but by no means its least—is to assist in the kindling of love and love's intelligence. It can only do this, however, when it is itself a work of religion, of faith instructed by and adhering to *this* God who works *thus*. In a theological culture in which such instruction and adherence are lived realities, anxiety or resentment about the creaturely condition may find relief.

Apprehensiveness that creation ex nihilo entails creaturely ignominy is both a cultural–historical condition and a spiritual malaise; theology cannot separate these. The cultural–historical factors demand exquisite inquiry, examining, for example, shifts in conceptions of motion inaugurated in the early modern period, initially in the philosophy of nature and derivatively in conceptions of human being and action. The shifts would include a narrowing of divine causality to efficient causality; decline of appeal to final causality in the explanation of nature, or the reorientation of final causality to human, not divine, purposes; a sense that natural motion is self-contained, not requiring talk of God's creative and providential operations to render it intelligible; in short, the retraction of the concept of a divine *source* for natural and human movement.[46] Alongside this, attention would

---

45 Aquinas, *Summa Contra Gentiles*, II.3.1.

46 See here J. Weisheipl, *Nature and Motion in the Middle Ages* (Washington, DC: Catholic University Press of America, 1985); R. Sorabji, *Matter, Space, and Motion: Theories in Antiquity and Their Sequel* (London: Duckworth, 1988); S. Oliver, *Philosophy, God and Motion* (London: Routledge, 2005).

need to be directed to loss of confidence in the explanatory power and innocence of appeal to first principles in making the natural and human world intelligible.[47] Appeal to principia rests in part upon a sense that the world is a *principiatum*—not just a given state of affairs but that which is what it is by virtue of its relation to its source—and in part upon trust that this source is benign plenitude. When this double assent is absent, the principium becomes that to which the *principiatum* can be reduced, broken down and so evacuated of substance. Of such destructive reduction, *creatio ex nihilo* may be judged the primary instance. Corresponding to shifts in causality and in the explanatory value of first principles is a loss of a sense of the interiority of things, that is, of the need for intelligence to penetrate through the surfaces of things in order to perceive that by which they are constituted. In the case of human creatures, interiority—a basic concomitant of creatureliness—is edged out by reflexivity in which human consciousness is, as Michael Buckley puts it, both its own source and its own term.[48]

These are crude characterizations, no more than an agenda for analytical work. The analysis would try to discover how there has arisen a condition in which the axiom "aut gloria Dei aut gloria homini" has gathered such cultural authority, one in which God and creatures are natural antagonists, "two units in a symmetrical or asymmetrical relationship, each poised in such contradiction that one must sink if the other is to rise."[49] Theology will, however, go further. Errors about creatures are symptomatic of spiritual disorder, the entry of some evil into the creature's relation to God. Thinking about the world and ourselves in relation to God as source and sustainer is always a way of disposing ourselves in relation to God; *nolens volens* it always takes up an attitude. This is not to reduce thought to passion (a vulgar polemical trick), but rather to say that thought may not be detached from religion and religious failure manifest as mistrust, resentment, impatience, pride, love of some untruth. We may not exclude the possibility of *caecitas mentis*, mental blindness; we may need the healing and illumination of intelligence if we are to know and love our created condition.

As theology displays how it can be that creation out of nothing is not a matter of the creature's dispossession but rather the conferral of good, it begins from its principal part, the doctrine of God, determinations of the Creator's identity and act constituting the ground on which all else rests.

Creation is a work of wholly adequate love. Part of this love's adequacy is its voluntary character: it is fully spontaneous and self-original, nothing more than God's will being required for creatures to come to be. But creative divine volition

---

47 On this, see A. MacIntyre, *First Principles, Final Ends and Contemporary Philosophical Issues* (Milwaukee: Marquette University Press, 1990), and especially the remarkable set of analytical exercises in K. L. Schmitz, *The Texture of Being: Essays in First Philosophy* (Washington, DC: Catholic University Press of America, 2007), esp. 21–73.

48 M. J. Buckley, *Denying and Disclosing God. The Ambiguous Progress of Modern Atheism* (New Haven, CT: Yale University Press, 2004), 84.

49 Buckley, *Denying and Disclosing God*, 94.

is not caprice but purpose, direction of entire capacity to another's good; and it is purposive *love*, most of all because this other does not antecede the gift of its own being but receives the gift of life from God. Love *gives* life, and love gives *life*. In willing to create, God wills the realization of life that is not his own: "Love is also a lover of life."[50] Only God can do this; only God can bring about a life that is derived yet possessed of intrinsic substance and worth. Because God is not one being and agent alongside others, and because he is in himself entirely realized and possesses perfect bliss, he has nothing to gain from creating. Precisely in the absence of divine self-interest, the creature gains everything; *because of* (not *in spite of*) the nonreciprocal character of the relation of Creator and creature, the creature has integrity. "The creatureliness of the creature (the received condition) is not a nullity, but is rather the ingress of the creature into being, so that, on the basis of that ingress, can be seen the absolute *nihil* that was the creature's nonontological predecessor. The creature is ex nihilo, that is, it stands *outside of* absolute privation by virtue of the creative generosity. The creative generosity is the ground of the absolute inequality between Creator and creature, that very inequality that has raised the threat to the creature's integrity. But that very creative generosity is also the ground for the very being of the creature."[51] Benevolent love establishes and safeguards the integrity of the beings that it creates.

Created integrity includes created act. God creates *agentia ordinem habentia*, "subordinated active things."[52] How do we free ourselves of the habit—spiritual as much as intellectual—of opposing (at least in our own case) subordination and proper agency? By reflecting on the character of God's creative action. In establishing another thing in being, God bestows finality, a tendency or active bent and movement toward the completion of that thing's nature. This bent and movement is an effect of God's initial donation of being, and is held and stirred by God's maintaining and governing presence to the creature. God is "in all things in the manner of an agent cause."[53] It is just at this point that scrupulous consideration (contemplation) of the divine creative action may not be relaxed. There is an overextension of the concept of God as cause of being and action (and a consequent overextension of the creature's causal dependence upon God) according to which "no creature has an active role in the production of natural effects."[54] To this, Aquinas advances four objections, each arising from attentiveness to the divine attributes, and, in particular, from a belief that anxieties about debasement of creatures may stem from insufficient consideration of what might be called the perfecting effect of God's perfection.

First, such is the divine wisdom that in its products there is nothing useless, no sheerly passive and redundant creature. "It is contrary to the rational character

---

50 Dorner, *A System of Christian Doctrine*, 2:15.

51 K. L. Schmitz, *The Gift: Creation* (Milwaukee: Marquette University Press, 1982), 74.

52 Aquinas, *Compendium of Theology*, §103.

53 Aquinas, *Summa Contra Gentiles*, III.68.12.

54 Aquinas, *Summa Contra Gentiles*, III.69.1.

of wisdom for there to be any thing useless in the activities of the possessor of wisdom. But, if created things could in no way operate to produce their effects, and if God alone worked all operations immediately, these other things would be employed in a useless way by him, for the production of these effects."[55] Second, in communicating his likeness to creatures, the Creator communicates not only being but also a proportionate agency: "if [God] has communicated his likeness, as far as actual being is concerned, to other things, by virtue of the fact that he has brought things into being, it follows that he has communicated his likeness, as far as acting is concerned, so that created things may also have their own actions."[56] Third—this is the most telling argument—perfect power communicates perfection, including perfection of action: "the perfection of the effect demonstrates the perfection of the cause, for a greater power brings about a more perfect effect. But God is the most perfect agent. Therefore, things created by him obtain perfection from him. So, to detract from the perfection of the creature is to detract from the perfection of divine power. But, if no creature has any active role in the production of any effect, much is detracted from the perfection of the creature. Indeed, it is part of the fullness of perfection to be able to communicate to another being the perfection one possesses. Therefore, this position detracts from the divine power."[57] Perfect power does not absorb, exclude, or overwhelm and dispossess other dependent powers and agents, but precisely the opposite: omnipotent power creates and perfects creaturely capacity and movement. Exclusive power is less than perfect and falls short of divinity. Fourth, as the highest good God makes "what is best";[58] the creatures of such a God therefore share in the self-communicative, active goodness of their Creator. "God so communicates his goodness to created beings that one thing which receives it can transfer it to another. Therefore, to take away their proper action from things is to disparage the divine goodness."[59]

In short, to attribute all created effects to God as omnicausal is not to rob creatures of their proper action, because what God in his perfect wisdom, power, and goodness causes is creatures who are themselves causes. The idea whose spell must be broken is that God is a supremely forceful agent in the same order of being as creatures, acting upon them and so depriving them of movement. What Aquinas commends here—something that Barth also reached toward in his theology of covenant and of God's evocation of active human partners—is that the plenitude of God apart from creatures does not entail the thought of God's segregation as sole cause but rather the opposite: God's perfection is seen also in bringing into being other agents. God bestows being and activity: this is part of the special sense of creation out of nothing in the Christian confession.

---

55 Aquinas, *Summa Contra Gentiles*, III.69.13.
56 Aquinas, *Summa Contra Gentiles*, III.69.14.
57 Aquinas, *Summa Contra Gentiles*, III.69.15.
58 Aquinas, *Summa Contra Gentiles*, III.69.16.
59 Aquinas, *Summa Contra Gentiles*, III.69.16.

Such specifications in theology proper show that affirmation of the world's integrity of being and movement does not require denial of creatureliness. All that is not God is out of nothing, and its existence is sheerly gratuitous, nonnecessary. From God's creative act there arises a condition of "absolute unconditioned inequality" in which God the donor of being is "the founder of the entire order within which the giver gives and the recipient receives."[60] Such inequality—so runs our anxious argumentation—humiliates the creature, because without genuine diversity of being and capacity for action there can be no relations of dignity. In the absence of Christian characterizations of the Creator, this would be so—if, for example, divine creative action were reduced to continuous retrieval of creatures from nothingness and not understood as bestowal of being, or if absolute contingency were all that needed to be said about creatureliness. But the Creator, once again, is benevolent and gives *being*: to be from nothing is not to be nothing but to *be*, instituted as an integral order of reality and given the capacity for operation.

From this may be drawn a double assertion about created acts. First, no created thing is the principle of its own action; the creature is a *moved* mover. In the order of operation no less than in the order of being, the creature possesses no capability for pure self-origination. "Created act is a received act."[61] This, because created substance is "determined in and through its radical participation in and relation to the Source of its existence. The supposit of the creature does not stand in any way "outside" of or "prior" to the ontological relation, not even as a possibility, but is brought into being within that relation."[62] "Even as art presupposes nature, so does nature presuppose God . . . Therefore God also operates in the operation of nature."[63] Second, the creature is a moved *mover*. God who is the creature's principle is the creature's source: not an abyss into which the creature tumbles but one who in conferring being also bequeaths act. The relation of creatureliness includes "nonpassive receptivity,"[64] a given capacity for becoming through the enactment of created life.

The reality and dignity of created act does not eradicate the nonreciprocal character of the Creator-creature relation but rather indicates that that relation is not malign. That which is ex nihilo and has being by divine gift adds nothing to what is uncreated; even after it has come into being, the creature is not a reality to which God is "other," some correlate in a common order. Just because this is so, the Creator does not displace the creature. To be created out of nothing is not to suffer deprivation but to be given a nature whose performance will certainly involve acts of courage and may include, for example, magnanimity and magnificence, the extension of spirit to great things, the performance of some great work.

60 Schmitz, *The Gift: Creation*, 62f.

61 Schmitz, *The Texture of Being*, 125.

62 Schmitz, *The Texture of Being*, 128.

63 Aquinas, *De potentia*, in *Quaestiones Disputatae* II (Turin: Marietti, 1965), III.7 s.c. 2.

64 Schmitz, *The Texture of Being*, 196.

Chapter 14

THE CHURCH AND THE CHRISTIAN: THEIR THEOLOGICAL INTERDEPENDENCE

Nicholas M. Healy

In this chapter I suggest that there could be significant benefits for the life of the church and contemporary theology if we were to retrieve certain elements of what we can call, following Lewis Ayres, the "pro-Nicene theological culture" of the late fourth century, as exemplified paradigmatically in the work of such theologians as Ambrose and Augustine, Athanasius and the Cappadocians, in spite of their differences.[1] While the focus here is on ecclesiology and theological anthropology, the discussion cannot be entirely restricted to these loci. For although the earlier theological culture and our own theological culture(s) have much in common— Scripture, the Creed, many practices, and much more besides, including much anthropology and ecclesiology—we differ with regard to significant assumptions, agenda, contexts, strategies, practices, and debates, all of which shape our respective theologies.

Consider a few simple examples. We usually write books on ecclesiology *or* anthropology, as if it were quite unremarkable that we treat them separately, and we assume it is possible for someone to be a scholarly expert in one but not the other area. We sometimes do bring the two loci very much together, but then it is usually to promote a theologically informed theory of relational identity over against contemporary individualism, a move that would have been meaningless within the earlier culture. More generally, most modern theology, including most contemporary ecclesiology and anthropology, is second-order discourse, and it seems to most of us quite reasonable to think that academic forms of theology are necessary, if perhaps not sufficient. But, as Frances Young reminds us, such forms usually come in "a critical and reflective mode foreign to the ethos of patristic

---

1 Ayres describes the "pro-Nicene" "theological culture" in chaps. 11–13 of his *Nicaea and its Legacy: An Approach to Fourth-Century Trinitarian Theology* (Oxford: Oxford University Press, 2004), 273–343. Note that it was a *theological* culture or ethos, one different from others of its time, such as that exemplified by Pelagius. I do not mean to suggest this culture was without its own problems.

theology, which was never divorced from prayer and the life of the church."[2] It could also be argued that there has been a marked tendency in the theology of the last hundred years (at least) to place comparatively greater emphasis upon the second Person and upon the church, and to pay rather less attention to the third Person and the individual Christian, at least when compared with the earlier pro-Nicene theology.[3] And while this may reflect a contemporary pro-Nicene concern to counter modernity's challenges to the very idea of authoritative religious doctrine, it, too, is a response to a problem not shared by the earlier culture, or not at all in the same way.

The idea here, then, is to offer an initial case for retrieving certain elements of the culture of patristic theology, as these are displayed in its treatment of anthropology and ecclesiology. We cannot, of course, simply import these elements wholesale. However earnestly we might try, we can never become anything like a late fourth-century Christian or church. Anything we retrieve from another culture—including a different contemporary Christian culture as well as one from the past—will necessarily be altered in the retrieval. What we can do, however, is to attempt to learn from the earlier culture by means of a critical appropriation between their Christian ethos and ours, here with special regard to ecclesiology and anthropology. Since both theological cultures are Christian, such a critical correlation will not take the form found in some modern theology, in which a particular second-order characterization of Christianity seeks critical distance on itself by engaging positively or negatively with a similar characterization of the prevailing non-Christian culture. Instead, the critical correlation here is intra-Christian: between a broad interpretation of the pro-Nicene theological culture of about 400 AD and some aspects of our own ecclesial culture. The earlier pro-Nicene ecclesiology cannot be simply taken on as our contemporary ecclesiology, nor can we adopt its particular kind of theological anthropology as normative for us. Instead, their usefulness lies in the way they are set within a theological culture that may in certain respects—but not all—be significantly better than ours, and so they may offer help for reforming the church and its members as well as improving our ecclesiology and anthropology.

Christian life: transformation

The pro-Nicene theological culture was different from the various strands of our own in large part by reason of its understanding of the Christian life—of what is the proper response of every Christian to God's gift of salvation in Jesus Christ, through the Holy Spirit, within the church. The proper response was above all to

---

2 Francis Young, *God's Presence: A Contemporary Recapitulation of Early Christianity* (Cambridge: Cambridge University Press, 2013), 3.

3 For an argument along these lines, see Eugene Rogers Jr., *After the Spirit: A Constructive Pneumatology from Resources Outside the Modern West* (Grand Rapids, MI: Eerdmans, 2005).

attempt to be transformed so as to become reflective of, and actualize in oneself, the true image of God that is Jesus Christ.[4] As a Christian, one was understood to be "oriented towards an ever-new future" and "capable of endless self-transcendence."[5] The development of a deeper and thus more personal relation with God was possible for any Christian, given suitable pastoral guidance and the prompting and aid of the Holy Spirit. Accordingly, patristic theologians read "the Bible as essentially a transformative text,"[6] and theology was primarily a pastoral practice oriented toward the Christian life.

Although a similar concern for transformation is by no means unknown within contemporary Christianity, it is rarely given such a central place, whether from the pulpit or by the theologian. Churches today generally direct their efforts less to helping their members achieve the joy and freedom of life in the Spirit, and rather more to moral guidance through teaching and enculturation. Some theologians seek to ally the church and its membership with a particular moral or social program, calling, for example, for us to see Christ in the poor and the victims of our societies or to challenge structural injustices. These efforts are right and good, and by contrast some patristic theological writings may strike us as one-sided, a bit too "all about me" and my road to heaven, and so "religious" in a bad sense as well as too arduous for the ordinary Christian.[7] But these and other concerns can be addressed by the distinctive way their theological culture situates the Christian life in relation to the individual Christian and the church.

Space is too limited here to build up a description of the pro-Nicene ethos directly from the sources. But it is not necessary, for the concern here is with the basic elements of the contrast between their and our theological cultures as seen in the two areas under discussion. So I will draw upon a summary account of the way this primary objective—transformation—plays out in relation to our two loci as developed by the great *ressourcement* theologian Henri de Lubac. The account comes from a rather obscure essay,[8] but de Lubac thought it one of his

---

4 For the patristics (and later for Erasmus, but far less so for Luther), "our grace-enabled imitation of Christ is a long healing process, renewing the faithful in God's image so as to culminate in union of lover and beloved . . . [an] assimilation of copy with original . . . like with like." Jennifer A. Herdt, *Putting on Virtue: The Legacy of the Splendid Vices* (Chicago: University of Chicago Press, 2008).

5 Young, *Presence*, 100.

6 Young, *Presence*, 5.

7 An example is a letter of Basil to Gregory of Nazianzen, which describes the ideal ascetic life and the joy to be had therein. See Basil, *Letters*, 2. Yet the letter is misleading if taken alone, since Basil was very active in Caesarea, building the "Basileias," a new "city" for the sick, the needy and visitors. See Andrew Radde-Gallwitz, *Basil of Caesarea* (Eugene, OR: Cascade, 2012), 94–5.

8 One part (of two) of this essay can be found in English as "Tripartite Anthropology," in *Theology in History*, trans. Anne Nash (San Francisco: Ignatius Press, 1996), 117–200, cited below in the text as *TA*. The other part is "Mysticism and Mystery," in *Theological Fragments* (San Francisco: Ignatius Press, 1989), 35–69. I have sketched its place within de

more important, and what he says there informs much of his other writing. The essay is ostensibly on theological anthropology, but for reasons that will become obvious, it is also on ecclesiology. The two loci are brought together and illumined by the basic aim and shape of the Christian life, and in such a way that they cannot be treated separately.

According to de Lubac, patristic pro-Nicene theological reflection upon the Christian person and the church can be described by means of a schema consisting of three triads, one each on anthropology and ecclesiology, and a third reflecting the shape and development of the Christian life. It may be helpful to see them together, at the risk of oversimplification:

	1	2	3
Anthropology:	body	soul	spirit
Christian Life:	ascesis	transformation	synthesis
Ecclesiology:	religion	morality	spirituality

The nine elements indicate the movement and shape of Christian transformation, which begins at the first vertical group (body, ascesis, religion), moves on into the second (soul, transformation, morality) and then on to the third (spirit, synthesis, spirituality). No element of any group can be left behind as the Christian develops; everything earlier remains fully necessary for any further transformation. Yet progress is genuine because transformation significantly affects the earlier elements. So, for example, the religion of one who has achieved some degree of synthesis will be more lively, loving, and God centered.

To forestall any concerns about individualism, we can begin with the third row, the ecclesiological. According to de Lubac, pro-Nicene patristic theologians had in mind something like three "domains," or social areas, in each of which it is necessary to dwell if we are to become Christian and grow in the Christian life. The Christian lives initially within the religious domain: the worshipping church. Here young or newly converted Christians learn how properly to orient themselves toward God by regular enactments of the church's cultic practices, by repeated recitation of the Creed, and by hearing the church's proclamation of Scripture. In this first domain the relation with God is primarily a personal one because it is mediated by worship rather than by the acquisition of a set of beliefs about God. Correct belief is subsequent to, and dependent upon, engaged participation in the church's right worship of the triune God.

This domain is correlated anthropologically with the "body." The pro-Nicenes understood the body to be good and of intrinsic value because it is created for us by God. But it must be trained by obedience and self-denial (ascesis). The distinction between the "body" and the rational "soul" of the next column

Lubac's work more generally in "Henri de Lubac and the Christian Life," *The T & T Clark Companion to Henri de Lubac*, ed. Jordan Hillebert (London: Bloomsbury/T & T Clark, 2016). Citations have been rendered inclusive.

should not be overstressed. It is not that they are two parts of the person that do different things, nor even that they do the same thing in different ways.[9] Rather, the point is that initially the new Christian must cultivate an unquestioning, or (as it were) "mindless," obedience.[10] There is no other Christian road to God and to the freedom of life in the Spirit than through simply accepting and becoming "physically" transformed by the church's religious practices. While this may seem odd to some Christians today—though it probably should not—this insistence on fundamental obedience can be appreciated more easily if we think of the way in which someone learns to play a musical instrument. The pupil must follow his teacher's instructions without questioning them if he is to learn from her and overcome his initial physical inadequacies, since only she knows the path forward. The more obedient he becomes, through careful listening and practice, the more progress he makes. Thereby he acquires the self-control to overcome spontaneous and erroneous bodily movements and feelings, learns how to listen musically, and so begins to play well.[11]

In the second stage the Christian moves into a somewhat less restricted but far more complex social domain: morality. We have been dwelling here to some extent from the beginning, of course, but this is indeed a new stage, for here we must learn how to be obedient in a more than merely "bodily" way. A response in charity to the other requires us to reason and thus involves our "rational soul" as well as our body, since, in the concrete, how I am to love my neighbor cannot be prescribed for me in advance. I might, for example, find myself in a situation where two or more moral teachings apply in seemingly incompatible ways, and so I must deliberate as to what course of action is appropriate. I gradually learn how to love

---

9 A contemporary retrieval of patristic anthropology would need to find a different way to express the main idea here. For a summary account of what he argues are the problems of premodern anthropologies, see David H. Kelsey, *Eccentric Existence: A Theological Anthropology* (Louisville: Westminster John Knox Press, 2009), 29–31 and 36–8; see also 562–6.

10 Ascesis and absolute obedience can, of course, be distorted, especially in combination. For an account of diverse and not always beneficial developments in the patristic ascetic tradition in relation to the governance of the church, see George E. Demacopoulos, *Models of Spiritual Direction in the Early Church* (Notre Dame, IN: University of Notre Dame Press, 2007). For a contemporary view of obedience within the religious life, see Sandra M. Schneiders, I. H. M., *Buying the Field: Catholic Religious Life in Mission to the World* (New York/Mahwah, NJ: Paulist Press, 2013), pt. 3, especially chap. 7, 355–424.

11 Nicholas Lash is right to say that modernity has left us with a "crisis of docility," and that much pedagogy is based on an "unreal antithesis" between truth, understood to be had only as we discover it for ourselves, and that which we get from learning from someone else, which is thought to be "at best unreliable, and at worst, degrading." See *Believing Three Ways in One God* (Notre Dame, IN: University of Notre Dame Press, 1993), 10. Yet there do remain some places where this antithesis does not pertain; in sports, for example, as well as music.

my neighbor over the course of repeated attempts to do so, and as I follow up each attempt by reflection and prayerful repentance for my inadequacies or failures. Every time we act more lovingly than sinfully or blindly, we are transformed to some degree and over time may acquire virtues and skill in discernment. The moral domain is not, then, one in which we unquestioningly follow God's laws, nor should we follow the church as if it were simply God's juridical representative. For my primary concern is my relation with my neighbor, in and through which I come to have a closer relation with Christ in the Spirit. The moral teaching of the church is necessary and an end in itself. But it is an integral part of the overarching goal of personal and communal transformative action.[12]

In and through our love of God, neighbor, and community we begin to move into the third domain, the spiritual, and therewith into the fullness of the Christian life. According to de Lubac, in spite of varying terminology the working anthropology of the pro-Nicene theological culture required in effect three components: body, soul, and spirit. This is "obviously not to be understood as implying three substances, or even three 'faculties,' in the person: it is discerned rather as a threefold zone of activity, from the periphery to the center" (*TA 177*). All three are and remain necessary for the "life of the spirit, in the Spirit" (*TA* 175), in contradistinction to the Flesh. De Lubac traces this anthropology to Paul, for example 1 Thes 5:23: "and may your entire being, spirit, soul and body, be kept safe and blameless for the coming of our Lord Jesus Christ" (*TA* 117). He argues that Paul's teaching—and following him, that of the pro-Nicenes—is that our spirit participates in the Holy Spirit such that the latter works in us not solely as an "event" of grace (de Lubac here amicably contradicts Karl Barth). Rather, our spirit is the "zone of [the Spirit's] activity." It is where the Spirit dwells, as it were, even though our spirit "does not appear completely like a constituent part of a person as such, like the body or the soul" (*TA* 129).

Although the pro-Nicene theologians developed the Pauline anthropological "ambiguity" (*TA* 129) in rather different ways, for all of them it is this spiritual relation that makes possible genuine self-realization or "synthesis." The spiritual relation is generative of holiness and is the source of a person's contribution to the transformation of the church and the world. In our spirit's relation to the Spirit (and therefore always also within the religious and moral domains), the Christian moves "from the periphery to the center, or, to use a traditional and irreplaceable word, to the 'heart,'" understood as "the most radical and the most authentic reality of the human being" (*TA* 117n2). While we never leave behind our sinfulness in this life, we can move beyond merely natural possibilities toward a relation with God wherein we each become more and more who we are called to be, as our spirit responds to the Spirit working within us.[13]

---

12 While the church's moral teaching is functional to this degree, the moral agent's action can never be. I cannot truly love my neighbor if my focus is on my relation to God. See Gareth Moore, OP, *Believing in God: A Philosophical Essay* (Edinburgh: T & T Clark, 1988), 144.

13 For some support from modern biblical scholars for something like this interpretation of Paul, see Gordon D. Fee, *God's Empowering Presence: The Holy Spirit in the Letters of*

In sum, for the pro-Nicene theological culture, the freedom to love and serve the Lord in holiness is the gift of the Spirit through and within the Body of Christ, the church. We could say, perhaps, that it is God's third gift to us, after our creation from nothing and our reconciliation in Jesus Christ. It is the gift in and through which the other gifts achieve their fullness, for the Cross and Resurrection not only reverse the effects of the Fall but also prepare us for the work of the Spirit in us. As a result of that work, some people may experience some foretaste of the kingdom even now. We remain very much within the world, nonetheless, since all nine elements of the schema continue to be necessary.

Keeping ecclesiology and anthropology formally and materially interdependent reminds of this. The church *in via* is the community where the faithful are to help one another worship, love, and be transformed. No Christian, as such, can be transformed outside the church. Thus when ecclesiology is associated with pro-Nicene theological anthropology, it becomes fundamentally pastoral in orientation. Its task is to reflect upon the church's religious, moral, and spiritual practices and teachings, and consider its institutions in view of their contribution to its members' transformation and, through them, the world's. The church's institutional structures, though necessary, are subsequent and primarily functional, even if they are not only so. The church is not constituted as the Body of Christ by its polity, whether hierarchical, episcopal, congregational, or any other kind. And the church cannot be reformed and purified unless it fosters in enough of its members some measure of holiness, as its history indicates.

Retrieval

How, then, might we retrieve these elements of the patristic pro-Nicene understanding of the person and the church? Clearly, it would likely require us to take on something like the patristic view of the Christian life and to develop appropriate pastoral practices to enrich and reform the various cultures of the churches, including their theological cultures and scholarly products.[14] Such an enrichment cannot be accomplished simply by means of theoretical blueprints of what the church and its culture ought to look like once such changes have been made.[15] We would misunderstand the point of de Lubac's schematic description of the pro-Nicene theological culture if our response were to try to turn it into a contemporary second-order ecclesiology and anthropology. That would be to

---

Paul (Peabody, MA: Hendrickson, 1994), 64–6 and 896–9. Also see James D. G. Dunn, "The Gospel According to St. Paul," in *The Blackwell Companion to Paul*, ed. Stephen Westerhom (Malden, MA: Blackwell, 2011), 148–52.

14 Congregational ethnographies may be an essential aid for such an effort; see *Perspectives on Ecclesiology and Ethnography*, ed. Pete Ward (Grand Rapids, MI: Eerdmans, 2012).

15 For an argument against "blueprint" ecclesiologies, see my *Church, World and the Christian Life* (Cambridge: Cambridge University Press, 2000).

recast a once-living theological culture into a theoretical proposal that, as a next step, we would somehow have to put into practice by changing our churches' theological cultures. Since it is this second step that is the more necessary and difficult, all our efforts, including our second-order theological analyses and proposals, should be oriented toward it from the outset.

Accordingly, a preliminary move might be to try to get a clear and detailed sense of where and how our contemporary church cultures differ from the earlier pro-Nicene theological culture. I cannot attempt such a massive undertaking here, but instead consider briefly a few common criticisms, made by some Christians as well as non-Christians, against certain cultural elements of the mainline churches, focusing here on the Roman Catholic church as a particular case.[16] I then suggest how a retrieval of elements of the earlier pro-Nicene theological culture could help to address such criticism.

One complaint is that the church's moral rules and principles are treated by ecclesiastical authorities as if they are beyond discussion. Yet, for example, teachings based upon natural law appear to many to be unconvincing in what they determine what "Nature intended" us to do and not do. They seem to rationalize the preservation of unjust and oppressive structures of a bygone society rather than reflect either the Gospel or common sense. More generally, the churches appear to some to be dehumanizing institutions that block certain reasonable aspirations—on the part of women, for example. The churches are characterized as rejecting freedom of religious expression, freedom to live according to conscience, and therefore the freedom of individuals to develop their unique relationship with God.

This complaint is often captured in the distinction between an "organized religion" and one's "personal spirituality."[17] Obviously, from a patristic perspective such a distinction makes little sense because, as we have seen, positive acknowledgment of the church's religious and moral authority is necessary to achieve any progress in spirituality. True freedom in the Spirit and authoritative church teaching are the

---

16 The churches differ considerably, and while I would argue the patristic schema would benefit all of them, it would do so in different ways. For an account of significantly different problems in Baptist churches to which the schema could arguably be applied, though differently, see Curtis Freeman, *Contesting Catholicity: Theology for Other Baptists* (Waco, TX: Baylor University Press, 2014).

17 For an ethnographically based theory of the reasons for this complaint in the United Kingdom, see Paul Heelas and Linda Woodhead, *The Spiritual Revolution: Why Religion Is Giving Way to Spirituality* (Malden, MA: Blackwell, 2005). On the United States, see David Masci and Michael Lipka, "Americans May Be Getting Less Religious, But Feelings of Spirituality Are on the Rise," at *Pew Research Center*, http://pewrsr.ch/1OzDbMu (accessed March 20, 2016). This complaint has been made before in other forms, for example the eleventh-century rejection of traditional monasticism by eremitical movements as mere pharisaism. See Gert Melville, *The World of Medieval Monasticism: Its History and Forms of Life*, trans. James D. Mixson (Collegeville, MN: Liturgical Press, 2016), 89–124.

product of each other by the working of the Holy Spirit, and therefore each should have the other always in view. Yet from that same perspective, such complaints may get some things right. Cultivating the desire for a renewed life in and through one's personal relation with God is an essential element of the Christianity of the patristic and medieval periods. The power of the Spirit is the necessary and, when need be, can be the sufficient condition for a person to reason and act lovingly in true freedom. The Roman Catholic church acknowledges this to some extent in its official teaching about the conscience,[18] but it is rare to hear from the pulpit that obedience to the church's religious and moral teaching, though necessary, is but the beginning of the Christian life, and that it is by no means sufficient for a right and loving response to God.

Accordingly, the church's reaction to these criticisms should not be simply to condemn them, and certainly not to accuse those who make them of narcissism and self-indulgent individualism. Such ad hominem arguments merely bolster resistance to its teaching, not least because in accusing critics of being sinful or ignorant, their proponents seem to claim the church is always spotless and right thinking, whereas, to many people, including not a few Christians, it plainly is not. Nor does it help to chide the latter—the church's internal critics—for their lack of critical distance from prevailing sociocultural attitudes, for these are just as much at work among the more contented members of the church and include those who do not appear to be in accord with the Gospel.

A better response to these and similar criticisms would be for the church to consider how it may reflect its failure to foster a pastoral and theological culture that engages its members with the fullness of the tradition. Our critics, we might say, are instruments through whom the Holy Spirit is working to effect the always-necessary and -ongoing reform of the church and the transformation of its members. Their criticisms are partly supported by the pro-Nicene theological culture, since a comparison indicates that too often we fail to preach and live, both as churches and as individual Christians, as people who know we are dependent upon the Holy Spirit's transforming action within us for our very existence as the Body of Christ. We fail to acknowledge sufficiently, in our theology and in our practices, the necessary relations among the three domains. For example, in some churches the second domain is so deformed that moral teachings are presented, first, as if they require the unquestioning, even quasi-mindless, obedience that is more appropriate for the religious domain; second, as if the moral were the primary domain; and, third, as if the Spirit were merely a function of the church and under its control.[19] As a result, the third domain

---

18 *Catechism of the Catholic Church*, Liguori, MO: Liguori, 1994, nos. 1781–82 and 1788. Far bolder is Aquinas on the New Law: *Summa Theologiae*, 1a2 107.4; 1a2 108.1; 2a2 93.2.

19 Yves Congar seems to relate this to the development of the doctrine of capital grace in the twelfth century and its subsequent adoption by Aquinas (*Summa Theologiae*, 3a 8). Prior to about 1160, he argues, the church was understood in "strongly pneumatological

has atrophied, and Christian spirituality has become a kind of optional extra for the unusually devout.[20]

So the first and perhaps most obvious area of retrieval in response to this set of issues would be to develop cultural forms that better acknowledge and support the church's task of producing "spiritual" individuals, people who are on their way toward some kind of "synthesis." Christians should hear from the pulpit about these traditional teachings on the Christian life and be offered church missions and workshops through which they may come to realize how joyful and self-actualizing it can be to grow into the life of the Spirit by our worship of God and love of neighbor. Pastoral moves in this direction can be found in some churches here and there, most notably in the person and work of Pope Francis. His spiritual maturity displays both the necessity and fruitfulness of the first two domains, and how they cannot be just a means to the goals of the third.[21] But he and other exemplary Christians also show that, while worship and love of neighbor are both ends in themselves, they should be productive of a spiritual life that renders them more Christlike.

With regard to ecclesiology, although proposals about new "models" of the church might be useful, it is cultural transformation that is arguably more urgent. Roberto Repole has explored church transformation under the rubric of "The Humility of the Church."[22] Theological reflection upon what makes a "humble" church can highlight practices and attitudes that display and acknowledge its dependence upon the Holy Spirit, without whom it cannot live as the Body of Christ. In the Spirit, the church becomes stronger the more it is humble and fragile, or "bruised, hurting and dirty," as Pope Francis has put it.[23] It lives as it should

terms," for it was "the Holy Spirit who made the body of which Christ was the Head." With grace now assigned to Christ as Head of the church, the church becomes the sole source of grace, and the Spirit is in effect under its control: Yves Congar, OP, *I Believe in the Holy Spirit*, trans. David Smith (New York: Crossroad, 1997), pt. 1, 116. Parallel developments were the consolidation of the power of the papacy within a more hierarchical and institutional church, and a shift in pastoral focus away from spiritual direction toward confession, and so from the third to the second domain; see John Mahoney, *The Making of Moral Theology: A Study of the Roman Catholic Tradition* (Oxford: Clarendon Press, 1987), 1–36.

20 It may well be that the more progress is made in the third domain, the more some (but maybe not all) of the more challenging of the church's moral teachings will appear reasonable, provided that they are taken to apply only to oneself. It is in counseling and legislating for others, especially those who have made less progress, that difficulties are likely to remain.

21 For an argument for why one cannot aim to become a spiritual person, see Moore, *Believing*, 153–9. For a moral theology more consonant with the pro-Nicene schema than many others, I would suggest Michael Banner, *The Ethics of Everyday Life: Moral Theology, Social Anthropology, and the Imagination of the Human* (Oxford: Oxford University Press, 2014).

22 Roberto Repole, *L'Umiltà della Chiesa* (Communità di Bose: Edizioni Qiqajon, 2010).

23 Pope Francis, Apostolic Exhortation, *Evangelii Gaudium*, at The Holy See, http://w2.vatican.va

when it is devoted to God and humanity without care for its safety, its rights, or its prestige as an institution. And so, as Repole argues, a further and always necessary task for ecclesiology is "to carry out an anti-ideological function,"[24] which would include reminding the church how different it actually is from what it should be and from what some of its members may assume it is.

One might respond to this by pointing out that the patristic church showed little or no humility of this kind, even though it placed a more pronounced emphasis on the Holy Spirit. In reply, we could point to a significant display of humility in the patristic churches that has been absent for some centuries. Then, as now, there were frequent and sometimes bitter theological arguments, but they were sustained by bishops rather than academic theologians. Their rank gave them authority, but they also had an independence today's bishops do not have, so they could and did publicly and vigorously disagree with one another. They were in turn challenged by emperors and by people whose holiness had an appeal and a de facto authority they themselves did not always have. Sometimes they were even shouted down by their congregations as they preached.[25] The church was a place where disputes over the interpretation of the Gospel were pursued with an urgency and passion that left little room for worries about the dignity of office or the faithful being scandalized. With a few significant exceptions, bishops in the Roman Catholic Church these days rarely engage in theological argument, and especially not in public. Nor do they often meet ordinary folk who disagree with them and dare to challenge them directly. Today's episcopal culture is largely administrative. Doctrinal and moral teachings are assumed to be settled and agreed upon by all in authority, enabling the bishops to present a united front against external and internal challenges to received doctrine and practice. By comparison, the bishops of the patristic period appeared far more fragile, more alone as leaders, and their difficulties in leading their church were on display for everyone to see.[26]

I have offered some reasons why the church should consider enriching its theological culture by retrieving suitably modified elements of the patristic pro-Nicene culture, and I have argued that if this were done, the distinction between spirituality and organized religion would no longer be justified. Yet even if this suggestion were taken up and were successful, this would not, of itself, resolve a significant theological question. There are now, as there always have been and will be, not a few church members who do not seem to be particularly interested in spiritual growth, and whose reasons for attending church lie to some varying degree outside the three domains. Some Christians seem to be happy enough with the way they are, and do not want religious, moral, and spiritual transformation

---

24 Repole, *L'Umiltà*, 107.

25 According to Peter Brown, Augustine's congregation sometimes challenged his sermons as he preached them. See Peter Brown, *Augustine of Hippo*, new ed. (Berkeley: University of California Press: 2000), 446–7.

26 To be sure, today's bishops perform important and necessary functions. This is merely a simplified picture made only to illustrate retrieval possibilities.

from their church. And what do we say to those who feel that in spite of some effort, they have remained largely the same in fifty or sixty years of being Christian, except perhaps in the particular ways they sin?[27]

This is a question that has received various answers over the centuries. One, developed mostly after the patristic period, was to institute something like a two-tier form of the Christian life. A minority, mostly the religious and clergy, oriented themselves through the first and second domains toward the third domain by a rigorous way of life involving frequent worship and prayer, celibacy and obedience, and, for some, personal poverty. The vast majority pursued a less stringent way of life, with suitably easier practices that led to some minor transformation but mostly only in the first and second domains. This would not have been acceptable to the patristic church, since everyone should be attempting to live the Christian life fully, commensurate with their abilities and opportunities. And so, if the contemporary church were to take on something like the pro-Nicene view of the Christian life, we too would have to refuse the two-tier approach, since the schema applies to everyone; it is not just for the especially devout.[28] It would seem, then, that we could not accept a view of the Christian life as one that can be ordinary and untransformed, and more or less contentedly so. Nor would such a view appear to be consistent with what is said about discipleship in the New Testament.

Does this mean, then, that our leaders must now demand from everyone that they had better become not only moral but also spiritual, or else? And what is the "else"? From some pulpits, we are still told that we get to heaven on the basis of our efforts in the first two domains, a teaching that, however carefully hedged about with talk about grace, too frequently boils down to a transactional quid pro quo. A renewed emphasis upon spiritual growth in the Christian life could end up similarly distorted into an individualistic pursuit of heaven, as it seems to have been in some cases in the monastic traditions and later devotional piety.[29]

If we follow the pro-Nicene theological tradition in keeping ecclesiology and anthropology more closely interdependent, we may have a better answer than the two-tier view or threats of judgment against those who do not try harder. Our two loci together promote the humility of the church, for we will need to preach, reflect theologically upon, and find ways to display our reliance upon the mercy and love of the triune God. As noted earlier, we have been give three great gifts, to none of which have we contributed, let alone earned: our existence from the Creator, forgiveness and reconciliation from our Redeemer, and the promise of a future in the kingdom. If this is correct, then the Christian life cannot be anything like a kind of test of our worthiness for heavenly life, to pass which requires effort

---

27 I also have in mind Frances Young's profound and profoundly important theological reflections in relation to her severely disabled son, Arthur, in Young, *Presence*, passim.

28 See Ayres's discussion of "ascetic portability" in his *Nicaea and Its Legacy*, 342–3.

29 For example, de Lubac detects a certain individualism in Bernard of Clairvaux, *Catholicism: Christ and the Common Destiny of Man* (San Francisco: Ignatius Press, 1988), 128. The worry over final perseverance indicates a similar problem.

in all three domains, or at least the first two. That gets everything the wrong way around. For instead of a requirement, we are in fact faced with an offer, one that should indeed prompt our response. But it is not an offer of heaven as such, for this is already ours in Jesus Christ. Rather it is the offer of a life lived in the joy of the Spirit's indwelling in our spirit, of a proleptic taste of the kingdom even now in faith, love, and hope. Not everyone in the churches will take up that offer, and perhaps only a few will devote their lives to it. For those of us who do not, that is our loss, to be sure. But it is not a fundamental loss, for transformation does not cease in heaven.

The point can be made—though necessarily far too simply—in terms of the two great analogies for the church that we and the patristics share: the "Temple of the Spirit" and the "Body of Christ." These should function interdependently and anti-ideologically. It is as the Spirit's Temple that the church makes it possible for each of us to be transformed. As we are transformed, we witness to the power of the Gospel and contribute to the church's transformation and renewal, and in this way we may at times give some evidence to the world that the church is indeed the Body of Christ. However, the church and most of its members are not transformed very much, and sometimes do not seem to be transformed at all. The often visible difference between the potential effect of the Spirit and its actual effect on the church and ourselves should cause the church and ourselves to be humble. As a properly humble church, we acknowledge the difference and find ourselves able to do little more than point to Christ and remind ourselves that it was he who achieved our salvation *pro nobis* and *extra nos*. As Christ's Body our salvation remains ours to have, irrespective of the quality of our response to the Gospel. Furthermore, if we acknowledge in practice and theory that the Body of Christ in some real way is made up of all humanity,[30] the very name "Body of Christ" is also anti-ideological, undermining any overreach in our self-understanding.

What the church offers us, as the Temple of the Spirit, is the wondrous possibility of making a genuine response to Christ, a response that is not required, in the sense of something I must do in order for Christ's work to be applied to me. It is "required" only in the sense that one would be foolish, ungrateful, and self-harming in not taking up that offer of the joy of the Gospel. Many of us are often just that. Yet we are members of the Body of Christ. And so in this way, the Gospel is the Good News of our triune God, and Good News for everyone.

---

30 Already in Aquinas, *Summa*, 3a.8.3. This is necessary to avoid any notion of "religious luck," the idea that some are saved just because they are lucky enough to have been members of a particular religious group, which is not only unjust but also surely incompatible with the triune God.

Part VI

A BROADENING CONVERSATION

Chapter 15

"YOU CAN'T GO HOME AGAIN": RETRIEVAL AND MULATTIC THEOLOGICAL METHOD

Brian Bantum

On a plantation, any plantation in the antebellum South, a young man stands on the steps of his father's grand house and says, "I am your son, white man!" His mother is still back in the slave quarters nursing yet another of his master's slave sons. A half brother and half sister are picking cotton in the field, grabbing glances of their brother, hoping the trouble will not come to them. "Why does he keep up this way?" That's never going be his house, master's never gonna see him as his son," they say. And the young man's other two half brothers watch him from above, laughing at his inflections, mocking the very assumption that they could all be kin.

Not far down the road is the church the master and his family, and his slaves all attend every Sunday. With the slaves in the back (the young man usually sits in the first pew of the colored section, right behind the white women and their children), they listen to a sermon that promises of a "hereafter" where all will be well and emphasizes obedience and compliance and the virtues of suffering.

But on the other side of the property, where the small forest meets the fields and shades the creek—after the sun goes down and all the lights are out in the master's large white house—the slaves gather and sing their own songs and read of Moses's calling and Israel's liberation.

Not all gather at night. Some are content with the service in the morning. Others simply remain in their quarters wondering what could possess their bonded kin to bend to anything associated with those white men and women.

The plantation, and the interrelated bodies that constitute it, serve as a sign, a crevice into which we can begin to see the challenges of theological reflection in a world so deeply shaped by the racial logic of white supremacy. The ubiquity and violence of this racial world require everyone to account for themselves once caught within its gravity. Being pulled deeper and deeper into its orbit, we must begin to account for ourselves as products of this world.

Race in the modern world is an economic, political, and social ordering of bodies. One of the most salient manifestations of this violent order was the American plantation. To consider the question of race, theology, and retrieval, the plantation is a good beginning. Not because it exemplifies what the entirety of the

American racial logic looked like but because on the plantation we see the whole economy working in one space. Throughout the American and the colonial world, dynamics of economic exploitation, theological justification, brutal violence, racial classification, and legal manipulation to sustain the system are all present in various ways. On the plantation they are total.

While the plantation was the most visible, its underlying logic and organization of bodies was the basis of the colonial project beginning as early as the fifteenth century. Race also functions as a religious phenomenon and within a theological space. Its social and economic arrangements are underwritten by a telos, a transcendent ideal that shapes the ways bodies are read, while also shaping what is possible (or impossible) for these bodies within the unfolding social spaces of the New World.

What is theological retrieval in the shadow of the plantation? Retrieval is a means of identification, a way of locating oneself and God in the world. But what should we remember? How should we remember? How do various projects of theological retrieval navigate the reality of our racialized world?

The plantation serves as a space from which to think about these questions. The locations, the bodies that navigated these spaces answered these questions in varying ways, drawing on sources and excluding others in order to articulate how they understood God and the world and navigated the challenges they perceived in the world. Movements such as Radical Orthodoxy are explicit attempts at theological retrieval, mining the structures and sources of a Christian tradition in order to account for a contemporary moment. But I wonder if this is really new. Is not Christian existence itself a retrieval project, a return to Judaic sources and structures while also reimagining them in their contemporary moment?

The reflex of retrieval is inherent in Christian thought and experience. The question of retrieval posed by schools of thought such as Radical Orthodoxy is more a question of which structures get retrieved. "Orthodoxy" is the key term here. While Radical Orthodoxy is considered a theological retrieval because of its emphasis on orthodoxy, so-called "contextual" theologies are the contrast, often understood as eschewing tradition and orthodoxy. In this chapter my concern is how theology can most faithfully articulate our contemporary moment truthfully. In a violently racialized world, where the legacy of the plantation, of economic exploitation, racial segregation, police brutality, and rampant inequality persist, how do we theologically speak? What are the resources and the methods we employ?

In this chapter I want to begin from the space of the plantation to suggest that retrieval is not a new theological method for black Christians, or for contextual theologians more broadly. While contextual theologies have pointed to the complicity of traditional doctrine or orthodoxy and the subjugation of dark bodies in colonization, they nonetheless press the question of *what* should be retrieved and how these various sources ought to be understood together as we imagine a way forward in our world. I want to suggest that we exist in a world where our bodies and lives have become interwoven in complex ways. Though these interconnections are varied, the plantation points to how race has deeply marked us all and yet also circumscribed our bodies into particular spaces within this new world.

Retrieval is a critical instinct in theological thought, but not because there is some ideal theological construction that will rehabilitate our sickened world. We cannot go home again. The first time we go home to see Mom or Dad with our partner, with children, "home" becomes something new. It is both familiar and strange. The rhythms and patterns of my life there have shaped me, but I cannot reproduce those patterns in the same way for my own kids, in my own life—at least not in the same ways or toward the same ends. Those practices, mundane rituals, values become altered as the ripple drifts away from the place where the stone was tossed into the lake. They retain the same shape for a while, but then the other ripples, the wind, the ebbs of boats all begin to disrupt the movement of "home" moving out into the world. But from its very beginnings the earliest followers of Jesus sought to reckon with the theological frame that located them in the world and the realities of the man who encountered them and would eventually be confessed as their Lord and Savior. They returned to the sources of their stories and saw them in new ways, began to tell the old stories with a different emphasis. Even when Christianity began to forget its Jewish beginnings, theological innovation was anathema. Heresy and orthodoxy were arguments about tradition, about reclamation.

Of course, retrieval is also a political process, a process of identification that looks back in order to make sense of the present, discerning how various lines of thought have shaped who we are and how those ideas might instruct us in discerning how we ought to shape our lives together.

We live in a moment where a singular tradition seems impossible, and yet we exist in a globalized world where no nation or people can be understood as disconnected from another. Like the plantation, we are caught in an economy of inequality and distorted kinship, while also being inextricably bound to one another. What does theological retrieval look like in this world? Christian existence is a curious process of re-creation. In an economy of death and resurrection retrieval is always a bodily process, an incarnational mode of being in the world that cannot extricate itself from the old but can never repeat it. The new body is new because of what has been added to it, what has been folded into its life, layer upon layer.

In this chapter I want to suggest theological retrieval in our racialized moment requires a mulattic theological mode. Less concerned with reclamation of the Nicene Creed or orthodox formulations, a mulattic theology begins at the intersections of bodies and the discourses that create them, but is never without the various descriptions of God and Jesus that preceded them. The creeds and confessions are themselves embodied responses to an encounter with the bodied God in a historical moment. A mulattic approach cannot dismiss these descriptions, but it cannot reproduce them either. The old and new become comingled in the contemporary body, disrupting the distorted claims of purity that concretize inequality and exclusion.

Retrieval is a necessary practice, a practice that seeks to discern the bodies, discourses, and histories that have constructed the bodily present. But a mullatic theological mode also exists within these dynamics of power and inequality. In this regard retrieval also necessitates the possibility of confession. And mullatic theology is necessarily open to reimagination, the possibility of new inflections of truth being born in the encounter of various bodies and traditions. Thinking from the context of the plantation we can begin to see theological retrieval as not only a return to a "classical" theological mode. Mulattic theology is a particular instantiation of black Christian existence, a reclamation of wholeness and humanity, drawing from the texts, bodies, land, rhythms, and songs that are on hand.

Approaches to retrieval from the plantation

From its very inception black diasporic Christianity was a retrieval project, of sorts. In the face of a colonial system and a theological framework that questioned whether black bodies even had souls, or the capacity to become Christian, slaves and free blacks would read Scripture and see bondage and liberation as an act of defiance toward a system and theological frame that sought to dehumanize their bodies. The early jeremiads of David Walker in the late eighteenth century are striking examples of how black Christians retrieved notions of liberation, freedom, and equality from the Bible, inverting notions of fidelity and "orthodoxy" as a mode of being in the world, how one responds to God's presence in the world. Not all black women and men would become Christian, however. Christianity signified the divine legitimization of their enslavement, a God who ordained their bondage. And in the midst of this were the minority of white Christians who opposed slavery (though most still doubted black equality) and the majority of white Christians who believed in a God who ordained white supremacy.

In all of these there are various retrieval projects, attempts at drawing from traditions and patterns to articulate a notion of fullness. Any contemporary consideration of retrieval must account for the plantation and the theological, political, and social forces that conceived it. Beginning with the plantation as a centering location, I would suggest three metaphors of retrieval in contemporary theologians: restoration, the blues, and excavation.

Restoration

The sermons of slave Christianity served the economic and imperial purposes of slave society. The ubiquity of retrieval as a restoration project is the normative mode of contemporary theological education. In these spaces theology is practiced often as though the plantation never existed or missionaries did not accompany conquistadors. In this way, contemporary theology skirts around the buildings of the plantation, perhaps believing it is not the building that was oppressive but its use, or perhaps the frame of the structure is worth keeping. Replace the rotted wood, switch out the windows. It is not the building or the creed but a distorted version of these. Or, some might say, "it is not even true belief at all . . . If it were true faith, that true doctrine might begin to see ourselves more clearly."

While occasionally pointing to the plantation, this "traditioned" retrieval by and large forgets the plantation. It might note its existence as an unfortunate anomaly. This is never done explicitly, of course. But of the major white theologians in the last fifty years at major doctoral institutions, how many consider whiteness, slavery, or racism as necessary aspects of their theological matrices? The problem of Constantinianism, neoliberalism, or capitalism all serve as major points of contestation that shape their theological projects. But how does race figure into these projects?

The Confederate flag becomes either an embarrassing aberration or a benign symbol of just another flawed culture. Theological retrieval that draws upon a canon, a tradition, without reckoning with the colonial realities of religion and race that formed the modern world constitutes a canon that is melancholic because "it excludes but cannot forget."[1] This "melancholy of race" described by Professor of English Anne Cheng, is not absent from our social lives but rather becomes a "mis-remembered" presence.

> While the formation of American culture may be said to be a history of legalized exclusions (Native Americans, African-Americans, Jews, Chinese-Americas, Japanese-Americans, etc.) it is, however, also a history of misremembering those denials . . . Because the American history of exclusions, imperialism, and colonization runs so diametrically opposed to the equally and particularly American narrative of liberty and individualism, cultural memory in America poses a continuously vexing problem: how to remember those transgressions without impeding the ethos of progress?[2]

Ignoring the exclusions that are constitutive of a society does not erase their presence. They remain.

The effects of this misremembering are so complete, so thorough that it is difficult to point to an exception in American Christian life where the realities of America's and Europe's racist and colonial ventures have not been fundamentally ignored in the imagination of Christian life or its theological education. Apart from the communities marginalized by colonial ambitions, Western Christianity seems to miraculously overlook its own overt, violent, and idolatrous existence in the so-called Western world.

Theologian Willie James Jennings describes how such misremembering is engrained in the very beginnings of the Western Christian world. Jennings presses the interrelationships between theology and imperialist modernity.

> that this crisis of theological tradition was not discerned by [Jesuit theologian Jose Peres de] Acosta, and for the most part has still not been discerned, as a crisis

1 Anne Anlin Cheng, "The Melancholy of Race," *Kenyon Review* 19 (1997): 51.
2 Cheng, "Melancholy of Race," 50–1.

of Christian tradition. From the moment Acosta (and those like him) placed his feet on the ground in Lima, the Christian tradition and its theologians conjured a form of practical rationality that locked theology in discourses of displacement from which it has never escaped . . . it would not alter the creedal substance of his doctrine of creation but the way in which its logic would be performed. The ground on which Acosta was to stand was disappearing and reappearing in a new way. His theological vision was formed in the midst of that transformation.[3]

The problem of contemporary projects of theological retrieval is not necessarily the source material but that such projects seem to retrieve so selectively. In the colonial moment an understanding of tradition exacerbated fundamentally flawed relationships to the land and cultivated a reconfiguration of bodies, detachments that formed new ways of identifying and imagining the world. For Jennings such detachment allowed whiteness to become the ground of Christian identity in the New World and subsequently shaped all other bodies in relationship to itself. "Detached from the land, oblivious to the ongoing decimation of native ecologies, deeply suspicious of native religious practices, and, most important, enclosed within Iberian whiteness, the performance of Christian theology would produce a new, deformed, and deforming intellectual circuit."[4]

When considering the relationship between a racialized world and theological retrieval, the question can never simply be which doctrines or practices should be retrieved, restored, rehabilitated. A theology of retrieval that does not consider where the materials that built the home came from, the land that the plantation was built upon, is a theology of forgetting, a theology of misremembering that must continually articulate why race, why the racialized and enslaved body is not a question, a central question for its theology, its understanding of the world we live within. Jennings points to a retrieval where the form of creeds remained the same, but they were performed in the world in ways that were contrary to the encounters that gave rise to confession. This is not to say that the creeds were simply a mask for a distorted idolatry. Jennings points to a parasitic relationship between the colonial moment and traditioned strains of Christianity that accompanied and authorized it. I am not suggesting that retrieval is not a worthwhile exercise. It is an inevitable aspect of Christian practice. But any act of retrieval in a contemporary moment that seeks to go back without walking through the plantation, the slave auctions, and the slave ships, such disembodied retrievals are only a renewed intellectual colonialism.

The blues

Theologian James Cone inhabited a theological method grounded in the blues. The blues do not go around the plantation. Instead, the blues pick up the rhythms

---

3 Willie James Jennings, *The Christian Imagination: Theology and the Origins of Race* (New Haven, CT: Yale University Press, 2010), 72.

4 Jennings, *Christian Imagination*, 82.

of resistance present in the slave houses and hush harbors. The spirituals are not a retrieval of an intellectual system but rather an embodied freedom, a freedom that can both claim an encounter with the God of enslavers, while also rejecting the enslaver's religious idolatry.

Cone's retrieval project can only be understood within the tradition of black Christian prophetic disruption. He is one example of a contemporary black Christian who paradoxically holds on to signs that seemingly intend black dehumanization and, from those deathly tools, create songs of life. Black Christianity bears witness to traditions of resistance where retrieval is a complicated process of adoption and critique, or even critique through adoption of practices, belief, and ways of living that defied what was so often intended in a racist/imperialistic society. That is, black Christianity is grounded in encounter, encounters of Africans with a liberating God, in the very book that seemingly authorized their inhumanity. Retrieval is the reclamation of a tradition of resistance:

> To understand the history of black resistance, it is also necessary to know the black spirituals. They are historical songs which speak about the rupture of black lives; they tell us about a people in the land of bondage and what they did to hold themselves together and to fight back. We are told that the people of Israel could not sing the Lord's song in a strange land. But, for blacks, their Being depended upon a song. Through song, they built new structures for existence in an alien land. The spirituals enabled blacks to retain a measure of African identity while living in the midst of American slavery, providing both the substance and the rhythm to cope with human servitude.[5]

I still recall my first encounter with Cone's *Black Theology and Black Power* as an undergraduate student. In this book I discovered that a text could catch you in an unequivocal stare. It was a holy, furious, and prophetic stare, one that seemed to require you to account for yourself, to decide. Looking back upon this moment I am reminded that this is theology at its best—that a text is never a mere collection of words, but that when one wields them skillfully and with passion and insight they cut us to the quick, require us to examine ourselves, our commitments, our hopes. What does it mean to stand within this tradition? But as well, what is the relationship of this tradition to other expressions of Christian existence?

From its very inception, black theology has been an attempt to liberate the black body from the oppressive vestiges of Western economic, social, and theological hegemony. At its heart, the theological work of the earliest black Christians in America sought to articulate wholeness. Cone writes, "The slave has another concern, centered on the faithfulness of the community of believers in a world full of trouble. He wonders not whether God is just and right but whether the sadness and pain of the world will cause him to lose heart and thus fall prey to the ways

---

5 James Cone, "Black Spirituals: A Theological Interpretation," *Theology Today* 29 (1971): 58.

of evil. He is concerned about the togetherness of the community of sufferers."[6] At the heart of this project has been a reappropriation and reevaluation of what sources are determinative in casting a theological vision of black experience in the West and particularly in the United States, but all for the sake of articulating the humanity of their community.

However, even Cone's invocation of the slave spirituals is not a simple process of uncovering and retrieving old sources. Victor Anderson has brilliantly pointed out in his work *Beyond Ontological Blackness*, that the retrieval project of the black Christian tradition (namely the slave spirituals and narratives) aimed to buttress the lineage of black theology's primary concerns within a broader African American Christian narrative. As well, Anderson points to the difficulty in locating a coherent narrative from within these various disparate sources, especially regarding their often contentious relationship to the white-dominated abolitionist movement. Anderson's critique is representative of an inherent difficulty in black theology's seemingly perpetual tension regarding which sources are faithful and expressive of the African diasporic reality and which sources represent colonial modulations that gave rise to that diasporic reality.

To think through this tension it is helpful to turn briefly to Cone's navigation of this challenge. While black theology certainly cannot be distilled to Cone, his negotiation of this challenge highlights one of the fundamental marks of black theological reflection that does not reach past the plantation but reincorporates varied realities encountered in that present and redeploys them to articulate black humanity and Christian existence.

In Cone's work the question of sources became a prophetic display of swords turned to plowshares (or perhaps plowshares turned into swords) as the theological conceptions of Jesus's humanity and divinity resisted becoming parroted repetitions of a Western "orthodoxy." Instead Cone ventured into this "Christo-logic" so deeply that he broke open new ways of imagining the "classical." Speaking of Jesus's life and ministry, he recenters bodily freedom as the soteriological focus of the incarnation.

> Simply stated, freedom is not doing what I will but becoming what I should. A man is free when he sees clearly the fulfillment of his being and is thus capable of making the envisioned self a reality. This is "Black Power!" They want the grip of white power removed . . . Is this not why God became man in Jesus Christ so that man might become what he is?[7]

Cone's conceives the deification of the black body through the logic of the *communicatio idiomatum* and thereby articulates the presence of all oppressed dark bodies in Jesus's body. This reimagination of theological claims continued the theological tradition of black Christian thought and life in its creative appropriation

---

6 Cone, "Black Spirituals," 64.
7 James Cone, *Black Theology and Black Power* (Maryknoll, NY: Orbis, 1997), 39.

of oppressive ideologies and turning them into modulations of Christian resistance and liberation.

He turned the *Sound of Music* into jazz, if you will; he Coltrane-ified the Christological formulations of "creedal" theological ideas. Cone displays a fundamental rhythm of black theology as a praxis of creative reappropriation, reinterpretation, and redeployment. In this way black theology, as an improvisational performativity, seeks to both articulate God's work in the world and for the world. But even more, black theology has done so out of a deep commitment to the embodied moment from which our speech concerning God must arise.

Yet, like so many projects that attempt to retrieve, the creative invocations of ancient rhythms with contextual claims also exhibit limitations of sight. Womanist theologians have quite rightly pointed to the dismissal or erasure of black women's contributions to these "blues songs" of black Christian thought and life. Absent from Cone's early accounts were struggles to reconcile the language of racial equality with the continuation of patriarchal structures of the black church and theological spaces.

Tracing the historical gap between black Christian expressions of liberation and its marginalization of black women, theologian and historian Jacquelyn Grant has noted, "The conspiracy to keep women relegated to the background is also aided by the continuous psychological and political strategizing that keeps women from realizing their own potential power in the church."[8] Theologians such as Grant display the limitations of retrieval that cannot acknowledge the limitations of one's sight.

Retrieval must be willing to examine the fullness of its own story and the complicated interconnections and oppressions that have been constructed upon the land. The sources of this work cannot only be songs or theological patterns but also the realities of the bodies that fed and sustained communities upon the land. Their legacies and power are not present in creeds or theological treatises or debates about heresy and orthodoxy. Retrieval is the recognition of the bodies that made our lives possible and the retrieving of the practices and commitments to communal flourishing.

Theologian Emilie Townes highlights this embodiment of retrieval in her closing invitation in *Womanist Ethics and the Cultural Production of Evil*, inviting readers to *"live your faith deeply.* This is not a quest for perfection, but for what we call in Christian ethics the everydayness of moral acts. It is what we do every day that shapes us and where both the fantastic hegemonic imagination and the challenge and hope to dismantle it are found."[9] Townes's call displays a tradition of presence in the black community, and especially in the black church, exemplified by black women whose labor maintained the community even while being rendered invisible by formal male leadership.

---

8 Jacquelyn Grant, "Black Theology and the Black Woman," in *Black Theology: A Documentary History*, ed. Gayraud S. Wilmore and James H. Cone (Maryknoll, NY: Orbis, 1993), 328.

9 Emilie M. Townes, *Womanist Ethics and the Cultural Production of Evil* (New York: Palgrave Macmillan, 2006), 164; italics added.

The blues express a theological retrieval that is attentive to the formal traditions of songs passed from generation to generation that convey the hope and possibility of a people's faith. But the blues also suggest the bodied realities of communities that lived day to day, supported, nurtured, fought, and sacrificed for the sake of one another's survival and flourishing.

Excavation

Lastly, I want to consider a mode of retrieval that wrestles with the relationship between Christianity and slavery. Seeing clearly the complicity of Christianity in the Atlantic slave trade and the colonial development of the Americas, religious consciousness cannot be found solely in Western Christianity. From this vantage point retrieval requires dismantling the structures of oppression and finding the truth deep beneath or perhaps beyond the confines of the plantation. Perhaps the most influential work of this mode is that of Professor of Religion Charles Long. In his groundbreaking work, *Significations*, Long suggested

> the transcendent meaning in the notion of God is dethroned in favor of defin-able human structures; the worker and the economic order in the case of Marx, and the authority principle that lies behind pulsations of desire within the social context for Freud. A new primordium that is universal within the actualities of history rather than mind is brought to the fore. These ideologies not only counter the older Western theological notions but serve as well to deconstruct the Enlightenment primordium of reason and rationality.[10]

Long's retrieval began with the bodies and experiences of the "opaque ones," the dark bodies of the world whose lives had been continually pressed and decon-structed by the preeminent notions of rationality that legitimated their bondage. But even more his retrieval reached to the broadest corners of the black Diaspora and the various instances of black religious experience. From these, "this god has evoked a new beat, a new rhythm, a new movement. It is a god that must be com-mensurate with both the agony of oppression and the freedom of all persons."[11]

In the corners of the world where Christianity served as a legitimizing frame-work to enslave black bodies, retrieval is reaching beneath the structures of oppression, dismantling the edifices that housed the oppressor and the shacks that sheltered the enslaved.[12] Retrieval forms new rhythms from the "factual symbol

---

10 Charles H. Long, *Significations: Signs, Symbols and Images in the Interpretation of Religion* (Aurora, CO: Davies Group Publishers, 1999), 211.

11 Long, *Significations*, 212.

12 Interestingly, J. Kameron Carter suggests that Long's analysis is ultimately trapped within a modernist (and Western) rationality where Long "reinscribes a thoroughly mod-ernist, rational aesthetics. It differs from rational aesthetics only in this: rather than being positioned next to the beautiful as the index of the moral capacities of the human being in its

of these oppressed ones."[13] Long's project echoes the theological questionings and wrestling with the realities black bodies faced in America. Marcus Garvey, founder of the Universal Negro Improvement Association and the Black Star Line, sought an "African Fundamentalism" where "we must canonize our own saints, create our own martyrs, and elevate to positions of fame and honor black men and women who have made their distinct contributions to our racial history."[14] Garvey's retrieval sought to bypass or go through the Eurocentric ideologies and religions that oppressed dark bodies. The retrieval pointed to an idea or a reality more primordial than the present constructions of Christianity or colonial imagination.

When confronted by an evil so ubiquitous and complete as the plantation or the Atlantic Slave trade, retrieval of an identity or sources that precede this reality make sense. Garvey's and, subsequently, Long's work served to highlight the international reality of the black diaspora and how colonialism reproduced deathly patterns wherever it became rooted. The retrieval projects fostered deeper insights into the historical realities of African civilization, cultivated historical awareness about the richness of black existence in the world. But in a way it also functioned as a restoration project, a restoration that required excavation of the land but ultimately sought a conception of the black self unhinged from the historical realities of slavery, colonization, and just how American black women and men were.

The question of retrieval from this point of view is a question of how one begins to account for the formations and attachments that life in a particular land has created. Is it possible to go "home again?"

A mulattic mode of retrieval

Retrieval is a critical exercise in any accounting of oneself in the world. The idea that we exist in a vacuum, that we can construct identities out of nothing would seem ridiculous to most. At the same time, when considering how colonial society

universal powers of cognition, it champions a vision of the sublime that is positioned now to the oppugnant, the opaque, the grotesque." See J. Kameron Carter, *Race: A Theological Account* (Oxford: Oxford University Press, 2008), 221. Carter's press against Long must be understood in relationship to sympathy with Long's concern. In the end, liberation and the ability to flourish are the aim. Long's account is not insufficient because it does not attend to tradition. Long's account is critiqued because it does not escape the rationality of "the religious" that brackets black Christian experience, thus reinscribing a colonialist project. This is a critical nuance. To read Carter's use of theological figures central to what is commonly understood as the Tradition (such as Ireneaus of Lyon or Maximus the Confessor) without also reading the contextual reality of black bondage is to misread his entire project. Carter draws upon multiple sources, traditions, and theological modes in order to articulate a theological present. In this regard Carter's work bears a strong resemblance to Cone's blues project.

13 Long, *Significations*, 211.

14 Robert A. Hill, Marcus Garvey, and Universal Negro Improvement Association. *The Marcus Garvey and Universal Negro Improvement Association Papers* (Berkeley: University of California Press, 2006), 318.

fundamentally structured all bodies within a racial economy, any consideration of retrieval that does not account for the complicated interrelationships between confession, bodies, and cultural contingencies seems equally mythological.

Mulatto theology navigates a complicated space of multiplicity, seeking to make sense of how people can be entangled in attachments to both the regimes of power and the marginalized. Here the language of mulatto is intentional and guides an overarching methodological conviction. "Mulatto"—as a term inherited from a colonial system of classification that raped dark women and then deployed both the women and their children within the domestic economy—points to bodies that were both the product of exploitation but that also inhabited these spaces in complicated and conflicted ways.

On the one hand these bodies were unequivocally "colored," not white, and suffered the perpetual terror and humiliation of their fellow black brothers and sisters. On the other hand, in the midst of this there also emerged societies and implicit (or explicit) biases regarding light and dark. The mulatto was certainly a victim, but they also embodied and deployed a certain power within a racialized society where light and dark were a type of currency.

What "mulatta" in a mulattic theological framework suggests is not the valorization of the mixed race body nor the marginalization of the mixed race body.[15] Rather, mulatta gestures toward the situatedness of bodies in a racial world where a person and a people occupy multiple spaces at once. The life of discipleship is navigating these various realities, discovering patterns of unfaithfulness as well as the continual possibilities that stand before us. Mulatta theology suggests that we stand in a space that is both transgressive and transgressed, that we cannot separate ourselves from the realities of our tragic beginnings, but that these realities do not exonerate us or protect us from perpetuating old terrors in new ways. We are children of mothers and fathers with complicated and tragic stories, but we cannot excise ourselves from them. A mulattic theology seeks to exist between these realities and to discern patterns of faithfulness in their midst. Out of this reality a mulatto theology does not work to establish a cultural space or retrieve a tradition. Retrieval suggests an idea can be redeployed, restored in some sense to give clarity or to shape our contemporary cultural space.

But a mulattic theological space begins with the presupposition that the past cannot be reproduced, nor can one's body be understood without the contingencies, the realities of that history present in one's body. In *Redeeming Mulatto* I suggest,

> The lives of these new creatures are political through their presence, for they refuse to be named within the confines of racial or ethnic singularity, for these ideas cannot attune themselves to the songs of their ecclesial being. The names of cultural and racial personhood must resist innovation and change to preserve

---

15 While I use the term "mulatto" throughout *Redeeming Mulatto*, I have recently begun to use "mulatta" as well to gesture toward the gendered realities that lay beneath mulattic life.

them. Yet the Christian life is one perpetuated by its adaptation, its continual impressing and openness to being impressed upon. It is a community marked by prayer, by baptism, by a feast of flesh and blood. It is a people marked by songs and new songs. It is a people whose lives are not marked by the certainty of their melody but by the possibility of improvisation.[16]

In a way, mulatta theology seeks to work against itself. Liberation is the creation of space where particularities become intermingled, where sources and tradition become bound to aliens and strangers. Its aim is to make possible a vibrant and vital space where humanity's possibilities become reimagined in the various encounters of races and cultures but above all in the ongoing encounters between God and humanity. In these encounters humanity becomes new again and again, being added to, molded, shaped, cut and knit together. But because it speaks out of the interspaces, in the midst of a whole made from the many, mulatto theology is a modulation of possibility whose outlines are reinscribed as we encounter others whose stories and realities find resonances in our stories.

And thus mulatta theology is irrevocably tied to slave spirituals and Walker's jeremiads, and to Cone's confession of a Jesus who ontologically identifies with black experience. But it is also tied to the liminal reality of the migrant worker and to the perpetual foreignness of the Asian American. Mulatta theology stands bound to the courage and insights and wisdom of black theological tradition. But in relationship to this tradition mulatto theology also embraces the neither/nor and the ways in which these interstitial realities make space for new improvisations, new songs. The mulatta is bound to the confessions and the creeds, but by acknowledging the ways in which their bodies had been pitted against the darker bodies of field workers, it resists the recapitulation of proper confession as a mode of domination.

The mulattic rhythm of this theological retrieval is grounded in the embodiment of the Word made flesh, the contingency of ethnic and religious particularity, and the disruptions that emanated from how Jesus lived and preached in the world. Willie Jennings's *Christian Imagination* displays this mode of retrieval as it accounts for a historic contextuality, centralizing Jesus as an ethnic, social, and religious body.

Jennings articulates a way forward in terms of belonging and joining. But in order for a joining not to be the distortion of colonial rape or the deformation of social space encapsulated in slave society (and which reverberates throughout Western society), we must begin to account for creation, for bodily life in a new way. This new way must run through the bodily life of Israel. More specifically, Jennings situates the question between the difficulty of Israel as chosen and the goyim, or those outside the "intimate knowledge of the ways and struggles of life inside."[17]

This understanding of Israel begins with understanding how God's creation of and interaction with Israel creates a particular relationship of peoplehood to land.

---

16 Brian Bantum, *Redeeming Mulatto: A Theology of Race and Christian Hybridity* (Waco, TX: Baylor University Press, 2010), 186.

17 Jennings, *Christian Imagination*, 252.

"From Mount Sinai, through the revelation of the law, through the rehearsal of covenants, through the eruptions of disobedience, the story reveals a God who stands between the land and Israel. This enfolds the holy people in the truth that YHWH, not the land, is the giver of life; YHWH, not the land defines their identity ... But word and land are bound together as the realities that constitute the stage of life for Israel. They live between the word spoken and the land given."[18]

In this position, Israel reveals a particular relationship to land and a new conception of personhood to the world. For the Gentiles, articulations of power, nation, and identity cannot be construed directly to the land but also not apart from the land. Just as Israel's very existence mediates, reveals God's word to the world, so too does reception of the word require an understanding of one's relationship to God, to one another and to land as necessarily contingent. In other words, we are fundamentally bound to one another in such a way that knowledge of God and knowledge of ourselves is continually bound to a Word spoken to us through a particular bodied people. Our words about God, our language about God (and ourselves) are perpetually received through the vernacular of Jewish bodies in Israel culminating in the divine translation of the Divine Word into our own human existence.

This translation does not leave Jesus's occupation and existence within Jewish space. In this space, "he recapitulates the reality of Israel in a fallen world in order to overcome the power of the world in Israel. By calling Israel to receive the presence of their God through his teachings, he is also taking them to witness to its absolute embodiment in him. And the Gentiles from the centurion to the Canaanite woman overhear. Gentile inclusion is born out of this overhearing."[19]

Jennings's outlining of Christian existence bound to the Jewish body of Jesus as an accounting of the historical, economic, and social forces that recreated the land beneath our feet, and the creative retrievals of marginalized bodies have been the heart of black Christian existence from their very beginnings.

Jennings's reading of the Canaanite woman is an example of what is at stake in this mode of retrieval: a decentering of all bodies—the Canaanite woman is all of us—and yet we are all in different positions in this recentering. Those with power will be humbled, while those on the edges will be brought near. While Jennings reaches back for descriptions of Christian life that are bound to both the contextual and experiential realities of early Christians, creedal confessions, and liberative interpretive lenses, his retrieval also resists cleaning the mud from the bones of these seemingly lost ancestors. Emphasizing not only Jesus's Jewish identity but also the scandal of Gentile inclusion as inherent to Christian identity, Christian confessions must struggle with questions of cultural inclusion and communal reconfiguration as their central mode of being in the world. When confessions and creeds function to reify patterns of exclusion, to buttress social or economic

---

18 Jennings, *Christian Imagination*, 256.
19 Jennings, *Christian Imagination*, 263.

patterns of oppression, they attempt to separate belief from the material realities that we exist in and that Jesus entered into.

Retrieval in a mulattic mode is fundamentally a confessional practice that seeks to understand the myopic sight, the failings, the violence as well as the possibilities that these traditions might point to.

Retrieval of traditions is necessary in that these descriptions are like my mother, my father, my grandfather . . . I am caught with them. And my confession of Christ as my beginning and my end means that they testify something about who God is and who we are. In the same way that the early traditions resisted confessions of Christ without a true body or a true body without divinity, true Christian confession cannot look to a past devoid of bodies, histories, buildings, land, native peoples and believe it is retrieving anything true. Such attempts are as much constructions as race itself. Christian discipleship is a wrestling with the redemption Jesus has sown into our bodies and the ways in which we resist God's work or twist it into a tool for our misconceived ends.[20]

While traditions serve to shape particular peoples and cultures, their effectiveness lies in processes of differentiation as much as constructive identities. Traditions and cultures give birth to new traditions and cultures as peoples begin to describe their present in new ways.

The plantation is a critical moment in a reflection upon tradition and retrieval because it does not allow us easy resolutions. The Christianity of the slaveholder was not a true Christianity, some might say. Orthodoxy is not present without orthopraxy, others may press. We can find our truest selves in African tribal religions, in a deeper black consciousness that can escape the orbit of white supremacy.

Retrieval in a hybrid world suggests that our orthodoxies (whichever they might be) are caught within contextual contingencies. Put differently, there is no tradition without a history, and there is no history without bodies and land.

One of black theology's enduring contributions to theology is the insistence on enacting theology from within the situation of the black body. In the midst of this

---

20 In *Redeeming Mulatto*, I discuss race as a mode of discipleship, a way of being in the world where we are both formed by ideas and the social realities of our world, while we also navigate and live into or out of racialized realities. To say that race is a social construction is not to say it is not real. Social construction is a process of formation, a mode of discipleship. "Race as a social construction and race as essential: each approach offers some important insights and neither can be easily dismissed in the acuity of its approach or the reality of the condition. The notion of discipleship mitigates these two approaches by suggesting that race/ethnicity is a way of being in the world that seeks to live into something beyond itself. In doing so, it enacts, adopts, and implicitly absorbs certain practices, habits, and desires that allow the person to enter into this aim. The life of discipleship is one that is cognizant of its personhood, but also bound to a certain community. This life of following and being formed is the negotiation of what it means to be a part of a people and how their individual desires, gifts, and such are to participate within the wider aims, hopes, and desires of their community, nation, and race. Discipleship is the deliberate conforming to certain aims,

contribution, black Christian intellectuals also demonstrate how the black church was an exercise of the bodily commitment and presence of Jesus in the world. This commitment can be seen in the subsequent movements from black theology and the important contributions of womanist scholars. It is in relationship to this deep commitment to the body that my own work is both connected to black theological reflection and seeks to reimagine the particularity of the body in our contemporary moment.

My own work in *Redeeming Mulatto* took up the situatedness of the black body in the American context but sought to complicate both the creation of the black body and its concomitant relation to the white body. *Redeeming Mulatto* did this through a theological examination of the mulatto or interracial body as a lens through which to explore how race works as a theological construct, but also how we might begin to theologically articulate difference (be it racial, ethnic, cultural) in more fluid and nuanced ways. This exploration culminates in reenvisaging of Christ through a mulattic personhood where difference is not an either/or (either black or white) but a new possibility of wholeness made through the incarnation and the life and practices of the church.

In this way the methodological center of *Redeeming Mulatto* is working out of the rearticulation of themes, plunging more deeply into a particular Christian logic with a commitment to the bodily spaces that these theological claims occupy. But it is this commitment to bodily space that also creates a reconfiguration of this bodily space and hence a "mulatto theology."

A mulatto theology articulates the significance of the body in relationship to the particularity of the multiple or the "in-between." One particularity within this space is the reality of race and ethnicity, the constitutive reality that our bodies are marked by race, a matrix of interpretation wherein the meaning of my body is both given to me—flowing toward me through various cultural, institutional, and interpersonal realities—and within which I attempt to live and be. Race is a reciprocal performativity that I am at once performing out of and which is performing upon me.

Understood as a process, mulatto theology articulates identity within the multiplicity, seeking to improvise and reconfigure in the midst of various realities that constitute one's life and body. Among these are race, ethnicity, and gender. But as a theological exercise mulatto theology also articulates the fact of createdness, of Jesus's particular body and life and identity as a reality that constitutes and performs upon individuals and humanity as a whole.

Retrieval, if done in a mulattic key, brings us back to Cheng's observation regarding the melancholy of race and the dangers of misremembering. Pointing to a possible way forward in Ralph Ellison's *Invisible Man*, Cheng suggests, "*Invisible Man* hints that the first solution to that melancholic condition is not to recover a presence that never was, but to recognize the disembodiment that is both the

---

but it is also a more subtle process of being formed to become a citizen or a participant."
Bantum, *Redeeming Mulatto*, 18.

master and the slave."[21] Such recognition allows the possibility that we are filled with both "weal and woe," to borrow from Julian of Norwich. From this confessional space, "you carry the foreigner inside. This malady of doubleness, I argue, is the melancholy of race, a dis-ease of location and memory, a persistent fantasy of identification that *cleaves* and *cleaves to* the marginalized and the master."[22]

A mulattic mode of retrieval begins with the realities of white supremacy that conceived its body, its body in the field or in the house. It begins to reckon with the formations and discourses that legitimate its lighter body in one space while marginalizing it in another. A mulattic mode resists the temptation to see the master's recognition as its ultimate telos but also wrestles with the privilege inherent in its body (its maleness, its heterosexuality, its whiteness, its ability). Retrieval cannot extricate itself from the legacy of the plantation, but it is also not bound to reproducing it.

Ultimately, a mulattic mode of retrieval is not contingent on a biracial identity. The language of mulattic is intentional in this regard. Mulattic retrieval gestures toward the increasingly interconnected, intersectional, globalized world where our identities are at once overlapped and distinct. It is clear that we cannot be "post" anything (racial, gender, Christian, liberal), but we also cannot go home again. We must navigate the world, our bodies, our histories as they are, confessing the ways white supremacy has so deeply distorted our sight, while also negotiating the ways in which our lives are bound together. We cannot do theology as though the plantation never existed. Retrieval in a mulattic mode means that our histories, our theologies, our starting points, and our canons must tell a fuller story in order to point us to a future where we can all flourish.

---

21 Cheng, "Melancholy of Race," 58–9.
22 Cheng, "Melancholy of Race," 60.

Chapter 16

ON GENDER AND THEOLOGY IN THE MODE
OF RETRIEVAL

Ruth Jackson

Mary's gender, produced and perceived

In a sermon preached at the University of Oxford, on the occasion of Candlemas 1843, the then-Anglican John Henry Newman opened up the subject of Christian doctrine in its historical development by extolling the Virgin Mary as the pattern for Christian faith. Mary is our pattern, he explains, not because she is the apotheotic example of quiet passivity and total submission to the will of God—an image we may form if we rest simply with her response to the Angel's message "let it be to me" (Luke 1:38). Rather, Mary is the pattern for faith in Newman's eyes because of her remarkable behavior—because she commits to both the reception and the study of Divine Truth. Her willingness to submit to divine command is an *active* willingness. She accepts her appointed task but she also bears, contributes to, and reflects on it.

Mary is a figure whom, despite her great legacy as a global Christian symbol, we hear very little about in the New Testament. And in this sermonic context Newman's grounds for asserting her exemplarity for faith amount to a single line of text—a sentence describing her response to the angelic announcement, reported by shepherds, that her son is the Messiah. The phrase is this: "Mary kept all these things and pondered them in her heart" (Lk 2:19). And indeed, matching traditional pictorial depictions of her at the event of the Annunciation, where she is imagined as pouring over the Scriptures while paying heed to the angel, Newman interprets this line about Mary as an indication of her deep capacity for reflection, with which she takes up and examines the good news, having received it in faith. He writes,

> She does not think it enough to accept, she dwells upon it; not enough to possess, she uses it; not enough to assent, she developes it; not enough to submit the Reason, she reasons upon it; not indeed reasoning first, and believing afterwards, with Zacharias, yet first believing without reasoning, next from love and reverence, reasoning after believing. And thus she symbolizes to us, not only

the faith of the unlearned, but of the doctors of the Church also, who have to investigate, and weigh, and define, as well as to profess the Gospel; to draw the line between truth and heresy; to anticipate or remedy the various aberrations of wrong reason; to combat pride and recklessness with their own arms; and thus to triumph over the sophist and the innovator.[1]

For Newman, then, Mary's active, reflective, and "developed" faith is the symbol and guide for all believers—both the "unlearned" and the very "doctors of the Church."

I begin with Newman's sermonic appraisal of Mary because it provides us with a road into the question of how gender might be a concern for theologies in the mode of retrieval. It does so because it invites us to consider how Mary's own gender relates to the role Newman allots her here as the model of faith for *all* Christian believers across time, place, and culture. It prompts us to ask how the issue of gender—perceived and performed—relates to the development and transmission of Christian teaching, as this takes place through history, and relies upon shared narratives, language, and acts of remembrance. And as it prompts these questions, it also helps set out the position that this chapter as a whole will contend. This is the following: that although issues of gender are vital considerations for theology, which impinge on its method and on its mode of approach, such issues must nevertheless sit within and be contextualized by more basic questions concerning the task of theology, and concerning the relation between God and God's creation. This chapter suggests that belief in a unity *beyond* gendered difference should underlie and inform all theologies of retrieval that wish to attend to the issue of gender, including those of gender relations of difference and power.

For indeed, the above passage from Newman suggests that he does not understand Mary's ability to fulfill her role as a question of "identity." Her being the model of faith for all believers is not something specifically dependent upon her being a woman or upon her having essentially female qualities or "womanly" features, which Christians should replicate or participate in as they repeat the pattern of her faithfulness. Rather, it is the details of Mary's actions as someone who believes in order to understand, we might say, or her commitment to dwelling on what has been revealed to her, to which Newman draws attention. To put this another way: this sustained practice of *dwelling-having-received* for which Newman lauds Mary, and that makes her the pattern for faith for every particular member of the historical Christian community, is not something that can be universalized or hypothesized as a gendered disposition or gendered structure. Indeed, Newman's appeal to Mary as exemplar here thus seems to confound the popular polarized tropes of passive femininity set against active masculinity, and feminine emotion set against masculine reason, which were written into the paradigms and structures

---

1 John Henry Newman, "The Theory of Developments in Religious Doctrine," in *Fifteen Sermons Preached before the University of Oxford*, ed. James David Earnest and Gerard Tracey (Oxford: Oxford University Press, 2006), 211.

of Christian theology in the Middle Ages,[2] and which rose to new prominence in the nineteenth century with the notion of the "feminine soul."[3]

What should we make of this? The invitation is perhaps to see in Newman's lines, this vision of Mary, this idea that belonging to the Christian faith community—that is, to the body of Christ—constitutes a membership across historical and cultural boundaries that in its truest sense (and one we cannot grasp or fully comprehend in this life) is not arranged or defined by those differences indicated by categories like "male" and "female." This is a prospect sustained by the oft quoted line from St. Paul, that "there is neither Jew nor Greek, there is neither slave nor free, there is neither male nor female; for you are all one in Christ Jesus" (Gal 3:28). Framed in these terms, the suggestion is that each particular member of the church community is fundamentally and before everything else a creature related to Christ: a creature grasped hold of and transformed by the Gospel. And indeed, as Newman continues this sermon by describing the development of Christian teaching as an endless occupation—since what thoroughly finite minds seek to represent and elaborate here are radically transcendent truths—it seems that he is elaborating a vision of theology as a task that cannot be grounded in any particular vision of human identity, and cannot take its foundation in any sure account of the human "subject." Rather, and in the sense that it means quite literally "words about God," theological inquiry is confirmed here as a properly humble exercise, and is defined instead by its stretching toward truth that it cannot encapsulate, toward God who is the source and end of humanity. Newman's sermon on Mary's practice of reasoning only *after* believing thereby develops into an account of the task facing Christian teachers and dogmaticians as one of constant refining, constant purification of terms and ideas—a task that "makes no beginning" and is framed by human "feebleness." And at the close of his address, Newman confirms the following:

> not even the Catholic reasonings and conclusions, as contained in Confessions, and most thoroughly received by us, are worthy of the Divine Verities which they represent, but are the truth only in as full a measure as our minds can admit it; the truth as far as they go, and under the conditions of thought which human feebleness imposes . . . Reason can but ascertain the profound difficulties of our condition, it cannot remove them; it has no work, it makes no beginning, it does but continually fall back, till it is content to be a little child, and to follow where Faith guides it.[4]

---

2 See Julia O'Faolain and Lauro Martines, eds., *Not in God's Image* (New York: Harper and Row, 1973), and Eleanor C. McLaughlin, "Equality of Souls, Inequality of Sexes: Women in Medieval Theology," in *Religion and Sexism: Images of Women in the Jewish and Christian Traditions*, ed. Rosemary Ruether (New York: Simon & Schuster, 1974), 213–66.

3 See Marilyn Chapin Massey, "Religion, Gender, and Ideology: A Historical Exploration," *Journal of Religion* 67 (1987): 151–63.

4 Newman, "Theory of Developments," 235.

What we have proposed is that when Newman invokes Mary to introduce the specific topic of doctrinal development through history, and the rational investigation of Christian teaching, he seems to avoid including her gender in this analysis as an "essential" attribute or category. He resists defining it here, in this specific context, as an atemporal, ahistorical, and fixed part of Mary's person. Furthermore, theology itself is introduced here as a finite discipline for finite creatures that can only asymptotically approach its intellectual end. And yet, having used Newman's sermon as a surface against which to make these tentative comments about the significance of Mary's gender in this particular role,[5] and about the possibility of a radical Christian unity that lies *beyond* gendered difference (we shall return to this prospect in our concluding section), we must now turn to face the obvious material and historical counterpoint to these theological postulations. An obvious counterpoint, indeed, which has occupied feminists of all stripes for several decades. This includes not only theologian feminists like Tina Beattie, whose constructive work on the place of the female body in Christian soteriology defended classical and patristic Marian theology as a body of texts that can be fruitfully reclaimed in the twenty-first century, and that can be mined to develop a properly gynocentric narrative of salvation.[6] They also include those, like Mary Daly, whose criticisms of the Christian tradition as unjust and oppressive in its treatment of women have prompted them to sit outside or to look askance at it. This point begins with the detail that Mary's gender—a "womanhood" perceived, developed, and symbolized as virginal motherhood—is itself presented and received in Christianity as an integral part of its narratives of incarnation and redemption. Christians (including Newman, with his later Roman Catholic vision of Mary as the "daughter of Eve, unfallen"[7]) who encounter

---

5   It is worthwhile underscoring how my opening comments do not purport to represent Newman's theology in toto. They merely draw upon this specific sermon as a source to open up our themes of theology and gender. For a comprehensive appraisal of Newman's attitude toward Mary, both in his Anglican ministry and in his later Roman Catholic ministry, see John Henry Newman, *Mary: The Virgin Mary in the Life and Writings of John Henry Newman*, ed. Philip Boyce (Leominster, Hertfordshire: Gracing Publishing; Grand Rapids, MI: William B. Eerdmans, 2001).

6   See Tina Beattie, *God's Mother, Eve's Advocate: A Marian Narrative of Women's Salvation* (London: Continuum, 1999/2002), 5–6: "Rather than offering a systematic critique of Marian theology and doctrine, I insinuate myself into the cracks and gaps, developing a gynocentric narrative out of the discarded scraps of patristic theology that have been neglected or rejected in the construction of Marian theology," and 10: "Women do not need to declare death to the tradition. There is a more fertile way of understanding. Rather than silencing the Father, I approach them as a woman mimicking innocence, in a garden where humankind believes that it walks again in the presence of God because through an ancient conspiracy between a serpent, a dove and two women, original goodness has been restored to creation."

7   See Newman's letter to the Rev. E. B. Pusey, written in December 1865, in *Mary: The Virgin Mary*, 226.

Mary in Scripture mediated though the praxis and tradition of the Roman and Orthodox Churches, respectively, meet a figure who as obedient, sexually pure, mother is allotted a theological and salvific role in Christian life as intercessor and advocate of Eve.[8] As *Theotokos*—a title endorsed at the Council of Ephesus in 431 and echoed in Byzantine art and iconography—Mary became a pillar and symbol for asserting the divinity of Christ.[9] And as the Virgin, Mary is globally named in terms of sexual purity, but in the Roman Catholic tradition especially she has been represented with bridal imagery too, as in Bernard of Clairvaux's numerous sermonic commentaries on the *Song of Songs* (which he began in 1135), in which she is allegorically interpreted as the Bride featured in the text. Just as the angel announces to Mary in Scripture, "blessed art thou among women" (Lk 1:28), so too does Mary's cousin Elisabeth greet her in pregnancy in these terms: "blessed art thou among women, and blessed is the fruit of thy womb" (Lk 1:42).[10] Mary's perceived and portrayed "womanhood"—which in its symbolic quality takes up her behavior as reckoned in Scripture and in apocryphal texts, her perceived societal and familial role, and her reproductive capacity—is thus in itself manifestly a central and generative category for the church's multifaceted vision of her, and the shape of her legacy that has been accrued through history via apologetic theological texts, art, song, public devotion, and festival.[11] In short, when faced with the figure of Mary, the theologian cannot, as it were, *get past* her gender, her virginal motherhood.

The figure of Mary as received and portrayed in the church—inspired by the scant Marian passages in Scripture, but quickly developed and compiled by classical and patristic authors—reoccupies feminists because it has been so developed and

8 Irenaeus calls Mary the "patroness" or "advocate" (*advocata*) of Eve, for the former's obedience balanced and thus set aright the latter's disobedience. See Irenaeus, "Against Heresies," in *The Ante-Nicene Fathers,* vol. 1, *The Apostolic Fathers with Justin Martyr and Irenaeus* (Grand Rapids, MI: Eerdmans), 547.

9 See Henry Chadwick, *The Early Church,* rev. ed. (London: Penguin Books, 1993), 192–8. Regarding the significance of the title *Theotokos* and its place in fifth-century Christological debates, Kallistos Ware summarizes that it "is not an optional title of devotion, but the touchstone of true faith in the Incarnation." Ware, *Mary Theotokos in the Orthodox Tradition* (Wallington, NJ: Ecumenical Society of the Blessed Virgin Mary, 1997), 8.

10 Significantly, where Newman cites these words from Elisabeth at the beginning of the sermon we have been working from, he does not pick up on Mary's position "among women." Instead, he describes Elisabeth as "speaking with an apparent allusion to the contrast thus exhibited between her own highly-favoured husband, righteous Zacharias, and the still more highly-favoured Mary." See Newman, "Theory of Developments," 211.

11 For an ecumenical study of Mary's polyvalent resonance and role in Christian doctrine, see George Henry Tavard, *The Thousand Faces of the Virgin Mary* (Collegeville, MN: Liturgical Press, 1996). See also H. Graef, *Mary: A History of Doctrine and Devotion* (Notre Dame, IN: Ave Maria Press, 2009).

compiled by theologians operating under androcentric assumptions, and from a patriarchal cultural perspective. To put it another way: from a feminist standpoint, the Mary envisioned and taught within Christian sources ancient and medieval is one generated and reflected on by theologians who perpetuated a narrative of male superiority, whether uncritically or not. In 1949, Simone de Beauvoir tore into this patriarchally mediated portrait of Mary with her negative and eminently *unchristian* comparison of the submissive Saint against the ancient goddesses Ishtar, Astarte, and Cybele. Of Mary, Beauvoir wrote,

> This is the first time a mother kneels before her son; she freely acknowledges her inferiority. The supreme masculine victory is consummated in the worship of Mary: it is the rehabilitation of woman by the achievement of her defeat.[12]

Following Beauvoir, and while second-wave feminist criticism was gathering momentum in the early 1970s, Daly's book *Beyond God the Father* also drew out how Mary's role was one mediated and approved by masculine or patriarchal symbolism. Despite the image of Mary as Virgin inherently carrying a signal of female independence, for instance—in the sense that it means she is not defined by her relationships with men—Daly maintained that this imagery has nevertheless been consistently interpreted by male theologians in a *relational* way, "having significance only as tied to the male savior and the male God."[13] Yes, Mary is privileged and promoted by the tradition, but for Daly this celebration is of a *relatively* powerless, instrumentally maternal woman, who is rendered a symbol of obedience through systematic patriarchal commentary. For Maria Warner too, whose study of the Cult of the Virgin Mary (1976) engaged the Roman Catholic Christian tradition as a critic and outsider, this Cult of Mary instrumentalized the saint as the instantiation of Christian teachings. Indeed, the assessment drawn by the broad sweep of Warner's historical survey is that the shifting roles allotted to Mary—Virgin, Queen of Heaven, Bride, Mother, and Intercessor—came into play as responses to the social and political pressures in the communities that looked to her for inspiration.[14]

In the 1970s, both Daly and Warner—as well as others working at this time from within the Christian tradition and accepting the authority and determinative quality of its texts, like the radical feminist theologian Elisabeth Schüssler Fiorenza—illustrated and underscored how the Cult of Mary has its roots and development in a "male, clerical, and ascetic culture and theology."[15] As such, they

---

12 See Simone de Beauvoir, *The Second Sex*, trans. H. M. Parshley (London: Jonathan Cape, 1960), 160.

13 Mary Daly, *Beyond God the Father: Toward a Philosophy of Women's Liberation* (Boston: Beacon Press, 1985), 84.

14 See Maria Warner, *Alone of All Her Sex: The Cult of the Virgin Mary* (Oxford: Oxford University Press, 2016).

15 Elisabeth Schüssler Fiorenza, "Feminist Theology as a Critical Theology of Liberation," *Theological Studies* 36 (1975): 621.

saw that far from being seized as an opportunity to promote the independence or flourishing of women in the Christian tradition (as was its potential, its resonances with ancient goddess mythologies), Mary's womanhood has been portrayed in such a way as to naturalize the idea of female subordination. And in Roman Catholic theology specifically, Schüssler Fiorenza asserted, this myth of the "virginal mother" functions to promote a disjunction between body and soul, between the realm of the spiritual and that of necessity, and to restrict the possible ecclesiastical roles for women to the dualistic option "mother" or "nun."[16]

In the view of these twentieth-century critics, Mary's "womanhood" was theologically and symbolically co-opted by theologians of the early church working under androcentric assumptions. And yet—to turn back to Newman's appraisal of Mary's faith—feminist analysis has also criticized what Daly refers to as "spiritualization": the practice of unshackling figures like Mary and indeed Jesus from their historical and embodied identity and glorifying them instead in terms of their faith, in terms that are noncorporeal.[17] The argument here is that stripping Mary of her body—the fleshly "thisness" and sensuality of her femininity—is not a cause for Mary's liberation so much as a way to "shift focus away from the patriarchal implications of Christian discourse" while subsuming the spiritualized Mary under the terms of a universal (and perfect) masculine subject. Addressing those lines from St. Paul that we mentioned earlier—"There is neither . . . male nor female" (Gal 3:28)—Beattie has drawn attention to the androcentric context for Paul's seemingly egalitarian remarks, and has pointed out that the grammatically masculine language he uses in this context cannot be assumed to be neutrally generic, to be "inclusive" of both male and female. Indeed, she explains, the radical egalitarian connotations of this passage are put into relief by Paul's preceding line (Gal 3:26): "you are, all of you, *sons* of God through faith in Jesus Christ."[18] In short, then, the feminist theologians and critics we have listed problematize the notion that we should seek to look "beyond" Mary's gender or to overlook it as a matter for appraisal and critique, precisely because her portrayal in the tradition is so fraught with issues of power, so ripe with concerns about the body.

Strategies and strategists for drawing on the past

This brief and selective appraisal of critical feminist approaches to Marian theology demonstrates nevertheless how such approaches proceed from the following, broader point: that as a historical discipline, theology is a finite and culturally conditioned discourse, prone in the generation of its texts, language, and symbolism

---

16 Fiorenza, "Feminist Theology," 623.

17 Daly, *Beyond God the Father*, 5 and 80.

18 Italics added. See also Kari Vogt, " 'Becoming Male': A Gnostic and Early Christian Metaphor," in *The Image of God: Gender Models in Judeo-Christian Tradition*, ed. Kari Elisabeth Børresen (Minneapolis: Fortress Press, 1995), 170–86.

to participate in and to perpetuate the structural biases and prejudices of its cultural and intellectual environment. For a great many theologian feminists like Schüssler Fiorenza, however, the critical practice of drawing out the androcentric and patriarchal assumptions operating in the texts of one's own theological tradition does not dictate that one should dispense entirely with the texts in question—which are of course considered foundational, authoritative, and formative for the tradition. It does not occur as an option to Schüssler Fiorenza to reject wholesale the Christian Scriptures or to abandon the writings of the church fathers or to endeavor to sit *outside* the tradition itself. Indeed, and after Paul Ricoeur, her own declared approach in the 1970s and 1980s was to suggest instead that in reading these texts, and evaluating them to ask how they promote and encourage human flourishing, feminist theology and biblical commentary develop a hermeneutic of suspicion.[19] In Schüssler Fiorenza's view, such a "consciousness-raising" approach demands of theologians and commentators that they scrutinize their own prejudices and assumptions as they read traditional texts as well as apply such scrutiny to the sources themselves. Using this mode of hermeneutical approach, the feminist theologian can *filter* the Christian canon, while still remaining in the tradition more broadly. She can examine and excavate each individual text (and each translation), in each case asking whether it contains androcentric symbolism and imagery that should be should be protested and revised.[20] Indeed, Schüssler Fiorenza's view of such a hermeneutical practice also casts the critical reader or hermeneutist as a person involved in the process or event of divine revelation itself. To put it another way, the work of rereading traditional texts in a feminist key—a task that means filtering and revising the canon—is work that gets us closer to the truth. It is work that breaks open, and that peels away, dead material. She asserts,

> Biblical revelation and truth are given only in those texts and interpretive models that transcend critically their patriarchal frameworks and allow for a vision of Christian women as historical and theological subjects and actors.[21]

Here then, Schüssler Fiorenza describes how feminist theologians approach the biblical canon as a body of texts that must be scrutinized and deconstructed—that must be purged of problematic symbols and imagery, and filtered in the interests of allowing the oppressed to flourish. According to her model, the task for the Christian feminist wanting to "get in touch with their own roots and tradition" is thus not so much one of "retrieval" as it is of *revision-toward-liberation*. The need, she explains, is to "rewrite the Christian tradition and theology in such a way that

---

19 Elisabeth Schüssler Fiorenza, "Missionaries, Apostles, Co-workers: Romans 16 and the Reconstruction of Women's Early Christian History," in *Feminist Theology: A Reader*, ed. Ann Loades (Louisville: Westminster John Knox, 1990), 57–71.

20 See Dawn Llewellyn, *Reading, Feminism, and Spirituality: Troubling the Waves* (New York: Palgrave Macmillan, 2005), 31–64.

21 Elisabeth Schüssler Fiorenza, *In Memory of Her* (New York: Crossroad, 1985), 30.

it becomes not only his-story but as well her-story recorded and analyzed from a feminist point of view."[22] The promise, seemingly, is of writing over troubled ground and building new futures from flawed and oppressive *yet* shared beginnings.

As stated, written into Schüssler Fiorenza's late-twentieth-century critical feminist "theology of liberation" is the notion that the theologian interpreter should be ever suspicious of their own bias and suppositions. The feminist theologian herself in this way cannot claim access to any final, fixed, or privileged theological pathway. Schüssler Fiorenza is also careful to explain that she understands patriarchal oppression in terms of a "pyramidal system and hierarchical structure of society and church," in which "women's oppression is specified not only in terms of race and class but also in terms of "marital status."[23] Her vision of such oppression is thus that it occurs along complex institutional, economic, and systemic lines. There can be no simple account, she suggests, of active and powerful "male oppressors" working against a passive group of "female oppressed."

Despite these qualifications, however, by speaking in terms of liberating "Christian women" from their standing as the second sex,[24] and of provoking a "feminist consciousness" among such women capable of transcending patriarchal norms and structures, Schüssler Fiorenza's proposal for feminist theological study of the past nevertheless falls prey to criticisms and considerations that have been taken up in the development of queer theory and intersectional theory respectively. These criticisms are that the ambition to liberate women, to appeal to a "feminist consciousness" inevitably grounded in bounded experiential claims,[25] and to revise and reread texts using such experience as a starting point are all aims that in practice actually risk treating "women" or "the feminine" as a homogenous grouping or fixed category—a category that, under criticism, can only fracture into ever smaller fixed and bounded experiential fields: "Christian women"; "Jewish women"; "Christian women of color." The concern here is that a feminist theological approach incorporating these reactionary, liberating aims would thereby risk occluding the rich diversity, complexity, and intricacy belonging to lived, portrayed, and performed gender and sexuality. In other words, by orienting itself in reactionary terms—as a *response* to the conditions of patriarchal society aimed at the liberation of women shown injustice and oppression—Schüssler Fiorenza's approach risks fronting a method for critically rereading theological

---

22 Schüssler Fiorenza, "Feminist Theology," 611.

23 Elisabeth Schüssler Fiorenza, *Bread Not Stone: The Challenge of Feminist Biblical Interpretation* (Boston: Beacon Press, 1995), 5.

24 Schüssler Fiorenza, *Bread Not Stone*, 6: "A feminist theology of liberation must remain first and foremost a critical theology of liberation as long as women suffer the injustice and oppression of patriarchal structures. This theology explores the particular experiences of women struggling for liberation from systemic patriarchy and at the same time indicts all patriarchal structures and texts, especially those of biblical religion."

25 The concept is explored in Sandra Lee Bartky, "Toward a Phenomenology of Feminist Consciousness," *Social Theory and Practice* 3 (1975): 425–39.

texts on the assumption of a blanket commonality of oppression among this group "women," experienced under androcentric norms.

In the face of all of this, the question remains as to how a retrieval approach to theology might work when concerns about gender become prominent. If we turn to the work of Beattie—who is wary of proceeding in theological enquiry via an appeal to "women's experience,"[26] wary of pledging uncomplicated confidence in human power to effect ethical and social transformation,[27] and unwilling to treat "women" as a uniform group on behalf of which she herself might speak—the psychoanalytic theoretical approaches of Luce Irigaray and Jacques Lacan have been an important catalyst in this regard. Beattie's work (over the course of three books) has considered how feminist insights might encourage a renewed attention to the relevance of Marian theology, Thomas Aquinas, and the doctrine of the Trinity within contemporary theology and practice. But by engaging with psychoanalytic approaches, Beattie has nevertheless avoided making theology simply *answerable* to feminist thought, conceived perhaps as a series of clear external claims and agendas for social and political change. Instead, Beattie has sought to emphasize the sheer depth and labyrinthine quality of the Christian story itself, in terms of its textual origins and its development. Indeed, she writes,

> One must go beyond any moralistic formulation of right and wrong, true and false, to recognize the pervasive and insurmountable instability of the Christian story, particularly in its Catholic version. This story is a weaving together of multiple "texts," performative narratives of faith extending in time and space across two thousand years of histories and localities—and it must be read simultaneously as a narrative of damnation and redemption, of poison and cure.[28]

The point here is that for Beattie, the Christian story greatly exceeds whatever we might make of it—and such is its power that to inhabit it and try to abide by it comes at the risk of one's soul. According to this understanding, then, the Christian tradition is no single monolithic document, no resolute and conservative stone under which new directions and innovations might be stamped out. Rather, it is

---

26 See also Mary McClintock Fulkerson, *Women's Discourses and Feminist Theology* (Minneapolis: Fortress, 1994), for a critique of the appeal to women's experience, as in the theologies of Daly and Schüssler Fiorenza but also Sallie McFague and Rosemary Radeford Ruether.

27 For a critique of the feminist theological approaches of Schüssler Fiorenza and Ruether on account of their overinvestment in human power for change, see Susan Frank Parsons, "Accounting for Hope: Feminist Theology as Fundamental Theology," in *Challenging Women's Orthodoxies in the Context of Faith*, ed. Susan Frank Parsons (Aldershot: Ashgate, 2000), 1–20.

28 Tina Beattie, *New Catholic Feminism: Theology and Theory* (London and New York: Routledge, 2006), 4.

in view of this depth and excess that Beattie sees it unnecessary to look for textual support extrinsic to the tradition in order to prescribe change to current Christian practices, and to its social order, which feminist analysis finds to be unjust and oppressive: "one has only to look clearly at what is already there [in the Christian narrative]," she writes, "to bring out its full potential for women and men."[29] The emphasis here is thus upon reading, attending to, and as it were listening to the sources themselves, to the end of retrieving a history there not yet opened up and having one's expectations challenged.

And yet, while Beattie's psychoanalytic approach leads her to thus appreciate the deep and ambivalent mystery of Christianity's historical tradition and its immanent force—the crisscrossing annals and paths-not-taken within Catholicism's past—this is not something she pursues at the expense of an appeal to the transcendent. Her approach is one mounted in light of the eschatological hope of the Christian narrative. In her 2013 work *Theology after Postmodernity*, she speaks in the following way of being led:

> I have been guided by both Thomas and Lacan with regard to the elusive relationship between language, desire, the material world within which we belong, and the unattainable Other who calls to us in and through language from beyond all the horizons of time and space with a persistent, unnameable sense of loss and longing.[30]

Thus framed, it is clear that Beattie's approach to doing theology in the mode of retrieval involves no presumption that present thought or experience should or even *could* unilaterally dictate our approach to the past. Rather, Beattie's theological approach allows her to indwell her own Roman Catholic tradition, because she is interested in "asking how core doctrines of the Christian faith *reveal their truthfulness anew* within the changing conditions and times within which we find ourselves."[31]

Beattie's stress upon the unstable history of the Christian faith ("a narrative of damnation and redemption") as well as her invocation of Christian eschatological hope as intrinsic to her approach (i.e., feminist theology is not a utopian discourse) prompt us to introduce another related point here about feminist strategies for studying or retrieving the Christian past. This point is that such strategies should be suspicious of what we might call a program of women's "inclusion" or "representation" in the writing, teaching, and retrieving of Christian history. In other words, we should be wary of a push toward making women's voices, behaviors, and bodies more prominent in Christian narratives, where such a push is not also accompanied, first, by an appreciation of those societal,

---

29 Beattie, *God's Mother*, 6.

30 Tina Beattie, *Theology after Postmodernity: Divining the Void—A Lacanian Reading of Thomas Aquinas* (Oxford: Oxford University Press: 2013), 12.

31 Beattie, *Theology after Postmodernity*, 3; italics added.

economic, and religious structures that gave rise to the silencing or occlusion of these bodies, voices, and practices in the first place, and, secondly, by an effort to take account of the *particularity* of these occluded women, their bodies, and the distinctive nature of their practices and behaviors. Here, we not only need to ask whether increasing female representation in the practice of teaching and narrating of Christian history is something that writes over the past, eclipsing and misleading readers and students about the reach of women's voices as well as the platform and attention afforded them. We also note that *in itself*, the act of seeking to include more women writers in one's timeline or syllabus of Christian history will not effect a challenge to the symbolic power of gender as inscribed and received in Christian doctrine and Christian narratives, nor will it disrupt and call into question the way that gendered difference and sexual difference has been imported into theological patterns of imagination as well as inscribed into Christian interpretive and linguistic structures. For indeed, what does the sex or gender of a given author matter, if—as Virginia Burrus puts it, "discourse . . . may prove the most stubborn mediator of the constraints of patriarchy?"[32]

In place of a simple and naive impulse toward inclusion and representation, then, a much subtler, reflective, and indeed constructive approach is warranted, which takes account of how gender relations of power inform Christian thought and practice. And here I think it is worth mentioning Caroline Walker Bynum's historical work on gender and the human body in medieval religion. For this, I venture, affords an example of how the writing of history might attend positively to female particularity and to the distinctive nature of women's religious devotion, while at the same time working constructively to produce a deeper and more complex picture of medieval society as a whole.[33] Alongside social scientists like Pierre Bourdieu and Michel de Certeau, Bynum treats as a working assumption the point that "marginal and disadvantaged groups in society appropriate that society's dominant symbols and ideas in ways that revise and undercut them."[34] And in her book *Holy Feast and Holy Fast*, she gives us an example of such a revision and appropriation of ideas, as she explores the great significance that food as well as the practice of eating had as religious motifs for medieval women in particular. Through their social role as preparers of food, Bynum explains, and via their corporeal identification with food in their capacity as nurses and biological (rather than merely socially construed) mothers, medieval women envisaged and experienced themselves as united with Christ in the sacrament of the Eucharist. In other words, food and eating practices functioned as a medium through which

32 Virginia Burrus, "Is Macrina a Woman? Gregory of Nyssa's Dialogue on the Soul and Resurrection," in *The Blackwell Companion to Postmodern Theology*, ed. Graham Ward (Oxford: Blackwell, 2001), 250.

33 On this front, see also Ann W. Astell, *Eating Beauty: The Eucharist and the Spiritual Arts of the Middle Ages* (Ithaca: Cornell University Press, 2006).

34 Caroline Walker Bynum, *Fragmentation and Redemption: Essays on Gender and the Human Body in Medieval Religion* (New York: Zone Books, 1991), 14.

women could consider themselves part of the body of Christ and could attain communion with God, while emphasizing their own physicality and continuing to carry out those roles conventional to their gender.[35]

Here and elsewhere—as in her collection of essays *Fragmentation and Redemption*—Bynum's investigations into the creativity of medieval women's bodies and voices frustrates unthinking appeals to thick and totalizing categories like "medieval religion" or "the oppression of women." Medieval gender imagery was misogynistic, and male writers would mockingly characterize women for their fleshly appetites, for their lust, emotionality, and disorder. Yet Bynum has explained that this did not provoke a religious subculture among women, defined by a *response* to such mocking characterization. Nor, interestingly, did the Virgin Mary—a symbol of chastity—seem to feature prominently as a mediating figure or role model for women. Indeed, she argues, women's practices not only shared common characteristics with men's (asceticism, mysticism, and eucharistic piety increased in the period among both sexes), but women also understood that they could *retain their womanhood* in the imitation of Christ, which was—as it was of course for men too—their "immediate spiritual motive."[36] In other words, spiritual progress for medieval women did not mean "becoming male."[37]

With Bynum's work, we have an example of how looking to the past can not only challenge one's preconceived ideas about the power and resonance of traditional Christian symbols and practices but also, here, where the past is presented as offering a complex and multilayered picture of Christian community, help break open one's theological imagination. Bynum's essays on gender and the medieval body explore the following, she explains:

> how some women manipulated the dominant tradition to free themselves from the burdens of fertility yet made female fertility a powerful symbol; how some women extricated themselves from family yet served society in the stinking streets of medieval towns; how some used Christian dichotomies of male/female, powerful/poor to facilitate their own *imitatio Christi*, yet undercut these dichotomies by subsuming all dichotomy into *humanitas*.[38]

Bynum's detailed exploration of women's piety (and particularly its somatic quality) works on theological expectations and imaginations, challenges our categories, and contributes to our understanding of the tradition. Yet it is *history* that she is writing, and it is for this reason, and at this point, that the theologian must be careful to differentiate her own task. For whereas Bynum investigates how her subjects sought to come into relation with God, and shows how medieval

---

35 Caroline Walker Bynum, *Holy Feast and Holy Fast: The Religious Significance of Food to Medieval Women* (Berkeley: University of California Press, 1987).

36 Bynum, *Fragmentation and Redemption*, 152–5.

37 Bynum, *Fragmentation and Redemption*, 167.

38 Bynum, *Fragmentation and Redemption*, 17–18.

images of Christ and of Mary were tangled up with matters of human desire and power, the work of the theologian is of course to take this seeking Christ—this journeying toward God—to be her own final labor and purpose. Theology does not rest content with the tying and untying of historical knots and narratives. The materials, the perspectives, the past, that the theologian retrieves are thus resourced and recovered toward the greater end of making—as Sarah Coakley refers to the task of theology—*a recommendation for life.*[39]

This chapter began with a sermon from Newman, which introduced dogmatic theology as a human, historical, and ever developing discipline, unworthy of the divine truth that it seeks to represent; theology as a stretching toward that which it cannot comprehend. And what we have subsequently highlighted, in our survey of theologies that attend to the past in order to think through gender, is that inevitably (precisely *because* they are human), words about God and words about knowing God are enmeshed in matters social, political, and material. Seeking God is a seeking affected by relations of power, it is a journey scored through with desire, and—as we have been focusing on here—it is inevitably tied up with concerns about human difference. Having discussed what a retrieval approach to theology might look like when concerns about gender become prominent, then, in a final short section I now wish to draw back, returning to the following wider and more fundamental question: what is it that enables and makes possible such an approach? The point I wish to make here is that, for a theology of retrieval to fruitfully attend to gendered difference, without its attentions simply fracturing into an exercise in treating isolated and fractured groupings—without, in other words, becoming a politics of experience and identity—it requires and must be undergirded by a vision of human community where there is believed to be a unity persisting beyond all difference. Such an account of unity beyond difference is delivered in those Christian doctrines concerning redemption, eschatology, and the resurrection of the body, according to which those who have faith in Christ are, through grace, saved in Christ, who is the Word of God. Christian hope is that by grace working upon nature, these faithful persons will be united in eternal communion with one another as members of Christ's body. For the purposes of this chapter, however, I focus on another Christian doctrine that delivers an account of unity beyond difference, namely that of *creatio ex nihilo*: the teaching that every worldly creature is held in being by the transcendent creator God (who is in Godself without difference). Here, this unity amounts to the proposal that before everything else in life it belongs to humans that they are *created*—the proposal that without exception, each and every human depends absolutely upon God for their existence.

In order to suggest that such perceived unity enables a fruitful account of difference, I finish just as we began: with the musings of a nineteenth-century theologian.

---

39 Sarah Coakley, *God, Sexuality, and the Self: An Essay on the Trinity* (Cambridge: Cambridge University Press), 18.

Created difference yet unity in creation

The nineteenth-century theologian I wish to look to here is Friedrich Schleiermacher. Yet rather than take from one of Schleiermacher's sermons, or from his great dogmatic project *The Christian Faith*, the passage I am interested in is from his early, romantic, and irreverent work *On Religion: Speeches to Its Cultured Despisers* (1799). This passage is a particular favorite of my *Doktormutter*, Janet Soskice, and I am indebted to her reading of it.[40] In it, the young scholar offers a short retelling of the creation myth.

Indeed, what I find significant about Schleiermacher's playful reenvisioning of the story of human origins is its suggestion that the human ability to know God and to respond to God (the task of theology in its very germination) is found, sourced, and borne out from the relationships that a person has with other humans. In this passage Schleiermacher presents unity between humans as a loving gift from God, while he also presents created difference between humans as that, strikingly, which actually enables them to know and love their Creator. We read,

> As long as the first man was alone with himself and nature, the deity did indeed rule over him; it addressed the man in various ways, but he did not understand it, for he did not answer it; his paradise was beautiful and the stars shone down on him from a beautiful heaven, but the sense for world did not open up within him; he did not even develop within his soul; but his heart was moved by a longing for a world . . . Since the deity recognized that his world would be nothing so long as man was alone, it created for him a partner [*Gehülfin*],[41] and now, for the first time, loving and spiritual tones stirred within him; now, for the first time, the world rose before his eyes. In the flesh and bone of humanity he discovered humanity, and in humanity the world; from this moment on he became capable of hearing the voice of the deity and of answering it, and the most sacrilegious transgressions of its laws from now on no longer precluded him from association with the eternal being.[42]

At the climax of this passage, Schleiermacher reveals to us that it is only in fellowship with another human—who wrought in him the ability to love and a sense of the spiritual—that the first person became able to speak to, and of, the deity who created him. Before this first man was given a "helpmate," we read, and before he could thus share his thoughts and ideas and feelings in human discourse,

---

40 See Janet Soskice, "The Word Became Flesh and Dwelt among Us: Incarnation, Speech and Sociality: Schleiermacher and Augustine," in *Incarnation*, ed. Marco M. Olivetti (Padua: CEDAM, 1999), 565–76.

41 Whereas the English translation "partner" is nongendered, Schleiermacher's original term does indicate a female helpmate.

42 Friedrich Schleiermacher, *On Religion: Speeches to Its Cultured Despisers*, trans. Richard Crouter (Cambridge: Cambridge University Press, 1996), 37.

even his soul remained unformed, and his appreciation of the world around him was shallow. The world was, Schleiermacher explains, "nothing" to him. Yet what is also significant here, is that Schleiermacher's narrative establishes how even prior to that fortifying relationship with the divine, which was made possible only through human dialogue, the first man is nevertheless bound to his Creator and is addressed by him. In other words, the tale assumes the existence of a prelinguistic relationship between human and divine—a relationship characterized (to use that famous term employed by the mature Schleiermacher) by the "absolute dependence" of the human upon God. Absolutely everything that this first man might claim to own has, in reality, been given to him. And this is true about him even before he can respond to his Creator. God is the beginning and end of human life without question or qualification, and each human being is thus united before their differences in the fact of their being given existence by God. But in order to *understand* the significance of this gift of life, to realize the beauty and wonder of God's creation, and to offer thanks and praise to God for it: for all these things a human needs society. To know God, Schleiermacher hints—and even to *become human*, to gain one's soul—a human needs to enter into reciprocal and fruitful relationship with those who have been created other to him or her.

How to apply Schleiermacher's little story to our question concerning the issue of gender and theologies of retrieval? Since Schleiermacher suggests how reciprocal human communication—communication across difference—is integral to the task of seeking and knowing God, what we find here is a reminder that theology should not sideline questions of human difference, as if these are not inextricably bound up with it. It is true that *prioritizing* human concerns in one's search for God leads to idolatry. But to be aware of such human concerns—to be aware, in our case, of how issues of gender and power permeate the theological past we are studying and the ancient symbols and narratives that we draw upon: this is a vital part of doing responsible and ethically sound theological work.

Moreover, Schleiermacher's retelling of the creation myth, in which we glimpse an unfallen humanity, also reminds us of the important distinction between finitude on the one hand (as the "natural" condition of humanity), and sin on the other (as the disordered state into which humanity has fallen).[43] In Schleiermacher's story we see how finite difference, including sexual difference, is written into creation, and how such finite difference alone—and not relationships corrupted and disordered through sin and suffering—provides the conditions for Adam to gain his soul and to "discover humanity."

Schleiermacher's Adam, who is *changed from without* by finite otherness, is thereby also defined here as a character who emerges through time and is constantly interacting with the world around him—as well as with his companion—for the development of his nature. There is no appeal to a fixed or static human essence here, and no sense carved out either of a (fully) active male against a (fully) passive

---

43 The importance of the distinction between sin and finitude when attending to matters of gender in theology is carefully laid out in Tonstad, *God and Difference*.

female. Schleiermacher portrays Adam as partially dependent on, and partially independent from, the conditions of his environment, and describes how this continually reciprocal dependence and independence within human society is enabled by the creative power of God, who holds everything in being.

How do we proceed with a theology of retrieval that is especially attentive to the issue of gender? What is it that underlies and makes possible such an approach? We began with an image of Mary as the pattern of faith—an image that called us to look beyond Mary's gender but that quickly became weighty, problematic, and complex, as we heard about the difficult nature of this task: how Mary's gender simply cannot be forgotten, since it has been produced, instrumentalized for theological teaching, and harnessed as a tool of female oppression in the Christian tradition. How Mary's gender *should* not be forgotten, indeed—for to seek to look beyond it is also to ignore her particularity, to occlude her fleshly nature. What we have found in this chapter is that for theologians, the business of studying the past means challenging our assumptions and expectations, refining our shared narratives, and examining the dynamics of power produced and perpetuated historically in our communities. And yet, in light of Schleiermacher's indication of a human unity beyond all human difference—a unity entailed in the doctrine of *creation ex nihilo*—I finish with the proposal that a belief in such unity should underlie and form all theologies of retrieval that wish to attend to the issue of gender.

What Schleiermacher's little narrative also suggested, of course, is that it is unavoidable to do anything else as a theologian than to begin with the particularity of one's person. The "thisness" of my experience, the shape of my body and what my body is capable of, the matter of how I am perceived and received because of the gender that I live out through time in the world: none of these specific, placed, and temporal factors can simply be "got over" or "got beyond." As Bynum puts our specificity emphatically, "however we construct it and whatever it stands for to us, body is what we've got."[44] Nevertheless, what we cling to when we believe in a unity beyond difference—when, on the most fundamental level, we hold each and every person to be a person capable of hearing the Gospel—is the point that faith in God is not something that comes down to our gender, as if this were an essential part of our being a Christian. Christians, in other words, need take up no particular role in order to come to Christ—they need not "become male"; they need not transcend their bodily status. And it is with this, and while heavy with the weight of staring at present injustices, that our labor in attending to the past might be done in light of Paul's radical promise concerning the body of Christ: "there is no difference" (Gal 3:28).

---

44 Bynum, *Fragmentation and Redemption*, 19.

Chapter 17

RETRIEVAL AND RELIGIONS: ROMAN CATHOLIC CHRISTIANS AND THE JEWISH PEOPLE AFTER THE HOLOCAUST

Gavin D'Costa

Introduction

The Roman Catholic tradition[1] along with all Christian denominations faces a deep challenge. Will its particular traditional sources for authority—the Bible, tradition, and the magisterium—be credible today in the light of these apparently retrospective norms of "authority" to engage with issues in the modern world? The collapse of its authority along with its membership in Europe is often cited as an indication of this lack of credibility. Its stances on contemporary issues such as homosexuality, same-sex marriage, the exclusion of women from the priesthood, and embryo research are cited as examples of its backward-looking conservatism and its inability to engage with the modern world. Likewise, there is its stance on other religions, and especially Judaism, let alone its view that Catholicism is itself the true religion. These too are markers of what is seen as a backward and parochial outlook by many secular commentators and those from other religions. While one must concede that there is an inherent conservatism (in terms of conserving the truths that have been handed down) in the Catholic tradition, there is also, I contest, a radical and challenging outlook that is able to engage with, criticize, learn from, and serve the modern world. Being committed to retrieval is also being committed to doctrinal development and reform but not at the cost of failing to take seriously its authoritative sources. It seems right to argue the case not only in theory but also in practice, as the claim is both about theological resourcefulness and the importance of retrieval as is actually displayed in the largest Christian denomination in the world.

The Catholic view on the Jewish people will form a test case in this chapter. The test: to see if my claim above seems credible. Why this case? Because of the extent of Christian complicity and specifically Catholic complicity in the Holocaust and nearly two thousand years of anti-Jewish thinking and practice. The Jewish people

---

1   For shorthand, I shall use "Catholic" from now on.

and their persecution by Catholics raises the serious question as to how deeply Scripture, tradition, and the magisterium are guilty of anti-Semitism. Some argue that the rot reaches down to the core: Scripture itself is guilty of anti-Jewishness, let alone the other "authority" sources. In contrast, others, like myself, contest this level of revisionism especially regarding Scripture. They acknowledge that the tradition, understood in a particular way, contains deep elements of anti-Semitism (subsequently lowercase tradition), but that "formally authoritative tradition" (subsequently uppercase Tradition), in contrast, can be defended, as can formal pronouncements of the papal magisterium. I use this test case to show how the Catholic Church in the modern world, specifically at the Second Vatican Council (1963–65), has faced the Jewish question, precisely through retrieval as a means of renewal. Such a study could extend to examine the manner in which the Catholic Church has dealt with other religions at the Council and engaged in interfaith dialogue after the Council, but that is beyond my remit.

Let me define these three sources of retrieval more precisely before proceeding. One might ask, why pose the question in terms of three sources, when only one seems to have precedence and real authority—Scripture? An abbreviated answer within mainstream Catholicism might run along the following lines. There are analogical arguments in most Christian denominations that accept the ancient creeds. True authority for the Catholic is God's self-revelation in Jesus Christ. We know Christ through testimony in Holy Scripture. But the very notion of "Holy Scripture" requires a community (a specific tradition) authorized (a magisterium—a formal teaching office) to declare what is Scripture and, indeed, that Scripture has such authority as is being claimed. The authority and existence of "Scripture" requires an authority within the community in naming the right books that constitute Scripture and helping in the guidance of reading those books correctly when controversies arise so as to make present, to witness to, the truth and reality of Jesus Christ. The Tradition in the shape of church councils came up with creeds that were explications of the truth of Scripture. Scripture's meaning is then extrapolated by the Tradition, authoritatively in terms of the ecumenical councils—twenty-one according to the Roman Catholic tradition; and with lesser authority in the traditions of liturgies of the church that can be reformed; and with even lesser authority by the traditions that are formed by the doctors and saints of the church. These latter can be wrong about a lot of things, both in terms of practical judgments and matters of doctrine, but they are seen as fundamentally learned and wise in the case of the doctors of the church and are viewed as holy in the case of the saints. Saintly doctors should clearly be particularly respected. In Catholicism, St. Thomas Aquinas has special status in this respect and is viewed as a preeminent saintly doctor. The teaching "magisterium" is primarily the pope either on his own in his extraordinary capacity or with the councils (acting with the bishops) when they formally proclaim on matters of doctrine and morality. The pope could for instance claim that the Boston Red Sox are the best baseball team in the world. No Catholic would be obliged to agree. If the pope were to claim this with special authority, he would have to demonstrate how this was to be found explicitly or implicitly in Scripture. If he could not, then he might be rightly asked by what authority he teaches this, especially if it is not a doctrine or related to morality. Fortunately, no pope has advanced such a teaching.[2]

Finally, before turning to my test case, I want to suggest that the kind of tradition that is Catholicism, is in principle no different from any other tradition of inquiry, religious or nonreligious, that participates in the contemporary public square. It has the same epistemic standing. The philosophers Alastair MacIntyre and Alvin Plantinga have made this case with some rigor, but the debate obviously continues.[3] I am deeply sympathetic with their positions. All religious and nonreligious traditions, they argue, have a formal logic about their modes of inquiry with differing authority sources operating within each tradition. The Enlightenment has its canon, its authorities, and its modes of argument, as do postmodern cultures and pre-modern cultures. Sometimes these sources of authority overlap in name (for example, "reason"), and sometimes they have unique authority sources (for example, the Buddha, the Qur'an, disembodied reason, natural sciences, Jesus Christ, and so on). Second, viewing these authority sources in Catholicism as backward looking is potentially a failure to understand how these norms operate in practice: they are forward looking, as I shall show, committed to engaging in rational debate with contesting worldviews, concerned with the common good, and having a developmental and reform character about them. Not only do they have the same epistemic status as other worldviews but they also have a claim that their views are important in shaping the common good in pluralist societies, for they are fully committed to the common good. Third, these authority sources are grounded in "truth," the truth of God's self-revelation in Jesus Christ whose mystical body resides in the "church," understood as its sacramental nature and in its magisterial teaching function. The "truth" for some other group might be expressed as upholding the ultimate values of freedom, conscience, and equality, or for another group, the truth of the dharma upheld in the law codes of Manu and the ancient Hindu scriptures. Those who believe this truth, the Catholic version, have no other option than to operate in such a rational manner and uphold the vitality and rationality of their tradition. Retrieval thus operates to sustain the dynamism of the tradition, committed to the development of doctrine and the reform of the church, while upholding the authority of Scripture, Tradition, and the magisterium.

2 See Avery Dulles, *Magisterium: Teacher and Guardian of the Faith* (Naples, FL: Sapientia Press, 2007) and, in contrast, but with significant overlap: Francis A. Sullivan, *Creative Fidelity: Weighing and Interpreting Documents of the Magisterium* (Eugene, OR: Wipf & Stock, 2003).

3 See Alasdair MacIntyre, *After Virtue: A Study in Moral Theory*, 2nd ed. (London: Duckworth, 1994) and Alvin Plantinga, *Warranted Christian Belief* (New York: Oxford University Press, 2000).

Test case: the Jewish people

The history of anti-Jewishness within Catholic culture makes for painful reading for Catholics and clearly for Jews.[4] Historically, Catholic cultures were involved in persecution of Jewish people: there were forced conversions, there were all sorts of laws restricting Jewish freedoms and rights, and sometimes there were straightforward outbreaks of violent persecution against the Jewish people. One short snapshot: seventh-century Visigothic Spain is known for its anti-Jewish legislation. For example canon 57 of the Fourth Council of Toledo promulgated that Jews should not be forced to convert but that Jews who had been forced to convert under the reign of King Sisebut had to be forced to remain Christians. This canon eventually entered the second recession of Gratian's *Decretum* and led to complex discussions about absolute and conditional compulsion. Innocent III gave a judgment on this in his letter *Maiores Ecclesiae causas* (1201) that effectively meant that any Jew who had not chosen death over conversion had to remain a Christian even though they were baptized against their will. Another canon of the Fourth Council of Toledo ruled that children of forcibly converted Jews should be taken away and put into monasteries or with "good" Catholic families to get a proper Christian upbringing. Later canonists argued that Jewish children should be taken away from their parents to be baptized. Others, such as Aquinas, opposed this.

Most importantly, and perhaps the central motor behind Christian anti-Jewishness, the Jews were accused of deicide (killing God), and the "blood libel" of Mt 27:24–25[5] was very often interpreted from the second century on as the Jewish people deserving punishment and suffering because of this ancient crime. Christian anti-Semitism runs like a dark red line of blood throughout Christian history, with variations and respite and complexity, but nevertheless relentlessly. Some argue that Nazism was an outgrowth of this Christian anti-Semitism.[6] Others, in my view rightly, contest this claim arguing that ultimately Nazism

---

4 See Edward H. Flannery, *The Anguish of the Jews: Twenty-Three Centuries of Antisemitism* (New York: Paulist, 1985) from a Catholic angle, and Jules Isaac, *The Teaching of Contempt: Christian Roots of Anti-Semitism* (New York: Holt, Rinehart and Winston, 1964), a classic and influential Jewish statement, and Jeremy Cohen, *Christ Killers: The Jews and the Passion from the Bible to the Big Screen* (New York: Oxford University Press, 2007) from a more recent Jewish angle. "Angle" is a limited metaphor as there is much overlap in the actual material evidence.

5 "When Pilate saw that he was getting nowhere, but that instead an uproar was starting, he took water and washed his hands in front of the crowd. 'I am innocent of this man's blood,' he said. 'It is your responsibility!' All the people answered, 'His blood is on us and on our children!'" During Easter, the attacks against Jews would often increase due to this text being central to the Easter liturgy.

6 This is the position advanced by Rosemary Radford Ruether, *Faith and Fratricide: The Theological Roots of Anti-Semitism* (New York: Seabury Press, 1974).

intended the destruction of Christians who opposed its racial and pagan creeds.[7] Nevertheless, there can be no question that with the destruction of nearly a third of world Jewry within "Christian Europe," Catholic culture and Catholics themselves must share some responsibility for the Holocaust for facilitating and perpetuating deeply negative views about the Jewish people.

In the 1960s the Second Vatican Council was convened by Pope John XXIII. The Council, the twenty-first in Catholic counting, would form the traditions and Tradition by which Catholics would have to orient themselves. The Council attended to the question of anti-Jewish theologies by focusing on one initial question, conflating the deicide and blood libel issues: were the Jews responsible for Christ's death and thus cursed through all generations? Many of the great doctors of the church had answered yes, and many Christian liturgies and cultures perpetuated this answer. Jules Isaac, the Jewish historian and author of the influential work *L'enseignement du mepris* (1962), had argued that this one central teaching generated and perpetuated Christian anti-Semitism.[8] Isaac argued that orthodox Christianity did not stand or fall on this belief, so it was reformable and was not a doctrinal rock. Isaac, unlike some Christians, did not argue that the Scriptures were corrupt. Isaac had an audience with Pope John XXIII and apparently suggested that were this one teaching to be dismantled a new era of Catholic–Jewish relations could unfold.[9] Prior to his becoming Pope John XXIII, in his role of nuncio, Angelo Roncalli was responsible during the war for helping many Jews escape from the Nazis.[10] As Pope he sought to purge his church of anti-Semitic traditions. He asked that this matter be on the Council's agenda and entrusted it to Cardinal Augustin Bea. I cannot here trace how treating of this topic eventually started a chain reaction whereby Muslims were also addressed by the Council (to counter any sense of preference for Israel in the Middle East disputes currently raging at the time). Because of this, later on, Hindus and Buddhists (as requested by Asian bishops) were also addressed. Hence an era of interfaith dialogue arose out of a concern to address a single question regarding the Jews.

The Council's teachings on the Jewish people occur in two documents: *The Dogmatic Constitution on the Church* 1964, para 16 (*Lumen Gentium = LG*) and

---

7 See Zygmunt Bauman, *Modernity and the Holocaust* (Ithaca: Cornell University Press, 1989) and Andre Mineau, *The Making of the Holocaust: Ideology and Ethics in the Systems Perspective* (Amsterdam: Rodopi, 1999).

8 See note 4 above.

9 John Connelly, *From Enemy to Brother: The Revolution in Catholic Teaching on the Jews, 1933–1965* (Cambridge, MA: Harvard University Press, 2012), 175–81. He places Isaac in a wider context, showing two key Catholic voices advocating for this issue to be addressed: the Pontifical Biblical Institute and Seaton Hall in the United States, where Fr. John Oesterreicher was director. Oesterreicher was a key architect in drawing up *Nostra Aetate* and was himself Jewish.

10 See Dina Porat and David Bankier, *Roncalli and the Jews during the Holocaust: Concern and Efforts to Help* (Jerusalem: Yad Vashem Publications, 2014).

the *Declaration on the Relationship of the Church to non-Christian Religions*, 1965, para 4 (*Nostra Aetate* = *NA*). The title *Dogmatic Constitution* indicates that the contents relate to dogma and doctrinal teachings of the highest status, whereas a "Declaration" is not normally thought to contain doctrines, but in this case, was understood to be an unfolding of the *Dogmatic Constitution*'s teaching in its pastoral and theological implications. Since there is much controversy as to what these documents actually taught, I recommend the reader go to the originals and some of the various interpretations. I am unable to address the complex hermeneutical debate here.[11]

LG was not concerned with Judaism per se, but mentions it when discussing the nature of the Catholic Church as the church founded by Christ (14) and its relation to other Christian churches (15) and to non-Christians, both religious and non-religious (16). *LG* was not addressing Isaac's question. *NA* would do that. *LG* 16 walked the tightrope of trying to signal the positive features of Judaism that were deeply valued by the Catholic Church and that made its monotheism the closest religion to Christianity, while at the same time retaining the view that this monotheism, while true, was also lacking Christ. In examining these two Vatican documents we see the Catholic Church retrieving ancient traditions and using them to develop positive attitudes to the Jewish people. The main concern of this chapter is to look at these two documents to inspect the dynamics of retrieval in this particular case. A new world of Catholic ecumenism and interreligious dialogue[12] begins to emerge through the Council—which would be developed and elaborated upon after the Council.

LG 14 reiterated the ancient teaching: that the church "is necessary for salvation" because Christ is present to the world in this form, but added that this necessity only obtains "if they are aware that the catholic church was founded by God through Jesus Christ as a necessity for salvation." (*LG* 14). Hence, it kept intact the central teaching of Christianity: that Christ brings salvation into the world for all people, but it did not apply it negatively to all non-Christians. This qualification regarding those invincibly ignorant of the Gospel entered the formal magisterial tradition in 1854 (in Pope Pius IX's encyclical *Singularai Quadam*), but has roots much earlier in the discovery of the New World in the sixteenth century.[13] There,

---

11 See my discussion of this debate in *Vatican II: Catholic Doctrines on Jews and Muslims* (Oxford: Oxford University Press, 2014), 10–58.

12 See Ann Michele Nolan, *A Privileged Moment: Dialogue in the Language of the Second Vatican Council 1962–65* (Berlin: Peter Lang, 2006). Nolan shows through close textual analysis of Paul VI's texts and the Council texts that "dialogue" was not understood in a dialectical fashion as a movement toward a truth not known but rather in a missiological and evangelical context. This is the position advanced incisively (and polemically) by John Milbank, "The End of Dialogue," in *Christian Uniqueness Reconsidered*, ed. Gavin D'Costa (Maryknoll, NY: Orbis, 1990), 174–91.

13 See Francis A. Sullivan, *Salvation outside the Church? Tracing the History of the Catholic Response* (London: Geoffrey Chapman, 1992), 63–82, and Stephen Bullivant, "*Sine culpa? Vatican II and Inculpable Ignorance*," *Theological Studies* 72 (2011): 70–86.

Christians came to terms with two interesting factors: peoples who had never heard the Gospel through no fault of their own, and profoundly cultured and moral civilizations that had existed over hundreds of years. Previously, there had been a presumption that all non-Christians had actually rejected Christ. Such a presumption was no longer possible. It was in this context—that the Jews had willfully rejected Jesus Christ—that many of the negative teachings on Judaism were propounded. *LG* 15 then addressed other Christians showing differentiated levels of relation to them but a deep unity in baptism and Trinitarian belief that would require full visible unity for total communion. Then comes para. 16. Here we see retrieval of the past at its best and most creative.

LG 16 prefaces the sentence on Judaism (and other religions and nonreligions) with Aquinas's notion of a universal orientation (*ordinantur*) to Christ in every single human being. "Finally, those who have not yet accepted the gospel are related [*ordinantur*] to the people of God in various ways. Reference given to Thomas Aquinas, *Summa Theologiae*, III, q. 8, art. 3, ad. 1." In this part of the *Summa,* Aquinas is arguing all creation has Christ as its head. He challenges the view that some people do not have this relationship. In citing Aquinas, the Catholic Church is retrieving its heritage to theologically cast this new relationship in doctrinal terms in a way not done before. Aquinas argues this relationship exists in two modes: potentiality and actuality. Actuality involves baptism and inner conversion; potentiality indicates that this is desired for all people, who are in different stages of potential orientation toward Christ. Those who believe in God, for example, have a greater closeness than those who do not, but no one is without conscience, which is the manner in which God is present to all at the subjective level. This indicates a twofold manner of relationship: inner, through conscience, and outer, through external elements in a religion that can be considered as true (not salvific, as Christ alone is that). After this Thomistic reference to the universal *ordinantur,* we then get the sentence on the Jewish people, which if read in Latin and with the Vulgate nearby, one would immediately recognize is taken verbatim from St. Paul's letter to the Romans, in a cut-and-paste manner from Romans 9–11. Both sections of the cut texts are cited. "In the first place, there is the people to whom the testaments and promises were given and from whom Christ was born according to the flesh (see Rom. 9.4–5), a people according to their election most dear because of their ancestors: for God never goes back on his gifts and his calling (see Rom. 11.28–9)."

Five points should be noted about this quotation. First, Judaism is given prime place precisely because of this biblical valuation and affirmation found in St. Paul. Second, this positive valuation is achieved by foregrounding Romans 9–11, which was being recovered by some theologians at the time of the Council as a main resource to rethink the church's attitude toward Judaism. Soon after the Council in the 1970s biblical scholarship on Romans 9–11 became a major enterprise by Christian exegetes seeking to mine the tradition for a better understanding of a positive relation to the Jewish people.[14] For Catholic exegetes, this foregrounding

---

14 See Joseph Sievers, "A History of the Interpretation of Romans 11.29," *Annali di storia dell'esegesi* 14 (1997): 381–442.

was a real support to show the way forward for rethinking the newly emerging relationship.[15] However, the seeds of that scholarly exegetical retrieval were present before the Council, and John Connelly has done an important job in laying bare these seeds.[16] Interestingly, Connelly also shows the importance of Jewish converts in this avant-garde movement. Third, it was left to *NA* to unpack this reference because as it stood in *LG* 16 it was left entirely uninterpreted. No one could contest what St. Paul had said in Scripture. *LG* 16 simply cited Paul to indicate the basis for this special relationship (*ordinantur*), the only interpretative context for the Pauline quote. The real task was unpacking Paul in the light of the profoundly problematic way in which Catholicism had always related to Judaism. The retrieval of Scripture was central for this reformation within Catholicism. Fourth, after the Council this sentence/quotation and *NA*'s sentences became a central focus for development in Catholic theology on the matter. Many interpreted this statement and *NA*'s reference to Romans as granting covenantal and salvific legitimacy to Judaism.[17] However, this is quite anachronistic as such a claim would have been deeply contested at the Council and there is no evidence in the discussions by the Council Fathers that this was their intention. One might argue, with the benefit of hindsight, that too many read into these early statements what later theologians were exegeting from Romans 9–11. While this hermeneutical question of both the Council documents and St. Paul's passage are deeply contested, it is interesting that a magisterial organ, the Pontifical Commission for Religious Relations with the Jews, *"The gifts and the calling of God are irrevocable" (Rom 11:29). A Reflection on Theological Questions Pertaining to Catholic–Jewish Relations on the Occasion of the 50th Anniversary of "Nostra Aetate" (no.4)*, not speaking with magisterial authority, actually said of *NA*: "the Conciliar text is not infrequently over-interpreted, and things are read into it which it does not in fact contain. An important example of over-interpretation would be the following: that the covenant that God made with his people Israel perdures and is never invalidated. Although this statement is true,

---

15 The Lutheran exegete Krister Stendahl, *Paul among Jews and Gentiles and Other Essays* (Philadelphia: Fortress, 1976), esp. "The Apostle Paul and the Introspective Conscience of the West," 78–96, is a key figure in his influence, although he is now criticized by some (for instance, Ben R. Meyer, "Election-Historical Thinking in Romans 9–11, and Ourselves," *Ex Auditu* 4 (1988): 1–7). Franz Mussner and Clemens Thoma are early Catholic exegetes on this matter, respectively: *Tractate on the Jews: The Significance of Judaism for Christian Faith*, trans. Leonard Swidler (Philadelphia: Fortress, 1984); *A Christian Theology of Judaism*, trans. Helga Croner (New York: Paulist, 1980). Ruether, *Faith and Fratricide,* was one of the earliest Catholic theologians to develop the dual covenant position.

16 Connelly, *From Enemy to Brother.*

17 See, for example, Connelly in the note above and also Philip A. Cunningham, "Official Ecclesial Documents to Implement Vatican II on Relations with Jews: Study Them, Become Immersed in Them, and Put Them into Practice," *Studies in Christian-Jewish Relations* 4 (2009): 1–36.

it cannot be explicitly read into *Nostra Aetate* (No.4)."[18] Fifth, the end of para. 16, ends with the call for mission to all those who do not know Christ, and para. 17 is devoted to the universal mission: "the church prays and works at the same time so that the fullness of the whole world may move into the people of God, the body of the Lord and the temple of the Holy Spirit, and that all honour and glory be rendered in Christ, the head of all, to the creator and Father of all" (17).

The doctrinal development in affirming that objective elements of Judaism (and Islam explicitly mentioned in *LG* 16) are valued and affirmed by the church is an important step forward. This affirmation of Judaism is achieved by retrieval of both Aquinas and St. Paul in a delicate rethinking that has only just begun in Catholicism. Of course, for some theologians this step is too small, too grudging, and too late. However, for most, it is a move toward taking Judaism seriously for profound theological reasons rather than on grounds of tolerance or equality, grounds granted by, for example, secular Enlightenment thought, but not persuasive for the Christian mind.[19] The reaction of Jews to the Council is another matter entirely and one that is most important given that the documents are related to the Jewish people. However, that complicated phenomenon cannot be addressed here, although it is an important element in interpreting the reception of the Council teachings, both within the Catholic Church and outside it.[20]

What did *NA* add? A considerable amount, while explicating Paul still further. This document, as indicated earlier, was only intended to address the deicide and blood libel charge. In the end, it addresses "non-Christian religions" as well as the Jewish roots of Christianity and the Jewishness of the earliest ecclesia. The first paragraph of *NA* expresses the pastoral intent of trying to seek for what the church and others have "in common and what things tend to bring them together" (1). One should recall the pastoral orientation of the Council set by Pope John XXIII, who wanted to deal positively with wider cultures and societies, not to engage in anathemas and condemnations of non-Christian or Christian groups.[21] This is not to say that Pope John XXIII wanted to sweep difference and disagreement under the carpet but that he prudentially thought that a positive outreach would require affirmative language and a seeking for what is shared.

18 Commission for Religious Relations with the Jews, The Holy See, http://www.vatican.va/roman_curia/pontifical_councils/chrstuni/relations-jews-docs/rc_pc_chrstuni_doc_20151210_ebraismo-nostra-aetate_en.html (accessed January 20, 2017). See esp. para. 39. Subsequently: *Gifts*.

19 See my *The Meeting of Religions and the Trinity* (Maryknoll, NY: Orbis, 2000), 19–52.

20 See my forthcoming "*Nostra Aetate* (The Relations of the Church to Non-Christian Religions)," in *The Reception of Vatican II*, ed. Matthew Levering and Matthew Lamb, (Oxford: Oxford University Press, 2017), chap.16.

21 See the original text: The Holy See, "Concilium Oecumenicum Vaticanum II Sollemniter Inchoatur," https://w2.vatican.va/content/john-xxiii/la/speeches/1962/documents/hf_j-xxiii_spe_19621011_opening-council.html (accessed January 20, 2017).

This could form the basis for conversation and engagement, and apologetics and mission.[22] Some Catholics would later push this pastoral approach into a lower common denominator theological approach, and others would deny status to *NA* entirely.[23] Different readings of Councils is the norm, as is deep dispute and controversy. Such discussion eventually helps better clarify more accurate readings of the documents. The living magisterium sometimes has to intervene in such debates to help make clarifications or guide a discussion, even though their intervening is sometimes criticized as closing off debate or not allowing for intellectual freedom[24] Such situations are sometimes inevitably fraught but are not new, and the behavior of the magisterium is itself not beyond reproach, although in the modern period the autonomy of the theologian especially, because of their location within the university rather than the church, has generated complex tensions.[25]

Tanner's translation breaks para 4 of *NA* into eight sections, which are not found in the original document, but helpfully indicates the different issues that it covers.[26] Section 1 recalls the spiritual unity of the church with the "descendants of Abraham." This link with Abraham that both religions share is important for two reasons. First, there is a link with Abraham made in the previous paragraph in relation to Islam, thus generating an exploration of the notion of "Abrahamic

---

22 See Nolan, *A Privileged Moment*; and again, through close textual analysis of all the pertinent documents: William R. Burrows, "The Roman Catholic Magisterium on Other Religious Ways: Analysis and Critique From a Postmodern Perspective" (PhD diss., University of Chicago, 1987). Burrows's position in the 1990s changed radically on this matter but without textual attention to his earlier position. While Connelly's *From Enemy to Brothers* is an important work, one of its central arguments is deeply flawed. He argues that Vatican II taught that there could be no mission to the Jews because Judaism constitutes a valid covenant. While the latter has actually been called into question by the Pontifical Council for the Jews (see above), the former is claimed with no textual evidence from the Council, apart from the removal of a text that made mission explicit and its replacement with a text that Connelly himself admits that the drafter, Oesterreicher, allowed for different interpretations (245). From this slender basis, Connelly then calls into question Pope Benedict XVI's liturgical prayers that indicate the hope of the Jewish people recognizing their messiah.

23 See my "Pluralist Arguments: Prominent Tendencies and Methods," in *Catholic Engagement with World Religions*, ed. Karl Josef Becker and Ilaria Morali (Maryknoll, NY: Orbis, 2010), 329–44 for treatment of the first group and my *Vatican II*, 38–41.

24 See the collection of essays, especially the closing one of Richard R. Gailardetz, ed., *When the Magisterium Intervenes: The Magisterium and Theologians in Today's Church* (Collegeville, MN: Liturgical Press, 2012).

25 See Congregation for the Doctrine of the Faith, *Instruction on the Ecclesial Vocation of the Theologian* (London/Dublin: CTS/Veritas, 1990).

26 Throughout, I have relied on Tanner's excellent English translation. See Norman Tanner, *Decrees of the Ecumenical Councils*, vol. 2 (London: Sheed & Ward, 1990).

religions," an avenue that is not unproblematic.[27] Second, this sharing of the covenant marks the real sharing of a common scriptural and historical tradition that makes identity possible. Section 2 then returns to Paul (citing not only Rom 11:17–24 but also Gal 3:7 and Eph 2:14–16) in a Pauline scriptural mosaic of retrieval, showing that the church's own roots are to be found in the "ancient covenant," the revelation of the "Old Testament" and that the Gentile church is "grafted" onto this covenant. This retrieval is novel in historical terms (given that many theologians previously taught that Israel was invalid after the time of Christ and had forfeited its right to a covenant relationship), but clearly very biblical and thus very ancient. While radical, it certainly does not go quite as far as some later interpreters would, who suggest two valid covenants, two ways of salvation being affirmed in St. Paul.[28] The section finishes by noting that "Christ our peace reconciled Jews and gentiles and made us both one in himself through the cross." At the Council, it is difficult to see that Jews were being described in their own terms (as many of them pointed out with dismay), but rather they were presented once again through Christian tropes, most problematically, through the cross—which for so many Jews had been and still is a symbol of dark and extended oppression. This raises a difficult question that remains unresolved. While it is important to understand a religion in its own terms so as to avoid misunderstanding of what it means to its adherents, the Catholic Church is not concerned with promoting "religious studies" (understood as a comprehensive descriptive task) but rather with undertaking a religious/theological appraisal of another religion, which requires religious studies so understood but also theological evaluation. In the case of Judaism, it uniquely also happens to be understood as "Christianity" in its pre-Christ days, in terms of the root upon which the now Gentile branch is grafted. This particular problem still bedevils current debates in the Catholic Church even in the fiftieth anniversary document to celebrate *NA*, already mentioned, *Gifts*.

Section 3 returns solely to Rom 9:4–5 and now repeats the full verse section that is only partially cited in *LG*: "and to them belong the adoption as children, the glory, the covenant, the giving of the law, the worship and the promise; to them belong the patriarchs, and of their race, according to the flesh, is Christ."

---

27 Aaron W. Hughes, *Abrahamic Religions: On the Uses and Abuses of History* (New York: Oxford University Press, 2012) does an excellent job of calling into question the very notion of "Abrahamic religions," showing the term's genealogy and abuses. See particularly pages 65–71 on *NA*, although he attributes too much to Massignon's influence. A more rigorous biblical engagement, namely, Jews and Christians, is to be found in Jon D. Levenson, *Inheriting Abraham: The Legacy of the Patriarch in Judaism, Christianity and Islam* (Princeton: Princeton University Press, 2014). Regarding Islam and a partial background to the Council's assumptions, see Neal Robinson: "Massignon, Vatican II and Islam as an Abrahamic religion," in *Islam and Christian–Muslim Relations* 2 (1991): 182–205—and my criticism of the overreading of Massignon in *Vatican II*, 165–72.

28 See above Ruether. See *Gifts* blocking this option as had the Congregation for the Doctrine of Faith (2000): *Dominus Iesus* previously.

The Jewishness of Jesus, his mother, and the first apostles is emphasized, an emphasis that would bear great fruit after the Council in recovering and exploring the Jewish roots of Christianity. In fact, fifty years later, *Gifts* would speak of the "*ecclesia ex circumcisione* and the *ecclesia ex gentibus*, one Church originating from Judaism, the other from the Gentiles, who however together constituted the one and only Church of Jesus Christ" (16). This slow recognition of the Jewish roots of Christianity in *Gifts* also indicates that good relations with the Jewish people would inevitably raise the thorny and difficult question—for both Jews and Catholics—of Jews who have become Catholics and wish to retain their religious heritage as was the practice of Jesus Christ and his early disciples and Jesus's mother, Mary. Such Jewish Catholics are slowly being recognized by the Catholic Church as an indispensable element of retrieval, but balancing this with interfaith relations with Jews and the State of Israel (which does not recognize the right to return of Jews who have become Christians) is a complex and very difficult manner. The Catholic Church for years kept discussions with Messianic Jewish groups at an informal level because of this complexity.[29] Its own Hebrew Catholic movement, which is a small minority but most important, raises similar challenges.[30]

Section 4 begins the retrieval that attempts to expunge the deicide charge and the blood libel from Christian veins, while keeping faithful to the actual Scripture. The deepest opposition to *NA* from within the Council revolved around sections 4–6.[31] Section 4 begins by acknowledging what many Council Fathers felt was being denied in the attempted reversal of anti-Semitism within Catholicism. This sentence granted those who felt Scripture was being obscured at the cost of good

29 See the autobiographical comments by the messianic Jew Mark S. Kinzer, *Searching Her Own Mystery: Nostra Aetate, the Jewish People, and the Identity of the Church* (Eugene, OR: Cascade, 2015), who has been involved in this dialogue, and also Peter Hocken, *Azusa, Rome, and Zion: Pentecostal Faith, Catholic Reform, and Jewish Roots* (Eugene, OR: Pickwick, 2015), pt 3.

30 See Elias Friedman, *Jewish Identity* (New York: Miriam, 1987), and Nechma Tec, *In the Lion's Den: The Life of Oswald Rufeisen* (New York: Oxford University Press, 1990). These two remarkable Jewish converts were concerned about retaining their Jewish identity while remaining Catholic. Rufeisen, a Catholic monk, famously went to the Supreme Court to get Israeli nationality and was refused, as he would become a Christian, although in his view he had not left Judaism. In 1962 the Supreme Court upheld the government's decision: any Jew converting to another religion would lose their preferential access to Israeli citizenship (Rufeisen v. Minister of the Interior, (1962) 16 PD 2428).

31 See the deeply informed accounts by two authors who had a close hand in the drafting and seeing through of *NA*. Their accounts do not always tally. John M. Oesterreicher, "Declaration on the Relation of the Church to Non-Christian Religions," *Commentary on the Documents of Vatican II*, vol. 3, ed. Herbert Vorgrimler (London: Burns & Oates, 1968): 1–154; and Augustin Bea, *The Church and Jewish People: A Commentary on the Second Vatican Council's Declaration on the Relation of the Church to Non-Christian Religions* (London: Geoffrey Chapman, 1966).

relations with Jews the clarity that they desired—an acknowledgement that some Jews did reject Jesus Christ and the Gospel and some Jews were guilty of his death. But the "some" does not here distinguish them from the Jews who believed in Christ, but rather the majority who had little knowledge, if any, of this first century internal Jewish movement who followed Jesus of Nazareth. But it accepts head on, a real rejection: "Jerusalem did not know the time of its visitation, and for the most part the Jews did not accept the gospel, indeed many of them opposed its dissemin-ation (Rom. 11.28)." Without this sentence, which reflects the historical narrative, as perceived, there would have been no chance to advance the goal of removing the wrong interpretation of Scripture regarding the deicide charge and the blood libel. The arguments that raged over the use of the word "deicide" that was used in an earlier draft of the document, then removed, then returned and finally edited out again meant a growing recognition by Cardinal Bea. To flatly deny the deicide charge would amount to saying Scripture was wrong, so instead he steered a docu-ment that denied the Jewish communal guilt over the matter, which was what was really at stake, rather than expunge the word deicide from discourse—which is what he argued was nevertheless achieved, even if not explicitly.[32]

Section 6 begins with another concession to those who were resisting this retrieval and reconfiguration. Again, the truth of history should not be obscured: "Although the Jewish authorities with their followers pressed for the death of Christ, (Jn 19.6)," the major goal was achieved in the continuation of the same sentence: "still those things which were perpetrated during his passion can-not be ascribed indiscriminately to all the Jews living at the time nor to the Jews of today. Although the church is the new people of God, the Jews should not be represented as rejected by God or accursed [reprobate neque et maledicti], as if that follows from holy scripture." It is difficult to imagine the struggle over these two paragraphs and the achievement of these two sentences. Only a close read-ing of the account of each draft and the changes made and the debate that was had can convey the passion and deep conviction on different sides of the debate. While there was genuine anti-Jewishness displayed by some of the Fathers present, including the circulation of vile texts about a Jewish-Masonic conspiracy at the Council, there was something more profound at stake: the retrieval of Scripture that would overthrow many theological traditions (lowercase "t"). Eventual schism would take place because of the deep commitments over this matter, where some felt that the Council was becoming heretical and inauthentic by overthrowing previous liturgical traditions. In the case of the documents on religious freedom, the same group argued that there was a reversal of magisterial teachings, a much more significant and profound charge and one that cannot be examined within the scope of this chapter.[33]

32 See Bea, *The Church and Jewish People*, 66–88, on this matter.

33 David L. Schindler and Nicholas J. Healy, *Freedom, Truth and Human Dignity; The Second Vatican Council's Declaration on Religious Freedom: A New Translation, Redaction History, and Interpretation of* Dignitatis Humanae (Grand Rapids, MI: Eerdmans, 2015). The interpretative history is most illuminating regarding the theme of retrieval being explored

What is important to understand is that the retrieval of Scripture shorn of a long tradition of interpretation was at stake here. There is a profound cost to some aspects of retrieval, and that involves questioning the interpretation of much of the tradition, even some of the great doctors and saints of the Church. This kind of recognition is found in *Gifts*: "On the part of many of the Church Fathers the so-called replacement theory or supersessionism steadily gained favour until in the Middle Ages it represented the standard theological foundation of the relationship with Judaism: the promises and commitments of God would no longer apply to Israel because it had not recognised Jesus as the Messiah and the Son of God, but had been transferred to the Church of Jesus Christ which was now the true 'new Israel,' the new chosen people of God" (17). *Gifts* rejects replacement theory and supersessionism, which says that Israel/Judaism after the time of Christ is invalid and without covenant. It advocates "fulfillment" instead, which itself is not entirely unproblematic. Once the process of retrieval begins, it opens up new vistas that require exploration, practices, the going down of false paths, and eventual assimilation once there is enough of a common mind (sometimes called the *sensus fidelium*) or a prophetic mind (from leading theologians or ecclesiastics). Once such moves get consolidated, they may eventually enter into the magisterial teaching tradition.

In Section 8 *NA* achieves its other goal, to condemn anti-Semitism. Some commentators, both Catholic and Jewish, regretted that there was no explicit recognition of the Catholic Church's complicity in anti-Semitism. This was a recognition that was required by a church that was so profoundly European in its Roman/Latin-centeredness. The need for repentance of Catholic anti-Semitism had to wait until 1998 when the Catholic Commission for Religious Relations with the Jews issued its *We Remember: A Reflection on the Shoah*. In section 5, it says, "At the end of this Millennium the Catholic Church desires to express her deep sorrow for the failures of her sons and daughters in every age. This is an act of repentance (*teshuva*), since, as members of the Church, we are linked to the sins as well as the merits of all her children. The Church approaches with deep respect and great compassion the experience of extermination, the *Shoah*, suffered by the Jewish people during the Second World War. It is not a matter of mere words, but indeed of binding commitment. 'We would risk causing the victims of the most atrocious deaths to die again if we do not have an ardent desire for justice, if we do not commit ourselves to ensure that evil does not prevail over good as it did for millions of the children of the Jewish people . . . Humanity cannot permit all that to happen again' (citing Pope John Paul II, *Address on the Occasion of a Commemoration of the Shoah*, April 7, 1994, 3: *Insegnamenti* 171, 1994, 897 and 893.)"[34] This repentance, markedly and clearly, was on behalf of many Catholics,

---

here. For the argument that the Council overturned previous magisterial teachings, see Marcel Lefebvre, *Religious Liberty Questioned* (Kansas City, MO: Angelus Press, 2002).

34 Text available on Vatican website: http://www.vatican.va/roman_curia/pontifical_councils/chrstuni/documents/rc_pc_chrstuni_doc_16031998_shoah_en.html (accessed January 20, 2017).

not the "church" per se. This caused profound disquiet among some Catholics and Jews. The reason for this is that formally speaking, the church per se is the mystical body of Christ—in its sacraments and the formal teaching office. In the eyes of many there was no evidence that the church in this sense formally erred on the matter doctrinally. At one level, the ongoing debate about Pius XII's being less helpful than he could have in saving Jewish lives or in more strident public criticism of the Nazis' policy toward the Jews, while utterly important in terms of a historical question, does not pertain to the sources of authority that are being discussed in this chapter. If, for example, it is found he could have done more and that he sheltered anti-Jewish sentiments, while deeply regretful, this would not be a matter that indicts him as erring in his formal teaching capacity.

What lessons are there to be learned about the process of retrieval when examining the Council? First, it is an ongoing task. The same Scripture that was the source of Jewish persecution, the blood libel and the deicide charge, becomes the source of working for closer relationships of trust, respect, and reverence toward the Jewish people. Second, the same tradition that produced persecution of the Jewish people is, after the Council, being mined to advance and develop a closer relationship to the Jewish people. The tradition is rather like a mosaic whereupon some parts are recovered to bring to the fore old themes and wisdom to help the church move forward. For example, before the Council, Aquinas's view that the law was dead and deadening, a mortal sin to follow in the light of the Messiah's coming, was part of a tradition that seemed to help in negative images. After the Council, Aquinas's reading of Romans, his understanding of the Jews, is being revisited with vigor, because of the confidence that great thinkers of the church may still speak imaginatively.[35] Aquinas's assumption that following the law after Christ is "mortal sin" is part and parcel of his view that the Jews knew their Messiah had come in Jesus Christ. Once one removes the assumption of willful disobedience and knowing rejection of the Gospel and replace those assumptions with invincible ignorance (forgetting the pejorative nature of the term "ignorance" but remembering it simply means that a person may in principle choose other than the Gospel in entirely good faith), the reality of Judaism takes on a different coloring in the work of Aquinas. It is precisely in those ancient traditions that deeply affirmative and important insights arise about the legitimate covenant that the Jews enjoy, that their devotion and relationship to the true and living God is central to their own religious observance—and if this is the case, Christians have much to learn through keen attention to their elder brothers. Third, the magisterium's authority behind the Conciliar teachings is guarantee, at least for Catholics, that the church is being drawn into greater truth by its formal teaching

---

35 For example, see Matthew Levering, *Christ's Fulfillment of Torah and Temple: Salvation According to Thomas Aquinas* (Notre Dame, IN: University of Notre Dame Press, 2002) and Stephen C. Boguslawski, OP, *Thomas Aquinas on the Jews: Insights into His Commentary on Romans 9–11* (New York: Paulist Press, 2008), and Matthew A. Tapie, *Aquinas on Israel and the Church: The Question of Supersessionism in the Theology of Thomas Aquinas* (Eugene, OR: Pickwick Publications, 2014), who is critical of both.

body and offers witnesses to the condemnation of Christian anti-Semitism, the affirmation that this ancient religion partakes in God's revelation through its rooting in the Hebrew Bible (Old Testament), and that the promises made to Abraham and his descendants are never revoked. Fourth, one of the great ironies of the Council is that its central achievement regarding the dispelling of the blood libel through reexamining its scripture was hardly an issue by the time the Council ended. The World Council of Churches had already done this in 1948. The real debate regarding the reception of the Council moved to a more pressing issue for the post-Conciliar church regarding the status of contemporary Judaism: was its covenant still valid and, if it was, did this mean that it was a salvific religion? Fifth, the retrieval of the Jewish nature of early Christianity has moved along two separate tracks. On the one hand, the voice of living Jewry becomes important for the church's own consciousness. This was evidenced at the launch of *Gifts*, where two distinguished Jewish leaders (Dr. Ed Kessler and Rabbi David Rosen) shared the stage with Catholic cardinals, and both expressed praise for the document along with some of their reservations. This marked an important moment in the gestural symbolics of interfaith dialogue. On the other hand, the recovery of early Jewish Christianity has increased attention to the Jewish Christian ecclesia within the Catholic Church, the *ecclesia ex circumcisione*. Both these elements promise to open many vistas that are hardly charted in the current discussion. Retrieval is deeply open-ended, which itself is being open to God's drawing the church into deeper truths, but not without struggle, wrong-footedness, and stupidity. But without returning to the sources of authority in the light of the Holy Spirit's leading the church into deeper truth, such development and reform would not be possible.

Part VII

CRITICAL APPRAISALS

Chapter 18

DAVID TRACY: A CRITICAL THEOLOGY OF RETRIEVAL

William E. Myatt

All those involved in interpreting our situation and all those aware of our
need for solidarity may continue to risk interpreting all the classics of all the
traditions. And in that effort to interpret lie both resistance and hope.

—David Tracy[1]

Introduction

At issue in the current volume is a discussion on how best to appropriate, or
retrieve, historic theological texts. There is indeed something compelling about
the past for Christians. Christians believe the one God not only speaks in history
but also has been fully revealed at a historic moment in a historic person. This
moment should be recovered with as little manipulation as possible. Tertullian
expressed this sensitivity when he said

> any group of things must be classified according to its origin. Therefore, although
> the Churches are so many and so great, there is but the one primitive Church of
> the Apostles, from which all others are derived. . . . If the Lord Jesus Christ sent
> the Apostles to preach, no others ought to be received except those appointed by
> Christ. For no one knows the Father except the Son, and him to whom the Son
> gives a revelation.[2]

For Tertullian, if we are to locate the most pristine theological truths that mirror
the pristine unity of the God of Jesus, it is imperative to retrieve those pure pieces
of history that are closest to God's revelation in Jesus.

---

1 David Tracy, *Plurality and Ambiguity* (Chicago: University of Chicago Press,
1994), 114.

2 Tertullian, "Apology: The Demurrer Against the Heretics," in *The Faith of the Early
Fathers*, vol. 1 (Collegeville, MN: Liturgical Press, 1970), 120.

But are historical methods of retrieval like Tertullian's most adequate to our situation? Has the rise of historical consciousness in twentieth-century thought hamstrung Tertullian's quest? If so, why continue to prioritize it? Why look to the past at all? Why not try instead to anticipate God's future? Or, if one does insist on retrieval, how might one go about it? Should one follow the methodologies of retrieval that are retrieved from the past? Or are there new methods, informed by new sensitivities, that are more adequate for today?

In addition to such hermeneutical issues, there are dynamics of power at play. The project of retrieval, like the project of history, requires "connecting the dots." The retriever is presented with a series of moments. In order to make sense of those moments, she must act upon them in the task of interpretation. Such action is influenced not only by historical accidents like the location, time, and language of the interpreter but also by all the anxieties, hopes, desires, and assumptions any interpreter brings to the table. When the interpreter is acting from a position of power, it is all too easy to perpetuate that power and, in turn, to perpetuate the marginalization of those outside that power. If a Christian theologian believes in the claim that God's power is made perfect in weakness (2 Cor 12:19), then the act of perpetuating power, even through something as seemingly banal as history, is indeed a problem.

My proposed point of entry into this complex discussion is to survey someone whose entire theological career can be considered an exploration of the best form of theological retrieval, the Roman Catholic theologian David Tracy. Tracy's earliest writings appear in the 1960s, during a time of political, social, and theological upheaval. Critical philosophies of history and a general awareness of historical consciousness[3] challenged the easy connections made between historical expressions of faith and contemporary appropriations thereof. In response to the sense of relativism that emerged in the twentieth century, Tracy turned to disciplines like transcendental philosophy, phenomenology, and hermeneutics to suggest shared methodologies that would maintain theology's unique task of making and evaluating truth claims. But Tracy was likewise aware that theology was very subjective, perhaps *the* most subjective of all academic disciplines, and he was uniquely sensitive to critiques of his work, particularly from theologies at the margins.[4] Tracy knew that any theology hoping to situate its systematic claims in

---

3 The idea of historical consciousness was very important for Tracy's earliest hermeneutical sensitivities. See, for example, Tracy's review of *A New Catechism: Catholic Faith for Adults* (New York: Herder and Herder, 1967), *Theology Today* (1968): 402; "Why Orthodoxy in a Personalist Age?" *Catholic Theological Society of America Proceedings* 25 (1970): 78–86.

4 For example, Juan Luis Segundo, *Faith and Ideologies*, trans. John Drury (Maryknoll, NY: Orbis, 1984), 34–40. For Tracy's discussion with feminists, see, inter alia, David Tracy, "Theoria and Praxis: A Partial Response [to E. Farley and R. W. Lynn]," *Theological Education* 17 (1981): 167–74; David Tracy, "Reply to 'The Influence of Feminist Theory on My Theological Work,' by F. S. Fiorenza," *Journal of Feminist Studies in Religion* 7

a demonstrably "true" foundation was at risk of subsuming all particularities into an all-encompassing framework.

What eventually emerged was an approach to retrieval founded on the assumption that theology must continue the difficult task of truth telling, but this pursuit of truth must always run through multiple experiences of faith, and particularly through the experiences of faith that emerge from suffering. When this happens, theology is transformed into critique. It does not merely invoke the God of Christianity, a God whose universality requires risking claims to truth; theology is about Christology, a Christ whose revolutionary life and teachings upended what was typically thought to be true. This Christ blew apart all tendencies toward domination, and the most appropriate way to retrieve Christ today is by energizing the various Christological forms that likewise speak against power from the margins. In David Tracy's approach to retrieval, the Christ form emerges as fragment. A God-centered, Christomorphic theology thus continues to hope for truth by appropriating the fragmentary classics of Christian expression and empowering similarly fragmentary forms of expression today. The very nature of Christianity's God and the Jesus to whom Christianity gives witness demand nothing less.

Our survey is divided into three sections that together demonstrate how retrieval can function as a centralizing idea for understanding Tracy's lengthy and impressive career. We begin with a brief summary of four recognizable periods in Tracy's development and show how "the early Tracy" understood retrieval as an aspect of the theologian's search for truth in a situation of relativity. Second, we see Tracy forge a path toward meaningfulness by locating the theological project in the experience of self that gave rise to authentic theological expression. This creates a series of foundational-theological categories for systematic theology to retrieve central Christian symbols like God, Jesus Christ, and sin. For Tracy, the best forms of theological retrieval animated the latent dialectics at work when fundamental and systematic theologies converged. Third, we see that the religious classic, and later the fragment, animated a unique instantiation of the natural tension at work between such dialectics as fundamental and systematic theology, God and Jesus Christ, and "common human experience" and "the Christian fact." Here, retrieval emerges as the practice of enabling fragmentary expressions to remain as alive in their re-presentation as they were when first expressed. Fragmentary theological expressions disclose the deeply human passion for freedom, love, resistance, and even revolt. It was these forms that Tracy's revisionary methodology ultimately empowered.

(1991): 122–5; David Tracy, *On Naming the Present: Reflections on God, Hermeneutics, and Church* (Maryknoll, NY: Orbis, 1994); David Tracy and Elisabeth Schüssler-Fiorenza, "Editorial," in *Concilium* 1984/5. For a survey of works written in response to Tracy's earlier writings, see T. Howland Sanks, "David Tracy's Theological Project: An Overview and Some Implications," *Theological Studies* 54 (1993): 698–727.

Relativism and meaning

Tracy's academic writing can be separated into four recognizable periods. The first, located in the late 1960s and the early 1970s, can be characterized as an attempt to stabilize a rather chaotic, post–Vatican II theological milieu. With the theology of his mentor Bernard Lonergan serving as a guide,[5] Tracy confronted the unfettered use of the theological imagination by constructing a transcendental critique of religious expression. The early period culminated in his publication of *Blessed Rage for Order* in 1975, in which Tracy called for "an explicitly transcendental or metaphysical mode of reflection" to determine the "truth-status" of the theological project.[6] The second period, located in the late 1970s and the 1980s, is characterized by an increasing attention to publicness as a nuanced continuation of Tracy's earlier concerns. The pursuit of a transcendental critique is still present, but now it is complemented by a more robustly hermeneutical approach to phenomenology. The explicit mentioning of "public theology," an idea typically associated with Tracy, began appearing almost immediately after the publication of *Blessed Rage for Order* and culminated famously in Tracy's longest project to date, *The Analogical Imagination.*[7] In this latter work the public trajectory of theology was mediated by way of the "religious classic." Borrowing from Hans-Georg Gadamer,[8]

5 For "the early Tracy" on Lonergan, see David Tracy, "The Development of the Notion of Theological Methodology in the Works of Bernard J. Lonergan, S.J." (PhD diss., Gregorian University, 1969) and David William Tracy, "Lonergan's Interpretation of St. Thomas Aquinas: The Intellective Nature of Speculative Theology: excerpta ex dissertatione ad Lauream in Facultate Theologica Pontificaiae Universitatis Gregorianae" (Rome: Pontificia Universitate Gregoriana, 1969), where Tracy says, "It would be difficult to find another contemporary theologian who has kept both needs [of contemporary adequacy and historical appropriation] so clearly in mind as has Father Lonergan from his earliest to his latest work" (5). See also David Tracy, *Achievement of Bernard Lonergan* (New York: Herder and Herder, 1970) 232–69; "Lonergan's Foundational Theology: An Interpretation and Critique," in *Foundations of Theology: Papers from the International Lonergan Conference 1970,* ed. Philip McShane (Notre Dame, IN: University of Notre Dame, 1972), 197–222.Tracy later called Lonergan the Gregorian professor who was "excellent . . . above all." "Tribute to Bernard McGinn," *Continuum* 42 (2003): 41–2. Cf. also Gaspar Martinez, *Confronting the Mystery of God: Political, Liberation, and Public Theologies* (New York: Continuum, 2001), 176–8. Martinez stresses the fact that Lonergan's hermeneutical enterprise was especially influential for Tracy. Cf. *Plurality and Ambiguity,* 115, where Tracy says readers "will recognize [Lonergan's] presence here and elsewhere in this work—a presence for which I remain all the more thankful despite the obvious differences on 'language' and understanding and thereby interpretation."

6 David Tracy, *Blessed Rage for Order: The New Pluralism in Theology* (New York: Seabury, 1975), 52–6.

7 David Tracy, *Analogical Imagination* (New York: Crossroad, 1981).

8 For Tracy on Gadamer, see especially *Analogical Imagination,* 99–153. Of primary importance for Tracy is Hans-Georg Gadamer, *Truth and Method* (New York: Seabury,

Tracy suggested that a retrieval of the conversations with classics, informed by an inclusivist Christology, functioned as a foundation on which to construct systematic theology.[9] The third period began immediately after his publication of *Analogical Imagination* and continued into the 1990s. As with the second, the concerns of this period were not new developments but do include shifts in vocabulary and emphasis.[10] Tracy's concerns here can be characterized as extended reflections on conversation as a form for theological reflection, an idea that is especially present in Tracy's third major work, *Plurality and Ambiguity*.[11] Although a willingness to enter deeply and vulnerably into conversation was certainly present in the first two periods, *Plurality and Ambiguity* brought criticism through conversation to a determinative position in his project. The centrality of conversation is also discernible in Tracy's last major work to date, *Dialogue with the Other*.[12] Informed by the Christian–Buddhist dialogue in which Tracy was participating at the time of its publication, *Dialogue with the Other* brings a phenomenology of conversation to the very forefront of the theological task. The fourth period, which began in the mid-1990s and has continued into Tracy's present writings, lectures, and graduate courses, can be characterized by two noticeable themes: first, the trajectory toward "truth" that was present in *Blessed Rage for Order* and *Analogical Imagination* reaches its culmination not in "christocentric" but "theocentric," "christomorphic" categories[13] mediated by

---

1975). Gadamer's attention to the "question of truth as it emerges in art" (*Truth and Method*, 1–171) and his "theory of hermeneutic experience" (*Truth and Method*, 267–382) are especially important.

   9 Tracy originally published *Blessed Rage for Order* anticipating that it would be the first of a three-volume series covering fundamental, systematic, and practical theologies. Cf. *Blessed Rage for Order* 56n1 and 64. For a helpful self-critique of the differences between these two works, see *Analogical Imagination*, 96, 84–85n28, and 337–8.

   10 The foci of each period are not exclusive. Instead, they represent relative points of stress that stand out as uniquely representative concerns guiding Tracy during that particular time. Stephen Okey, "The Plural and Ambiguous Self: The Theological Anthropology of David Tracy" (PhD diss., Boston College, 2013), traces key aspects of Tracy's theological anthropology throughout Tracy's career. Okey's thesis is that the points of stress relative to each shift are a result of the respective conversation partners Tracy had in mind during each period. See also Gerald M. Boodoo, *Development and Consolidation: The Use of Theological Method in the Works of David Tracy* (PhD diss., Catholic University of Leuven, 1991), esp. pp. 50–87; Younhee Kim, *The Quest for Plausible Christian Discourse in a World of Pluralities: The Evolution of David Tracy's Understanding of "Public Theology"* (New York: Peter Lang, 2008).

   11 The title given to the German translation of this work connotes its dependence on the idea of conversation. Cf. David Tracy, *Theologie als Gespräch: Eine postmoderne Hermeneutik*, trans. Susanne Klinger (Mainz: Matthias Grünewald Verlag, 1993).

   12 David Tracy, *Dialogue with the Other: The Inter-Religious Dialogue* (Louvain: Peeters, 1990).

   13 David Tracy, "Theology and the Many Faces of Postmodernity," *Theology Today* 51 (1994): 104–14, at 111. For early versions of Tracy's Christological ruminations, cf. *Blessed Rage for Order*, 204–36; *Analogical Imagination*, 421–29.

"the fragment" as religious form.[14] Paralleling the trajectory from metaphysics in *Blessed Rage for Order* to publicness in *Analogical Imagination*, the fragment represents a nuanced uptake of *Analogical Imagination*'s classic, especially when the notion of the classic is run through the robust and deep appropriation of critical conversation expressed in *Plurality and Ambiguity* and *Dialogue with the Other*.[15]

The crisis of meaning in the twentieth century

In Tracy's earliest writings, beginning in the late 1960s and continuing into the early 1970s, a concern for truth stood at the center of his proposals for theological methodology. Tracy was among a group of young Catholic theologians who hoped to bring methodological order to an otherwise chaotic theological scene in a post–Vatican-II era. Doing so would help temper the undisciplined use of an active theological imagination, thus allowing theology to remain a respectable academic discipline, but it would also protect theology from creating new forms of oppression through the myopic appropriation of problematic traditions. The primary issues exacerbating the chaos after Vatican II were fourfold.

The first revolved around an awareness of "historical consciousness." The project of theological retrieval—and the hope for pursuing truth through retrieval—were no longer available from an objective, vacuum-sealed point of view. The increasing use of hermeneutics in all disciplines revealed numerous interpretational factors influencing the reading of texts and the construction of meaning. "Accidentals" like language, socioeconomic location, ethnic identity, and philosophical assumptions

---

14 See, inter alia, "Fragments: The Spiritual Situation of Our Times," in *God, the Gift, and Postmodernism*, ed. John D. Caputo and Michael J. Scanlon (Bloomington/Indianapolis: Indiana University Press, 1999), 170–84; "Form and Fragment: The Recovery of the Hidden and Incomprehensible God," *Reflections: Center of Theological Inquiry* 3 (1999): 62–89; "Fragments and Forms: Universality and Particularity Today," in *The Church in Fragments: Towards What Kind of Unity*, ed. G. Ruggieri and M. Tomka (Maryknoll, NY: Orbis, 1997); "Fragment and Form," *Concilium* 23 (1997): 122–9; "Fragments of Synthesis? The Hopeful Paradox of Dupré's Modernity," in *Christian Spirituality and the Culture of Modernity: The Thought of Louis Dupré*, ed. Peter J. Casarella and George P. Schner, SJ (Grand Rapids, MI: Eerdmans, 1998); "African American Thought: The Discovery of Fragments," in *Black Faith and Public Talk: Critical Essays on James H. Cone's Black Theology and Black Power*, ed. Dwight N. Hopkins (Maryknoll, NY: Orbis, 1999), 29–40.

15 Including all these categories allows us to move beyond the revisionist approach to theology associated with *Blessed Rage for Order* into Tracy's later uptake of conversation and fragment as central to the theological task. In this way, we move beyond an essay like that of Ian Markham, "Revisionism," in *The Oxford Handbook of Systematic Theology*, ed. John Webster, Kathryn Tanner, and Iain Torrance (Oxford: Oxford University Press, 2007), 600–16.

were among the increasing factors considered not merely influential for the writer but constitutive. This meant that the approach to theological retrieval had to change. Tracy wrote that the scholastic debates mirroring medieval *aggiornamento* "seem[ed] like an age of theoretical innocence—attractive, indeed, but no longer possible."[16] What theologians needed was a more careful, hermeneutically attentive, and methodologically sound approach.

Second, Tracy observed a "mystic alchemy" in his own religious tradition, Roman Catholicism. The Second Vatican Council had set free a renewed sense of the theological imagination that could in its worst forms actually exacerbate whatever problems had been caused by the *aggiornamento* of medieval theology. Late twentieth-century theology was making strides in the right direction. It was progressive, and Tracy was appreciative that new frontiers were being opened,[17] but he was likewise cautious of the increasingly arbitrary means by which the theological imagination was applied. And if it could be applied in one direction, it could easily be applied in another. For Tracy, the "most important" and "most difficult" question for theologians was "just how one may critically vindicate the very possibility of theological language" in an increasingly relativized situation. Theologians did not merely need a creative return to the sources but also some way of locating "the conditions of the possibility of whether such a return was possible at all."[18]

Third, Tracy realized that it was not possible merely to insert methodological requirements into the most subjective of all disciplines. Theological expression transcended methodology. In its best forms, theology mirrored religion, a form of human expression that was passionate, awe inspired, expressive, poetic, and fully human. To preserve these emergent qualities of religion, Tracy needed help from reflective disciplines that enabled access to the "experience of the self as a self," the "non-sensuous," or "supra-sensuous" experience of self. Tracy wrote, "We seek aid for understanding, for raising to explicit consciousness—in a word, for mediating—the immediacy of that experience by our own powers of intelligent and critical introspection."[19] This more elusive, indeed "primordial," disclosure of self was expressed in ways not typically associated with theology: mood, feeling, tone, music, poetry, and embodiment. If it was to be preserved in the academy, adequate modes of reflection must be located. Recent forms of phenomenology and transcendental critique, especially when run through a hermeneutical lens, provided this access and thereby preserved theology's academic respectability without compromising the deeply subjective nature of authentic theological expression.

16 Tracy, "Horizon Analysis," 167.

17 David Tracy, "Method as Foundation for Theology: Bernard Lonergan's Option," *Journal of Religion* 50 (1970): 307.

18 David Tracy, "Horizon Analysis and Eschatology," *Continuum* 6 (1968): 167. See also David Tracy, "Holy Spirit as Philosophical Problem," *Commonweal* 89 (1968): 205–13.

19 Tracy, *Blessed Rage for Order*, 66.

And finally, an increasingly global awareness of pluralism gave way to a sense of relativism among theologians who still believed it was important to risk and evaluate claims to truth. On the one hand, pluralism was a "fundamental enrichment" of the twentieth-century situation; on the other, it created a confusing, diffusing experience. No theologian authentically committed to the truth-claims of her tradition could allow the theological project to be reduced either to some religious, "lowest common denominator" or to a marginal instantiation of "one interesting but purely private option."[20] The former did not enable an authentic appropriation of history; the latter did not enable authentic participation in a global society. Neither option approached the problem of truth with any seriousness. The necessary task for the theologian was to construct an "inevitably complex" strategy for confronting pluralism that would avoid both privatism—a retreat into traditionalism and merely traditional forms of retrieval—and relativism—a retreat into the cognitive nihilism that was so concerning for Tracy's younger self.

Foundational and systematic theology

Foundational theology as revision

As a response to all these crises of meaning, Tracy followed the lead of his mentor, Bernard Lonergan.[21] Lonergan's major methodological insight was to suggest that there is a similar form, or isomorphism, between "the structure of knowing and the structure of the known."[22] If there were any possibility of bringing order to the theological discipline, without rushing through hermeneutical barriers or compromising theology's uniquely subjective nature, it would be achieved by attending to the one constructing theological claims in an eschatological hope for truth. Understanding the theological subject through self-reflection enabled a unifying sense of self-knowledge that could be used to understand theological knowledge and thus understand the nature of theological truth and the possibility of appropriately retrieving theologies of the past. The self-reflective theologian was able to explicate "the ground, the basis, the fundament"[23] of the phenomena appearing to the theological consciousness and would thus construct a referential framework for doing theology. A subject recognized a claim, a word, a sound, or even feeling as something that resonated with oneself, a recollection. To recognize something as true was to regather aspects of oneself that had been otherwise dispersed (cf. Augustine, *Confessions*, II.1.i). This experience of truth as a unifying

---

20 Tracy, *Analogical Imagination*, xi.

21 Tracy's dependence on Lonergan is well documented and was, of course, the subject of his first published book, *Achievement of Bernard Lonergan* (New York: Herder and Herder, 1970). See also Gaspar Martinez, *Confronting the Mystery of God*, 176–8. Martinez stresses the fact that Lonergan's hermeneutical enterprise was especially influential for Tracy.

22 Lonergan, *Insight*, 399.

23 Tracy, *Blessed Rage for Order*, 67.

moment was not unlike the unifying experience of selfhood that occurred when theological truth was recognized—an experience that transcendental phenomenology helped the reflective theologian understand.

Further, if it was granted that the experience of selfhood was a true event, then the claims made by theologians should be able to account for that experience, and vice versa. Theologies that could not demonstrably account for a contemporary experience of self (i.e., "truth") must be considered suspect. They may be in continuity with a particular faith tradition, but to the degree that an appropriation of tradition was out of touch with what Tracy called "common human experience," one must ask whether that appropriation was true. Tracy operated under the assumption that truth was essentially a unifying event. If a particular accounting of truth could not demonstrate unity with the unified sense of self disclosed in phenomenological reflection, the theologian should question its truth. This was, in fact, a promising exercise for the theologian. By opening up theology to critique from publicly available criteria, theologians achieved a new sense of freedom. They would not have to rely simply on the authoritarian claim "the Tradition teaches us" and risk perpetuating collective blind spots in their theological community. Running theological construction through something like "what we all know" built an accountability framework directly into the theological task and protected it from the lazy tendency toward blind, uninformed, and ultimately dangerous faith.

However, the theologian was not merely subservient to the newest and most imaginative understandings of self. Correction went the other way as well. By situating the theological project in a shared space, theologians could speak *to* non-theological forms of expression. This was prophecy. In its best forms, theology would correct the various tendencies toward technocracy, toward the flattening of human self-understanding, and toward the merely scientific approach to truth that emerged out of modernity and that continued in various forms of postmodern thought. Theology was the most subjective, hope-filled, quintessentially human of any expression. It provided a dense instance of the "religious dimension" to life that motivated humans to search for truth at all. Science, poetry, music, history, philosophy, civil rights, the march toward freedom, and other modes of expression demonstrated an orientation toward the limit of existence, a limit toward which religion itself was oriented. Religion expressed a hope to move beyond the various limits that bound our current situations. Preserving the originary sense of faith that exploded into earth-shattering, limit-oriented expressions protected the self from being subsumed into any all-encompassing framework. Tracy called this expression "the Christian fact."

When the theological conversation moved in both directions, there was an opening to revise both Christian self-understanding and common self-understanding. His fundamental method was therefore called "revisionist." Tracy famously offered the following five theses to clarify the "principal meanings" a revisionist theology involved:

(1) The two principal sources for theology are Christian texts and common human experience. (2) The theological task will involve a critical correlation

of the results of the investigations of the two sources of theology. (3) The principal method of investigation of the source "common human experience and language" can be described as a phenomenology of the "religious dimension" present in everyday and scientific experience and language. (4) The principal method of investigation of the source "the Christian tradition" can be described as an historical and hermeneutical investigation of classic Christian texts. (5) To determine the truth status of the results of one's investigations into the meaning of both common human experience and Christian texts, the theologian should employ an explicitly transcendental or metaphysical mode of reflection.[24]

In brief, Tracy's unique contribution to the project of retrieval was initially based on his assumption that there was still something valuable about truth. Indeed, the only Christian theology worthy of its name was one bold enough to risk making truth claims. But in contrast to so many theologians who assumed the tradition itself maintained a monopoly on truth, Tracy was sensitive to the manner in which historical consciousness had problematized the easy and unnuanced appropriation of tradition. Further, he was sensitive to the manner in which authentic theological and religious expression was irreducibly subjective. And further still, he was sensitive to the manner in which theology kept all disciplines from reducing the human to an object to be explored through mere objectivity. The human qua subject was singularly expressive, and theology was a discipline perfectly suited for preserving that subjective sense of singularity—a singularity unique to those beings willing to risk telling the truth.

Systematic theology as Christomorphic retrieval

The purpose of Tracy's second major work, *Analogical Imagination*, was to construct a systematic theology on basis of the fundamental theology of *Blessed Rage for Order*. In *Analogical Imagination*, Tracy claimed that it was not merely expedient for twentieth-century theologians to pursue universally recognizable criteria for theological construction. It was necessary. Publicness may have been occasioned by the rise of a historical and sociological consciousness, but publicness was caused by the most central theological symbols. For the sake of this chapter, we highlight three.

First, systematic theology began with God. Tracy claimed, "Christianity, when true to its heritage, cannot but recognize that its fundamental faith, its most radical trust and loyalty, is to the all-pervasive reality of the God of love and power disclosed in Jesus Christ."[25] Any Christian theology—"whether classical, process,

---

24 Tracy, *Blessed Rage for Order*, 43–56. The five theses laid out in *Blessed Rage for Order*, chap. 3 are also found in David Tracy, "The Task of Fundamental Theology," *Journal of Religion* 54 (1974): 13–34.

25 Tracy, *Blessed Rage for Order*, 43–56.

liberationist or liberal"—affirmed "the strict universality of the divine reality."[26] Theological speech that was private or particularist was unworthy of the God to whom it gave witness. In contrast to scholars in religious studies, theologians had to face the questions of meaning and truth "by the intrinsic demands of their discipline."[27] Tracy's God was the God whose life-giving presence infused all existence. God was both source and goal of theological expression, and God is one. Theologies that made false claims compromised the singularity of God by dividing the theological project into multiplicity. Theology was *logos* on *theos*, rational discourse on God, or faith seeking understanding. If theologians did not want to forfeit their most central identities, they had to demonstrate an isomorphic singularity between the God who stood at the center of their projects and the theologies they were constructing.

Second, the theological symbol of Jesus Christ tempered any universalizing tendencies based on Christianity's God. The truth of God revealed in Jesus is a challenging truth, one that speaks against power, that calls out hypocrisy, and that is present among "the least of these" (Mt 25:40). Jesus lived a life "at the limit," as it were, and the New Testament disclosed Jesus's life as "a certain limit-mode-of-being-in-the-world . . . a new, an agapic, a self-sacrificing righteousness willing to risk living at that limit where one seems in the presence of the righteous, loving, gracious God."[28] This radicalness could be philosophically clarified as a concentration of that fundamental trust in existence explored in Tracy's earlier works. All of the hopes and passions, dreams for justice and authenticity, expressions of singularity and desire—in other words, all of those quintessentially human expressions disclosed through a phenomenological account of selfhood—were in fact concentrated in the Christian recollection of Jesus Christ. And if Christ re-presented the radical limit nature of fundamental trust, then an appropriate retrieval of Christ in systematic theology must incorporate limit-oriented, even disruptive, expressions that communicate with contemporary society.

Third, notions such as sin, idolatry, fallenness, and confession served to keep the systematic theologian humble. Departing from a position of faith, the systematic theologian believed that all expressions—including theologies of retrieval—were radically affected by the finitude of the one retrieving history and of her or his faith community. No retrieval occurs apart from the anxieties, wills to power, and tribalistic tendencies of us all. The systematic theologian engaging in retrieval could thus build a kind of protective measure into the very infrastructure of theological method and provide an extra layer of plausibility. The "concrete" systematic form and the "abstract" fundamental form existed in a mutually critical correlation, protecting against the easy perpetuation of oppressive traditions. Insofar as the fundamental theologian explicated "the general, abstract, necessary (i.e., metaphysical) characteristics of any coherent concept of God," she was able

---

26 Tracy, *Analogical Imagination*, 51.
27 Tracy, *Analogical Imagination*, 20 and 55.
28 Tracy, *Blessed Rage for Order*, 221.

to "inform and, where necessary, correct the fuller, more concrete expressions of systematic theology."[29] But at the same time, concrete expressions of intense particularity retrieved as Christological forms kept the fundamental theological project from devolving into mere abstractions. Systematic theology pushed fundamental theology's "abstract, metaphysical notions of God . . . in the direction of greater concreteness."[30]

The religious classic and fragment

Retrieval and conversations with the religious classic

There was no more fruitful place to engage the fundamental–systematic dialectic than in those unique expressions of singularity that burgeoned into a universe of meaning. Tracy called these expressions "religious classics." For Tracy, religious classics functioned as a singular expression embodying a dialectical moment. The universalizing trajectory toward truth was held in tension with the singularity of the classic expression itself. Although religious classics were expressed "on a particular journey in a particular tradition," they nevertheless disclosed "permanent possibilities for human existence both personal and communal." Religious classics were individual, unique, and singular, but they were likewise "always public, never private."[31] Further, although Tracy was aware that the symbols, language, and grammar of religions often devolved into banality, the classics themselves— those original, "intense" moments of productive distanciation—are perpetually interruptive. The classics eluded easy assimilation. They were no more predictable than the plurality of interpretations to which they gave rise. When retrieved and re-presented in a manner consistent with their "permanent timeliness,"[32] religious classics enabled the resistance necessary to inform retrieval. To interpret a tradition's religious classics appropriately, one must "allow them to challenge what we presently consider possible."[33] Religious classics "entice us to hope for some other and different, yet possible, ways of thinking."

When organized into a kind of analogical framework revolving around the event of Jesus Christ, and when allowed to maintain the originary dialectic between singularity and universality, religious classics empowered conversation. Classics could facilitate new awareness, like a living metaphor in which two unassociated ideas were brought together and thus created meaning. The religious classics were like multiplied expressions of individuality dancing together in a semantic universe empowered by the Christ event. Continuing a trajectory of mystical theology, in

29 Tracy, *Analogical Imagination*, 90.
30 Tracy, *Analogical Imagination*, 91.
31 Tracy, *Analogical Imagination*, 14.
32 Tracy, *Analogical Imagination*, 102.
33 Tracy, *Plurality and Ambiguity*, 84.

which the life of prayer provided the language for theological construction, Tracy risked engaging the theological imagination by bringing together multiple, often disparate theologies into an imaginative and often tense conversation. When gathered in this way, religious classics would clash with one another and set off sparks of new meaning. Systematic theology became something like a symphony of multiple voices reflecting the plurality of twentieth-century society. Indeed, Tracy saw his role, perhaps "born of an irenic temperament,"[34] as something like a moderator, perhaps a mediator, or even a priest. The plurality of the twentieth-century situation—a plurality both internal and external to Christian theology—was thus reformulated as an enrichment of the theological project.

Indeed, for those who gave themselves over fully to the activity of conversation, there was the play of a "game." Tracy was well aware that conversation was "a game with some hard rules."[35] His early concern with methodology bespoke nothing less. But for the conversant who entered fully into the game of dialogue, not unlike the participants in the great philosophical dialogues of history, the experience was not unlike getting lost, freeing oneself from oneself. In such instances conversation participants got "in the zone."[36] They were taken over by the question being explored, and their conversation transformed into an authentic "exploration of possibilities in the search for truth."[37]

The problem Tracy readily admitted with this optimistic account was that in actual conversation, it was rare, "even for Socrates,"[38] to refrain from rhetorical domination. Ideological distortion, othering, fear, and unconfessed pathologies could keep conversants from achieving their intended goal—mutual, sympathetic engagement in a shared pursuit of truth. When conversation diverged from its ideal parameters, the "hope for conversation" dissolved, and conversation partners would find it necessary to inject "radical interruptions"[39] into the conversation being facilitated. Doing so kept the conversation from becoming merely disparate and increasingly disconnected options. By centralizing those intense religious expressions that eluded easy interpretation, the theologian provided a preemptive strike, ironically building interruption into the theological conversation itself. In so doing, she was less likely to reduce the individual to the universal and maintain the

---

34 Tracy, *Analogical Imagination*, 80. Tracy's student Stephen H. Webb wrote of his mentor, "David Tracy was an irenic and benevolent graduate school advisor who encouraged his students to follow their own paths." Stephen H. Webb, "On Mentors and the Making of a Useful Theology: A Retrospective on the Work of William C. Placher," *Reviews in Religion and Theology*, 13, no. 2 (2006): 237–43.

35 Tracy, *Plurality and Ambiguity*, 19.

36 David Tracy, "Western Hermeneutics and Inter-Religious Dialogue," unpublished paper presented September 25, 2009, at Boston College and April 8, 2011, at Loyola University Chicago.

37 Tracy, *Plurality and Ambiguity*, 20.

38 Tracy, *Plurality and Ambiguity*, 18.

39 Tracy, *Plurality and Ambiguity*, 32.

sui generis quality that religious classics expressed. The "first key" of an authentic religious classic was its function "as a final, now gracious, now frightening, now trustworthy, now absurd, always uncontrollable limit-of the very meaning of existence itself."[40] There was no better way to protect theological conversation from banality than by allowing all expressions that bespoke this absurdity to remain as absurd today as they have always been.

Tracy suggested that various "political theologies of praxis—of hope, of liberation, even of revolution"—could provide a contemporary retrieval of historic theological expressions worthy of the name "Christological." These expressions not only "strongly informed the present theological moment."[41] They also demanded a critique of society and a critique of the critique itself—a critique of the symbols, categories, truths, and language of the theological point of view from which societal critiques emerge. "A critical reappropriation of the symbols of Christian eschatological liberation, once united to a critical reformulation of the symbols God, Christ, and revelation, might free the imagination of the politically committed Christian and non-Christian alike to find symbols representative of their struggle for full-scale liberation."[42] The revisionist theologian aimed to expand previous theological limitations by way of new resources in social, philosophical, historical, and scientific disciplines.

An authentic appropriation of those Christomorphic religious classics highlighted the explicitly religious urge "to focus, confirm, correct, challenge, confront, and transform my present questions, expectations, reflections on life and all my attempts to live a life worthy of the name 'human.'"[43] For Tracy, preserving the uncanniness of the Christ protected against our tendency to forget the many repressed voices that were in actuality closest to the "pristine" Christology of Tertullian. Forms of expression allowing an appropriate retrieval of this disruptive Christology included the so-called "masters of suspicion," critical philosophers, apocalyptic theologians, marginalized narratives, black spirituals, theologies of liberation, Martin Luther's dialectics, and the apophatic theologies of Christian mystics. The Christ event was best retrieved by empowering such critical expressions and making them alive in newly disruptive moments today.

The religious classic as fragment: retrieval as critique

In Tracy's most recent reflections on theological form, he has engaged fully with this disruptive nature of the religious classic by shifting his terminology. Instead of using his earlier "religious classics," Tracy refers now to intense religious expression as "fragment." Still utilizing a version of the transcendental–phenomenological mode of analysis that has informed so much of his theological career, Tracy calls fragments

---

40 Tracy, *Blessed Rage for Order*, 108.
41 Tracy, *Blessed Rage for Order*, 240.
42 Tracy, *Blessed Rage for Order*, 247.
43 Tracy, *Analogical Imagination*, 326.

the "spiritual situation of our times."[44] The existence of fragments reminds the philosopher–theologian that we no longer live in a situation of modern essentialism. "There is no longer a Western cultural center with margins. There are many centers now."[45] This means that the categories "postmodernity" and "modernity" need to be rethought according to the variety of repressed narratives that have informed our understanding. Instead of facilitating a conversation where such forms remain on the margins, revolving around centers of power, the stereotypically marginalized are brought into the center of discussion. They are the discussion.

Such historically excluded forms of religious expression inform theology in two ways. First, fragments embody a "negative" function, insofar as they "show the need to shatter any reigning totality system."[46] Aware of the connection between totalizing frameworks and marginalization, defenders of the fragment maintain, "any form which attempts totality or closure . . . needs fragmentation."[47] Second, fragments serve a "positive" function. They point to "a break out of totality into infinity" by disclosing "one's own routes and one's own traditions."[48] Fragments are narratival, experiential, and emotive. They function as a unitary moment of productive distanciation, where form and content are united in an explosive expression of particularity. When such portrayals are received with sympathy, the interpreter may discern a means by which "all the others and the different" function "as possible disclosures of infinity."[49] Through a fragmentary form of expression, the subject insists, "Do not reduce me or anyone else to your narrative."[50]

Fragmentary religious expressions provide the most non-reductive space for theological retrieval, so long as they preserve the intensity and disruptive nature of Christology. For example, Tracy says, in "the intense religion of the black church traditions," one finds the "unassimilatable other," where "repressed, intense, saturated, and fragmentary religious forms" break through in an explosive claim to recognition.[51] Exemplified in the demand for liberation and justice, "the God of black religion is a fragmentary, liberating God."[52] Here, the fragment engenders not only "a shattering of any totality system" but also "the possibility of positive rediscovery of the intense presence of infinity in religious forms."[53] It is not accurate to assume that religion "must always enter the rooms of modernity without warmth and leave without regret."[54] That, Tracy says, "is not religion."[55] Religion

44 Tracy, "Fragments: The Spiritual Situation of Our Times," 170–84.
45 Tracy, "Fragments: The Spiritual Situation of Our Times," 170.
46 Tracy, "African-American Thought," 29–30.
47 Tracy, "Form and Fragment," 64–5.
48 Tracy, "African-American Thought," 30.
49 Tracy, "African-American Thought," 30
50 Tracy, "Fragments and Form," 124.
51 Tracy, "African-American Thought," 30.
52 Tracy, "African-American Thought," 30.
53 Tracy, "African-American Thought," 30.
54 Tracy, "African-American Thought," 33.
55 Tracy, "African-American Thought," 33.

is vibrant, particularly in its most disruptive, excessive forms (gospel songs, love mystics, cabalists, Sufis, and gospel music), and it is indeed the recovery of these excessive forms that has energized so many recent projects of resistance.

When gathered together into new modes of Christomorphism, these expressions are not merely anti-totalities but "fragments of hope."[56] They demand redemption and motivate believing communities toward resistance of oppressive structures. Fragmentary narratives—more typically forgotten than centralized— provide "hints and guesses of hope . . . glimpses of light and redemption."[57] It is particularly these narratives that provide an appropriate resource for "our desiccated public realm"[58] and that empower a potent corrective to the universalizing tendencies of so many other modes of retrieval. It is only in preserving that fragmentary form that appropriate forms of retrieval can take place today. By representing such Christomorphic expressions, the theologian helps reorient our shared conversations to that fundamental dimension of life in which we sense a "wholeness of meaning to all our basic activities."[59] Fragmentary religious classics disclose hope-filled modes of existence that lay dormant in our ownmost but unrecognized potential. And by highlighting isomorphic and analogous tendencies among them, including those in the present, the theologian is able to facilitate numerous, always-arriving, never-arrived moments of agreement in the ongoing conversation that we call Christian theology.

Conclusion

Including David Tracy in a consideration of theologies of retrieval opens up the way to a theology of retrieval as critique. Tracy's career began with a concern to protect the unique trajectory toward truth that characterized the theological project. But it concluded with an awareness that truth may be best preserved by centralizing modes of expression that are not often given a place at the theological table. Tracy refused to compromise the irreducibility of both historic and contemporary religious expressions by placing openness and self-critique at the center of theological method. If the desire to protect a particular tradition results in an inability to engage that tradition in substantial dialogue, then that tradition must be considered suspect. Further, if the desire to open up a tradition to critical

---

56 This phrase is borrowed from Susan Ross, "Evil and Hope: Foundational Moral Perspectives," *CTSA Proceedings* 50 (1995): 46–63. In this response to Tracy, Ross observes that even in the profound suffering recalled in the passion narratives, the attentive reader may find "fragments of hope." Such fragments inform a "hope for moral responses that are both cognizant of the ambiguity of all of human efforts in the face of evil yet refuse to let evil have the final say" (60).

57 Tracy, "African-American Thought," 37–8.

58 Tracy, "African-American Thought," 37–8.

59 Tracy, *Blessed Rage for Order*, 134.

evaluation results in an uncritical uptake of dominating forms of history—theological or otherwise—then that desire must also be considered suspect. However, if retrieval rests within the mutually critical space where a trajectory toward shared awareness meets a trajectory toward criticism, where universality and particularity engage, then the theologian can engage in a theology of retrieval that is simultaneously historical and contemporary, fundamental and systematic, God centered and Christomorphic.

As stated at the outset of this chapter, there is indeed something about the past that is compelling for Christians. Christians believe that, in spite of the many abuses of history, God is made present in and through history and can be discerned by appropriately retrieving history. Tracy provides a helpful corrective to theologies of retrieval that exacerbate new forms of marginalization. As a fundamental theologian, Tracy insists that theologies of retrieval engage in the difficult task of making and evaluating truth claims, including a critical evaluation of the very theologies being retrieved. But as a systematic theologian, Tracy inserts particular theological concepts into the potentially dominating universal tendencies of fundamental theology. An attentiveness to truth can—indeed, should—be carried out in dialogue with those "uncanny" religious expressions that we now see broke through the easy perpetuation of "more of the same." Historic moments of explosive, always timely, and consistently disruptive expressions of authentic religion provide fodder for a re-presentation of Christianity's central theological concepts, including God, Jesus Christ, and sin. Such concepts are best retrieved by re-appropriating those classic religious expressions that elude easy assimilation and that empower movements of resistance and hope today. For theologians who intend to retrieve the quintessentially Christian expression of faith, namely the life and resurrection of the Christ they worship, they would do well to follow Tracy's lead—insisting that all theologies of retrieval be as conversant, disruptive, and true as the God they believe Jesus revealed.

Chapter 19

RESTORATION, RETRIEVAL, AND RENEWAL: RECOVERING HEALING MINISTRY IN THE CHURCH— SOME CRITICAL REFLECTIONS*

The Very Reverend Professor Martyn Percy, dean of Christ Church, Oxford

One of the defining hallmarks of fundamentalist communities is the claim to be "biblical." The reasoning runs simply and clearly, and as follows: things that were practiced and believed in the time of the apostles are now, once again, to be found among the "chosen" or the sanctified gathering of the faithful. Put another way, it has taken this new group of true believers to recover or retrieve a lost element or authentic practice from the early church—one that the wider church had either forgotten, neglected, or perhaps even repressed. Thus, the wider church, typically, is narrated as heterodox, distracted, or, at best, lacking in focus. But in the new community of the sanctified—the newly inaugurated biblical church—God's original intentions and blessing are restored.

This chapter is concerned with a trinity of practical-pastoral theological questions. First, to what extent are the healing ministries—ones that are so prevalent in contemporary charismatic evangelicalism—different from those practiced in the Gospels? Second, can the claims to have restored or retrieved the charism of healing ministry in the ministry of Jesus, and in that of the early church, really be corroborated? Third, are the healings of the late twentieth-century and early twenty-first-century evangelicalism and revivalism really the same kind of phenomena that might have been witnessed in the eighteenth century? To help us pursue this investigation, we draw, both empathetically and critically, on the work and ministry of John Wimber (1934–1997), a key figure in charismatic evangelicalism, revivalism, and healing ministries, who enjoyed a particular international following in the latter half of the twentieth century. Wimber articulated his theological rationale as follows:

---

* This chapter draws upon and develops ideas originally aired in my earlier M. Percy, *Words, Wonders and Power: Understanding Contemporary Christian Fundamentalism and Revivalism* (London: SPCK, 1996) and *Power and the Church: Ecclesiology in an Age of Transition* (London: Cassell, 1997).

One of the Protestant Reformation's key contributions to the church was the recovery of the centrality of the Bible in the Christian life . . . If we are serious about the Reformation doctrine—an idea found in the scripture—that the church reformed is always reforming, we must make room for practices like divine healing in the modern church. Divine healing undeniably was part of Christ's ministry and something that he expected the church to experience (today).[1]

Such reasoning found its purest expression in the United Kingdom within (so-called) restorationism—a movement that gave birth to house churches and other forms of communitarian Christianity from the 1960s. Restorationists believed that God no longer had much purpose for mainstream denominations. Instead, claimed those within the restorationist movement, God was restoring his kingdom in these latter days, and new, purer forms of Christian discipleship would emerge, in preparation for and anticipation of Christ's imminent return. Restorationists stressed separatism (from other churches) and claimed to be restoring the original, true church that God had intended from the time of the apostles. The new house churches emphasized charismatic epiphenomena such as healing, deliverance, and speaking in tongues. They also stressed the restoration of "original" patterns of church leadership, including apostles, prophets, and healers.[2]

Alongside the development of restorationism, and from the postwar era onward, the emergence of charismatic evangelicals also led to a renewed interest in prophecy, deliverance and healing ministries—and in particular, there being some sense in which divine healing could be reclaimed as a fundamental charism of the true church. My doctoral study focused on fundamentalism and revivalism, and part of this work involved the habitual attending of healing meetings—as an observer, observing participant, participant observer, and sometimes just participant. I kept notes. I was absorbed by the dynamics of the gatherings and by the claims.

My purpose was not to investigate whether or not the claims to be healed were true or false—for theologians cannot know such things.[3] Rather, the question was, what do these healing encounters and stories *mean* to those who are gathered? I would listen to eloquent sermons and testimonies from healers, who would tell you that Jesus could heal anyone and anything. (I would then watch them take off their spectacles, put them carefully in their top pocket, and invite people to come to the front for ministry—so the failing sight of the preacher seemed not to bother

---

1   John Wimber, *Power Healing* (London: Hodder & Stoughton, 1986), 245.

2   On this, see Andrew Walker, *Restoring the Kingdom* (London: Hodder & Stoughton, 1985).

3   There are studies that purport to "prove" miracles, and since the late twentieth-century, sympathetic treatises that explore claims of healing have been undertaken by, among others, David Lewis, *Healing: Fiction, Fantasy or Fact?* (London: Hodder & Stoughton, 1986) and Rex Gardner, *Healing Miracles? A Doctor Investigates* (London: Darton, Longman and Todd, 1986).

them or their audience). I would puzzle over how illnesses were described and addressed. Some of the things I saw and heard were profoundly moving. Some were troubling and disturbing. Others were risible or just plain odd. Testimonies varied in scope, ranging from minor illnesses, diseases, or conditions cured to stupendous claims of lost organs regrown (e.g., eyes, arms, and so on), cancers removed, and the dead raised.[4]

But I suppose what caused me to struggle was the refusal of most speakers and preachers to readily acknowledge the relationship between cause and effect, unless it could be tied to something personal and moral. Yet according to the World Health Organization, well over 90 percent of the illnesses and diseases on this planet have a single cause: poverty. We lose five million children a year, under the age of two, to perfectly preventable malaria-related fever. Clean the nearby water supply, and you eradicate the breeding grounds for the mosquitos that spread the disease. I sat through many healing meetings that described many individuals recovering instantly and miraculously from a fever. But inside I protested all the while that, even if that were true, it was quite pointless when the *causes* of fever were not addressed.

In the United Kingdom, obesity is now one of our biggest threats to health, and one of our biggest killers. Yet it is not a disease of the rich but the poor. Maps of the United Kingdom spell out the demographics of obesity plainly. The concentrations of obesity lie in our poorest and most disadvantaged communities. I have attended many healing meetings that have been beautiful, pastoral, and powerful. But I have never visited one in which anyone returned to their home ten stone lighter. (The dieting industry would be ruined if this happened). A recent map of Scotland, produced in September 2014,[5] showed that the concentrations of population voting "yes" to independence correlated precisely with earlier maps that chart concentrations of obesity (i.e., parts of Glasgow, Dundee, and so on).[6] In turn, those maps of obesity also correlated precisely with indices of poverty and unemployment. And the maps charting the related consequences—cancers, heart conditions, and diabetes—follow in their wake. The areas in Scotland that voted "no" to independence were, unsurprisingly, the wealthiest and healthiest.

Yet one of the most interesting things about the Gospels and the New Testament is the way in which they play with our sense of perspective. They make us see ourselves differently—and others, and the wider world. We are asked to read more deeply, and see relations, cause and effect, consequences, and the like, differently, more wisely, and with deeper compassion. Perhaps it is this that makes us pause and reflect, and adopt some appropriate caution (note, not doubt) in relation those

4 See Ian Cotton, *The Hallelujah Revolution* (London: Little-Brown Publishing, 1995), ix–xiii.

5 Christine Jeavens, "In Maps: How Close Was the Scottish Referendum Vote?" BBC News, September 19, 2014, http://www.bbc.co.uk/news/uk-scotland-scotland-politics-29255449.

6 "Map Highlights 'Obesity Hotspots," BBC News, August 27, 2008, http://news.bbc.co.uk/1/hi/health/7584191.stm

exponents of healing ministries that would claim to read the Bible "literally," and as a "program" or "blueprint" for how to heal today, and how to retrieve the healing ministries of Jesus and the first apostles.

Our chapter began with a quote from Wimber, and the claims made in his key books *Power Evangelism* (1985) and *Power Healing* (1986), and in many of his conferences and recorded talks, suggest that he read the epiphenomena that were present in his own revivalist gatherings and "healing clinics" as more or less identical to the observations made at the revival meetings of John and Charles Wesley, Jonathan Edwards, George Whitefield, Charles Finney, and others.[7] But close attention to detail highlights some interesting differences:

CONTRASTS IN REVIVALS

Phenomena	Eighteenth- and Nineteenth-Century Revivals	Late Twentieth- and Twenty-First-Century Revivals
Particular aspect of God being focused upon:	The holiness of God and the need for individuals/the church to likewise have sins forgiven	The healing power of God, and the need for individuals/the church to likewise
Primary needs of respondents to message:	To have sins forgiven	To be physically/emotionally healed and/or empowered
Falling down at meetings or being "slain in the Spirit":	Individuals usually fall on their faces, as in the Bible (Mt 7:16; Lk 5:8; Acts 9:4; 1 Cor 14:25	Individuals usually fall on their backs
When manifestation occurred:	During preaching	During a "clinic"/ministry
Attitude of preacher:	Wesley did not encourage the phenomenon, often ignoring it	Very much encouraged
Congregational proxemics:	People fell down on their own, sometimes involuntarily, or as a conscious response to a particular conviction	Individuals fall down once others have gathered around them and prayed for them during a clinic
Reaction of preacher to people being "slain in the Spirit":	Wesley claims he ignored them or had them carried away	Fallen person becomes focus of activity, since this is where the Spirit is "resting"

7 See John Wimber, *Power Evangelism* (London: Hodder & Stoughton, 1985), 37.

Of course, this table does not mean late twentieth- and early twenty-first-century revivals are bogus in their claims to divine power. It simply shows the discrepancies in social and historical hermeneutics. So the questions I seek to raise in this chapter are particularly important when one considers the emphasis placed on miracles by some movements within contemporary Christianity. Since the early 1980s, the influential Signs and Wonders movement has held that public demonstrations of the miraculous may be a preeminent form of evangelism. Those at the hub of the movement urged churches to practice the miraculous in their congregations and beyond, in order to verify that the power and presence of God was manifestly within them. The premise was that this represented a restoration—or the retrieval—of God's purposes for the church and the world in these "latter days." Sometimes, the claims made by such groups in respect of being able to reproduce the miraculous lay beyond boundaries of credibility. Claims were made that the dead were raised, the chronically and terminally ill healed, the handicapped "made whole," and global disasters accurately predicted, with revivals following.[8]

Contemporary charismatic renewal has witnessed a surge in specifically spiritual healing methods. A number of healers claimed that they were operating within a "revival tradition" that can be traced back to the New Testament but pointed to specific periods of history when the church had retrieved its healing mandate. However, this account of history depends more than a little on literal and naive readings of the past. Although relatively little has been done in terms of intellectual evaluation of the revival, the field is wide open for a range of assessments.[9]

Granted, evaluating the effectiveness of methods of healing is an important medical, theological, and phenomenological task. But my main contention is that the Signs and Wonders movement was not a retrieval of the lost charism of healing to the church. Rather, it was a bourgeois spiritualization of divine power, focused on individuals rather than on those alienating social, religious, and political cultures that Jesus's healings invariably challenged. The "Signs and Wonders" movement primarily blessed those who already had health, wealth, status—and more besides. Jesus's healings were very seldom directed toward individuals within such societal strata.

I am conscious that this is a serious charge, but it can be defended by attending to the following hypothetical example. Suppose a middle-aged man attends a healing meeting at which charismatic healing ministry is offered. At the close of

---

8 The Signs and Wonders movement saw itself as part of the "Third Wave" of the Holy Spirit in the twentieth century, and with the Second Wave being the charismatic renewal of the 1960s and 1970s. The Signs and Wonders movement regarded healing miracles as the fount of a growing, successful church, and promoted revival and renewal across denominational boundaries. Leading exponents included Wimber, Peter Wagner, Bill Surbritzky, and Morris Cerullo. More recently, the revivalist preacher Todd Bentley has claimed that dozens of people have been raised form the dead through his ministry, with other healings including divine liver transplants and cancers eliminated.

9 See Stephen Pattison, *Alive and Kicking* (London: SCM, 1989), 50

the meeting he is approached by someone who claims to have a word from God for him, about his chest pains. The man is astonished at the accuracy of the prophecy; he does indeed suffer acute chest pains. He is prayed for, feels "touched by God," and returns home rejoicing. But his problems really begin here: he returns to his home, which happens to be on one of the most depressed and crime-ridden housing estates; unemployment is very high, community amenities scarce, and debt and stress-related poor health common. He takes up smoking again, and his pains soon return: his smoking is related to his stress, which is in turn related to his social conditions. Globally, the biggest single cause of illness and disease is poverty.

In the example above, the pain may well be psychosomatic, but no true healing can take root until the social conditions are materially transformed. (If this is true for the man in our example, how much more true is it for the millions who suffer illness because of experiencing malnutrition, living in slum conditions, or being the victims of war). In contrast, a Signs and Wonders approach to healing generally dealt with inner or unseen transformations in middle-class groupings. The kind of healings claimed were usually for things that could neither be seen nor tested: headaches, backaches, heart problems, or depression were typical. Mention of social transformation, however, as a basis for any healing, especially for the poor, was very rare.

But my purpose here for the moment is not to examine whether or not modern Christian healing methods "work." Clearly, many people believe they do. What is perhaps of more importance is to inquire into the original purpose of miracles, particularly those in the Gospels. I wish to argue that the task of miracles in the Gospels primarily has more to do with social, political, and ethical considerations rather than with naked demonstrations of divine power simply intervening in often tragic human situations—with consequent implications for their audiences and the disciples, and, therefore, for the church today.[10]

Rereading healing in the Gospels: comparing and contrasting

Jesus's healing ministry as recorded in the Gospels appears to be extremely discriminating. On only four occasions is a healing recorded in a building used for religious purposes (see Mk 1:23–27, Mk 3:1–5, Mt 21:14, and Lk 13:10–13, and their synoptic parallels). In two of these four cases, it is a woman who is healed, whose actual right to be there must be in some question. In every other case, healings by Jesus take place outside any community of faith, except where "crowds" or the poor are deemed by an evangelist to constitute a group of faithful

---

10 In saying "primarily," I would like to make it clear from the outset that I am not claiming to have constructed a complete scheme for interpreting miracles in the Gospels; there will be exceptions to the rule. Equally, miracles in the Old Testament and in Acts have not been considered, which some readers may also find problematic

people.[11] Jesus's friends or relatives are not usually the beneficiaries of his healing power either.[12] In fact, of those who are healed, we know little, not even a name, and certainly nothing of the long-term response of those who are healed.

This may be partly due to the fact that those who are healed are either poor, voiceless, marginalized, or despised within society. The form of healing as engendered by Jesus is also ambiguous, extending well beyond physical changes in a person. So, Zacchaeus has his status within his community challenged through a symbolic gesture initiated by Christ, which called into question the "demonizing" tendencies of a hostile public in response to an unfair tax (Lk 19:1–10).[13]

Others are forgiven before they can even confess their sin (e.g., Lk 7:36ff and Jn 8:1–11), resulting in a form of healing. Where some would indict the individual sinner, Jesus seems to recognize the corporate and societal pressures that create the wrong. The equation between sin and suffering is one that Jesus seems to question rather than endorse.[14]

11 On this, see Stefan Alkier and Annette Weissenrieder, eds., *Miracles Revisited: New Testament Miracle Stories and Their Concept of Reality* (Berlin: De Gruyter, 2013).

12 Exceptions to what I have stated above are few. Peter's mother-in-law is possibly a friend of Jesus and is healed (Mt 8:14–15; Mk 1:30–31; Lk 4:38–39). However, she may have been a widow, and therefore her status as that may be more significant. Mary Magdalene is healed (Lk 8:2), but the precise nature of her affliction is unclear. Lazarus is raised to life (Jn 11:1–44), and is, according to John, "beloved" of Jesus. However, caution should be exercised when reading parts of the Gospel of John: its allegorical and apologetic directionality suggest that it is not always to be treated as "literal history" (see 1:1–18, 20:30–31, 21:24–25, and so on). This is not to say that the Gospel is "untrue", just the contrary. The Fourth Evangelist is clearly aiming at revealing the Truth (i.e., Christ) in his work, while being faithful to the historical Jesus. Yet the Gospel is more than history. The "I AM" sayings are, I think, more allegorical than historical, and the raising of Lazarus may be a "myth" (i.e., a story that is "true" on the inside but not necessarily on the outside, like a parable) that is a vehicle for affirming Jesus as the Resurrection and the Life—a "confessional story," in effect. We should note that John the Baptist is not healed by Jesus, in spite of their closeness (Mt 14:1, Mk 6:14, Lk 9:7ff). Nor should we forget that Jesus seems to be unable to heal the victims of natural disasters (Lk 13:1–5) or massacres (Mt 3: 16ff). These instances raise important theological questions about the limits of Jesus's healing ministry: what sort of things could he not do?

13 We should note that Zacchaeus does not concede that he has cheated the public in taxation. Luke records Zacchaeus as saying, "if" he has overcharged anyone on tax—note, "if"—he will repay fourfold. He also volunteers half his wealth to the poor. The text clearly implies that although the crowd thinks Zacchaeus is a crook, he is in fact an honest tax collector, grateful that Jesus has refused to collude with his demonization and marginalization.

14 For further reflection, see the discussion of Lk 13:1–5, especially verse 2, "Do you suppose that these Galileans were greater sinners than all the others in Galilee, because they suffered this fate?", in Joseph Fitzmyer's commentary (*The Gospel According to Luke*

In virtually every healing story—and there are over forty in the Gospels—the person healed is politically, socially, or religiously disadvantaged—unloved or unnoticed by the majority of onlookers or witnesses. The Gospel miracles, then, are a record of Christ reaching out to the marginalized, dispossessed, cast out, and cursed in society and from faith communities. Christ seems to embrace those that society deems to be untouchable. There is even a sense of urgency about this within the context of the Messianic mission. The woman healed of a crippling infirmity in Lk 13:10–17 is healed on the Sabbath: first-century Rabbinism allowed for such healing, but only when there was danger of death, which the narrative strongly suggests was not the case. Fitzmyer describes this healing as "the welfare of a human being [taking] precedence over . . . religious obligations."[15] The thrust of the narrative is to contrast the jealousy or skepticism of the "leader of the synagogue" (v. 14) with the plight of the "daughter of Abraham": Jesus emerges as Lord of the synagogue and Sabbath in the space of seven verses—a healer whose responsiveness and urgency of ministry reflects his overall mission.

Other commentators have suggested that the link between healing and the forgiveness of sins must be linked to the perceptions of onlookers. In effect, it is only for this reason that the Gospels reflect the linkage: they are not trying to make a theological point but rather to subvert a commonly held premise.[16] Not only that, but authors such as Anton Fridrichsen, Norman Geisler, and Ernst and Marie-Luise Keller suggest that the act of repeating a miracle may diminish its value, relegating it to the ranks of thaumaturgy.[17]

The Kellers' exegetical readings allow them to see miracles as "signs" that had a unique function, which in turn have been imbued with a unique status.[18] But their shrewd analysis of the treatment of miracles in philosophical theology and biblical literature places them in a good position to discuss the "reality" of miracles. They see them as something localized [from] beyond this world . . . concentrated in mysterious centres of action. They are primarily revelations that point to the ultimate dissolution between the "natural" and "supernatural" order, but this dissolution is held in the crucified, raised, and ascended Christ, which is not always consonant with the activity of the church.[19] In short, they are part of the created order, but are not *supra*-creation in terms of eschatology. As such, critiques of their function and place are to be welcomed.

X–XXIV, Anchor Bible Commentary 28a (New York: Doubleday, 1985), 103ff). Fitzmyer points out that when the "sin-suffering equation" is pressed by Jesus's audience, Jesus turns the question on its head to speak about the need for all to repent. Cf. Lk 13:36ff.

15 Fitzmyer, *Gospel According to Luke X–XXIV*, 101.

16 See Anton Fridrichsen, *The Problem of Miracle in Early Christianity* (Minneapolis: Augsburg Publishing House, 1972).

17 See Norman Geisler, *Miracles and Modern Thought* (Grand Rapids, MI: Zondervan, 1982), and Ernst and Marie-Luise Keller, *Miracles in Dispute* (Philadelphia: Fortress Press, 1968).

18 Ernst and Marie-Luise Keller, *Miracles in Dispute*, 226–40.

19 Ernst and Marie-Luise Keller, *Miracles in Dispute*, 241ff.

By way of comparison, much of what passes for charismatic healing move-ments in today's church is very different. Evangelists and healers who offer min-istry usually do so in the context of a church or "faith gathering." The ministry on offer is inward looking, intended for those who join or become members. It largely leaves the dispossessed and marginalized of society alone. Where they are included, the terms are often strictly defined, whereas those who were encompassed by Jesus's healing ministry had no obstacles placed in their way, at least by him. The modern healing movement only appears to work for believ-ers, or to make people believe who would not otherwise. Frequently, those who claim to be healed already possess significant social, moral or religious status, whereas the healings of Jesus seem to be directed at people who are exactly the opposite.[20]

In fact, Jesus, both in parable (e.g., Luke 15—the prodigal son) and activity (Luke 7—the woman at Simon's house), demonstrates the importance of the assur-ance of forgiveness being offered *before* the respondent can speak or confess their sin. The Gospels seem to be saying that you can only truly confess once you have heard the words of absolution. In contrast, many exponents within contemporary charismatic healing movements would insist on confession of sin as a precondi-tion to being offered healing ministry.

In saying this, I am not dismissing accounts where sin and sickness are bound up together. For example, Mt 9:2–7 records the paralytic, where Jesus originally says to the man, "Your sins are forgiven." The teachers of the law, scandalized by this, question Jesus's authority to forgive, upon which Jesus simply instructs the man to walk, which he does. The social construction of reality concerning the relationship between sin and sickness in Jesus's day was complex, involving processes of hereditary curse, personal responsibility, third-party blaming, and psychosomatic causes. Jesus's attitude to the perceived cause-and-effect relation-ship between sin and sickness is, to say the least, ambiguous; he simultaneously rejects and accepts it, treating it almost playfully at times. It is not unfair to sug-gest that when he does appear to acknowledge it, agreement with the link is not necessarily implied.[21]

The disparities between the way in which Jesus conducted his healing min-istry and the way in which modern healers usually proceed are numerous. However, as the table below shows, what is perhaps more striking, when com-pared to the subsequent list of healing miracles, are the *types* of people healed by Jesus and the consequent implications for the church in "liberal" and "con-servative" spheres.

---

20 The question on the social status of people who are healed is a contentious one. Wimber's healing meetings seem to primarily cater to white American, European, and Commonwealth middle-class people. But other healers do operate in different racial and social contexts with equally dramatic effects. For a fuller discussion of this see my *Words, Wonders and Power* (London: SPCK, 1996).

21 Fitzmyer, *Gospel According to Luke X-XXIV*, 103ff.

TYPOLOGIES OF PEOPLE AND GROUPS HEALED IN THE GOSPELS

1 The "demonized" (by society?), the mentally ill, and therefore ostracized from society and faith community (1,9,17,21,22).
2. The handicapped—marginalized in society—due to inability to function or fit in "normally" (6,7,15,16,18,40).
3. Lepers and other "untouchables"—banned from society (5,11,34).
4. Children and widows—little social status (10,14,17,30,38). [Also single mothers: 14?,30]
5. Women adjudged "unclean" through sin/sickness (11,31,32; see also Luke 7, John 4 and John 8).
6. Others judged to be ill through sin (40; but possibly the case with most sickness—see John 9).
7. People of other faiths (14,19,34,38).
8. "Multitudes"—seemingly indiscriminate, except insofar as the Gospel writers use the term "multitude" to refer to those excluded from "normal" religious activity and the poor in society. They are to be distinguished from the religious of the day such as the Pharisee and Saducee "denominations" as well as elders, scribes, and priests (3, 13, 23, 24, 25, 26, 27, 28, 36, 37).

AN OVERVIEW OF THE HEALING MINISTRY OF JESUS

Description	Matt	Mark	Luke	John
1 Man with unclean spirit		1:21–28	4:31–37	
2 Peter's mother-in-law	8:14–15	1:30–31	4:38–39	
3 Multitudes	8:16–17	1:32–34	4:40–41	
4 Many demons		1:39		
5 Leper	8:2–4	1:40–42	5:12–13	
6 Man with palsy	9:2–8	2:3–12	5:17–26	
7 Man with withered hand	12:9–14	3:1–6	6:6–11	
8 Multitudes	12:15–16	3:10–11		
9 Gaderene demoniac	8:28–34	5:1–17	8:26–39	
10 Jairus's daughter	9:18–19, 23–26	5:22–24, 35–43	8:40–42, 49–56	
11 Woman with bleeding	9:20–22	5:24b–34	8:42b–48	

Description	Matt	Mark	Luke	John
12 A few sick people	13:58	6:5–6		
13 Multitudes	14:34–36	6:54–56		
14 Syrophoenician's daughter	15:21–28	7:24–30		
15 Deaf and dumb man		7:31–37		
16 Blind man		8:22–26		
17 Child with evil spirit	17:14–18	9:14–27	9:38–43	
18 Blind Bartemaeus	20:29–34	10:46–52	8:35–43	
19 Centurion's servant	8:5–13		7:1–10	
20 Two blind men	9:27–31			
21 Dumb demoniac	9:32–34			
22 Blind and dumb demoniac	12:22		11:14	
23 Multitudes	4:23		6:17–19	
24 Multitudes	9:35			
25 Multitudes	11:4–5		7:21–22	
26 Multitudes	14:14		9:11	6:2
27 Great multitudes	15:30			
28 Great multitudes	19:2			
29 Blind and lame in temple	21:14			
30 Widow's son			7:11–17	
31 Mary Magdalene + others			8:2	
32 Woman bound by Satan			13:10–13	
33 Man with dropsy			14:1–4	
34 Ten lepers			17:11–19	
35 Malchus's ear			22:49–51	
36 Multitudes			5:15	
37 Various persons			13:52	
38 Nobleman's son				4:46–53
39 Invalid man				5:1–9
40 Man born blind				9:1–7

The types of people and groups listed in the table have their modern equivalents, and it is clear that the overwhelming focus of Jesus's ministry lay with the poor, the unknown, and the excluded of his day. So, the healings themselves can be seen as activity that characterizes the love of God for the forsaken and the damned, especially those who are victims of religious, moral, and societal exclusion. This love even extends to including those of other faiths, with no conditions attached; nobody becomes a Christian in the Gospels or is compelled to believe anything because of a miracle. The activity therefore stands as a literal as well as a symbolic sign of God's love for the oppressed, and questions the role of religion and society in colluding with or instigating that oppression.

As Mary Grey says, the healings of Jesus are "characterised by a redemptive mutuality in which people come into their own."[22] This is endorsed in some of Jesus's encounters with others even where a physical healing does not take place. Mention has already been made of Zacchaeus, and, as Jean-Jacques Suurmond points out, the Gospels are full of playful political subversion and "social healings": "tax collectors become Robin Hoods who returned their money to the poor; common sluts become princesses of the resurrection preaching."[23]

Therefore to focus on repeating miracles as demonstrative acts and reifications of divine power for today—trying to retrieve or restore the performance and practice of healing miracles—essentially misses the original context and target of Jesus's healings, which had radical political, social, and religious dynamics that were usually missed in their day, but that should not be ignored for now.[24]

Healing as taking on affliction

There is a further dimension to the healings of Jesus that should be mentioned, which places his ministry in sharp contrast to much of today's charismatic healing movements. It is the notion that there is some sense in which Jesus takes on the suffering and affliction of the individuals he cures, such that it becomes

---

22 Mary Grey, *Redeeming the Dream* (London: SPCK, 1989), 51.

23 Although I dislike the word "slut" in this quote, it nonetheless serves its purpose. See Jean-Jacques Suurmond, *Word and Spirit at Play* (London: SCM, 1993), 51.

24 On this point, we note Richard Hooker's critique of the Puritans, dated to the late sixteenth century. In the preface to the *Lawes of Ecclesiastical Polity*, Hooker argues against the Puritan claim that church life should be based only on what is demonstrably proven by scriptural precedent. This endeavor, contends Hooker, is wrongly conceived and impossible to carry out:

> what was used in the Apostles' times, the Scripture fully declareth not; so that making their times the rule and canon of church-polity, ye make a rule, which being not possible to be fully known, is as impossible to be kept . . . in this general proposing of the Apostolical times, there is no certainty which should be followed: especially seeing that ye give us great cause to doubt how far ye allow these times. (Preface 4:3–4—see

part of him. This view would not have been strange to the early church fathers, whose progressive move toward a richly incarnational theology required them to conclude that what was not assumed could not be redeemed. So, Jesus risks social ostracization when he dines with Zacchaeus, consorts with sinners, and receives women of dubious repute into his company, precisely in order to take on their brokenness as well as take on the taboos of society that maintain structures that divorce the secular and sacred.

As Janet Soskice has pointed out, it is no different in the healing miracles themselves. Noting the story of the hemorrhaging woman in Lk 8:40–56 (compare Mk 5:21–43 and Mt 9:18–34), she points out that what is striking about it is Jesus's willingness to touch or be touched by an "impure" woman. Although modern readers of the text may find this aspect of the narrative difficult, the significance of Jesus's action should not be underestimated: "she defiled the teacher which, according to Levitical law, she would have done for she was in a state of permanent uncleanness, polluting everyone and everything with whom she came into contact."[25] Her poverty—"she had spent all she had"—is a direct result of her affliction. Yet Jesus, apart from healing her, also seems to challenge the social and religious forces that have rendered this woman "contagious." Jesus calls her "daughter" in all three accounts, and all three evangelists stress the woman's faith. Interestingly, the Synoptic accounts of the hemorrhaging woman are all paired with the raising of Jairus's daughter. Again, the issues of impurity (touching a corpse) and of menstruation occur: the girl is twelve, and her untimely death clearly prevents her from entering womanhood. Jesus declares her "not dead, but sleeping," and his touch, resulting in his defilement, raises the girl.

Frank Kermode's work has important resonances with the observations made by Soskice.[26] Kermode's discussion of the purity issues in Mark 5 picks up on the fact that the stories of the hemorrhaging woman and Jairus's daughter have been paired and conflated.[27] Kermode cites as evidence for this the undue prominence Mark gives to the narrative by the sharing of the number "twelve" (the girl is twelve, and the woman has also been ill for twelve years):

> this coincidence signifies a narrative relation of some kind between the woman and the girl . . . an older woman is cured of a menstrual disorder of twelve years'

Hooker's *Laws of Ecclesiastical Polity*, Everyman Edition, vol. 1 [London: J. M. Dent, 1954], 108–9); italics added.

25 I am indebted to Dr. Janet Soskice for some of these insights, in her (unpublished) paper "Blood and Defilement," given at the annual conference of the Society for the Study of Theology, Oxford, UK, April 1994.

26 See Frank Kermode, *The Genesis of Secrecy: On the Interpretation of Narrative* (Cambridge, MA: Harvard University Press, 1979).

27 See also Ched Myers, *Binding the Strong Man: A Political Reading of Mark's Story of Jesus* (Maryknoll, NY: Orbis Books, 1988/2012).

standing, and is sent back into society. A girl who has not yet reached puberty is reborn.[28]

Kermode presses his claim that the narrative is centered on gender-related taint with some force: "they take their complementary ways out of sickness into society, out of the unclean into the clean."[29] Jesus does not negate either of the women, nor does he "demonize" their afflictions or imply that they are unclean—the healing comes from their being accepted by him as they are: their "defilement" is done away with.

Modern readers might well struggle with these texts and wonder what all the fuss is about in relation to normal issues in "feminine hygiene." But contemporary society may not be quite as progressive as it imagines. The story of how the Samaritans began—the organization founded in 1953 by the Reverend Chad Varah—has some resonance with the story of Jairus's daughter. Varah's inspiration came from an experience he had had as a young curate in the city (and diocese) of Lincoln, United Kingdom. Varah had held a funeral for a girl of fourteen who had killed herself because she had begun menstruating, and was mortified that the girl had to be buried in unconsecrated ground, with parts of the burial liturgy redacted as it was a suicide. Varah became concerned about the state of sex education for teenagers in the city and started to work with young people, especially listening to those who were contemplating suicide. Varah's Samaritan movement grew rapidly when he subsequently moved to London. Within ten years, the Samaritans were a sizable charity, offering a supportive and empathetic listening service that is not political or religious.

So, the story of Jairus's daughter and that of the older woman (both women, note, are unnamed) are remarkable. The pairing of these two stories seems to turn everything around. A woman becomes a daughter, and a daughter becomes a woman. Moreover, we might also allow ourselves a little speculation. What precisely is the relationship between Jairus and the bleeding woman? Remember, Jairus is the synagogue ruler and would therefore have an instrumental role in policing its precincts, keeping the impure and undesirable out. So now we have a story about immediacy and patience. The woman has waited for twelve years—and probably been excluded from worship for the same period of time. One of the subtle yet blunt exercises of power is to make people wait or be kept waiting.

If you are in power, people wait to see you—or you keep them waiting. It is the powerless who must wait. For that appointment, the letter, the news, the interview—waiting is a form of powerlessness. Jairus kept this woman waiting for years, but he wants Jesus to heal his daughter, *now*. What does Jesus do? He gets distracted by an apparently pointless brush with a member of the crowd and keeps Jairus waiting—and too long too. Where is the lesson in this? This is a miracle with a moral. So, we are now in a position to understand the significance

28 Kermode, *Genesis of Secrecy*, 132.
29 Kermode, *Genesis of Secrecy*, 134.

of Jesus's encounter with the two women and their "healing," or, indeed, why Jesus bothered with lepers. When, in the midst of the dynamics of this particular understanding of the relationship between an "impure" body and the social body, Jesus reaches out and *touches* the unclean and declares them healed, he acts as an alternative boundary keeper in a way that is religiously and ritually subversive to the established procedures of his society. Jesus disrupts and undermines the social order that declares such people outcasts. Thus, Jesus makes possible a new community that now refuses to be founded upon the exclusion of the other.

While these elements in the Gospel accounts may be implicit in the text, or buried by "traditional" forms of exegesis, their uncovering raises serious issues for the contemporary church in its healing ministry. The taking on of another's affliction is not something many would contemplate, particularly if that requires the "healer" to then be regarded as also being "handicapped," "defiled," or a "sinner." Nowhere is this issue more acute than in the field of care for "victims" of HIV/AIDS-related cases, where "defilement" through touch has stalked the mind of society like a ghost. (Indeed, it is interesting that the "young man" Wimber obliquely refers to in his speeches and publications as bringing the first experience of dramatic renewal to his Vineyard churches—a Jesus Freak hippie by the name of Lonnie Frisbee and who was born in 1949—was an active homosexual. Wimber, of course, could not possibly acknowledge Frisbee's sexuality in public, as it would have alienated his evangelical followers. But Wimber was nonetheless willing and able to continue describing Frisbee as the channel and agent of God's Pentecostal blessing that had caused the Vineyard churches to become what they were. Frisbee died of AIDS in 1993).

My reading of this healing miracle in the Gospels therefore suggests three things. First, touching and embracing the afflicted, in the widest possible sense, is critical to Jesus's ministry. Secondly, judging the cause of sickness, or naming it as "sin," has no place in Jesus's ministry. Thirdly, (somehow) inculcating the sickness itself into the body of Jesus was important. I am aware that this is effectively a call for the church to live as though the "body of Christ has AIDS,"[30] fully assuming the personal, social, moral, medical, and political problems that arise for sufferers. But to do less than this would be to fall into the familiar dualist trap of seeing the body of Christ as pure and unassuming rather than being in engaged in complex, rich, suffering, and mutual intercourse with the world.

There is a fundamental sense, then, in which the suffering God needs to be brought alongside the Jesus of healing miracles. The crucified Christ needs to be placed firmly in the center of any theology of healing, not because Jesus's death somehow negates sickness but because the death itself is the ultimate fulfillment of those miracles. In death, Jesus becomes the man who is going nowhere, an emblem of hopelessness, betrayed, vilified, and cursed; he earns the scorn of

---

30 I have borrowed this phrase from Professor Anthony Dyson's (unpublished) paper delivered at the annual conference for the Society for the Study of Theology, Amersfoort, Netherlands, April 1992.

society, for "he saved others, but he cannot save himself" (Mt 27:42). So at the heart of the Gospel there is a profoundly broken person, who was prepared to be broken for others and ended up by paying the ultimate price. This vision of Jesus flies in the face of the usual portrayals one encounters in the majority of modern healing movements. The emphasis is typically on Christ's strength and his ability to accomplish all things. Those who are afflicted must lose what afflicts them before they can join the company of the redeemed: that same company will certainly not be joining them, descending to their level. So as far as the church is concerned, Paul's "kenotic" hymn of Philippians 2 is reversed: individuals and society must empty themselves and rise to meet God on another plateau. Yet at the heart of the Eucharist, it is the action of breaking bread that signifies Christ's solidarity with his people and points to the salvation beyond. When the church lives like this, as the broken body of Christ for the broken themselves, there is healing and redemption in abundance: the work of many communities and individuals testifies to this.[31]

Before looking finally at the task of miracles, it perhaps apposite to ask, "did Jesus actually heal, or are the miracles just 'signs'?" Part of the answer has to lie in locating the healing ministry of Jesus within the activity of incarnation, which, in some sense, is an ongoing process. In the incarnation, that which is symbolized in Christ is also actualized, and the hidden revealed: the church is called to live out this life too, relating the inner to the outer in all spheres. So the miracles of Jesus are real in the sense that all symbolic action became focused in activity that was observable, reifiable, and demonstrable. This apparently involves disturbing the laws of nature, but the laws are only subverted where they oppress or threaten, and Jesus's healing activity points to the importance of breaking through all oppressive barriers, be they legal, societal, or "natural." Again, this suggests that miracles can never be "proofs" or simple demonstrations of "power": they always have a social–transcendent function that is primary.[32]

The task of miracles

The social, moral, religious, and political impacts of Jesus's healing miracles are inescapable. Part of the value of these miracles in Jesus's ministry, besides healing individuals, seems to be in questioning society on its attitude to sickness itself. The sin of the individual as a cause is uniformly rejected by Jesus. Instead, he tends to challenge crowds and onlookers, questioning their implicit or explicit role in the person's misfortune. For Jesus, healing is never just an action for an individual: there are always wider, corporate implications.

---

31 See John Hadley, *Bread for the World* (London: DLT, 1989), 87.

32 I am grateful to the insights of Werner Kelber here, who originally set me thinking on this path. See *The Passion in Mark* (Philadelphia: Fortress Press, 1976), especially chaps. 2, 3, and 7.

This observation is particularly pertinent in the context of the changes taking place in health care at present. Besides the radical shake-ups in the financing of the National Health Service (they are perennial), there is also a political and moral shift taking place. People are increasingly encouraged to relate to a system as individuals in their own right, competing for funds, care, and treatment. Increasingly, the causes of disease are portrayed as matters of individual choice: those who might have poor diets or smoke too much in, say urban priority or inner city areas, are "blamed" for their own bad health. The rhetoric of "choice" somehow implies that those who are ill, disabled, or marginalized have partly become that through their own free will. Even at its best, such rhetoric reduces the patient to the status of a unit of consumption, a figure whose only significance is their place on the balance sheet.

So, the contemporary charismatic healing movement needs to bear in mind that the Gospels and the accounts of healing within them do not provide the reader with a kind of "manual" on how to heal or what to think about sickness. Leaving aside the worldview of first-century Palestinians, the healing stories of the Gospels are too symbolic to be read as aids to diagnosis and prognosis. (Presumably, one should be just as cautious about adopting the "demonology" of the first century as much as the pre-Copernican cosmology and "flat Earth" geography of Psalm 19). Accounts of healing cannot be read as a type of instruction book, any more than an artist's portrait should function as an anatomical guide for a surgeon about to perform an operation. "Healing stories" are "still-life" pictures, pregnant with meaning, including social and political, yet faithful to the original subject. What counts is our reaction to what we "see," not whether or not we can copy the picture.

Contemporary charismatic healing movements, for the most part, are correctly diagnosed by Jon Sobrino as being too "spiritualized" in their relation to the world.[33] There are, no doubt, many benefits in being part of the phenomenological escapism that many believe constitutes a revival.[34] Healing rallies and conventions will continue to come and go; healers who emphasize methods, texts, and types of faith will always abound; some will always be helped by such things, while others will be hindered. But the healing task of the church surely lies well beyond this horizon. What I am arguing for is a "reading" of the healing stories that involves eschewing literal or demythologized paths, conservative or liberal slants, seeking instead a shared agenda for social, moral, and political praxis. There are implicit imperatives in the healing ministry of Jesus that the church needs to heed.[35]

---

33 See Jon Sobrino, *Jesus the Liberator: A Historical Theological Reading of Jesus of Nazareth* (Maryknoll, NY: Orbis Books, 1993). See also Ernesto Cardenal, *The Gospel in Soltiname* (Maryknoll, NY: Orbis Books, 1970/2010). For a more devotional approach, see Jeffrey John, *The Meaning in the Miracles* (Norwich: Canterbury Press, 2001).

34 See Martyn Percy, *Words, Wonders and Power* (London: SPCK, 1996), chap. 8.

35 See Pattison, *Alive and Kicking*, 55ff. The theory that healing movements are a reflex response to secularization and postmodernism remains unchallenged. I have been especially

The retrieval of healing ministries to the church, I would suggest, will only come when there is a serious theology of "touch" in relation to pain. Moreover, this cannot just be for individuals. To refract an old saying, "Jesus was not just tough on disease but also tough on the causes of disease." When he heals a person, he also touches the social context and culture that frames the disorder and disease. Jesus hears the dumb; he speaks to the deaf; he sees the blind; and he touches the untouchable. The body of Christ is richly sensate.

Touching is one of the most basic forms of human communication, and one of the most personally experienced of all sensations. Our tactile sense is the genesis of our individual and social awareness. Closeness and physical intimacy play a major part in addressing pain: a hand extended in friendship or consolation, a hug or embrace can be more profound than a thousand words.[36] The remarkable story of Jesus's healings is his awareness of this dynamic: he was willing to touch and be touched—he expressed grace in his physicality. Individually and socially, the church needs to contemplate real touching in response to real alienation and pain. This engagement requires a deep reaching inside itself as well as a reaching out, drawing on the resources of the one whose incarnation is just that.

So, can the church retrieve the healing ministry of the Gospels, and restore it to the present church, so that renewal and revival will come? The answer must be "yes." But true revival will only come when the poor are accounted for and liberated. Renewal will only come when the culture that "blames" individuals for their sickness, along with the purchasing of "services" and "choices" in levels of treatment in health care, is subverted by a more corporate sense of responsibility and a spirit of true service. True Gospel healing will always be about addressing the causes of illness and disease and challenging the political and social forces that divide and demonize in our society. If the church wants to retrieve the healing miracles of Jesus, it cannot just do this personally for individuals. It will have to engage with the more subversive political motivations that lie behind Jesus's healings.

impressed with the work of Charles Davis in relation to some of these problems. See Charles Davis, *Religion and the Making of Society: Essays in Social Religion* (Cambridge: Cambridge University Press, 1994), 199–201, on religious hope and praxis.

36 Two very helpful books in this regard are Norman Autton's *Touch: An Exploration* (London: DLT, 1989) and *Pain: An Exploration* (London: DLT, 1986).

INDEX

Lightning Source UK Ltd.
Milton Keynes UK
UKHW020702240821
389378UK00006B/1248